DICTIONARY

OF THE

SYNONYMOUS WORDS

AND

TECHNICAL TERMS

IN THE

ENGLISH LANGUAGE.

———

By JAMES LESLIE.

A GREAT BOOK IS A GREAT EVIL.—ADDISON. SPEC. NO. 124.

Edinburgh:
PRINTED BY JOHN MOIR, ROYAL BANK CLOSE,
FOR THE AUTHOR,
AND SOLD BY S. CHEYNE, GEORGE STREET, EDINBURGH,
AND VERNOR & HOOD, POULTRY;
LONDON.
1806.

TO

THE RIGHT HONOURABLE

FRANCIS RAWDON HASTINGS,

EARL OF MOIRA,

MASTER-GENERAL OF THE ORDNANCE,

LORD LIEUTENANT, AND CUSTOS ROTULORUM

OF THE TOWER HAMLETS,

&c. &c. &c.

AND ONE OF

HIS MAJESTY'S

MOST HONOURABLE PRIVY COUNCIL,

THIS WORK

IS,

WITH GREAT DEFERENCE, DEDICATED,

WITH HIS LORDSHIP'S PERMISSION,

BY

THE AUTHOR.

PREFACE.

THE scheme on which this Dictionary is arranged, is totally different from that of any work bearing its name. The uniform plan
of Dictionaries of Synonymous Words has been to shew where
a word may, or may not, be used with propriety, by giving *one*,
two, or more examples of its application : A work done in the
manner just mentioned, could not contain *one-tenth* the number of words necessary to make it generally useful, every word
in the alphabetical arrangement requiring several lines of illus-
tration, by which the work would be necessarily rendered too
expensive for general use.

After much *care* and *labour*, the following arrangement is
now laid before the Public, viz. that having any common or
simple word in memory, every word which is synonymous with
that in question is instantly exhibited under it.

By this mode, it is evident a great variety of words is pre-
sented to the reader, either for composition or declamation,
which the most retentive memory could not otherwise embrace,
and thus enable him to avoid tautology or circumlocution.

The author thinks it proper to observe, that he makes no
pretensions to enter into the philological niceties of the language, or to distinguish under their respective heads those more
delicate shades of which the English tongue is susceptible : His
sole aim has been utility, by bringing before the eye, at one
glance, all the synonymes of a word, and thus afford to the
speaker and writer an infinite variety of expression, by which
he may avoid that periphrastical mode which fatigues and dis-
gusts.

Two objections may be urged against this mode of arrangement : *First, it may be asked,* what is understood by *Common*
or *Simple Words?* It must be confessed that it is somewhat

difficult to define these terms; for what is a *simple* word to a scholar, may be an uncommon word to one less learned; but it is hoped a short perusal of the work will remove this ambiguity: Thus, for example, the word " Clear" is a common word, which is found in the alphabetical arrangement, and which can be mistaken by none; whereas the words under it, in the Dictionary, are the opposite; and, although they are not uncommon to some, may nevertheless be so to others, while they assist the memory of all. The next objection may be, that there really are but few words which are truly synonymous, and therefore such as are found under their respective heads in alphabetical order, are not true and legitimate *synonyma*. In answer to this it is not maintained, that *every word* is the true synonyme of that under which it is found, as a scrupulous nicety in this particular would have entirely defeated the intention of the Author, the philological application being left to the taste and judgment of the reader.

In addition to this, it is perhaps sufficient to say, that the first authorities have been consulted in the selection and disposition of the matter in the following sheets; and it besides gives the Author much confidence to find a late writer of eminence, treating the subject nearly in the same way; but unluckily the work alluded to is too expensive for general use.

The judicious use of *technical terms* has often a happy effect; and as their application is indispensible in treating of any art or science, such technical terms as are commonly found in the best English Dictionaries, are here inserted: The Reader, however, is not to expect that an 8vo work, which is intended solely as a *Remembrancer*, should embrace *every term* in Art or Science, as this would be an Index to all books of knowledge extant!—*a thing impossible!*

The small number of words in the alphabetical arrangement will not, it is hoped, be objected to by the candid Reader, when he is informed that this work contains at least ten times the number of words more than Dictionaries of this nature of triple its cost; besides, such words were purposely left out as had synonymes applicable to them, but such as were as simple

as the words themselves, under which they would have fallen to
have been inserted.

There are upwards of *Five Thousand* words alphabetically arranged; under these will be found more than *Fifty Thousand*
Synonymes and Technical Terms; and where few words occur
under any head, such as the word, " Abandoned," (arising
from the nature of the work) references are made.

How this Work may be received, and what judgment may
be passed upon it, the Author presumes not to determine : He
trusts the Public will give him every candid allowance, and
assures the Reader, that where any dubiety occurred in the prosecution of the Work, the opinion of others has been consulted.

July 24, 1806.

✓ ERRATA.

A

DICTIONARY

OF THE

SYNONYMOUS WORDS

AND

TECHNICAL TERMS

IN THE

English Language.

ABS

ABANDONED. *a.* Profligate, reprobate, Rakehelly. (See wicked.)

ABATE. *v.* To Forzeve, to assuage, to allay, to deduce.

ABHOR. *v* To Absonate, to detest, to execrate, to loathe or lothe, to nauseate.

ABILITY. *s.* Efficiency, potency (See power capacity, skill.)

ABLE. *a.* Capable, potential. Able to do all things, omnivalent.

ABODE. *s.* Commorance, resiance, retirement, domicile; exchange of abode, intermigration.

ABOMINABLE. *a.* Detestable, execrable, nefandous, nefarious, odious.

ABOVE. *prep.* Placed above, empyrean, empyreal, supernal.

ABOUNDING. *p.* Flush, teeming; abounding or flowing from a spring, scatebrous.

ABRIDGEMENT. *s.* Abbreviate, abstract, compend, compendium, epitome, excerption, synopsis, summary.

ABRIDGER. *s.* Summarist, abbreviator. (See shorten.)

ABROAD. *ad.* A sending abroad as on an embassy; ablegation.

ABSOLUTE. *a.* Inconditionate, inconditional, indispensible, indispensable; absolute sovereignty, autocracy, despotism.

ABSOLUTELY. *ad.* Arbitrarily, categorically, peremptorily, point blank.

ABSTRACT. *v.* To prescind. (See to divide.)

ABSTRACT. *s.* Epitome, syllabus, synopsis. (See abridgment.)

ABSTRUSE. *a.* Recondite. (See difficult hidden.)

ABSURD. *a.* Absonous, absonant, illogical, implausible, incompatible, incompetible;

ACC

inconsistent, irrational; preposterous, sinistrous.

ABSURDITY. *s.* Alogy. (See unreasonableness, foolishness, folly.)

ABUNDANCE. *s.* Uberty, exundation, glut, foison, foizon; over-abundance, nimiety.

ABUNDANT. *a.* Inundant, opulent, affluent, copious, exuberant, fecund, prolific, feracious, ferile; nimious.

ABUSE. *v.* To vilify, to debase, to conviate.

ABUSE. *s.* Belowt; personal abuse, lampoon, libel.

ABUSED. *a.* Catachrestical.

ABUSIVE. *a.* Invective, libellous, scurrilous, affrontive; an abusive expression, catachresia.

ACCENT. *s.* Of syllables, that part of grammar which teaches the quantity and accent of syllables, prosody

ACCIDENT. *s.* Encounter, incident, incidence.

ACCIDENTAL. *a.* Adventitious, adventine, adventive, eventful, casual, circumstantial, contingent, hab-nab, fortuitous, vague, eventual.

ACCOMMODATE. *v.* To attemper, to quadrate; to accommodate or serve one, to bestead.

ACCOMPANY. *v.* To accompany by way of respect; to consort, to esquire.

ACCOMPLISHED. *a.* Polydore, quaint. (See complete, affected, elegant, nice.)

ACCOMPT. *s.* (See account.)

ACCOUNT. *v* To account or reckon, to addeem; to examine and settle an account, to adjust, to audit, to liquidate.

A

ACCOUNT. *s.* Writer of accounts, logographer; one who is behind in his accounts or affairs, reliquator; an account of the causes of diseases, &c etiology; account or description, enarration; verbal account of occurrences handed down from early periods; tradition.

ACCOUNTANT. *s.* Logist. (See reckoner, computer, calculate.)

ACCUSATION. *s.* Delation, dicæology. (See complain, charge.)

ACCUSE. *v.* To arraign to calumniate, to criminate, to delate, to denounce, to impeach, to incriminate; to accuse again in one's turn, to recriminate.

ACE. *s.* Two aces thrown at once, ambsace; ace of spades, spadille.

ACKNOWLEDGE. *v.* To agnize, to recognize. (See to confess, to grant.)

ACKNOWLEDGEMENT. *s.* Recognition, requital, agnition.

ACORN. *s.* Glans; bearing acorns, glandiferous.

ACQUIT. *v.* To absolve, to assoil, or, assoilzie.

ACROSS. *ad.* To sail across, to traverse; across, astraddle, athwart, kimbo; drawn across from corner to corner, diagonal; lying across, transverse.

ACT. *v.* To achieve; to operate; to bring out to act, to elicit.

ACT. *s.* Feat; capital act, master-stroke; act or deed, ministration.

ACTING. *p.* Acting together, co-efficiency, co-efficacy, simultaneous.

ACTION. *s.* To put in action, to actuate; action, feat, gesture; reason or cause of any action, motive. The animal or vital actions of the body, hegemonicæ.

ACTIVE. *a.* Agile, adroit, dapper, energetic, expedite, fleet, mercantile, volant, voluble, mercurial, quiver, strenuous, vivacious, vivid.

ACTIVITY. *s.* Mobility, navity, gnavity.

ACTUALLY. *ad. De facto,* L. (See really, verily, truly, certainly.)

ACUTENESS. *s.* Acuteness of intellect; acumen, sagacity, ingeny.

ADAM. *s.* Name given to those who deny Adam was the first man, præ-Adamites; done or made *before* the fall of Adam, supralapsary; done *after* it, sublapsary.

ADD. *v.* To ascervate, to affix, to annex, to eke, to ingeminate, to ingest, to annumerate, to append, to accumulate, to add over and above, to superadd, to superinduce.

ADDED. *a.* Added over and above, advenient, adscititious; that may be added, addible; added afterwards, postic; what is added, adjection, additament.

ADDITION. *s.* Annexation, annexion, ag-

gravation, exaggeration, appendant, appendage, appendix, apposition; the addition of matter, or, vamping up of an original writing, &c. interpolation, coming as an addition, survening.

ADDITIONAL. *a.* Adscititious, ascititious.

ADDRESS. *v.* To greet.

ADDRESS. *s.* Dedication, allocution, compellation, oration.

ADJUSTMENT. *s.* Adjustment of the parts of a body to each other, coaptation, juxtaposition.

ADMIRAL. *s.* Thalassiarch.

ADMIT. *v.* To adhibit, to coincide, to homologate, to induct, to initiate, to matriculate; to admit moisture, to imbibe.

ADMITTED. *p.* Very generally admitted or believed, receptory; which may be admitted, admittable.

ADMONISH. *v.* To monish (See persuade, advise, to warn, reprove.)

ADMONITION, *s.* Monition, parænesis, (See counsel, advice, hint, direction.)

ADOPTION. *s.* Co-optation; adoption of a son, affiliation.

ADORATION. *s.* Prostration (See respect.)

ADORN. *v.* To bedeck, to blazon, to decorate, to embellish, to emblaze, to enchase, to bedight, to bedizen, to dight, to fard, to invest, to garnish, to impaint, to plume, to prank.

ADORNED. *p.* Yclad (See deck, dress.)

ADORNING. *p.* Investient (See ornament)

ADVANCE. *v.* To promote, to promove; to advance the price of a commodity, to enhance.

ADVANCEMENT. *s.* Profection (See improvement, progression.)

ADVANCING. *p.* Adjutory, gradient, progressional.

ADVANTAGE. *s.* Avail, behoof, boot, bye-end, emolument, additament, lucre.

ADVANTAGEOUS. *a.* Beneficial, proficuous, lucrative, lucrific, lucriforous, lucrous.

ADVICE. *v.* To give one useless advice; to fig; to ask advice, to consult; advice by letter, aviso; hortation, rede, lore, counsel; a thoral advice from a wife to her husband, curtain-lecture.

ADVISE. *v.* To admonish, to exhort, to excite, to incite, to inculcate, to monish; to advise before hand, to premonish; to advise wrong, to misadvise; to advise against, to discounsel, to dehort, to dissuade.

ADVISING. *p.* Hortative, hortatory, protreptical.

ADULTERATE. *v.* To sophisticate (See to corrupt, mix.)

ADULTERY. *s.* Advowtry, avowtry.

ADVOCATE. *s.* Paraclete; acting the part of an advocate, dicæology

AFFECTATION. *s.* Coquetry, prudery. (See conceit.)

AFFECTED. *a.* Finical, spish, quaint, (See Gay.)

AFFECTEDNESS. *s.* Cacozelia. (See affectation, conceit, pride, vanity.)

AFFECTION. *n.* That peculiar affection we have to any particular thing, idiopathy, jemmard; the affection of parents to children, philostorgy. (See love.)

AFFIRMATION. *s.* Avouchment, averment, predication; most solemn affirmation, asseveration.

AFFIRMATIVE. *a.* Categorical, assertive. (See positive, absolute.)

AFFIRMING. *p.* Indicative, predicant; affirming for another on oath, compurgation.

AFFLICT. *v.* To disaster. (See to grieve, trouble, torment, vex.)

AFFLICTION. *s.* Tribulation, heartache, Thlipsis. (See grief, distress, misery, sorrow, pain.)

AFFORD. *v.* To subminister. (See to yield, produce, grant, sell, give.)

AFFRONT. *s.* Despite. (See insult, wrong, enrage, oppose.)

AFFRAID. *s.* Afeard, trepid. (See fearful, terrified, fright.)

AFTER. *prep.* Placed after, posterior. (See behind.)

AFTERNOON. *s.* Performed in the afternoon, postmeridian; nap or sleep in the afternoon, sest, *as to go to one's nest.*

AFTERWARDS. *ad.* Done afterwards, postic, postliminous.

AGAIN. *ad.* Encore, *Fr.*; to do again and again, to reiterate.

AGAINST. *prep.* Over-against, diametrically opposite.

AGE. *s.* To place or rank in the same age, to contemporize; ripe age, puberty, pubescence; those who have arrived at the age of puberty, hircosi; a vigorous old age, agerasy; old age, senectude; very great age, grandevity; term used of one who has arrived at his 15th year or thereby, ephebia; account of occurrences that have happened from age to age, tradition; worn out with age, superannuated; consequent on old age, senile; the old age of a woman, anility; of the same age, coetaneous, coeval, coevous, cotemporary, contemporary.

AGED. *a.* Longevous. (See old, ancient.)

AGEDNESS. *s.* Annosity.

AGENCY. *s.* Efficiency, ministration, function.

AGENT. *s.* Emissary, mediator, intercessor, procurator, syndic.

AGITATE. *v.* To bandy, to betoss, to conquassate. (See to move, shake, examine,

debate.)

AGREE. *v.* To congree, to correspond, to covenant, to advene, to stipulate, to tally, to cohere, to coincide, to combine, to concur, to fadge, to assent, to compound, to attour.

AGREE. *s.* Which does not agree, incondite,

AGREEABLE. *a.* Concordant, conformable, consentaneous, accordant; agreeable to the smell, fragrant; agreeable to the taste, gustful; agreeable, like, or similar, homologal.

AGREEMENT. *s.* Congruence, consension, contract, convention, coincidence, concert, composition, omology, pact, paction; mutual agreement, concert, harmony, concord; agreement of sound, consonance, chime, symphony; agreement of opinion, unanimity; agreement to exchange prisoners, cartel; the want of agreement disconformity, discongruity, inconcurrence, incondity. (See love, union, bargain, likeness.)

AGRICULTURE. *s.* The tackle used for the purposes of agriculture, gainage; relating to agriculture, geoponical, georgic; the art or science of agriculture, geoponics. (See husbandry, tillage.)

AGUE. *s.* Ague that returns every third day, tritæophyes or tertian ague; every fourth day, quartan; every day, quotidian; (See day.) Medicine applied round the wrist, to cure or prevent an ague, pericarpium.

AID. *v.* To adjute, to adjuvate, to abet, to propugn. (See to help, assist, support.)

AID. *s.* Opitulation, subsidy, subvention, adjument; aid in war, symmachy.

AIDING, *p.* Auxiliary, collateral, conducible, contributory, relevant, superadvenient, subsidiary. (See helping, assisting, succouring, relieving.)

AIM. *v.* To aspire, to soar; to aim at a target, to collimate. (See to endeavour, design, direct, guess.)

AIMING. *p.* Act of collimation, or collineation.

AIR. *s.* Air or manner, mien, aspect; instrument for measuring the moisture of the air, hygrometer; instrument for shewing the rarity or density of the air, manometer, manoscope, barometer, baroscope (See weather and glass.) instrument for measuring the different airs or gasses in chemical processes, gazometer; for ascertaining the purity of the atmospheric air, eudiometer, oximeter; machine tending to break a fall in passing through the air, parachute; the whole body of air circumverting the earth, atmosphere; the pure and light air in the higher regions, æther;

A 4

air-hole, suspiral, spiracle, ventilator; the doctrine of the air, pneumatics; the circulation of the air through chambers, &c. ventilation; change of air (term among physicians) metabole.

AIR. *v.* To walk in. or take the fresh air, to walk in fresco.

AIRY *a.* Highty-tighty, jovial, juvenile, modish, sportive, debonair; airy girl, coquette. (See light, brisk, gay, trifling.)

ALARM. *v.* To affright, to gallow, to ghast,

ALARM. *s.* Alarm given after a thief, hue and cry.

ALE. *s.* Sort of inferior vinegar made from sour ale, alegar; ale made from wheat, mum; posset or drink made from ale and milk, zythogala.

ALEXANDER. *s.* Alexander the Great's regal successors in Syria, Seleucidæ; name given to his famous horse Bucephalus.

ALGEBRA. *s.* Belonging or relating to, cossic, logistic; a quantity of one single term in algebra, monomial; of two, binomial, &c.; the division of the terms of an equation by a known quantity, that is involved in the first term, parabolism, thus

$$4x + n = b + c \text{ and } x = \frac{b + c - n}{4} \text{ Those}$$

numbers which are prefixed to the letters of the members of any power to be raised algebraically, unciæ, co-efficients; the agibraic method of enquiry, zetetics. (See equation.)

ALIEN. *s.* Allophylus. (See foreigner, stranger, foreign)

ALIENATE. *v.* To impropriate. (See to transfer to remove, to sell)

ALIKE. *ad.* Homologous. (See same, equal, proportional, similar.)

ALIMENT. *s.* Affording aliment, pabular. (See food, nourishment, support, victual, fuel.)

ALL. *a.* All, total, versal. (See whole, entire, complete.)

ALLOY. *s.* Lega, allay.

ALLOW. *v.* To dispense, to deign, to tolerate. (See to admit, to give, to pay, to grant, to yield, to praise)

ALLOWANCE. *s.* Toleration; allowance, or approbation of any act or deed in writing, by signing it, homologation; small allowance of money, &c., pittance. (See licence.)

ALLURE. *v.* To bait, to inveigle, to seduce. (See to entice, to decoy, to tempt, to wheedle.)

ALLUSION. *s.* Agnomination, implication. (See hint, reference, comparison, respect.)

ALLUSIVE. *a.* Hieroglyphical, emblematical.

ALMIGHTY. *a.* Omnipotent, omnivalent, pancratical.

ALMONDS. *s.* The quantity of two cwt. of almonds, seron; almonds of the ear or throat, amygdalæ, tonsils.

ALMS *s.* The distributor of alms, almoner, living on alms, eleemosynary; alms, corban, passade, passado, dole, sportule, sportula.

ALONE *a.* Living alone, monial, solitary, single, lonely.

ALTAR. *s.* Plate or dish used at the altar, paten; ornaments about an altar, parements

ALTER. *v* Alter from the original meaning, to detort; alter, to diversify, to metamorphose, to revocate, to repeal, to transmew; to alter or overturn, to renverse.

ALTERED. *p.* Not to be altered or bent, inflexible; not to be altered or changed, intransmutable.

ALTERABLE. *a.* Convertible.

ALTERATION. *s* Mutation, metabole; alteration for the better, emendation. (See change.)

ALTITUDE. *s.* Parallels of altitude are termed almacantars, almacanteras or almicanthers.

ALWAYS. *ad.* Ere, incessantly, indesinently.

AMASS. *v.* To congest. (See to heap up, collect, gather)

AMAZE. *v* To daunt, to gast or ghast.

AMAZED. *p.* Planet-struck, confounded. (See astonishment, fear.)

AMAZEMENT. *s.* Aghast.

AMAZING. *p.* Stupendous, prodigious, horrendous, astonishing. (See wonderful, fearful.)

AMBASSADOR. *s.* The Pope's ambassador, nuncio, legate or legatory; a resident ambassador, lieger, or ledger.

AMBASSAGE. *s.* Joint ambassage or mission, adlegation.

AMBER. *s.* Bearing or yielding amber, electriferous; of or belonging to amber, succineous.

AMBLING. *p.* Act of, tolutation.

AMBUSH. *s.* To lay in ambush, to belay, to waylay; ambush, illaqueation.

AMENDMENT. *s.* Resipiscence. (See correction, repentance.)

AMERICANS. *s.* The offspring of Americans and Spaniards, Mestisos.

AMMUNITION. *s.* Munition.

AMOROUS. *a.* To cast amorous glances, to gloat; amorous, buxom. (See fond, loving, kind)

AMOUNT. *s.* Quantum, amount of any sum, &c., mountenance. (See whole.)

AMUSE. *v.* To recreate, to solace. (See to entertain, deceive.)

AMUSEMENT. *s.* Pastime, recreation. (See toy, entertainment.)

ANALYSIS. *s.* Principiation, anastoichiasis, (See separation and resolution.)

ANATOMY. (See sarcology.)

ANATOMICAL. *a.* Anatomical description of the human body, anthropography. (See description and treatise.)

ANCHOR. *s.* Small anchor used in rivers, kedge, grapnel.

ANCIENT. *a.* Primitive, antique, immemorial, matronly, pristine, Gothic. (See old, past, former.)

ANGELIC. *a.* Cherubic.

ANGELS. *s.* The two angels who are supposed by the Mahometans to examine the souls of the departed, Munker and Neker.

ANGER. *s.* Chagrin, choler, despite, ire, stomachosity, exasperatedness; violent anger, excandescancy; easily provoked to anger, irascible; act of provoking to anger, lacession.

ANGLES. *s.* Angle among workmen, basil, bevel; drawn from angle to angle, diagonal; right angled, orthogonal, rectangular; angle (in fortification) the vertex of which points towards the besiegers, salient angle; having three acute angles, oxygonial; having an obtuse angle, amblygonial; having equal angles, equiangular; instruments for measuring angles, pantometer, theodolite, Jacob's staff; graphometer; the method of measuring angles, as proposed to the Royal Academy by M. D. Lagny, by means of a pair of compasses, without any scale, except an undivided semicircle, goniometry; instrument for laying down angles *in plano*, protractor.

Figure having 3 angles, triangular figure.

—— 4 ——		quadrangular,
—— 5 ——	{	quinquiangular, pentangular,
—— 6 ——	{	nexangular, or sexangular,
—— 7 ——	{	heptangular, or septangular,
—— 8 ——	{	octangular, or octogonal,
—— 9 ——		enneagonal,
—— 10 ——		decagonal,
—— 11 ——	{	undecagonal, hendecagonal,
—— 12 ——		dodecagonal,
		&c. &c.

having many angles, multangular, multagonal.

ANGRY. *a.* Act of growing angry, excandescence; soon angry, irascible; apt to be angry, testy; angry, froward, indignant, moody.

ANIMAL. *s.* A scientific treatise of animals, zoology; the producing of perfect living animals, zoogonia; animal in the womb not completely formed, fetus, fœtus, embryo; animal of doubtful gender, hermaphrodite, androgyne; collection of brute animals, menage or menagerie; of living animals of any kind, vivary; describer of animals, zoographer; animals which bring forth their young alive, viviparous; by eggs, oviparous; term for the natural heat or temperament of animals, biolychnium; term used for such animals as urine backwards, retromingents; the soundness of the body of an animal, ulumelia; the principle of life and vigour in an animal, archeus.

ANIMATE. *v.* To inanimate, to incite, to vivify. (See to quicken, stir up.)

ANNUL. *v.* To abolish, to abrogate, to blank, to cancel, to cassate, to disannul, to repeal. (See to make void, end, destroy.)

ANNULLING. *p.* Act of, defeasance.

ANOINT. *v.* To balm, to oint, to consecrate.

ANOINTED. *p.* Ceromatic, consecrated.

ANOINTING. *p.* Inunction, unction; physician who performs cures, by anointing and external applications only, iatroleptic physician. (See physician.)

ANSWER. *v.* To resolve, to respond.

ANSWER. *s.* Quietus, response; final answer, ultimatum; answer to a question, redditive; reply to an answer, rejoinder; witty answer, repartee; answer made by the parish clerk and people to certain parts of divine service, responsal; answer to a difficulty, enodation; full and complete answer, clencher; answer to a rejoinder, rebutter.

ANSWERABLE. *a.* Amenable, comptible, responsible.

ANSWERING. *p.* Responsion; act of answering difficulties, enucleation.

ANTECEDENT. *a.* Precedaneous, procatarctic; antecedent or previous to objections, proleptical.

ANTIC. *a.* Gestic. (See odd, ridiculous, wild.)

ANTIDOTE. *s.* Alexipharmic, alexiteric, preventive.

ANXIOUS. *a.* Intense, intent, solicitous; to be very anxious, to cark.

APATHY. *s.* Analgecy, indolence.

APOSTLE. *s.* False apostle, pseudapostle; name given to the apostles James and John, Boanerges.

APOTHECARY. *s.* Pharmacopolist, pharmacopœius, 'pothecary.

APPEARANCE. *s.* Having many appearances or forms, multiform; excuse for non-appearance in a court of law, essoin; appearance formed in the mind only, apparition, ostent, phasm. (See ghost.)

APPEAR. v. To appear as a ship at sea, to loom; to appear as buds, to pullulate; it appears to me, methinks. (See, to seem, look, answer, think.)

APPEARANCE. s. Any wonderful appearance of nature, phenomenon.

APPEASE. v. To allay, to placate. (See to quiet, pacify, calm.)

APPENDIX. s. Parergy. (See addition.)

APPETITE. s. Orexis; want of appetite, anorexy, dysorexy, inappetence; enormous appetite, bulimy, cynodes, eligurition, ingluvies; (see gluttony) medicines to help the appetite, embamma; term used for those who have no appetite, anorecti.

APPLAUSE. s. Acclamation, plaudit; act of catching at applause, captation. (See praise, commendation, credit.)

APPLES. s. Consisting of pomaceous; fragrant ointment made of apples, pomade; bearing apples, pomiferous.

APPLICATION. s. Application or disposition of any body to one near it, habitus.

APPLY. v. To adopt, to adhibit, to betake, to buckle; apply to, to dedicate. (See, to put in use, study, attend.)

APPOINT v. To assign, to constitute, to designate; appoint before hand, to preordain.

APPREHEND. v. To apprehend before hand, to presage.

APPREHENSION. s. Quickness of apprehension, sagacity, acumen.

APPRENTICE. s. Kid, tyro.

APPRENTICESHIP, s. Tyrociny.

APPROACH. v. To proximate.

APPROACH. s. Approximation, access.

APPROBATION. s. Approof, plaudit, acclamation, homologation.

APT. a. Pertinent. (See fit, ready, qualified)

ARBITRATOR. s. Umpire. (See governor, president.)

ARBOUR. s. Made of twigs and branches, cut and plaited together, topiary work.

ARCH. v. To arch over, to concamerate.

ARCH. a. Histrionic. (See mirth, waggish.)

ARCH. s. Cave, embowment; middle stone of an arch, keystone; any rising in the form of an arch, camarosis; chord of an arch, subtense; the number of degrees an arch wants of 180°, supplement; of 90°, complement; continuation of arches, arcades; the binding of an arch, contour.

ARCHED. p. Cambering, kimbo, camerated, testudinated.

ARCHITECTURE. s. The orders in architecture are five, viz:
The Tuscan.

The Doric.
Ionic.
Corinthian, and
Composite.

ARGUE. v. To ratiocinate; to argue again, to redargue.

ARGUMENT. v. To battle, to expostulate, to moot; to disprove by argument, to refel; to return an argument, to retort.

ARGUMENT. s. Elinch (See reasoning) argument composed and drawn from several previous ones, epichirema; false arguments are, ceratias, paralogy, paralogism, enthymeme, sophism, fallacy, pseudomenos, ceratine or sophistical; argument which contains the sum of a discourse, periocha; argument containing divers propositions, sorites; arguments that are probable, but do not convince or determine the mind to either side of the question, dialectical arguments; sophistical and fallacious argument, elenchus; that sort of argument, which, while it yields the point to the adverse party in a sneering manner, it then retorts, and cuts down his objections, synchoresis.

ARGUMENTATION. s. Disceptation. (See reasoning.)

ARGUMENTATIVE. a. Discursive.

ARISE. v. To ensue, to result.

ARISTOTLE. s. Aristotle's lectures on rhetoric, which every one had liberty to hear, exoterics; his lectures on the more difficult and nice parts of philosophy, to which only scholars and friends were admitted, acroatics; relating to Aristotle, peripatetic, stagyritical.

ARM. s. Relating to the arm, brachial; arm of the sea, estuary; a swathe which holds the arm when it is wounded or hurt, mitella; term used for the position of the arms when laid across, kembo or kimbo.

ARMING. p. An arming in defence of a country, &c. firdefare.

ARMED. p. Armed horseman, cataphract.

ARMIES. s. Armies or numbers, Sabaoth (Heb)

ARMOUR. s. Horseman in complete armour, cataphract; armour for the shoulders, mognions; complete armour, panoply.

ARMY. s. Army, host; the art of drawing up an army or body of men in any geometrical figure, for the immediate ascertaining of their number, stratarithmetry; the art of encamping an army, castrametation; said of an army or body of men secured by a fort, insconced; the commander in chief, or generalissimo of the army, archistrategus.

ARRANGE. v. To arraign.

2. Arranger or setter of types, compositor,

ARRANGEMENT. *s.* That certain arrangement in which simple terms or words are put in a series, predicament; the handsome and beautiful arrangement of things, eutaxy.

ARROGANT. *a.* Imperious, pragmatical, presumptuous, uppish.

ARROWS. *s.* Maker of bows and arrows, fletcher, (from fleche, F. an arrow); arrow, sagitta, bolt, missile; case for arrows, quiver; name of a poison used by the Indians on their arrows, which renders the wound inflicted incurable, toxica; divination by arrows, belomancy.

ART. *s.* Manual art, cunning (as a cunning workman); made by art (not natural) factitious; art or trick, expedient, expertness, farfetch, manœuvre; art or flattery, daubry, stratagem, ruse, sleight, tergiversation, finesse; not done with art, inartificial; art of making moulds for casting, proplastic.

Terms used in arts and sciences are called technical; circle of arts and sciences, cyclopædia, or encyclopædia; encourager of arts, philotechnus; the knowledge of many arts and sciences, polymathy.

The Arts and Sciences are,

Acoustics	Ethics
Aerology	Farriery
Aerostation	Fencing
Agriculture	Financing
Algebra	Fluxions
Amphibiology	Fortification
Anatomy	Gardening
Annuities	Gauging
Architecture	Geography
Arithmetic	Geometry
Astronomy	Grammar
Belles Lettres	Gunnery
Book-Keeping	Heraldry
Botany	History
Brewing	Husbandry
Catoptrics	Hydraulics
Chemistry	Hydrostatics
Chronology	Ichthyology
Commerce	Law
Comparative Anatomy	Logic
Conchology	Magnetism
Conics	Mathematics
Cosmography	Mechanics
Criticism	Medicine
Dialling	Mensuration
Dioptrics	Metallurgy
Distillation	Metaphysics
Drawing	Midwifery
Dying	Mineralogy
Electricity	Music
Engineering	Mythology
Engraving	Navigation
Entomology	Natural History
Optics	Politics
Oratory	Projectiles
Ornithology	Rhetoric
Painting	Sculpture
Perspective	Surgery
Pharmacy	Surveying
Philosophy	Tactics
Physic	Theology
Physiology	Trigonometry
Pneumatics	Vermeology
Poetry	Zoology

ARTFUL. *a.* Vulpinary, subdolous, political, quaint, shrewd.

ARTIFICE. *s.* Finesse, goby, elusion, ruse, stratagem, manœuvre, ingannation; mean artifice, malversation; done by artifice, insidiously.

ARTILLERY. *s.* Ordinance, ordnance, ordonance; artillery soldier next below the gunners, matross.

ARTIST. *s.* Artificer, artizan, manualist, opificer; artist of skill and eminence, adept, adeptist.

ASBESTOS. *s.* Plumealum, amiantus (See fire)

ASCENT. *s.* Ascent of a hill, &c. acclivity.

ASHES. *s.* Consisting of or resembling ashes, favillous, cineritious, cinerulent; reduce to ashes, to incinerate; ashes of melted brass, nill; ashes of melted metals in general, scoriæ or oxyd of the respective metal; a reducing into ashes, cinefaction, cineration; baked under the ashes, subcineratious; the hole below a fire into which the ashes fall, purgatory; hot ashes, embers.—

ASIDE. *ad.* To turn aside, to tralineate.

ASK. *v.* To ask earnestly, to crave; to implore, to invoke, to rogitate, to importune; to ask previously, to pre-require; to ask with great importunity, to conflagitate, to ask, to interrogate, to solicit.

ASKING. *p.* Act of asking often, rogitation.

ASS. *s.* Cuddy, donkey; belonging to an ass, assinary, asinine; fabulous monsters, having the upper parts like a man, and body like an ass, onocentaurs.

ASSAULT. *v.* To assail, to brush, to impugn.

ASSAULT. *s.* Sudden assault, superchery.

ASSEMBLE. *v.* To congregate, to convene, to muster.

ASSEMBLY. *s.* Concourse, conventicle, convocation, coterie, frequence, resort, conveniendum; assembly of cardinals, conclave; assembly of the people or district, folk-mote; private assembly, ruelle.

ASSERT. *v.* To vindicate; assert positively, to dogmatize.

ASSES *s.* Herd or company of, pace.

ASSIST. *v.* To adjute or adjuvate, to avail.

ASSISTANCE. *s.* Opitulation, adjument,

propugnation, sustentation; assistance in war, symmachy; mutual assistance, coadjument.

ASSISTING. *p.* Auxiliary, collateral, conducible, contributory, prompting, subsidiary, superadvenient.

ASSUAGE. *v.* To alleviate, to demulce. (see to ease, soften.)

ASSUAGING. *p.* Assuaging pain; anodyne. (See pain.)

ASSUME. *v.* To adopt, to arrogate.

ASSUMED. *p.* Certain principles in arts and sciences, which are so self evident that they are assumed to be true, postulates.

ASSUMING. *p.* Pragmatical. (See busy, impertinent.)

ASTONISHING. *p.* Marvellous, prodigious, stupendous.

ASTONISHMENT. *s.* Abashment, amaze, maze, consternation, stound.

ASTRAY. *ad.* A going astray, divagation.

ASTRIDE. *ad.* Astraddle, across.

ASTRONOMER. *s.* Uranoscopist.

ASTRONOMICAL *a.* Astronomical tables framed by Erasmus Rhinaldus a Prussian, prutanic tables. (See tables.)

ATOMS. *s.* Particles, minima, monades; poisonous atoms, miasma.

ATONE. *v.* To propitiate, to expiate.

ATONED. *p.* That cannot be atoned for, inexpiable.

ATROCIOUS. *a.* Piacular. (See crime and wicked.)

ATTACK. *v.* To bait, to brunt, to encounter, to assail, to beset, to impugn, to oppugn.

ATTACK. *s.* Aggression, incursion, sudden attack, illapse; a very fierce attack, onslaught; attack in the night time sometimes practised in war, in which the soldiers have their shirts over their coats, so as to be known to each other, camisade, or camisado.

ATTEMPT. *s.* Attempt or beginning, inception, inchoation, tentation, proffer, bout, effort, emprize, exploit, atchievement, enterprize, essay, or assay; Silly attempt or whim, fangle.

ATTEMPTING. *p.* Molition, innitent. (See endeavouring, trying.)

ATTEND. *v.* To attend to, to advert, to animadvert. (See to regard, heed, punish.)

ATTENDANCE. *s.* Assectation.

ATTENDANT. *a.* Attendant (following) sequacious, concomitant; attendant or footman, henchman; attendant or gallant, cicisbeo: attendants, retinue, meiny, equipage, suite

ATTENTION. *s.* Observance; done without attention, listlessly.

ATTENTIVE. *a* Assiduous, intentive, attent, aware, intense, observant, vigilant, wistful.

ATTRACTING. *a.* Attracting or drawing applications to the skin, epispastics. (See blister)

ATTRACTION. *s.* Attraction or charm, alliciency. (See charm.)

AUCTION. *s.* Licitation, vendue.

AVERSION. *s.* Antipathy reluctation, (See dislike, hatred, struggle, resistance.)

AUGURS. *s.* Sort of chair in which the Roman augurs sat, when they took their observations, sella solida. (See chair.)

AVOID. *v.* To absonate, to evade, to evitate, to beware; avoid by artifice, to elude, to eschew.

AVOIDED. *p.* Not to be avoided, uneschewable.

AWAKEN. *v.* To excite, to incite. (See rouse, stir, spur, urge, animate.)

AUSTERE. *s.* Acrimonious, ascetic. (See devout, sharp, tart, odd, strict.)

AUTHOR. *s.* Author, said of an author's works, when his sense and style are wilfully altered, travested author; author or writer, who snarls and carps at the works of others, latrant author or writer; disrespectful epithet given to a poor author, garreteer.

AUTHORITY. *s.* Control, gubernation, masterdom

AWAKE. *v.* To suscitate, to exsuscitate, or exuscitate; the causing to awake, expergefaction.

AWARD. *s.* Arbitration, arbitrement, arbitrage, laudum.

AWAY. *ad.* Avaunt, aroynt. (See absent, begone.)

AWEFUL. *a.* August, dread, tremendous, horrendous.

AWKWARD. *a.* Uncourtly, uncouth, ineloquent; awkward country girl, hoiden; awkward fellow, bumpkin, clod, knuff, looby.

AWKWARDLY. *ad.* Bunglingly, loobily, lubberly.

AWL. *s.* Formed as an awl, subulated.

AWRY. *ad.* Obliquely, aslant.

AX. *s.* Cooper's ax, adze. addice.

AXLETREE. *s.* The pins which keep the wheels of any carriage, on the axletree, linchpins.

B

BABBLING. *p.* Garrulity, inaniloquence, inaniloquous. (See talking.)

BACCHUS. *s.* The feigned god of wine and drunkards; a hymn anciently sung in honour of him, dithyrambus.

BACK. *s.* To write on the back, to endorse, or indorse; a going back again, regress, regression, regressive; to beat back, to repulse; fall back, to relapse; turning back of humours, revulsion.

BACK. *s.* Of or belonging to the back, dorsal; gout in the back, rhachisagra. (See gout); one who has a distorted back, blæsus, G.

BACKBITE. *v.* To malign, vitilitigate, to detract.

BACKBITER. *s.* Insectator.

BACKBONE. *s.* Chine; joints of the backbone, vertebræ or vertebres, spondyles, a distortion of the backbone, repandity, scoliasis; backbone of a hog broiled, grisken.

BACKWARD. *a.* Averse, fro', loth, or lothe, posterior, postic; a going backwards, retrocession, retrogression, retrogradation; act of looking backwards, retrospection; term used for such animals as make water backwards, retromingents; to kick backwards with the heels, to recalcitrate.

BACON. *s.* Gammon of bacon, perna, pestle; slice of bacon, rasher.

BAD. *a.* Egregious, errant, discommendable, facinereous, facinoreus, indefensible, incorrigble, indign, intolerable, finewed, fulsome, nauseous, obscene, jadish, ignominious, immoral, malefic, nocent, nocive, nocuous, peccant, peracute, reprehensible, retchless; bad action, malefaction; bad constitution of body, intemperament. (See difficult.)

BADGER. *s.* Brock, meles.

BAG. *s.* Cell, cist, cyst, nodule, poke, satchel; bag for carrying clothes, portmanteau; enclosed in a bag, encysted.

BAGGAGE. *s.* Luggage; to take away or unload baggage, to desarcinate.

BAGNIO. *s.* Balneary, bawdyhouse. (See bath and stew.)

BAIL. *s.* Surety; those persons who become bail or surety for others, and to whom the prisoner is delivered for appearance at a future period, mainpernors, mainprizers, or manucaptors; term used in law, when one is admitted to bail, upon finding surety, invadiatus.

BAILABLE. *a.* Mainpernable.

BAILIFFS. *s.* Bailiffs in the Isle of Man,
Moors.

BAIT. *s.* Inducement, inescation, lure, enticement. (See trap.)

BALANCE. *v.* To balance exactly, to trutinate, to equilibrate, to librate.

BALANCE. *s.* Steelyard, poise, lever; equal balance, equilibrium, equilibrity, equipoise; overbalance, preponderation; to overbalance, to preponder, to preponderate, to exuperate; balance or adjust an account, to liquidate; the Roman balance, statera; prop or support of a balance, fulciment, fulcrum, hypomochlion, obex.

BALCONY. *s.* Balcony or projecting gallery, mirador.

BALD. *a.* Implume, callow. (See bare.)

BALDNESS. *s.* Baldness of the head, madarosis, alopecy, glabrity.

BALL. *s.* Pellet; to gather into a ball, to glomerate, to conglomerate, to agglomerate, to conglobate; ball of worsted or thread, crewel; ball, assembly, junto, conventicle; term for a game at ball, pall-mall, or pell-mell; balls filled with hair, sometimes found in the stomachs of animals, ægagropili; small ball, spherule; term for one who plays at ball with a racket, spheristicus; the feigned inventress of balls and dancing, Terpsichore.

BALLAD. *s.* The burden of a ballad or song, refret.

BALLOT. *s.* The art or manner of choosing by ballot, to fill up the place of those who were before refused, subsortition.

BAN. *s.* Excommunication, fulmination, anathema, maranatha.

BAND. *s.* Brace, cincture, compress; band for uniting of bones together, ligament, syndesmus; band of ten soldiers, decury; to divide into bands, to decuriate.

BANDAGE. *s.* Perizoma, ligature, fillet; act of applying a bandage, fasciation; bandage so tied, that if it be pressed or drawn, it shuts up close, laqueus; bandage for a rupture, amma, truss; bandage for a wound, anadesma; bandage for the head, capistrum.

BANG. *v.* To lamm, to pommel, to sugillate, to thwack.

BANISH. *v.* To expel, to exulate, to deport, to eject, to proscribe, to relegate.

BANISHED. *a.* Expatriated; banished man, londless.

BANISHMENT. *s.* Exilement, deportation; banishment for a certain limited time, relegation; sort of banishment formerly used among the Athenians for 10 years, in which the person's name to be banished was written on an oyster-shell, hence called, ostracism.

BANK. *s.* Bank of a river, rivage; waters or rivers which run betwixt banks, in contradistinction to those which run in the plain, riparious; banks or islets formed by the shifting of the tides, &c. alluvia.

BANKRUPT. *s.* Insolvent; stone in Padua in Italy, resorted to by bankrupts, at which, if they openly declare their inability to pay, they are freed from prosecution, lapis opprobrii, *i. e.* the stone of reproach.

BANTER. *v.* To gleek, to illude, to gibe, to sneer, to rally.

BAPTISM. *s.* Surety or sponsor in baptism, gossip; one who is an enemy to baptism, catabaptist; bason used at baptism, font.

BAR. *s.* Boom, barricade, barricado, exclusion, obstacle, let, portcullis.

BARBAROUS. *a.* Ferine, gothic, ruthless, alabastical, truculent.

BARBARITY. *s.* immanity, barbarism.

BARBERRY. *s.* Oxycantha, or piperidge, the flower of the barberry-tree has the curious property of the sensitive plant, for if the lower part of the pistillum is pricked with a fine needle, the stamina will instantly collapse!

BARE. *a.* Pinfeathered, callow, incondite, thread-bare (often repeated) trite; make bare, to denude, to denudate; act of making bare, nudation, denudation; barefooted, excalceated.

BARGAIN. *v.* To chaffer, to contract, to covenant, to stipulate; bargain hard, to higgle; a deceitful mode of bargaining, when one sells property as his own, when not so, stellionate. (See selling.)

BARGAIN. *s.* Paction; settled by bargain, pactitious.

BARK. *v.* To bark as a dog, to allatrate, to bay, to oblatrate, to illatrate; to strip off the bark, to decorticate, to excorticate, to delibrate.

BARK. *s.* Bark of a tree, cortex; Jesuits or Peruvian bark, cina, cinæ, or quinquina; disease in trees when their bark falls off, defluvium; bark used by tanners, ouse.

BARKING, as a dog, latrant.

BARLEY MEAL. *s.* Divination by, alphitomancy.

BARM. *s.* Zest, or yeast.

BARREL. *s.* Barrel of wine, bombard; small barrel for fish, butter, &c. cade.

BARREN. *a.* Addle, infecund, sterile, infertile, saturnine, teemless.

BARTER. *v.* To swap, to swop, to truck.

BASE. *a.* Iniquitous, marble-hearted, atrocious, heinous, cuckoldly, ferine, flagitious, homicidal, ignoble, ignominious, illegal, illiberal, notorious, perfidious, putid, recreant, servile, sordid, venal, illaudable; base wretch, miscreant, catiff; base metal put into gold or silver, to encrease its hardness, alloy or allay; base, (bottom of any geometrical figure) hedra; the art of measuring figures standing on their bases, epipedometry.

BASENESS. *s.* Degradation, despicableness, improbity, pravity, degeneracy, depravity, turpitude, incorrigibility.

BASHFUL. *a.* Verecund, diffident, pudibund, timorous. (See modest, chaste, doubtful.)

BASKET. *s.* Corb, ped; baskets filled with earth, used in fortification, gabions.

BASKING. *p.* Basking in the sun, aprication, insolation.

BASON. *s.* Basin, posnet, porrenger, skillet; basin used at baptism, font; divination by water in a bason, leucanomancy. (See divination.)

BASSET. *s.* To play at basset, to punt.

BASTARDY. *s.* State of, illegitimacy, illegitimation; bastards, *nothi*, L.

BATH. *s.* Balneary; bath for the feet, pediluvium, psammismus; bath for the belly, encathisma; half bath in which the patient sits only up to the middle, semicubium, incessus; hot or warm baths, thermæ; cold baths, psychrolusia; the apartments in baths wherein the sweat was scraped off, detersoria.

BATHE. *v.* To embay, to foment.

BATHING-ROOM. Balneary; bathing with warm water, fomentation; a liquid application, between bathing and fomenting, lotion; the bathing in sea-water, pseucrolusion.

BATTLE. *s.* Hosting, combat; order of battle, battalia or battle-array; to arrange troops for battle, to d'arrain; battle, to contravent, to embattle; loss of battle, discomfiture; battle with a shadow, sciamachy; battle or combat on horseback, hippomachy; battle of the gods and giants, theomachy. (See combat and fight.)

BAWD. *s.* Procuress, lupanatrix; belonging to a bawd, lenonian.

BAWDY-HOUSE. *s.* Bordel, stew, brothel, bagnio, balneary; addicted to talk bawdy language, spurcidical.

BAWLING. *p.* Vociferation, obstreperous.

BAY. *s.* Small bay, creek, fleet, indraught, sinus.

BEACON. *s.* Pharos, cynosure.

BEADLE. *s.* Apparitor, paritor.

BEADS. *s.* A string of beads which the Roman Catholics use in saying their paternosters, chaplet; a set of beads used by them, containing 15 large beads, called pater-nosters, and 150 smaller, called ave Marias, rosary.

BEAK. *s.* Beak of a fowl, bill, neb; having a broad beak, latirostrous.

BEAM. *s.* The principal beam in a building, architrave; this also means that part of a column in architecture which lies immediately upon the capital; beam, joist, balk, boom; beam of timber placed next the ground in any building, groundsel, or groundsil; frame made up of beams and boards, contignation; the beams or shafts of any carriage in which the horse goes, thill; hence the term, thill-horse, or thiller-horse; beam of light, pencil; to dart out a beam of light, to irradiate, to radiate.

BEAN. *s.* Belonging to the bean, fabaceous; terms used for the bean and pea tribe, and generally for all plants having a papilionaceous flower, legumes, leguminn, pulse; kidney bean, phascolus.

BEAR. *v.* To bear or support, to prop; bear or suffer, to brook, to endure, to tolerate; bear or carry, to delate; bear down or awe, to browbeat. (See support, suffer, carry.)

BEARD. *s.* Barb; beard or down hanging at the ends of the husks of some plants, juba; an ingredient, of a composition, to take off the beard, without the trouble of shaving, rusma, or susma.

BEARER. *s.* Bearer of a sword before a prince or magistrate, port-glaive.

BEARING. *p.* Bearing or carrying, gerent; a bearing or falling down, delaption. Bearing fruit, fetiferous,
—— grain, graniferous,
—— grass, &c. graminiferous, &c.
act of bearing or carrying young, gestation; past bearing young, effete; a bearing of children, puerperous, puerperal; a difficulty in bearing children, dystochy.

BEAST. *s.* Term for any beast used in husbandry, jument; belonging to beasts of labour, jumentarious; den of a beast of prey, lair, or layer; dissector of beasts, zootomist; the dissection of the bodies of beasts, zootomy; shew of wild beasts let loose by the ancients to the people, pancarpus; term used for those beasts that have broad horns, platycerotes.

BEASTLY. *a.* Belluine, bestial, brutish.

BEAT. *v.* To pommel, to bang, to sugillate, to tew, to thwack, to trounce, to vanquish, to vapulate, to repercuss, to buffet, to curry, to firk, to fease or feaze, to lamm, to bray, to drub, to baste, to batter, to maul, to nubble, to belabour, to bump, to cane.

To beat or shake as sound, to verberate;

to beat out the brains, to excerebrate; to beat to and fro, to bandy; to beat small, to contund, to contuse; to beat flax or hemp, to hatchel; to beat out of cover, to indagate; to beat with the knuckles, to knubble; to beat or bray as in a mortar, to triturate; to beat or tew with a hammer, to tudiculate.

BEATEN. *p.* Beaten in, adacted; beaten to pieces, pertuse.

BEATING. *p.* Beating of the heart as from surprise, spit-pat; an excessive beating of the heart and arteries, arising from a nervous affection, palpitation; a beating into thin plates, lamination; a beating or bouncing, salient; act of beating or striking, vapulation; a beating back, recussion, repercussion; beating or thrusting away, depulsion.

BEAUTIFUL. *a.* Luculent, venust; beautiful progeny, callipædia.

BEAUTIFY. *v.* To embellish, to adorn, to decorate, to garnish; which last word means also, to load with irons.

BEAUTY. *s.* Pulchritude, comliness; giving beauty, commetic; preserving beauty, cosmetic.

BECOME. *v.* To befit, to beseem, to fadge.

BECOMING. *p.* Behovable, concinnous, decorous; not becoming, misbecoming.

BED. *s.* Bed filled with locks of wool, flock-bed; swinging beds used at sea, hammocks; that apparatus necessary for the care of sick persons in bed, lectisternium; said of a person whose distemper requires him to keep in bed, lectual, clinical; bed (relating to the rites of Venus) thoral; flakes of wool, down of plants, &c. used in stuffing of beds, tomentum; a low bed which runs underneath another, truckle-bed; a little bed with curtains, grabat; term used when a disease seizes one so violently as obliges him to take to his bed, decumbiture; bed or couch of a wild beast, lair or layer; bed or layer of sand, clay, or other matter, stratum; bed upon bed, stratification.

BEDTIME. *s.* Bed-time, or the act of visiting late, couchee.

BEECH. *s.* The fruit of the beech-tree, mast.

BEER. *s.* Cant phrase for bad small beer, rotgut; old strong beer, stingo.

BEES. *s.* Place where they are kept and reared, apiary; name of a bird which destroys bees, modwall.

BEFORE. *prep.* Afore, ere; going before, anterior, a-head, precedaneous; to go before, to precede, to antecede; thought of before, precogitation; knowledge acquired before hand, precognition; opinion formed before hand, preconcept; cause of a disease going before the immediate one, proegumena; act of going before, precession.

BEG. v. To supplicate, to crave, to implore, to invoke, to mendicate, to solicit, to beg incessantly, to importune, to obtest. (See beseech.)

BEGET. v. To engender, to procreate; unable to beget, effete.

BEGGAR. s. Mendicant; genteel beggar, mumper.

BEGGARLY. a. Beggarly scoundrel, bezonian.

BEGGARY. s. Mendicity. (See want.)

BEGGING. p. Mendicant, supplicating, obtesting.

BEGIN. v. To begin or enter on any appointment, to inaugurate; to begin again or anew, to resume, to recommence.

BEGINNER. s. Inceptor, novice, tyro.

BEGINNING. s. Beginnings or rudiments, of any language, accidence; eagerness acquired from a prosperous beginning, fleshment; beginning or attempt, inception; what is just beginning or rising, incipient; beginning of any work, or the drawing of any plane or solid figure, genesis; beginning of any work, particularly of a suit in law, inchoation; placed at the beginning, initial; beginning or entrance, arche, exordium; existing from the beginning, primordial, primordiate.

BEGONE. inter. Avaunt, aroynt.

BEGOTTEN. p. Self-begotten, autogenial; begotten between animals of different species, hybridous.

BEGUILE. v. To delude, to supplant, to gull. (See deceive, cheat, betray.)

BEHAVE. v. To demean, to deport; to comport.

BEHAVIOUR. s. Portance, comportance; nicety of, punctilio.

BEHEAD. v. To decapitate, to decollate, to guillotine.

BEING. s. Entity, essence; the doctrine of being, ontology.

BELCH. s. Eructation, oxyregmia, ructation.

BELIEF. s. Firm of belief, confidence, credence; easy of belief, credulous; hard of belief, incredulous; not to be believed, incredible; want of belief, miscreance; belief, creed.

BELIEVE. v. To opine.

BELL. s. Bell rung at 8 o'clock at night, first ordained by William the Conqueror, curfew, ignitegium; name for the substitute of a bell used by the Greeks, under the dominion of the Turks, who prohibit their use, hagiosidaere, i. e. holy iron.

BELLOWING. p. Blatant, mugient.

BELLY. s. Having a double belly or sto-

mach, diagastric; to rip up the belly, to eventerate; bath for the belly, encathisma; act of carrying young in the belly, gestation; binding in the belly, coprostacy, opstipatio; seated or felt in the lower belly, hypogastric; lower belly, abdomen; contents of the lower belly, encolia; the art of speaking as if from the belly, ventriloquy, ventriloquism; one who possesses that faculty, engastrimythos, gastromyth, ventriloquist; a cutting open the belly, gastrotomy; divination by the belly, gastromancy.

BELONGING. p. Belonging to, purtenance, appurtenance.

BELT. s. Baldric, cincture, perizoma, diazoma. (See girdle.)

BEMIRE. v. To bedash, to bedraggle, to bedaggle, to soil.

BEND. v. To buckle, to courb, to elbow, to juke, to knuckle, to curvate, to incurvate, to inflect; bend or plait as with branches, to pleach; to bend out and in, to sinuate.

BENDING. p. Inclinatory, deviating; the bending of the leg or arm, engonios; bending downwards and forwards, prone; bending backwards, reflectent, recurvant; bending out and in, sinuous.

BENEFICE. s. Incumbency; the right to present to one, advowson; the person who has the right of presenting to a benefice, avowee or advowee; a term used for the gift of a void benefice, by the death, &c. of the former incumbent, which, as it is sometimes given pro tempore to the clerk, is called a commendam; to put into possession of a benefice, to induct.

BENEFICIAL. a. Lucrative, lucrific, lucriforous, lucrous.

BENEFIT. s. Boot, avail, emolument, benefaction, lucre.

BENT. a. Curvated, kimbo, flexuous; bent like a hook, hamated; bent, bandyed; bent, or inclination from an even course, bias; bent, or turned quite from the subject, kam; bent like a scythe, falcated; bent and hollowed like a tile, imbricated; bent or inclined, proclive; easily bent, limber, pliant, flexile, flexible; bent back, recurvous, repandous.

BENUMBED. p. Torpent, torpescent, torpid.

BENUMBING. p. Benumbing fish, torpedo.

BERRIES. s. Bearing berries, bacciferous.

BESEECH. v. To impetrate, to implore, to invoke, to obtest, to supplicate, to invoke, to obsecrate.

BESIEGE. v. To beleaguer, to invest, to beset.

BESIEGING. p. Act of besieging, obsession.

BEST. a. Primal, prime; state of being

best, optimity.

BESTOW. *v.* To collate, to confer.

BESTOWING. *p.* Bestowing freely, act of, elargation.

BETRAY. *v.* To bewray. (See beguile.)

BETRAYER. *s.* Proditor.

BETROTHED. *p.* Affied or affianced, combinate.

BETTER. *a.* Not to be made better, shameless, irreclaimable; to make better, to meliorate; state of being better, meliority.

BEVERAGE. *s.* Made of ale and roasted apples, lamb's wool. (See drink.)

BEWITCH. *v.* To fascinate, to intoxicate, to infatuate, to effascinate.

BEWITCHING. *p.* As by poison, veneficial. (See charm.)

BIBLE. *s.* The first five books of the bible, written by Moses, pentateuch; a bible having one line of Latin translation printed between every two lines of the Hebrew and Greek originals, is termed, an interlineary bible; the Mahometan bible, alcoran.

BICKERING. *p.* Bickering or wrangling in words, velitation.

BIESTINGS. *s.* Colustrum.

BIG. *a.* Burly; exceeding big, enormous, gigantic, immane, huge; big or swelled, turgid; big with young, fetiferous, gravid, parturient, tumid.

BIGNESS. *s.* Hugeness; bigness or grossness of body, polysarchy, corpulency.

BILE. *s.* Choler: bile or imposthume, furuncle; medicines which purge bile, cholagogues.

BILL. *s.* Bill or beak; having a broad bill or beak, latirostrous; bill or advertisement either posted up or delivered, to give notice of some speech to be delivered, or ceremony performed in a public seminary or school, programma; the king's assent to a bill in parliament, is in the following words "*Soit fait droit, comme il est desiré.*"

BIND. *v.* Bind up; to embale, to faggot, to furl, to edder, to brace; bind fast with fetters, to gyve, to immanacle, to manacle; bind or hold in a string, to leash; to bind the hands in fetters, to manacle; to bind or enslave, to mancipate; bind or tie the arms as is done to malefactors, to pinion, to shackle; to bind to, to illigate; having or possessing power to bind, said of medicines, restringent, astringent; to bind one hand and foot, to faggot.

BINDING. *p.* Adstrictive, astrictive, constrictive, colligation, constringent, astringent; binding up of a wound, &c. deligation; any binding whatever, or what strengthens, ligation, ligature, clamp; act of binding, ligation; very hard binding, perligation; binding by contract, obligatory; binding or obligatory, valid; binding fast, religation; binding, unitive; binding together, adstriction, restringent, astringent, stegnotic; act of binding underneath, subligation.

BIRDS. *s.* Divination by the flight, singing or feeding of birds, augury, ornithomancy; the nest of a bird of prey, or where their nests are built, aerie or eyry; place where birds are reared, aviary; the bill of a bird, neb, beak; stomach of any bird, craw, choule, crop, gizzard, inghuvies; bird-catching, aucupation; to dung as birds, to mute; bird just hatched, nestling; name of a bird that being looked upon by one who has the yellow jaundice, is said to cure the person and die itself, loriot; the systematic description and account of birds, ornithology; omens drawn from the observation of birds, orniscopics; the talon of a bird of prey, pouncer; name given to such birds as have feathers on their feet, as the owl, plumipedes; the mocking bird of America, polyglotta; the stroke of a bird of prey, swoop; flight of birds, volery or volary; the name of a noisy ravenous bird, in Staffordshire, and Shropshire, preying on other birds, which, when they seize, they hang on a thorn and tear them in picés, wariangles (Bailey); name given to a bird by ornithologists, which is so light as to be blown about with every puff of wind, cepphus; name of the largest bird known and found in America, two of which, it is affirmed, will kill a bull, condor, or contor.

BIRD-LIME. *s.* Caught by bird-lime, viscated.

BIRTH. *s.* Producing one at a birth, uniparous; two, biparous; three, &c. triparous, &c.; birth, descent; of the same birth, congenite, connascence, connate; calculator of births, genethliac, genethilatic; related by birth on the father's side, consanguinean; on the mother's, uterine; on both sides, german; relating to a birth-day, natalitious; producing many at a birth, multiparous; relating to birth, natal; certain deities among the Romans, supposed to be the helpers of women in child-birth, nixidii; the after birth, placenta, secundines, heam; false birth, humourously alleged to be produced by the Dutch women, from sitting over their stoves, sooterkin.

BISHOP. *s.* Leave given by the king to choose a bishop, congé d'elire, *i. e.* leave to elect; letter sent by one bishop to another, in favour of one who stands candidate for holy orders in another diocese, demissory letter; a register or list of bishops or eminent men of the church, diptych; relating to bishops, episcopal, prelatical; the killing of a bishop, episcopicide; the seat or throne of a bishop within the chancel, faldisdroy.

BIT. *s.* Bit, or insignificant fragment, fet, iot, iota, tittle; bit or morsel of exquisite relish, titbit, bonbon, cates.

BITCH. *s.* Dogess; to copulate as dog and bitch, to ligne or line.

BITE. *v.* To champ, to knab, to knap, to bite or deceive, to conycatch.

BITE. *s.* Morsure; bite of any venomous creature, lyssa.

BITING. *p.* Mordacious, mordicant, acrid, poignant; act of biting, morsure.

BITTER. *a.* Acerb, acrid, breme, hepatical; bitter and malignant temper, virulency.

BITTERN. *s.* Bittern, or liquor remaining in the bullary, after the culinary salt is withdrawn, is termed sulphate of magnesia; bittern, (species of hawk) kite, puttoc.

BITTERNESS. *s.* Invectiveness, amaritude.

BITUMEN. *s.* Naphta; bitumen of Judea, pissaphaltus.

BITUMINOUS, asphaltic.

BLACK. *a.* Sable, atramentous, stygian, fuliginous, jetty; made black, collied, denigrated; to make black, to infuscate; black and blue, livid, lurid; black and blue spots on the body like the mark of blows, molopes; growing black, nigrescent; act of making black, nigrefaction; to cover over again with black, to redenigrate; black cattle, rother beasts, beeves; black-bird, merula, ouzel, ousel.

BLADDER. *s.* Like a bladder, vesicular; bladder, cyst, cist; enclosed in a bladder, encysted; medicines for breaking or dissolving the stone in the bladder, calcifragus, lithontriptic; to catch fresh water fish, especially pike, by means of a bladder, to hux.

BLAMABLE. *a.* Culpable, faulty, reprehensible, vituperable.

BLAME. *v.* To chide, to discommend, to exprobate, to reprehend, te reprimand; blame in return, to recriminate.

BLAME. *s.* Odium, censure, culpability, disapprobation, dispraise, public blame or censure, ostracism (See banishment.)

BLAMELESS. *a.* Inculpable, unculpable, irreprehensible.

BLAMING. *p.* Correptory. (See to chide, reprove, rebuke.)

BLANK. *a.* Blank paper sent to be filled up with such conditions as the person who receives it thinks proper, and is sometimes practised in sending a challenge, carte blanche, Fr.

BLAST. *s.* Explosion, afflation, blight, blore, disaster; blast from below, exsufflation; blast by cold, to chill.

BLASTED. *p.* Siderated, planet-struck, rubiginated; act of blasting, syderation, astrobolism.

BLAZE. *v.* Blaze away as a lighted candle set in a current of air, to sweal or swale.

BLEACHING. *p.* Bleaching in the sun, insolation, aprication; this last word is generally applied to basking in the sun; act of bleaching, dealbation.

BLEEDING. *p.* Venesection, phlebotomy; instrument used by farriers in bleeding of cattle, phleme; instrument used in bleeding, by which the blood is impelled to the part covered by the instrument, by means of the pressure of the atmosphere being taken off, cupping-glass, vesicatory, cucurbitula, ventose.

BLEMISH. *s.* Disfigurement, defacement, macula.

BLEND. *v.* To commingle. (See mix.)

BLESS. *s.* Laud. (See praise.)

BLESSEDNESS. *p.* Beatitude, to make blessed, to imparadize.

BLESSING. *p.* Benediction, benison.

BLIND. *v.* To hoodwink.

BLINDNESS. *s.* Cecity; tendency to blindness, cecutiency, caligation; act of making or rendering blind, occecation, occæcation, or occoecation; to make blind, to occoecate; the state of being purblind, eluscation.

BLIND-SIDE. *s.* Foible.

BLISTER. *v.* To vesicate. Full of blisters, papulosity; blister made of mustard, sinapism; blistering, epispastic, vesicatory.

BLOCK UP. *v.* To begird, to embar, to blockade, to beleaguer.

BLOCKHEAD. *s.* Asshead, jobbernowl, jolt-head, loggerhead, ninny, ninny-hammer, nincompoop, numskull.

BLOOD. *s.* Blood, the circulation of the blood is termed, cyclophorea sanguinis; blood let out of the veins, extravenate blood; clotted blood, gore, tabum; flux of blood from any part of the body, hæmorrhage or hemorrhagia; evacuation, common after the exclusion of the foetus and secundines, lochia; void of blood, exanguious, or exanguous; drenched with blood, insanguined, cruentate; medicines for stopping the blood, ischæma, enthemata, styptics, stiptics; an eruption of blood through the vessels, persultation, extravasation; the binding up of a wound to stop the blood, epidesis; to let blood, to phlebotomize; field of blood, aceldama; conveying or carrying off blood, as the veins and arteries, sanguiferous; medicines good for correcting the blood, anticachectics; the art of producing or turning into blood, sanguification; belonging to the weight or ponderosity of the blood, hæmastatical; flowing with blood, sanguifluous; abounding with blood (also brisk, forward, &c.) sanguine; blood-letting, venesection; bloodsucker, such as the leech, sanguisuga; the formation of blood into clots, thrombus; the thin or watery part of the blood, serum; to stop blood, to stanch; medicine for stopping blood, emæmon; spots under the skin, arising from the blood being extravasated, ecchymoma, ecchymosis, this in a less degree is termed thrombus; bloodshot in the eye, caused by a stroke, hyposphagma; the mode of conveying the blood of one living creature into another, transfusion; bloodstone, hæmatites; any uncommon flowing of the blood, hæmatochysis, hæmorrhage; a swelling of the navel, turgid with blood, hæmatomphalocele; the faculty or power of turning into blood, hæmatosis; one who is afraid of being let blood, hæmophobus; remedies against spitting of blood, hæmoptics; one who spits blood, hæmoptic; a spitting of blood from the lungs, hæmoptysis; related by blood, consanguineous.

BLOODY. a. Fell, butcherly, gladiatorial, cruentous, gory, homicidal, incompassionate, sanguinary, sanguinolent; bloodyflux, dysentery; bloody sweat, hæmatopedesis.

BLOOMING. p. Roseate, vernant, virent.

BLOT. v. To blot, to delete, to distain; to blot out, to efface, to expunge, to annihilate, to obliterate, to rase.

BLOT. s. Blur, inquination, solure.

BLOTTED. p. Not to be blotted out, indelible

BLOW. v. To blow through a pipe, &c. to perflate; blow up, or enlarge, to inflate, to sufflate; blow a trumpet, to buccinate;

BLOW. s. Dub, bang, bob, brunt, buffet, bump, dint, verberation, impetus, occursion

BLUE. a. Deep blue colour, mazarine; sky colour, azure, cerulean, ceruleous, planket colour; blue and black as from a stroke, livid; blue and black spots on the body, as from a stroke, molopes; blue and black, portending a storm, lurid; name of a very fine blue colour used in painting, ultramarine; it was formerly produced from lapis lazuli, but now can be made, according to De Morveau, from selenite loaded with iron, and decomposed by carbonaceous matter.

BLUNDER. v. To hallucinate.

BLUNDER. s. Bull, hallucination.

BLUNT. v. To blunt, to obtund, to rebate,

to retund.

BLUNT. a. Obtuse, disedged, hebitated; blunt fellow, chuff.

BLUSH. s. Erubescence; that never blushes or changes colour, chromatic; blushing, erubescent.

BLUSTER. v. To rhodomontade, to roist.

BLUSTER. s. Fanfaronade, bravado, gasconade.

BLUSTERER. s. Huffer, thraso.

BLUSTERING. p. Turbulent, blustrous, bluff, domineering, thrasonical; blustering fellow, cacafuego.

BOARDS. s. Boards and beams, made of, contignation; made of boards, planched.

BOAR. s. The couch of a boar, layer, or lair; the teeth or tusks of a boar, rasors; to copulate as a boar and sow, to brim; to grunt or growl as a boar at rutting time, to fream; boar's flesh rolled hard, and eat in thin slices, boar-brawn.

BOAST. v. To bluster, to bounce, to glory, to exult, to rhodomontade.

BOAST. s. (Speech of defiance) bravado, bravo, gasconade; boasted display or challenge, vendication.

BOASTER. s. Thraso, vaunter, jactator, crack, huffer, cacafuego, braggadocio, braggard, hector.

BOASTFUL. a. Ostentatious, thrasonical.

BOASTING. p. Vain boasting, jactation, venditation.

BOAT. s. Name given to a kind of boat made by the Indians, composed either of the bark of a tree sewed together, or made by hollowing the trunk, canoe or canoo; huge sort of boats used in the northern countries of Europe, for bringing flax, hemp, &c. down the rivers, prames; rowing or sailing-match with boats, as is practised at Venice, Regatta; sort of row-boats or galley, with three tier of oars on a side, trireme; with four, quadrireme, &c.; the wooden pins inserted in a boat's gunwale, to keep the oars steady, thowls; the rope by which a boat is dragged after a ship, gift-rope.

BODKIN. s. Formed as a bodkin, subulated.

BODY. s. To remove in a body as birds, to commigrate, to migrate; body-politic, community; to form into a body, to corporify, to incorporate, to incorpse, to concorporate; body of soldiers, corps; small body, corpuscle, monade; body or company of merchants, guild; (hence their hall in London is called Guildhall); ill habit of body, cachetical; bulkiness of the body, corpulency, polysarchy; to walk with the body half covered, or with the clothes very tight, so as to shew one's shapes, to walk in cuerpo; dead body, corpse, or corse; good and healthy state of the body, euchrasy or euchymy, ulomelia; the natural or preternatural state of the body of an animal, diathemis, diathesis; to remove from body to body, as the Jews and Chinese assert the souls of men do, in sometimes passing into the bodies of men, and sometimes of beasts, to metempsychose; the due proportion of the parts of an animal body, symmetry; any posture of the body, attitude; combat between soul and body, sychomachy; that happy modification of matter constituting a body (generally applied to the human) which qualifies it to be able to perform acts proper to it, entelechia, idiocracy (see fitness); that part of physic, which teaches how to acquire a good habit of body, evectica; the peculiar disposition of one body to another, habitus; having one body, or being formed with one body, unicorporal; with two, bicorporal; with three, &c. tricorporal, &c.; the art of measuring the contents of solid bodies, stereometry; the doctrine of bodies, somatology.

BOG. s. Morass, marsh, fen, marish, mizzy, quagmire, syrtis.

BOGGY. a. Wearish, marshy, gouty, marish, quaggy, swampy.

BOIL. v. To decoct, to ebulliate, to estuate.

BOIL. s. The ripening of a boil or tumour, suppuration.

BOILED. p. Term for wheat and milk boiled together, frumenty, furmenty; half boiled, parboiled.

BOILING. p. Bullition, ebullition, fervid, coction, concoction, exestuation, or exestication; boiling up with a hissing noise, as is the case in mixing an impure alkali and an acid, effervescence; boiling of plants for the purpose of extracting their medicinal virtues, elixation; to do or make by boiling, to excoct; a boiling or seething, also the concoction of the aliment in the stomach, pepsis.

BOISTEROUS. a. Frampold, pail-mail, rustic, turbulent, valorous, undaunted.

BOLD. a. Audacious, brave, confident, frontless, hyperbolical, intrepid, martial, masculine, battalious; hardy, malapert, pindaric, presuming, resolute, strenuous.

BOLDNESS. s. Brass, confidence, front, presumption, prowess.

BOLT. s. The act of shutting up by means of a bolt or key, obseration.

BOMBAST. s. Altiloquence, fustian, teratology, altisonance, sesquipedalian measure.

BOND. s. Obstriction, recognizance or recognisance.

BONDAGE. s. Captivity, servitude, thraldom.

BONES. s. Of, or belonging to the bones, bony; void of divested of bones, exosseous; boneless; receptacle or place for keeping bones, ossuary, charnel-house; the adhesion of two bones without the intervention of a joint, in which neither have a proper motion, epiphysis, symphysis; the reduction of dislocated bones, mochlia; general term for pains in the bones, osteocope; like, or made of, bones, osseous; little bone, ossicle; act of turning into bone, ossification; the power or faculty of breaking of bones, as is possessed by the jaws of the lion, &c. ossifrangous, ossifrangent; devouring of bones, ossivorous; description of the bones, osteology or synosteography; stone said to be of great use in the uniting of broken bones, osteocolla; those fishes which have bony fins, term used for them, osteopterugious; term used for a small fracture of a bone like a hair, trichismus; the articulation of one bone into the hollow socket of another, arthrodia; the setting of a bone that is out of joint, diaplasis; the rottenness of a bone, caries, teredum; the corrupting of a bone in the joint, pædarthrocace; the fitness of the bones discernible in their ar-articulation, paragoge; membrane of exquisite sense, surrounding almost all the bones of the body, except the teeth and a few more, periosteum; the spontaneous knitting together of broken bones, porosis; little rods of bone or ivory, invented by Baron Napier of Merchiston, for finding large products, quotients, powers and roots of quantities in arithmetic, art of computing by them is termed, rhabdology; medicines for knitting of broken bones, catagmatics; the articulation of two bones, when the round head of the one is received into the round hollow of the other, arthrosis; term used for the longitudinal fracture of a bone, scidaceum; the union of two bones which are joined by a tendon, syntenosis; the union of bones by the means of flesh, sysarcosis; term used for such a total fracture of a bone as quite divides it, and forces it out through the flesh, periclasis; that articulation of the bones, in which the head of one is received into the hollow of another, and again the head of the latter into the hollow of the former, ginglimus; term used when one bone is fastened to another, like a nail, as the teeth are in the jaws, gomphoma, gomphosis.

BOOK. s. Common-place book, adversaria, repertory; writer of books, bibliographer, book-keeper, countercaster; small book, manual, enchiridion; name given to such books, of which eighteen leaves make a Whole sheet,   -   octodecimo,

Twelve leaves, - duodecimo,
Eight leaves, - octavo,
Four leaves, - quarto,
Two leaves, folio.

The term folio is used also in speaking of merchants books, for one leaf, or two pages of their ledger. It is also used, in printing, for the figure set at the top of every page of letter-press.

Impression or copy of a book, edition; first book given to children, primer, horn-book; Romish service-book, lectionary, missal; the first five books of the bible, written by Moses, pentateuch; method used with books having a bad sale, of putting new and different titles to them, is termed, quacking of titles; a general name given to any portable book, vade-mecum; border of a book left blank for inserting notes, margin, margent.

BOOM. *s.* Boom of the mainsail; to shift the boom of the mainsail of a sloop rigged vessel, so as she may more easily go about, to jibe or jib.

BOOTS. *s.* Half-boots wore by the ancient tragedians, buskins; large boots, wore by horsemen, jack-boots; boots generally worn by soldiers, sabatans.

BOOTY. *s.* Boot, exuviæ; belonging to booty, manubial.

BORDER. *s.* Border of a country, &c. confines, frontier, purlieu; border of flowers, wreath, festoon; border, lege; border of a writing or book usually left blank, margin, or margent; bordered with fringes, fimbriated.

BORE. *v.* To perforate, to terebrate, to thrill, to drill.

BORE. *s.* Bore of a gun, caliber.

BORED. *a.* Foraminous; bored quite through, pertuse, transforated; that may be bored, forable; not bored, imperforate.

BORDERING. *p.* Adjacent, conterminous.

BORING *p.* Act of boring quite through, perterebration.

BORN. *s.* Born together, cognate, connate; born or produced after the death of the father, posthumous; this is also applied to publications after the author's death, hence the term, posthumous works; first born, primogenial; the being born again, palingenesia; dead-born, still-born; born of the earth, terrigenous; home-born inhabitants, or those who were originally of the country, autochtones, aborigines.

BORNE. *p.* Borne or carried by the waves, fluctigerous; that may be borne or suffered, patible.

BORROW. *v.* To borrow or choose, to desume.

BORROWED. *p.* Borrowed (foreign or counterfeit) adscititious or ascititious.

BORROWING. *p.* The act of borrowing or choosing, desumption or desumtion.

BOTANY. *s.* Phytology; those botanists who rank plants according to their parts of generation, as in the following scheme, sexualistæ.

Scheme of the Sexual System of Plants, according to Linnæus.

Classes.

1. Monandria, having one male or stamen in an hermaphrodite flower.
2. Diandria, - two males or stamina.
3. Triandria, - three ——
4. Tetrandria, - four ——
5. Pentandria, - five ——
6. Hexandria, - six ——
7. Heptandria, - seven ——
8. Octandria, - eight ——
9. Enneandria, - nine ——
10. Decandria, - ten ——
11. Dodecandria, - eleven ——
12. Icosandria, twenty or more males, inserted into the calix, but not into the receptacle.
13. Polyandria, all above twenty males inserted into the receptacle.
14. Didynamia, has four males, two of them uniformly shorter than the other two.
15. Tetradynamia; six males, two of which are uniformly shorter than the rest.
16. Monodelphia; the males or stamina united into one body by the filaments.
17. Diadelphia; when the stamina are united into two bodies by the filaments.
18. Polyadelphia; when united into three or more bodies by the filaments.
19. Syngenesia; when the stamina are united in a cylindrical form by the antheræ.
20. Gynandria; when the stamina are inserted in the pistillum.
21. Monoecia; when the male and female flowers are in the same plant.
22. Dioecia; when the male flowers are in one plant, and the females in another of the same species.
23. Polygamia; when the male, female, and hermaphrodite flowers, are in the same species.
24. Cryptogamia; when the flowers are invisible, so that they cannot be ranked ac-

C

cording to the parts of fructification.

The above classes are divided by botanists into orders, the orders into genera, the genera into species, and the species into varieties; for an exemplification of which, treatises on botany are to be consulted.

BOTTLE. *s.* Bottle of leather, in which the Spaniards bring their wine from the mountains, borachio; small glass bottle generally used by apothecaries, phial or vial.

BOTTOM. *s.* What falls to the botom of fluids, subsidence (see dregs); that has no bottom, abysmal.

BOUGHS. *s.* Boughs or branches of trees, ramage.

BOUGHT. *p.* That may be bought, mercatable, mercable.

BOUND. *v.* To bound or limit, to restrict, to stint, to terminate; to bound or leap, to curvet, to brow.

BOUND. *a.* Bound up, braced; bound in gratitude, beholden; constantly bound, indissoluble.

BOUNDARY. *s.* Abuttal, meer, mere, precinct, confine, frontier, barrier, bourne, but, circumscription; belonging to a boundary, limitaneous; placed at a boundary, limitary.

BOUNDING. *p.* Bounding or leaping up, subsultive.

BOUNDLESS. *a.* Illimitable, unlimitable, immeasurable, unmeasurable, immensurable, indefinite, undefinite, indeterminate, undeterminate.

BOUNTIFUL. *a.* Largifical, munificent (See liberal, kind.)

BOUNTY. *s.* Largess; relating to bounty, munerary, largifical.

BOUT. *s.* Tilt, veney, tournament, rencounter.

BOW. *v.* To bow, to buckle, to courb, to cringe; bow or bend inwards, to incurvate.

BOW. *s.* Obaisance, obeisance, congee.

BOWS. *s.* Maker of bows and arrows, fletcher, (from fleche, Fr.)

BOWED. *a.* Bowed or arched as the arms when laid across, kimbo; bowed or bent backwards, repandous.

BOWELS. *s.* Entrails, intestines, viscera, entera, encolia, garbage, offals; to take out the bowels, to exenterate, to viscerate, to eventerate; to take out the bowels of a hare or coney, to hulk; belonging to the small or lower bowels, iliac, iliacal; one whose bowels are preternaturally large, megalosplanchnos; treatise or discourse concerning the bowels, enterology, splanchnology (see sarcology,); name

for the coat that covers the bowels on the inside, peristoma, or peristroma; the membrane by which the bowels are tied to the back, and to each other, mesentery; membrane which incloses the bowels as in a bag, peritoneum; such medicines as are good for comforting and strengthening the bowels, splanchnica. (See guts.) The term bowels is used metaphorically for compassion.

BOX. *s.* Hollow as a box, capsular; the box that contains the host, pix or pyx; box containing all manner of miseries sent by Jupiter to Prometheus, used figuratively, means, misery, calamity, &c. and is termed, Pandora's box.

BOXER. *s.* Pugil, pugilist; the art of boxing, pugilism; relating to boxing, pugilistic; the exercise of boxing, pugillation.

BOY. *s.* Boy kept for unnatural purposes, pathic, ingle, catamite, ganymede, bardac; fat stupid boy, fub; relating to the actions of a boy, puerile.

BRAG. *v.* To vaunt, to gasconade, to rhodomontade or rodomontade.

BRAG. *s.* Brag or threat, bravado.

BRAGGER. *s.* Braggadocio, thraso, jactator, cacafuego.

BRAGGING *p.* Thrasonical, ventose. (See boaster.)

BRAMBLES. *s.* Full of or abounding in brambles, senticose, veprecose; place full of brambles, queach.

BRAN. *s.* Bran mixed with meal, pollard.

BRANCH. *s.* Sprout growing out of a branch which grew out itself but one year before, malleolus; term used in gardening when the branches of a tree are bent down to the ground, and covered with earth, so as to take root, laying; branch, bough; to separate into branches, to ramify; branches of trees, ramage; full of branches, ramose, ramous, sarmentous.

BRANDISH. *v.* To quassate, to vibrate. (See, to wave, to shake.)

BRANDY. *s.* Brandy mixt with wine, visné.

BRASS. *s.* Composition of brass or copper with tin, with which statues and different figures are made, bronze; brass, lattin or latten (see iron); writing on brass, chalcography or calcography; ashes of milled brass, nili; belonging to brass, erean.

BRAVE. *a.* Valorous, doughty, topping, intrepid, magnanimous, strenuous; brave man, hero; brave woman, heroine or heroess; most brave, provest.

BRAVERY. *s.* Hardihood, hardiment, hardiness, prowess, resoluteness.

BREACH. *s.* Disruption, ruption, fracas; breach or opening, hiatus, aperture, apertion, brack, discontinuance; breach of law, anomy.

BREAD. *s.* Unleavened bread, azimus; the art of making bread, zimotechnics; bread socked in fat, brewis; bread grated and mixt with marrow, moile; one who has the care of bread in a house, pantler or panter; marriage constituted by eating bread together, confarriation.

BREAK. *v.* Break off, to dissever, to disespouse; break through, to efforce; break as milk mixed with an acid, to posset; break, to fract, to fracture, to infract, to infringe; to break off short as brittle wood, to knap; break in pieces, to mammoc; break wind from the stomach, to eruct, to eructate.

BREAKING. *p.* Breaking in upon, irrumpent; breaking in by force, obtrusion; ready to break forth, erupturient; sudden breaking asunder, abruption, disruption, dissilition, eruption; house - breaking, burglary.

BREAST. *s.* Breasts, relating to them, mamary, pectoral, thoracic; kept in one's breast (secret), petto; an extension of the breasts by too great abundance of milk sparganosis, gynæcomaston; breast-bone, sternum, or sternon; a weaning from the breast, ablactation, delactation; that faculty of sequestering the milk in the breast, galactopletic faculty; term used of a man whose breasts are as large as a woman's, gynæcomastos; the red circle round the nipple of the breast, halo; piece of armour to guard the breast, habergeon, poitrel.

BREATHE. *v.* To spire, to respire; to breathe hard, to suspire; to breathe out, to expire to exhale.

BREATH. *s.* Act of drawing in breath, inspiration; out of breath, anhelose; to draw in the breath, to inhale.

BREATHING. *p.* Breathing upon, insufflation, afflation; difficulty in breathing, pneumatodes, anhelation, orthopnoia, dyspnois or dyspnoon; deep breathing, suspiration; act of breathing, respiration; quick breathing, ecphysesis; the faculty of breathing out, ecpneumatosis; that operation in surgery, where the fore part of the wind-pipe is divided, to assist breathing, as in quincy, laryngotomy, tracheotomy; the faculty of breathing with ease, eispnoe, eupnoea,

BREED. *s.* Breed, brood, clan, sept; one of a peculiar breed or turn of mind, is termed, 'one of a curious kidney.' (See brood.)

BREEDING. *p.* Breeding near wells, fontigenous; near the sea; maregenous, &c.; the breeding and bringing forth perfect animals, zoogonia.

BRIBE. *v.* To grease.

BRIBE. *v.* Relating to a bribe, munerary.

BRIDEMAID. *s.* Paranymph; the ceremony of bringing the bride and bridegroom to the bedchamber, enthalmization.

BRIDEWELL. *s.* Panopticon, penitentiary.

BRIDLES. *s.* Maker of, lorimer, loriner.

BRIEF. *a.* Compact, compendious, concise, laconic, succinct, summary, chilonian, chilonic.

BRIERY. *a.* Dumal, dumose, vepricose, sentecose.

BRIGHT. *a.* Dilucid, pellucid; very bright fulgent, effulgent, fulgid, effulgid, hyaline, præfulgid, limpid, lucent, transpicuous, luculent, luminous, lustrous, nitid, orient, pellucid, splendent, refulgent, resplendent; not bright, unlustrous. (See clear.)

BRIGHTNESS. *s.* Brilliancy, conspicuity, effulgence, irradiation, lucidity, lucidness, nitency, nitidity, serenity, sheen, splendour, splendor, clarity, refulgence.

BRIM. *s.* Labra; having a brim, labrose.

BRINE. *s.* Having the nature of brine, muriatic; consisting of brine, saline, garous,

BRING. *v.* Bring in as evidence, &c. to adduce; bring or lead in, to induct; to bring out to view, to educt, to educe, to elicit; to bring or train up, to nousil, to nourture, to educate; bring in over and above, to superinduce.

BRINGING. *p.* Bringing forth, parturient, act of parturition; act of bringing back, retroduction; difficulty of bringing forth young, dystochy.

BRINK. *s.* Brink or beim, labra, verge, having a brink or brim, labrose.

BRISK. *a.* Wanton, flippant, alert, drastic, juvenal, vivacious, airy, buxom, pert, sanguine, debonair; brisk or quick, (in music) allegro; brisk fellow, galliard

BRISTLES. *s.* Set with bristles, echinated, hirsute, hispid, setaceous

BROAD. *a.* Discous; to make broad, to distend; having a broad beak, latirostrous; having broad leaves, latifolious; term used for beasts that have broad horns, platycerotes.

BROIL. *v.* To carbonate, to embroil.

BROKEN. *a.* Abrupt, disrupt; easily broken, frangible, fragible, brittle, ruptile; broken down by sickness, crazy; broken off, discontinuous; not to be broken, infrangible; that cannot be broken or hurt, inviolable, irresoluble; medicines for knitting of broken bones, catagmatics.

BROILED *p.* Broiled oysters, escalop; what is broiled on the gridiron, grillade.

BROOD. *s.* Brood, bevy, covey; brood or

hatch eggs, to incubate; brood of pigs, litter, farrow; of pheasants, nide.

BROOK. *s.* Bourne, borne, rill, rillet, rivulet, streamlet.

BROTH. *s.* Sodden or stewed in broth, jussulent.

BROTHER. *s.* Brother by the father's side, brother consanguinean; by the mother's side, brother-uterine; by both sides, brother-german; term used for a younger brother, also for a gentleman volunteer, who serves in expectation of a commission, cadet, or cadee; false brother, pseudoadelphus; the murder, or murderer, of a brother, fratricide; religious brotherhood, confraternity; brotherly, fraternal.

BROUGHT. *p.* That cannot be brought or come at, impetible.

BROWN. *a.* Brown tawny colour, auburne eruginous, minim, bay, olivaster; brown colour as a dead leaf, philomot.

BRUISE. *v.* To contuse, to maul, to nubble, to pommel, to triturate; to bruise or beat with a hammer, to tudiculate.

BRUISED. *p.* Obtrite.

BRUSHWOOD. *s.* Chatwood,

BRUTAL. *a.* Belluine, boarish, cynical, doghearted, fell, barbarous, churlish; brutal language, ribaldry.

BRUTISHNESS. *s.* Ferity. (See barbarous.)

BUBBLE. *v.* To ebulliate, to estuate.

BUBBLING. *p.* Bubbling as a fluid set on the fire, ebullition; bubbling, accompanied with a hissing noise, produced by the mixture of an acid, and an impure alkali, effervescence; bubbling as a spring of water, scatebrous, scatebrosity, subsultive.

BUBOES. *s.* Venereal buboes in the groin, codoscelæ.

BUCK. *s.* Buck or male deer in his second year, pricket, spitter; term (in hunting) for the horns of a buck, attire; track of a buck in the forest, fusee.

BUD. *v.* To burgeon, to germinate, to pullulate, to egerminate; to bud again, to repullulate, to regerminate.

BUDS. *s.* Term used in botany in taking away superfluous buds, oculation; bud to be grafted, scutcheon.

BUFFOON. *s.* Harlequin, kick-shoe, mime, punchinello, antic, merry-Andrew, jack-pudding; the chief buffoon, archimime; general name used for buffoons, mammamouchi; name of the famous Italian buffoon or posture-master, who acted in England in 1673, scaramouch.

BUFFOONERY. *s.* Dicacity; writer on buffoonery and jesting, mimographer.

BUILD. *v.* To fabricate, to edify, to construct, to extruct, to erect.

BULKINESS. *s.* Bulkiness of the body, corpulency, polysarchy. (See body.)

BULKY. *a.* Burly, corpulent, gigantic, huge, massive, portly. (See great.)

BULL. *s.* To roar as a bull, to bellow; having horns like a bull, tauricornus; species of wild bull, bugle; shaped as a bull, tauriform; offspring of a bull and mare, jumart; strong gluey substance made of a bull's hide, taurocolla.

BULLY. *s.* To bluster, to bounce, to brave.

BULLY. *s.* Hector, huffer. (See bragger.)

BULRUSHES. *s.* Full of bulrushes, juncose, juncous.

BUNDLE. *v.* Fardel, kid, truss, fagot; act of forming into a bundle, enbaling; relating to bundles, fascicula.

BURDEN. *v.* To lade or laden, to onerate.

BURDEN. *s.* Or load, pregravation, cumbrance, degravation, encumberance; burden of a song or ballad, refret.

BURIAL. *s.* Funeral, sepulture; burialplace, catacomb, dormitory, sepulchre.

BURIED. *a.* Inhumed; not buried, inhummated; that may be buried or hidden, sepilible; the punishment of being buried alive, defossion.

BURLESQUED. *a.* Travested, travestile, travesty.

BURN. *v.* To burn away as a lighted candle placed in a current of air, to sweal or swale; burn, to cauterise, to cense; burn up, to adure; to burn, ustulate; burn to ashes, to incinerate.

BURN. *s.* Burn or scald, ambustion.

BURNING. *p.* Torrid, calid, fervid, caustic, escharotic, searing, phlegmonous; burning sensation in any part of the body, encauma; the burning or inflammable principle in nature, according to Stahl, phlogiston; having the quality of burning, ustorious; a burning or searing with a red-hot iron, ustion; the burning off impurities in a crucible, deflagration; a great burning, conflagration, empyrosis; burning of any combustible matter, cremation, incension, combustion; incantatory lines, written on a building which is believed by the vulgar will save it from burning, arse-verse (see charm); burning mountain, volcano, or vocano; burning away slowly as a substance which has not much vent, smouldering.

BURNT. *p.* Whole burnt sacrifice, holocaust; what is not capable of being burnt, incombustible, incremable, asbestine; burnt up, adusted, arid; half-burnt, semicombust, semiustulate; smelling as burnt substances, empyreumatic, empyreumatical; that burnt taste and smell of some oils, &c. after distillation, empyreuma.

BURSTING. *p.* Act of, diruption, dissilition, proruption, displosion, explosion, erup-

· tion. (See breaking.)

BURY. *v.* To enwomb, to inhumate or inhume, to inurn, to sepulchre, to inter, to tumulate; burying-place, coemetry or cemetery.

BUSHES. *s.* Full of bushes, dumose, dumal.

BUSTLE. *s.* Utis, accoil, clutter, coil, fuss, hurly-burly, pother, pudder, romage.

BUSY. *a.* Mercantile, officious, pragmatical, sedulous.

BUTCHER. *v.* To enecate, to excarnificate, to laniate, to massacre; butcher-meat, place where it is kept, larder.

BUTCHERY. *s.* Butchery (or murder) trucidation; butchery, or place where meat is sold, shambles.

BUTLER. *s* Skinker.

BUTTING. *p.* Butting as a ram, arietation.

BUTTON. *v.* To infibulate.

BUTTON. *s.* Tache or tach.

BUY. *v.* Buy off, to commute.

BUYING. *p.* Emption; buying and selling, chaffery; act of buying and selling, mercature; belonging to buying and selling, mercative; desire to be always buying, emacity, empturition; the act of buying up the whole quantity of any thing, coemption.

BUZZING. *p.* Buzzing noise, insusuration.

C

CABLE. *s.* A twist or turn of a cable, or any rope, bight; piece of an old cable of which oakum is made, junk; to tie small rope or twine round the cable to prevent fretting, to keckle; the twisting of a cable while veering out, knock; small ropes for seizing the large cables in great ships, nippers.

CAG. *s.* Cade, keg, casket. (See caski)

CAGE. *v.* To cage or confine, to coop, to crib, to mew.

CAGE. *s.* Mew; large cage for birds, so as they may have liberty to fly about, volery, volary.

CALAMITOUS. *a* Adverse, tragic, tragical. (See mournful and sad.)

CALAMITY. *s.* Disaster, affliction, bale, infelicity, mishap, tort.

CALCULATE. *v.* To suppute, to compute, to rythm; to calculate wrong. to miscast.

CALF. *s.* Cast calf, scink, or slink; bellowing as a calf, blatant; belonging to a calf, vituline; sea-calf (in zoology) phoca; belonging to, or like the calf of the leg, sural.

CALL. *v.* To call or summons, to accite; call together, to convocate, to convene; to call or name, to clepe; to call to, to hail; to call before a judge, to convent; to call back or entice gamehawks, to lure; to call in customers as men who attend sales do, to klick; to call upon, to invoke, to invocate; to call back, to remand, to revocate.

CALL. *s.* A call or summons before a judge, interpellation.

CALLED *p.* Behight, benempt, ycleped.

CALLING. *p.* Calling or employment, profession, vocation; a calling away, avocation, evocation; a calling down, devocation; calling aside, sevocation.

CALM. *v.* To calm, to appease, to soothe.

CALM. *a.* Equanimous, sedate, tranquillous, serene, temperate, imperturbed, breezeless, composed, considerate, dispassionate, halcyon, placid.

CALMED *p.* Pacated; that may be calmed or appeased, mulcible.

CALMNESS. *s.* Indisturbance, undisturbance, tranquillity.

CALUMNIATE. *v.* To asperse, to defame, to detract, to infame. (See to censure.)

CALUMNY. *s.* Medisance, obloquy. (See slander.)

CAMEL. *s.* The offspring between a lion and a camel, leucrocuta.

CANCEROUS. *a.* Carcinomatous.

CANDLE. *s.* Lucern; a large candle used on an altar, luminare.

CANDLE-LIGHT. *s.* Work or study done by candle-light, lucubration, elucubration; composed by candle-light, lucubratory; distemper when the patient can only see by candle-light, nyctalopia; this term is used in contradistinction to the distemper wherein the patient can only see in day-light, and is called, hemeralopia.

CANE *s.* Ring of metal put on the end of a cane or staff, to prevent wearing, verrel or verril.

CANNIBALS. *s* Anthropophagi.

CANNON. *s.* The squares or openings in a fort, through which cannon are pointed, embrasure; staff with a match affixed to it, for setting off cannon, linstoc or linstock; method of driving nails, generally of steel, into the touch-holes of cannon, to render them useless, spiking; the arms or projecting pieces of cannon, by which they rest on the carriage, trunnions. (See gun.)

The names of the several cannons are

in general;

Cannon-royal, or	-	48 pounder.
Demi-cannon, large,		36 pounder.
Demi-cannon, ordinary,		32 pounder.
Demi-cannon, least,		30 pounder.
Culverin, largest	-	20 pounder.
Do. ordinary	-	17 pounder.
Do. least,	-	15 pounder.
Demi-culverin, ordinary,		10 pounder.
Demi-culverin, least,		9 pounder.
Saker, ordinary	-	6 pounder.
Saker, least,	-	4 pounder.
Minion, largest,	-	3½ pounder.
Minion, ordinary,	-	3 pounder.
Falcon,	- -	2 pounder.
Falconet,	-	1½ pounder.
Rabinet,	- -	8 ounce ball.
Base,	- -	5 ounce ball.

Besides the above, there are pedereros, or, pettereros, carronades, &c. &c.

CANT. s. Cant words used by rogues, so contrived as to be known only among themselves, gibberish; this sort of language is sometimes termed, slang.

CANVASS. s. Sort of canvass fit for making sails, mildernix; canvass for wrapping wares in, sarplier, poledavy.

CAP. s. Horseman's cap, montero; cap worn by a priest, pluvial; cap in the form of a crown or diadem, tiar or tiara.

CAPACITY. s. Capability, comprehension, dimension, habilitation.

CAPE. s. Cape or head-land, promontory.

CAPITAL. a. Capital or principal, premier; capital performance, master-stroke, chef-d'œuvre, Fr.

CAPTIOUS. a. Latrant, carping, criticising; captious beyond reason, hypercritical.

CARDS. s. The names of the games which are generally played at cards.

Whist
Cribbage
Lansquenet
Loo or lu
Ombre
Gleek
Quadrille
Cassini
Piquet
Primero
Basset.

Any spot or mark on cards, pip; term at whist for four privileged cards, which are incidentally used in betting, swobber; a deal at cards that wins the whole tricks, vole; deal of cards all of one suit, flush; four cards of one suit, murnival or a quaternion; term used when one plays at certain games at cards, such as basset or ombre, to punt; one who cheats at cards by slight of hand, palmer; one who cuts out at cards, scink or skink.

CARDINAL. s. Cardinal virtues are; Prudence, Temperance, Justice, and Fortitude; the cardinal points of the compass are, East, West, North and South; the four cardinal points of the ecliptic are, the signs Aries and Libra, which are the Equinoctial; and Cancer and Capricorn, which are the Solstitial.

CARE. s. Chariness, circumspection, considerateness, assiduity, prospicience, forecast, indoctrination; care or government of another's actions, tutelage, tuition, gubernation; care or trouble, tribulation; previous care or thought, precogitation; great care or anxiety, cark; to care for, to reck.

CAREFUL. a. Matronly, notable, prospective, scrupulous, scrutinous, sedulous, solicitous, vigilant, circumspect, intensive, chary.

CARELESS. a. Supine, cursory or cursorary, luke-warm, improvident, inaccurate, inadvertent, incautious, inconsiderate, incurious indolent, listless, perfunctory, reckless, remiss, retchless, unaccurate, uncautious, unconsiderate

CARELESSNESS. s. Invigilancy, oscitancy or oscitation; dressed with carelessness, dishabile.

CARGO. s. The person employed to take charge and dispose of a ship's cargo in foreign parts, supercargo.

CARNAL. a. Bestial; carnal desire, appetency; not carnal, uncarnate, incarnate.

CARRIAGE. s. Carriage or demeanour. (see behaviour); carriage from place to place, vection, vectitation, vecture; secret conveyance or carriage, subvection; carriage or conveyance by water or air, waftage; wheeled carriage of any kind, vehicle, voiture; the sudden shake of any carriage, jolt; the art of driving any wheeled carriage, aurigation.

CARRIED. p. That may or can be carried, portable, portative, vectible.

CARRIER. s. Carrier of corn or victuals up and down to sell, kidder or kiddyer, cadger.

CARRYING. p. Deferent, gerent; act of carrying young in the belly, gestation; act of carrying from place to place, vection, vectitation, vecture; act of carrying over, transvection; act of carrying underneath, subvection. (See bearing.)

CART. s. Car, tumbril or tumbrel; the black grease of a cart or carriage wheels, gome; the rails on the top of a cart, raers.

CARTER. s. Auriga.

CARVE. *v.* To insculp, to sculp, to incise; carve or cut up a fowl, to untach.

CARVER. *s.* Sculptor, statuary.

CARVING. *p.* Art of carving on wood, glyphice; on stone, colaptice; on plate, anaglyphice, or the anaglyphic art; carving in general, statuary.

CASCADE. *s.* Cataract.

CASE. *s.* Case, or what contains matter, water, &c. cist or cyst; case for pocket-instruments, etwee; case of a watch, &c. of a green colour, made from, or in imitation of the skin of the shark or ass, shagreen.

The use of one case in grammar for another, antiptosis; noun which is not declined with cases, aptote or aptoton; with one case, monoptote, monoptoton; with two cases, diptote, diptoton; with three cases, triptote, triptoton; with four cases, tetraptote, tetraptoton; with five cases, pentaptote, pentaptoton; with six, or all its cases, hexaptote or hexaptoton.

CASK. *s.* Large cask, puncheon, bombard; frame or stand for a cask, gauntree; what a cask wants of being full, ullage.

CAST. *v.* To cast or cheat, to jockey; to cast down or make sorrowful, to deject; to cast away, to eject, to reject; to cast out evil spirits, to exorcise; to cast hair, feathers, &c. to moult, to mew, to shed; to cast forward with violence, to traject, or project; to cast or throw out of the stomach, to puke; cast or convicted, pight; cast off as worthless, perdulous; cast or melted, molten.

CASTLE. *s.* Citadel; the jurisdiction of a castle, chattelany.

CASUAL. *a.* Fortuitous, adventitious, vague, accidental, incidental; the casual killing of a man, chance-medely. (See chance.)

CAT. *s.* Old worn-out cat, gib-cat; he-cat, boar-cat, or kaarle-cat; very old woman, gib-cat or grimalkin; a company of cats (among hunters) is called a kinder; a destroyer or killer of cats, also the act itself, catacide.

CATALOGUE. *s.* File; relating to a catalogue, inventorial.

CATAMITE. *s.* Bardac, ingle, pathic, ganymede.

CATCH. *v.* To bend, to illaqueate; to catch with a hook, to inuncate; to catch in a net, to mesh or immesh; to catch pike by means of a bladder, to hux.

CATCH. *s.* Tache, or tach.

CATECHISED. *p.* Term given for a person who is just catechised, and is yet in the first rudiments of Christianity, catechumen.

CATTLE. *s.* Black cattle comprehends bulls, oxen, and cows, and are termed, beeves, rother beasts, or neat cattle; herds of cattle are termed creaght, (Irish word); A buyer and seller of cattle for others, is termed, a jobber; plague or epidemical distemper among cattle, murrain; general term for the physic given to cattle, veterinaria medicina; cattle taken in to graze by the week, &c. egistment; small cattle, tits, *G.*

CAVALRY. *s.* A four pronged instrument, having, when thrown upon the ground, always one prong pointing upwards, and and is used to annoy and lame an enemy's cavalry, caltrops.

CAVE. *s.* Den, antre, cell, grot, grotto, cavern; places full of caves, are termed, leiry places (Bailey); one who inhabits the caves of the earth, troglodyte.

CAVITY. *s.* Chasm, fosse, foss, hiatus, lisne; cavity of the belly, abdomen; cavity of the breast, thorax.

CAUSE. *s.* Causes preceding others, proegumena, procatarctics; account or description of causes in general, more especially of distempers, etiology or ætiology. (See reason and motive); joint cause, concause; that causes or procures, conficient.

CAUSTIC. *a.* Medicine, ruptory; gentle and easy caustics, are termed, tryphera.

CAUTION. *v.* To admonish, to exhort, to monish.

CAUTION. *s.* Caution, circumspection, caveat, item, monitory, proviso, purview; want of caution, incircumspection, improvidence, indiscretion; unnecessary caution in any undertaking, periergy.

CAUTIOUS. *a.* Deliberative, presageful, aware, cautelous, scrupulous, chary, provident, discreet.

CAUTIOUSLY. *ad.* Gingerly. (See care and careful.)

CEASE. *v.* See (to stop.)

CELEBRATE. *v.* To carol, to commemorate. (See, to praise.)

CEMENT. *v.* (See to glue.)

CELL. *s.* Having one cell, uniscapsular.
——— two cells, bicapsular.
——— three, &c. tricapsular, &c.
——— many cells, multicapsular.

CENSURE. *v.* To censure with great acrimony, to accurse; to censure, to traduce, to vituperate, to reprehend, to syndicate, to carp, to discommend, to dispraise, to exprobrate, to infame.

CENSURE. *s.* Odium, reflection, reproach, anathema, maranatha, fulmination, disapprobation, animadversion, imputation; public censure, ostracism. (see banishment)

CENTRE or CENTER. *s.* Flying off from the centre, centrifugal; tending to the centre, centripetal; deviation from the centre, eccentricity; having the same centre as the earth, geocentric; same centre as the sun, heliocentric; having a common centre, homocentrical; relating to the centre of gravity, centrobarycal; a deviating from the centre of attraction, paracentric or paracentrical.

CENTURY. *s.* Secle. (obsolete) See age.

CEREMONIOUS. *a.* Punctilious, ritual.

CEREMONY. *s.* A religious ceremony; rite or solemnity; funeral ceremony, exequies; nice point of ceremony, puncto or punctilio; notification of some ceremony or speech to be delivered in a public school or seminary, programma.

CERTAIN. *a.* Apparent, definite, infallible, assured, avoidless, cocksure, fiducial, fiduciary, confident, incontestible, incontrovertible, indubitous, indubious, indubitable, irrefragable, irrefutable, luculent, uncontestible or uncontestable, indubitate, inevitable, unevitable, uncontrovertible, undubitable, positive, absolute, veritable, undefeasible, uneschewable, indefesible.

CHACE. *v.* and *s.* (See chase.)

CHAFF. *s.* Achne; full of chaff, paleous, paleated; to clear from chaff, to deventilate, to winnow, to ventilate.

CHAIN. *v.* To chain the hands, to manacle, to handcuff; relating to a chain, catenarian; to chain, to catenate; to chain or connect together, to concatenate.

CHAIN. *s.* Chain or collar of jewels for the neck, carcanet; chains or shackles, gyves.

CHAIRMAN. *s.* Prolocutor, president.

CHAIR. *s.* The chair of state among the Romans, in which the chief magistrate sat, and had a right to be carried in a chariot, sella curulis, or curule chair; chair or seat made of a piece of wood on which the Roman augurs sat, when they took their observations, sella solida; chair carried by men, for the conveniency of infirm people, or to avoid the inclemency of the weather, sedan; those used in the eastern countries born by slaves, are called, palanquins.

CHALLENGE. *v.* To brave, to champion, to defy, to challenge (or claim) to vendicate.

CHALK. *s.* Chalk is termed, carbonate of lime (new chym.); chalky concretion formed in some waters, also found in the joints of gouty people, tophus.

CHALKY. *a.* Cretaceous, calcareous.

CHAMBER. *s.* The first chamber in a house, antichamber.

CHAMBER-POT. *s.* Jorden or jurden.

CHAMPION. *s.* Pugil, pugilist, agonistes; belonging to a champion, agonistic, agonistical.

CHANCE. *s.* Accident, hazard, peril, ballot, babnab, hap, hap-hazard; what happens by chance, casual, peradventure, percase, paravaunt, fortuitous, contingent, windfall, incidental; bad chance or luck, mishap; the chance killing of a man, chance-medley.

CHANGE. *v.* To permute, to modify, to convert, to innovate, to metamorphose; to change or barter, to swop or swap, to scource, to scoss, to transmew, to transmute, to transpose; to change into another substance, to transubstantiate.

CHANGE. *s.* Change of nouns, declension; change or distance of the sun from the equator, declination; change or variety, diversification, change (figure of grammar) enallage; change of affection, alienation; change from one state to another, conversion; change or amendment, emendation; change of one disease into another less dangerous, diadoche; change of one disease into another more dangerous, metastasis or metaptosis; change or transposition, metathesis, metabole, mutation; change or exchange of one thing for another, permutation; change of place, migration, emigration or transition; change of mind or opinion, metanoia, retractation, retraction or recantation; change of expression, in which the first appearing too weak, the orator uses a stronger, epanorthosis; change of sex, transexion; change of weather, &c. vicissitude; change into another matter or substance, transmutation; change of place by carriage, transportance; the god of change and gardens, Vertumnus; liable to change, eventful.

CHANGEABLE. *a.* Alterable, commutable, instable, unstable, mutable, variant, volatile.

CHANGED. *p.* Not to be changed, intransmutable, inconvertible, irreversible, indefesible, undefeasible; that may be changed, transmutable, convertible, reversible, defeasible.

CHANGING. *p.* Changing or removing, remotion; remedies for changing of humours from one part of the body to another, antispastics. (See change.)

CHANNEL. *s.* Channel or drain, sough; channels or groves in the shells of marine animals, striæ.

CHAOS. *s.* Chaos or original matter, hyle.

CHARGE. *v.* To accuse, to criminate, to exprobate, to incriminate, to upbraid; charge with blame in return, to recriminate; to charge with any tax, to assess.

CHARGE. *s.* Charge or commission, mandate; charge or office, function. (See blame and censure.)

CHARGEABLE. *a.* Chargeable upon or to any person or thing, imputable.

CHARGED. *p.* Fraught.

CHARIOT. *s.* Chariot drawn by three horses, triga.

CHARITY. *s.* Almsdeed, dilection ; living on charity, eleemosynary. (See alms.)

CHARM. *v.* To charm, to spell, to bewitch, to captivate, to enchant, to fascinate ; (See bewitch.)

CHARM. *s.* Charm suspended about the neck by a thread, composed of the following letters in a triangular form.

Abracadabra
Abracadabr
Abracadab
Abracada
Abracad
Abraca
Abrac
Abra
Abr
Ab
A

said to be a cure of the hœmitritœus, or kind of remittent fever, abracadabra ; charms used for the cure or prevention of diseases, are generally termed, amulets, phylacteries, periamma, periapta, sigils or alexicaca ; act of charming, incantation, alliciency, fascination.

CHASE. *v.* To chace, to enthase ; to chase into a thicket, to imboss, to emboss.

CHASE. *s.* Relating to the chase, venatic ; the sport of the chase, venery ; act of chasing or hunting, venation.

CHASM. *s.* Hiatus, aperture, apertion. (See cleft and gap.)

CHASTE. *a.* Continent, coy, unlibidinous, platonic, pudicous.

CHASTITY. *s.* Chastity of women, pudency, pudicity ; a hole in the church of Rippon in Yorkshire, where in old times, the chastity of women was ascertained, the chaste getting through, the unchaste not, St Wilfred's needle.

CHASTISE. *v.* Chastise, to verberate. (See to beat.)

CHATTERING. *p.* Garrulous. (See talkative.)

CHEAPNESS. *s.* Vility. (See meanness.)

CHEAT. *v.* To falsify, to geck, to jockey, to bam, to bite, to bob, to bubble, to circumvent, to coneycatch, to cozen, to crossbite, to defraud, to dupe, to elude, to flamm, to fobb, to gull, to juggle, to fub, to lurch, to mountebank, to palm, to peculate, to shark, to trounce.

CHEAT. *s.* Delusion, imposition, fourbe, hocus-pocus, imposture, deception.

CHEATER. *s.* Filcher, geomancer, gipsy, gobby, hiccius-doccius, hocus pocus, impostor, losel, palmer ; cheater of the public, peculator, depeculator ; cheater or impostor in medicine, mountebank, sal

timbanco or saltinbanco, empiric?

CHEATING. *p.* Act of cheating, expilation, prestigiation, juggling, rookery.

CHECK. *v.* To reprimand, to rebate. (See to reprove, chide, curb, stop.)

CHECK. *s.* Coercion, control ; check or rebuke (in rhetoric) epitemesia, epiplexis.

CHEEK. *s.* The face or cheek, jole or jowl.

CHEER. *v.* To make or render cheerful, to exhilirate, to comfort, to revive, to solace.

CHEERFUL. *a.* Boon, complacent, genial, gleeful, joyous, facetious, jolly, jovial, mellow ; abounding in good cheer, dapatical. (See merry, gay, lively.)

CHEERFULNESS. *s.* Hilarity, alacrity, festivity, pleasantry ; cheerfulness of the mind, ecthymosis.

CHEERING. *p.* (See comforting.)

CHEESE. *s.* Sort of costly and delicate cheese made at Parma in Italy, Parmesan or Parmasan ; the curdling of milk in the stomachs of animals into a substance resembling cheese, tyrosis ; name of very large cheeses, so weighty as to require two men to place one of them on the table, chedders, so named from Chedder, a village in Somersetshire, where they are made.

CHEESY. *a.* Caseous.

CHEMIST. *s.* The workmen or assistant of a chemist, laborant ; a lover of chemists, philochemist ; a hater of chemists, misochemist.

CHEMISTRY. *s.* Chymistry (Johnson) the art of, is termed, the spagiric art. (See chymist.)

CHEQUERED. *p.* Chequered by squares, tessellated.

CHERISH. *v.* To nestle, to focillate, to refocillate.

CHEW. *v.* To manducate ; general name for medicines given to be chewed, masticatories ; to chew the cud, to ruminate.

CHEWING. *p.* Act of chewing, mastication.

CHIDE. *v.* To reprehend, to reprimand, to upbraid, to huff, to jobe, to objurgate. (See blame.)

CHIDING. *p.* Act of chiding, increpation ; a rhetorical chiding, in an easy way, which tends to convince, epiplexis.

CHIEF. *a.* Premier, primal, supreme, topping, arch, especial, fundamental, prime ; chief physician, archiater, archiatrus ; chief secretary, archigrapher ; chief of a sacred order, hierarch ; chief heretic, heresiarch ; chief poet, laureate or poetlaureate ; chief end or purpose, crownet ; chief or principle in power, meridional, paramount ; chief city of an empire or kingdom, metropolis ; of, or belonging to a chief city, metropolitan or metropoliti

D

cal; the commander in chief of an army, archistrategus, generalissimo; chief or principal of a college, gymnasiarch.

CHILD. s. Little child, bantling, collop, kid; young male child, manikin; child that dies within a month after its birth, chrisom or chrisam; child yet indistinctly formed, embryo; the act of bearing or carrying a child or young in the belly, gestation; big with child or young, gravid; goddess who presides over child-bearing, Lucina; certain deities among the Romans, supposed to be the helpers of women in their child-birth throws, Nixidii; the first excrements of a child, from resembling the colour of opium or poppy, is called, meconium; the dissection of a child newly formed, embryotomy; to cry as a young child, to mewl; child that has a meagre starved appearance, chitteface; the longing of women with child, malacia; medicines which assist in difficult cases of child-bearing, ecbolica; name of a wild beast, called the crier, from its cries resembling those of a child, ejulator; child born after the death of its father, posthumous child; hook for drawing a dead child out of its mother's womb, uncus, ungula; a getting with child or young, ingravidation, impregnation; the operation of cutting a child out of its mother's womb, hysterotomia, hysterotomatocia, or Cæsarian operation or section, so called, as Julius Cæsar was brought into the world this way; child born when the parents are old, swill-pow or dilling.

CHILDBED. s. Woman in child-bed, enixa.
CHILDBIRTH. s. Labour, travel or travail.
CHILDISH. a. Infantile, puerile.
CHILDLESS. a. Orbate.
CHILDREN. s. Prayer book in which children are taught to read, primer; the first book usually given to children, commonly covered with horn, horn-book; that part of physic which concerns the management of children, pædodica; that beareth children, puerperous, puerperal; the valley where the Ammonites sacrificed their children to their god Moloch, Tophet, (i. e. a drum) as drums were beat to hinder their cries from being heard; name given to those children who are brought into the world by the Cæsarian operation, Cæsares or Cæsones; the illegal practice of stealing children for the purpose of transporting and selling them, kidnapping; those children who are brought into the world with their feet foremost, as was the case with Agrippa, are termed, Agrippæ; young children who have not got teeth, are termed, nefrendes.
CHILL. v. To infrigidate.

CHILL. a. Very chill, algid, gelid.
CHIMERICAL. a. Utopian. (See fancy.)
CHIMNEY. s. The pipe or passage for the conveyance of the smoke of a chimney, funnel, tunnel, flue; the side supporters of a chimney, jambs; work done or placed on a chimney, mantel.
CHINA. s. Name given for china-ware in general, porcelain.
CHINCOUGH. s. (See cough.)
CHINK. s. Chap, cranny; full of chinks, rimous, rimose. (See cleft and gap.)
CHOICE. s. Election, arbitrament; cant phrase, used when a person has no choice or alternative, Hobson's choice.—This phrase is said to have had its origin from one Hobson who kept horses for hire, and who obliged every customer to take the horse which stood next the door; double choice, dilemma, alternative; the choice or preference of one thing before another, predilection; choice (excellent) eximious, eminent, exquisite; to make choice of, to affiliate, to select. (See to choose.)
CHOKE. v. To suffocate, to chouk, to strangle.
CHOOSE. v. To elect, to select, to cull, to chuse; the power to choose, volitive.
CHOOSING. p. Choosing at will, eclectic or eclectick; act of choosing, volition. (See to gather.)
CHORD. s. Chord of an arch, subtense.
CHRIST. s. The Immanuel; Theanthropos (Kames); the reign of Christ on earth for 1000 years, millenium; one who maintains that Christ will reign on earth a thousand years, millenarian; (Anno C. 71.) who denied the divinity of Christ, Homuncionists, Ebionites; heretics who denied that Christ was the Son of God, Marcionists; heretics, in the third century, who affirmed there were two Christs, Elcesacitæ; term used among divines, signifying, of the same nature and essence as Christ, homoousion; ceremony performed in the church of Rome, on the Wednesday, Thursday, and Friday before Easter, in representation of the agony of Christ, and darkness in the garden, tenebræ, tenebres; those who maintain the omnipresence of Christ's body, ubiquitarians; the napkin of St Veronica, on which the Papists pretend the face of Christ is represented, vernicle.
CHRISTMAS. s. Ule; the custom of young people going about from house to house, or on the streets, with warm beverage at this season, wassail or wassel; those who practise the above, are called, wassellers.
CHRONOLOGY. s. False chronology, antichronism; error in chronology, parachron-

ism, metachronism; prochronism.

CHURCH. s. Any magnificent church or hall, basilic or basalick; the eastern part of a church, in which the altar is placed, chancel; any church or temple consecrated to religion, fane; walk or alley in a church, ile, isle, aisle; gift left to a church at one's death, mortuary; two terms used for the most sacred part of a church or temple, bema and agiasma; the middle part of a church distinct from the aisles, nave or nef; the inclosed seats in a church, pews; the porch of a church or temple, pronaos or portico; plate where church vestments are kept, revestiary, revestry, or vestry; the keeper of these vestments, plate, and other valuables pertaining a church, cimeliarch; robbery or stealth from a church, sacrilege; churchman, ecclesian; church-lands, glebe; church-lands in the possession of a layman, is termed, impropriation; but when they are in the hands of a bishop, college, or religious house, it is termed, appropriation; church-bell used by the Greeks under the dominion of the Turks, hagiosidere, i. e. holy iron, as being a substitute for a bell, which is prohibited; church-yard, coemetery or cemetery; the gate of a church-yard through which funerals pass, lich-gate.

CHURLISH. a. Cynical. (See rude.)

CHURN. s. Quern or querne.

CHYMIST. s. The assistant or workman in a chymical laboratory, laborant; those who profess themselves enemies to chymists, misochymists; a lover of chymists, philochymist; professor of chymistry, spagirist; relating to chymical philosophy, spagirical; physician who performs cures upon chymical principles, iatrochymic. (See physician.)

CIDER. s. The refuse or dregs of cider after making, coom.

CINDERS. s. Breeze or breeze, gled; bad cinders, clinker; hot cinders, embers; pit coal burnt to cinders, coke; cinders of melted brass or iron, spodium.

CIRCLE. s. The circles of the sphere are as follow: viz.

Horizon, horison, or finitos.	Rational, or sensible.
Meridians.	
Equinoctial or equator, by seamen termed the Line.	Termed immutable Circles.
Zodiac or Ecliptic.	
Equinoctial and Solstitial Colures.	

The four circles termed lesser, are, the tropics of Cancer and Capricorn, and the Arctic and Antarctic Circles; called also Polar Circles.

Besides these, some add, the five following:

1st, Hour Circles, which are so many meridians.

2d, Azimuths or Vertical Circles.

3d, Almacantars, Or Parallel Circles of Almicanthars, Altitude.

4th, Circles of Longitude.

5th, Circles or Parallels of Declination or Latitude.

The act of describing a circle with a pair of compasses, circination, decircination; the squaring of a circle, term used by geometricians, tetragonism; the fourth part of a circle, quadrant; the line which passes through the centre of a circle terminated by the circumference, diameter; the half of the diameter is termed, the radius; half of any circle, semicircle, demicircle; circle or extent, compass; to encompass as with a circle, to encircle; circle of the knowledge of arts and sciences, cyclopædia, encyclopædia; circle described by any body in motion, or in an orbit, gyre or gire; a divination performed by walking in a circle, gyromancy.

CIRCUIT. s. Ambit; circuit or multiplicity of words, circumlocution, ambages, periphrasis; the court of justices in England, or the lords commissioners of justiciary in Scotland going their circuits, eyre.

CIRCULAR. a. Encyclical, rotund, armillary; the circular motions of a fluid for want of wind, eddy; the placing of things in a circular order, circumposition; the circular rising of any figure, convexity; the circular descending of any body, such as the curls of the hair, downgyred.

CIRCULATION. s. Circulation of the blood is termed, cyclophoria sanguinis.

CIRCUMFERENCE. s. Such figures as have equal circumferences or perimeters, isoperimetrical; circumference of any figure, perimeter, periphery, ambit; the half circumference, semicircumference, semiperiphery.

CITIZEN. s. Denisen or denizen; citizen of the world, cosmopolite.

CITY. s. A female inhabitant of a city, citess; belonging to a city, municipal; carried quite round a city, as a wall or ditch, ambarbial; act of casting up fortifications round a besieged city, circumvallation.

CIVIL. a. Compliant, complimental, ceremonial, complacent, complaisant, courteous; doctor of civil law, civilian, jurist; relating to civil honours, civic or civick.

CIVILITY. *s.* Urbanity, affability; act of civility, devoir; want of civility, incomity. (See kindness and politeness.)

CLAD. *p.* Pranked or prankt, yelad. (See adorn.)

CLAIM. *s.* To assert, to accuse, to vindicate; to claim unjustly the honour or merit of doing a thing, to arrogate.

CLAIM. *s.* Appropriation. (See demand.)

CLAMOROUS. *a.* Obstreperous. (See clamour.)

CLAMOUR. *v.* To clamour, to brabble, to clapperclaw. (See, to chide, abuse, scold.)

CLAMOUR. *s.* Clamour, vociferation, clutter, hue and cry.

CLAMMY. *a.* Adhesive, lentous, ropy, viscous, viscid, unctuous, glutinous, tenacious, depectible. (See glue.)

CLAN. *s.* Horde, sept. (See race and set.)

CLANDESTINE. *a.* Clancular. (See secret, private, hidden.)

CLASH. *v.* To clash, to collide, to hurtle, to impinge, to occur.

CLASH. *s.* Check, collision, rencounter, occursion.

CLASP. *v.* To clasp or fasten as with a button, to infibulate.

CLASP. *s.* Clasp or hug of kindness, embracement.

CLAUSE. *s.* Providing clause, purview, proviso.

CLAW. *s.* Claw of a shell-fish, chely; the claw of a bird of prey, talon, pouncer.

CLAY. *v.* To close up the junction or insertions of chymical vessels with clay, to lute.

CLAY. *s.* Argile; made of clay, fictile, figulate; like clay, lutarious; sort of clay with which crucibles are made, tasco; composed of clay, luteous.

CLEAN. *v.* To defecate, to depurate, to elute, to furbish, to burnish; to clean or weed, to sarcle; to clean or arrange feathers, as birds do, to preen; to dress or clean a horse, to curry.

CLEAN. *a.* Clean and bright, nitid; clean and neat, tidy.

CLEANSE. *v.* To endew, to fey, to lustrate, to mundify, to rinse; to cleanse by wiping, to absterge, to absterse.

CLEANSING. *p.* Act of cleansing or washing, ablution, lavation; cleansing, purificative, purificatory, detergent, abstergent; general name for cleansing or scouring medicines, rhyptics, cathartics; act of cleansing from spots, emaculation; cleansing, expurgatory.

CLEAR. *v.* To clear or acquit, to assoil or assoilzie, to exculpate, to justify, to vindicate; to clear from muddiness, to clarify; to clear out or drain, to deoppilate, to enswhge; to clear from water, to dephlegmate; to clear off any liquor, to filter or filtrate; to clear from intricacy, to disentangle, to discuss, to garble; to disembroil, to develope or disvelope, to elucidate, to expound, to illustrate, to explicate, to interpret, to extricate; to clear away or lessen debts, to liquidate; to clear a place from stones, to elapidate, to dilapidate.

CLEAR. *a.* Clear or bright, dilucid, exhibilous, hyaline, limpid, lucid, luculent, meracious, pellucid, relucent, serene, tralucid, tralucent, translucid, translucent, transpicuous, diaphanous, transparent, diaphanstick; clear or evident, articulate, distinct, obvious, perspicuous, conspicuous, declarative, demonstrable, intuitive, legible, incontestible, uncontestable or uncontestible; clear or distinct, significant, (see certain); not clear, (muddy) turbid; not sufficiently clean, inevident, imperspicuous, inconspicuous. (See doubt and doubtful.)

CLEARING. *p.* Act of clearing obstructions, deoppilation; term for such medicines as have the above power, deobstruents, deoppilatives.

CLEARLY. *ad.* Clearly drawn or laid down, graphic or graphical.

CLEAVE. *v.* To fissure. (See cleft.)

CLEAVING. *p.* Cleaving or sticking to, inhesion, adhesion; cleaving to a party, adherence; the act of cleaving or splitting, diffission.

CLEFT. *s.* Chasm, fissure, scissure, sinus, cranny, crevice, hiatus, aperture, apertion; that may be cleft, fissile, findible; having many clefts, multifidous, rimose, rimous.

CLERGY. *s.* Term for the dress of the clergy while performing their religious duty, canonicals; of or belonging to the clergy, clerical; those distinguished from the clergy, laity; of or belonging to such, laic or laical.

CLERGYMAN. *s.* Cleic, pastor, reverend, incumbent; nickname given to a clergyman who bestirs himself only for preferment, tantivy; term in law, used when the clergyman or incumbent suffers any edifices of his ecclesiastical living to go to ruin or decay, dilapidation.

CLERK. *s.* Clerk of a court, actuary; in a shop, cliker; lawyer's clerk, logographer.

CLIMBING. *p.* Scandent; act of climbing, conscension; a climbing up or scanning, scansion.

CLOAK. *s.* Bavaroy, huke.

CLOCK. *s.* Horologe, pendulus, horodix; clock which shews the time by means of water, clepsydra.

CLOD. s. Abounding in clods, glebous, gleby, glebulent; the breaking or harrowing of clods, occation.

CLOG. v. To cumber, to clamm, to embarrass, to encumber. (See distress.)

CLOSE. v. (Or engage) to engrapple; to close, to imbound, to instop, to occlude, to expire, to collapse, to condense; to close, join, or connect, to pan.

CLOSE. a. Adjacent, intentive, spiss, succinct, compact, contiguous dense; lying close, latitant; close or severe (resembling a monk) monachal; close fight or combat, half-sword.

CLOSE. s. The close of the day, eve; the close of an oration, peroration.

CLOSED. p. Closed up as the upper end of a barometer, hermetically sealed.

CLOSELY. ad. To lie closely in wait on the belly, to lie perdue.

CLOSENESS. s. Compactness, imporosity, spissitude; closeness of application, intenseness, intentness.

CLOTH. s. Term given to cloth that was never coloured or dyed, ray-cloth; sort of cloth made of hair and silk, grogram, grogeram or grogran; name of a coarse sort of woollen cloth, penistone; canvas cloth used for making sails, mildernix; sort of linen cloth used for table-cloths, coverlets, &c. huckaback; cant phrases used by taylors for stealing fragments of cloth, to cabbage, to prig.

CLOTHES. s. Clothes, habiliment, apparel, attire, investment; to mend clothes, to sarcinate; act of trimming up old clothes, mangonism; place where old clothes are vamped up and sold, frippery; room or apartment where clothes are washed, &c. laundry; to clothe again, to revest.

CLOT. v. To coagulate, to feltre. (See to curdle.)

CLOTHING. p. Investient. (See, to adorn.)

CLOTTED. p. Clotted blood, gore, tabum.

CLOUD. v. To bedim, to eclipse, to nubilate, to opacate, to obnubilate, to obnumbrate, to obfuscate or offuscate.

CLOUD. s. Two small clouds not far from the south pole, Magellan's clouds; producing clouds, nabiferous, nubigerous; produced by clouds, nubigenous; free from clouds, enubilous, innubilous; the contents of the urine or other liquor which float about in the middle resembling a cloud, enæorema. (See shade.)

CLOUDY. a. Murky, caliginous, nebulous, nebulose, nubilose, nubilous, sombre.

CLOVEN. a. Cloven-footed, bisulcous; animal whose feet are not cloven, solidungulous, solipedous, solipedal; cloven in two, bifid; in three, trifid; in four, &c.

quadrifid, &c.

CLOWN. s. Boor, bumpkin, clod, countryput, knuff, cuddy, looby, lubbard, lubber.

CLOWNISH. a. Agrestic, boorish, campestral, chuffy, inurbane, roynish.

CLUMP. s. Dallop. (See heap.)

CLUMSY. a. Loobily, loutish, lubberly, maladroit. (See awkward.).

CLUSTER. s. Boss, group; act of growing in a cluster as grapes, racemation.

COARSE. a. Faxed, chuffy, crass, palpable, recrementitious; coarse and rude behaviour, impoliteness, unpoliteness; coarse and rude fellow, macaroon.

COARSENESS. s. Crassitude, squalor. (See gross, grossness, nasty, nastiness.)

COAST. s. Rivage; to extend as a coast, to trend.

COAT. s. The coat or bag containing a tumour, cist or cyst; short coat with sleeves, palletoque or pallecote.

COAX. v. To glaver, to cajole, to inveigle. (See flatter and flatterer.)

COBWEB. s. Like a cobweb, araneous.

COCK. s. Divination by cocks, alectryomancy; the testicles a cock, waddles; the red fleshy substance that hangs under a cock or turkey cock's neck, wattles; cock, chanticleer; young cock, cockerel; cock which is conquered, craven; cockfighting, alectryomachy; artificial spurs for cocks, gaffles or gablocks; term used in cock-fighting, when measuring the girth of a cock's body by the grasp of the hand and fingers, hancling.

COCOA. s. Cacao or cocao. (Chambers)

COD. s. Cod-fish dried and salted, haberdine.

COFFIN. s. The velvet cloth which covers a coffin during the procession of a funeral, pall; sort of stone coffin used anciently, which quickly consumed the corpse, sarcophagus or sarcophagum.

COIN. s. The space just within the edge of a coin, on which the motto is written, exergue or exergum; coin, moneta; alloy mixt in coin, lega; the words round the edge of coins, medals, &c. legend; a description of ancient coins and medals, numismatography.

COLD. s. Bleak, chill, algid, frigid, rigor, rigour; very cold, gelid, hyperborean; producing cold, frigorific; cold treatment or reception, discountenance; cold (not of a lively turn of mind) phlegmatic; to make cold, to egelidate, to infrigidate; cold baths, psychrolusia; instruments for ascertaining the degree of cold and heat, psychrometer, thermometer; an aversion for cold things, psychrophoby.

OLIC. s. Colics are reckoned by Quincy of

four kinds, viz. bilious, flatulent, hysterical and nervous; term given to any of the former, when the patient is so pained as to excite compassion in the bystanders, *miserere mei.*

COLLECT. *v.* To compose, to congest, to congregate, to levy. (See to gather.)

COLLECTED. *a.* Aggregated, collectitious; collected into a ball, conglomerated, agglomerated; fragments collected from several authors, analects, analecta, cento; collected or gathered together, congregate.

COLLECTION. *s.* Complex, assemblage cluster, compilation, huddle, congeries; collection of matter in a boil or sore, core; collection made slowly and laboriously, glean; collection of various things or subjects, miscellany; collection of flowers, devotions, or poems, anthology

COLLEGE. *s.* University, seminary; the treasurer of a college, bursar; to admit or enter as a member of an university, to matriculate; notification of something to be performed in a college or public seminary, programma; the principal of a college, gymnasiarch.

COLOR. *s.* Colour, hue; picture of one colour, cameo, monochroma; producing colour, colorific; of one colour, concolour; to mark with various colours, to dapple; pale green colour, glaucous; pale yellow colour, like a dead leaf, feuillemort, filemot, or philemot; chesnut colour, bay; term in heraldry for a mixture of different colours, missile; what changes colour as the cameleon, versi-coloured; stone with which colours are ground on a marble slab, mullar stone; picture drawn only in lines without colours, monographic; of many colours, piebald or pybald; never changing in colour, chromatic; the act of beautifying with many colours, variegation. (See the respective colours, green, blue, &c. and the article paint.)

COLT. *s.* Herd of colts (among hunters) rag; name given to the famous poison or love dose, used by the ancients, which was taken from the forehead of a young colt, hippomanes.

COMB. *v.* To pheeze, to tose, to phese, to feaze.

COMB. *s.* Comb for dressing hemp or flax, hitchel or hatchel; like a honey-comb, faviform; formed like a comb, pectinal, pectinated.

COMBAT. *s.* Very close combat, half-sword; combat with knives, snick and snee; single combat, monomachy or duel; combat or fight on horseback, hippomachy; combat betwixt soul and body; psychomachy; combat for the trial of skill, agonism; sudden combat or onset, rencounter; place railed in for seeing a combat, steccado (Span.) (See fight, battle and attack.)

COMBINATION. *s.* League; combination of circumstances, conjuncture; combination or set of people for any purpose, generally applied to some illegal measure, junto, convention. (See set and party.)

COME. *v.* To come or, happen, to occur; to come between, to intervene; to come unexpected, to supervene; not to be come at, impetible.

COMEDY. *s.* That part of a comedy in which the plot lies, catastasis.

COMLINESS. *s.* Pulchritude. (See beauty and grace.)

COMFORT. *v.* To cheer, to cherish, to consolate, to console, to solace. (See, to amuse.)

COMFORTER. *s.* Paraclete.

COMFORTING. *p.* Analeptic, cordial, cardiacal, paregoric or paragoric; comforting medicines are termed, in general, roborantia. (See cordial.)

COMING *p.* Coming into, introvenient; coming between, intermedial, intermediate. (See, to come.)

COMMAND. *v.* To impose, to adjure, to enjoin or injoin; to command back, as to prison, &c. to remand.

COMMAND. *s.* Injunction, mandate, precept, behest, bidding, hest; solemn command, conjurement; relating to commands, preceptal, mandatory.

COMMANDER. *s.* Commander of 10 men, decurion or lancepesade, (Bailey); commander of 50 men, pentecontarch; of 100, centurion; of 10,000, myriarch or chiliarch; commander in chief, generalissimo, archicontarch.

COMMANDING. *p.* Coercive, imperative, mandatory. (See command.)

COMMANDMENTS. *s.* The ten commandments are termed, the decalogue.

COMMENCE. *v.* To inchoate. (See begin.)

COMMENCING. *p.* Incipient; a commencing, inception. (See beginning.)

COMMENDATION. *s.* Applause, laud, præconomy or præcony.

COMMENDER. *s.* Encomiast, panegyrist. (See praise.)

COMMENDING. *p.* Epainetic, plauditory. (See praising.)

COMMENT. *v.* To gloze.

COMMENT. *s.* Annotation, postil, elucidation, gloss.

COMMENTATOR. *s.* Glossator glossographer, scholiast, commenter, glosser.

COMMISSION. *s.* Legation, mandate, mission.

COMMON. *s.* Customary, appellative, brief, obvious, trite; common or vile, triobolar, trivial; the common people, canaille, the plebeians; one of the common people, or belonging to them, plebian; passing or descending to the common people, as dresses which are become unfashionable among the great, volgivagant; common birth, or a growing up together, connascence; common to both sexes, epicene.

COMMON-PLACE-BOOK. *s.* Adversaria.

COMMONWEALTH. *s.* (See governments.)

COMMUNICATE. *v.* To impart; to communicate mutually, to intercommunicate; those who communicate at the Lord's Supper, are called, husselters, husselling people, or communicants.

COMMUNICATION. *s.* Intercourse, fellowship, sodality. (See society.)

COMMUNITY. *s.* Dwelling in community, cenobitical. (See society.)

COMPACT. *s.* Comart, compromise, convention, concordate.

COMPACT. *a.* Not compact, incompact, uncompact, imporous. (See contract.)

COMPANION. *s.* Associate, camerade, comerade, comate, concomitant, puefellow, stainsmate, consort, chum; companion of worth and learning, tanquam.

COMPANY. *s.* Fraternity, hive, horde, band, bevy, clan, meine; company or assemblage of all knights, gentlemen, yeomen, labourers, &c. in a county, in defence thereof, is termed, posse comitatus, i. e the power of the county; company of goats (among hunters), trip; of colts, rag; of foxes, sculk; of wolves, rout; of cats, kinder; of birds, covey; of insects, foule; an immense number or company is termed, by Milton, a myriad.

COMPARE. *v.* To collate, to paragon, to confront, to confer. (See, to examine.)

COMPARISON. *s.* Collation, similitude, simile. (See like and likeness.)

COMPASS. *v.* To inviron or environ; to bring within a compass or extent, to decircinate.

COMPASS. *s.* The mariner's compass is called, pyxis nautica; the double rings in which the mariner's compass is hung, which allow it always to retain its horizontal position, gimbals; the Greek, Latin, and English names, used for the points of the compass, are as follow.

North, Septentrio.
N. by E. Hypaquilo, hyperborera.
NNE. Aquilo Gallicus.
NE. by N. Mesaquilo Mesoboreas.
NE. Supernas Borrhapeliotes.
NE. by E. Etesias.
ENE. Cæcias, Carbas.
E. by N. Mesocæcius.
East, Oriens, Subsolanus.
E. by S. Hypeurus, Hypereurus.
ESE. Vulturnus.
SE. by E. Meseurus.
SE. Euro Auster, vulgarly, Notapeliotes.
SE. by S. Hypophœnia, Hypereanotus.
SSE. Euronotus.
S. by E. Mesophœnix, Meseuronotus.
South, Auster.
S. by W. Mesolibonotus.
SSW. Austroafricus.
SW. by S. Hypolibonotus, Hyperlibonotus.
SW. Notolibycus, Austro-Zephyrus.
SW. by W. Mesafricus, Mesolopus.
WSW. Africus Subvesperus.
W. by S. Hypafricus.
West, Favonius, Subvespertinus, Occidens.
W. by N. Mesocorus, Mesargestes.
WNW. Corus, Caurus.
NW. by N. Hypocorus, Hyperargestes.
NW. Corus Etesiæ, Zephyroboreas.
NW. by W. Hypocircius, Mesothracias.
NNW. Circius.
N. by W. Mesocircius.

COMPASSES. *s.* To make or describe a circle with a pair of compasses, to circinate, to decircinate; sort of compasses, with bent legs for ascertaining the diameters of bodies, calipers.

COMPASSION. *s.* Commiseration, sympathy; to feel compassion, to relent; the word *bowels* is also used allegorically for compassion (Clarendon). (See pity.)

COMPENDIOUS. *a.* Chilonian, chilonic, concise, summary. (See short.)

COMPENDIUM. *s.* Breviat. (See abridgement.)

COMPETITOR. *s.* Adversary, candidate, corrival, opponent, antagonist.

COMPLAIN. *v.* To murmur; to complain angrily, on being approached, as a wild beast, to growl.

COMPLAINING. *p.* Plaintful, querimonious, querulous, plaintive or plaintiff.

COMPLAISANT. *a.* Affable, morigerous, condescending. (See kind; civil.)

COMPLETE. *a.* Compleat, absolute, accomplished, consummate, exquisite, integral. (See full.)

COMPLETELY. *ad.* Plenarily. (See fullness.)

COMPLIMENTARY. *a.* Congratulatory, dedicatory, adulatory, complimental.

COMPOSE. *v.* To compose a letter or writing, to indite; to compose or arrange as a bird does its feathers, to preen.

COMPOSING. *p.* Composing; (easing), sedative. (See comforting.)

COMPOSITION. *s.* Composition of music

in two parts, duetto or duetti; in three parts, trio; in four parts, quartetto; composition in mathematics, is termed, synthesis, or the synthetical method of demonstrating; composition (mean rate or medium) agistment. (See collection and mixture.)

COMPOUND. *s.* Compound of any kind, commixion; compound interest, anatocism; a compound resulting from the mixture of any two substances, producing something very different from either, is termed, a tertium quid. (See mixture.)

COMPUTER. *s.* Accomptant, computist.

CONCAVE. *a.* (See hollow and glass.)

CONCEAL. *v.* To disguise, to enambush, to enwomb, to immask, to obduce; to conceal (not to tell) to suppress; to conceal in the hand as jugglers do, to palm; to conceal or cover from danger, to shroud.

CONCEALED. *p.* Dormant, cryptical, latent, latitant, miching; to lye concealed, to miche; what cannot be concealed, inconcealable; that may be concealed by burying, sepilible.

CONCEALMENT. *s.* State of concealment, incognito or incog; act of concealment or darkening, occultation; concealment by silence, reticence; concealment or mask for the face, visor.

CONCEIT. *s.* Crank, crotchet, fantasy, fume, conception, contrivance, conundrum, trangram. (See fancy.)

CONCEIVE. *v.* To apprehend, to comprehend, to deprehend.

CONCEIVABLE. *a.* Conceptible, comprehensible, deprehensible.

CONCEIVED. *p.* Notional; conceived beforehand, prepense; that may be conceived, deprehensible; not to be conceived, incomprehensible, inconceptible, uncomprehensive.

CONCEPTION. *s.* Term for any medicine which prevents conception, atocium; a second conception before the first is brought forth, superfetation, epicyema, epicyesis.

CONCISE. *a.* Laconic. (See short.)

CONCISENESS. *s.* Brevity, briefness, syntomy; conciseness of speech, brachylogy.

CONCLUDING. *p.* Desitive. (See end and endless.)

CONCLUSION. *s.* Inference, closure, illation, result, termination, perclose, finis; unhappy conclusion, catastrophe.

CONCLUSIVE. *a.* Determinate, definitive, consequential. (See determination and end.)

CONCUBINE. *s.* Leman, this word is also used for a gallant, from l'aimant, *Fr.*

CONDEMN. *v.* To censure, to syndicate, to dispraise, to doom; to condemn beforehand, to prejudge. (See to blame.)

CONDUCT. *s.* Comportment, deportment, portance comportance.

CONE. *s.* A cone is termed right-angled, when the fixed side (round which the triangle revolving generates the cone) is equal to the side containing the right angle; obtuse, if the fixed side be less, and acute, if greater; a cone is termed, scalenous, or oblique, or imperfect, when the axis is not at right angles with the plane of its base, (Ward); the part of a cone cut off by a plane parallel to its base, is called a frustum; a cone thus cut is called a truncated cone, or a decacuminated cone.

CONFECTION. *s.* Confiture; confection made of the berry called, kermes, alkermes.

CONFEDERATE. *v.* To confederate, to complot, to consociate.

CONFEDERATE. *s.* Ally, accomplice, fedary or federary, leaguer.

CONFERENCE. *s.* Parle, or parley, interlocution, colloquy.

CONFESS. *v.* To agnize. (See to acknowledge.)

CONFESSEDLY. *ad.* Avowedly, indisputably. (See certain.)

CONFESSING. *p.* A person in the act of confessing, confitent.

CONFESSION. *s.* To make confession to a priest, to shrive.

CONFESSOR. *s.* Penitentiary.

CONFIDENCE. *s.* Reliance, affiance, creaunce, sanguineness, sanguinity, presumption, assurance; want of confidence, diffidence.

CONFINE. *v.* To brow, to cage, to circumscribe, to coarct, to coop, to immure, to cloister, to incloister, to mew, to engaol, to incarcerate, to impound, to imbound; to confine between, to jam; to confine or intrap, to nousel; to confine or limit, to scant, to stint, to restrict, to retrench, to crib.

CONFINEMENT. *s.* Enclosure, closure, clausure, coarctation, constraint, detention, duresse.

CONFIRM. *v.* To affear, to affirm, to assure, to clinch, to insinew, to verify. (See to strengthen.)

CONFIRMATION. *s.* Avouchment, corroboration; confirmation by the signing of any deed, homologation; the confirmation of any man's veracity by the testimony of another, compurgation.

CONFLAGRATION. *s.* Empyrosis. (See burning.)

CONFOUND. *v.* To baffle, to blast, to puzzle or empuzzle, to nonplus. (See to disturb.)

CONFUSE. *v.* To embroil, to perturbate. (See to confound.)

CONFUSED. *p.* Inarticulate, indiscriminate, mazy, promiscuous, rigmarole, distraught, macaronic, chaotic, tumultuary, turbulent; confused mixture, farrago.

CONFUSEDLY. *ad.* Higgledy-piggledy, immethodically, pell-mell.

CONFUSION. *s.* Disarray, distraction, garboil, anomy, huddle, hurly-burly, maze, misrule, mizmaze, anarchy; the apparent confusion of the humours of the eye from a violent ophthalmia, synchysis.

CONGRATULATE. *v.* To gratulate, to greet. (See, to salute.)

CONGREGATION. *s.* Congregation or gathering together of people, synaxis.

CONICAL. *a.* Turbinated; conical on one side, and plain on the other, plano-conical.

CONJUNCTION. *s.* Coagmentation, coalition. (See union.)

CONNECTION. *s.* Cohesion, connexion, catenation, concatenation; having connexion, connexive; want of connexion, incoherence, incongruity; done without connexion, inconnexity. (See, to join.)

CONNIVANCE. *s.* Connictation. (See wink.)

CONQUER. *v.* To prevail, to subdue, to subjugate, to vanquish; to conquer or take by assault, to expugn. (See, to overcome, to ruin.)

CONQUERABLE. *a.* Exuperable.

CONQUERED. *p.* That may be conquered or excelled, superable, vincible.

CONQUEROR. *s.* Victor; female who conquers, victress.

CONQUEST. *s.* Mastery, masterdom. (See victory and triumph.)

CONSCIENCE. *s.* Studier of cases of conscience, casuist; check or sting of conscience, remorse, synteresis.

CONSENT. *s.* Accord, acquiescence; consent or harmony of voices, consent or concert; consent or agreement in opinion, unanimity; consent by smiling, arrision.

CONSEQUENCE. *s.* Result, ultimity; of no consequence, importless, inconsequent, inconcludent, unconcludent; train of consequences, consecution.

CONSEQUENTIAL. *a.* Eventual. (See Accidental.

CONSIDER. *v.* To advise, to deliberate, to meditate, to muse, to pensitate, to ponder, to cogitate, to speculate, to trutinate. (See to examine.)

CONSIDERATION. *s.* The serious consideration of any subject, perpensation, perpension, trutination; said of any subject under consideration, *sur le tapis, i. e.*

upon the carpet; done without consideration, indiscreet, undiscreet.

CONSISTENT. *a.* Coherent, compatible, competible, comportable, consentaneous, consonant, congruous.

CONSPICUOUS. *a.* (See Clear.)

CONSPIRE. *v.* To band, to complot, to league. (See to assemble.)

CONSTANCY. *s.* Insisture. (Shakespeare.)

CONSTANT. *a.* Assiduous, perpetual, immutable, immarcessible, incessant, indefatigable, persistive, perseverant.

CONSTITUTION. *s.* That due mixture of humours which is best adapted to the constitution of an individual, crasis; bad constitution or habit of the body, cachexis, cachexy, intemperament; a fixed and permanent constitution of body either good or bad, hexis; this word is opposed to the terms diathesis and schesis, which mean transient dispositions, (See Body.) Constitution of good laws, eunomy.

CONSUME. *v.* To absume, to dispend, to erode; to consume or turn to ashes, to incinerate.

CONSUMED. *p.* That cannot be consumed; incombustible, incremable, asbestine.

CONSUMING. *p.* Corroding, eroding, esurine; consuming or wasting in the fire; deflagrable. (See burn, burning, and burnt.)

CONSUMPTION. *s.* Consumption arising from want of due nourishment, atrophy or oligotrophy; consumption of the lungs, Phthisis; consumption without any manifest evacuation, catharesis; consumption accompanied with excessive leanness, marasmus; general name for a consumption, tabes; those persons who are liable to consumption from having narrow chests, stenothoraces; a consumption which is induced by the too great attenuation of the fluids, syntexis; that induces consumption, tabific.

CONTEMPT. *s.* Contempt, scoff, derision, foutra, contumacy, disparagement; mark of contempt, by not entering into one's excuse, &c., hoot; contempt or concealment, misprision, as "misprision of trea-" "son," &c.; one held in contempt, pilgarlic; mark of contempt practised by the Italians, shewn by the snapping or pointing of the fingers, fico.

CONTENT. *s.* Superficial content, area; solid content, cubature.

CONTENT. *a.* Incapable of giving content or satisfaction, dissatisfactory; insatisfactory, unsatisfactory.

CONTENTION. *s.* Base, emulation; con-

E

tention by words, logomachy. (See strife, debate, quarrel.)

CONTENTMENT. *s.* Allubescency, contentation.

CONTEST. *s.* Brabble, brangle, colluctation, competition, luctation; contest at law, litigation. (See dispute.)

CONTINUAL. *a.* Hectic, incessant, perpetual, sempiternal. (See constant.)

CONTINUANCE. *s.* Endurance, durance, duration; distemper of long continuance, chronical, chronic, inveterate; long continuance, perduration, permanence, permension, persistence, persistency; continuance of order, series.

CONTINUE. *v.* To dure, to prolong; continue in pay, to retain.

CONTRACT. *v.* To abridge; to contract into less room, to condense, to astrict; to contract, or agree, to stipulate; to contract in marriage, to desponsate; to contract, or draw up, to furl; to contract, or draw together, to constrict.

CONTRACT. *s.* Contract, or agreement, affiance, compact, convention; the contract or convention between the King of Spain and other powers, for furnishing the Spanish dominions with slaves, assiento, (Span); one who is bound by a contract, obligee; contract, confederacy, covenant; relating to a contract, federal; the first draught of a deed or contract, protocol.

CONTRACTED. *p.* Concise, illiberal, constringed; contracted into wrinkles, cockled, corrugated. (See to contract, and abridgment).

CONTRACTION. *s.* Contraction of the left ventricle of the heart, during which the blood is driven into the aorta, systole; (See heart); a painful contraction of the frænum, chordæ, or chordee; rigid contraction of several parts of the body, bending it into different positions, the terms used according to the part affected are, I. Tetanus, *i. e.* when the body is rigidly held in an upright manner. II. Emprosthotonos, *i. e.* when the body is rigidly bent forwards. III. Opisthotonos, *i. e.* when the body is rigidly bent backwards. IV. Pleurosthotonos, *i. e.* when the body is rigidly held to one side. And, V. Trismus, *i. e.* when the under-jaw is so drawn towards the upper, that the mouth cannot be opened; this last is called locked jaw; contraction of any space or thing, coarctation. (See confinement.)

CONTRADICT. *v.* To disavouch, or disvouch; to militate, to repeal, to reverse; one who is much disposed to contradict another in conversation, antiloquist. (See to deny.)

CONTRADICTION. *s.* Contradiction between any words and passages in an au-

thor, antilogy; contradiction between two or more laws, antinomy; contradictions are termed antilegomena, antithets, or antitheses.

CONTRARY. *s.* and *a.* Adverse, converse, reverse, contradictory, dissentaneous, inverse, inconsistent, inconsisting, inimical, repugnant, retrograde; directly contrary; diametrically opposite; contrary to, counter; to act contrary to, to counteract; on the contrary, vice versa L.

CONTRIBUTION. *s.* Done by contribution, collatitious. (See gift.)

CONTRIVE. *v.* To devise, to machinate, to meditate, to premeditate, to brew, to concert, to plod, to conspire, to project. (See to plot, to think, to examine.)

CONTRIVANCE. *s.* Device, project, machination, invention; quick at contrivance, inventive. (See trick.)

CONTRIVED. *p.* Contrived before-hand, prepense.

CONTRIVING. *p.* Studious in contriving, plodding. (See to study.)

CONTROVERT. *v.* To agitate, to canvass. (See to debate, to dispute.)

CONTROVERSIAL. *a.* Polemical, eristical. (See dispute.)

CONVENIENCE. *s.* Vantage. (See gain.)

CONVENIENT. *a.* Advantageous, idoneous, opportune, pat. (See fit.)

CONVERSABLE. *a.* Homiletical, conversive, conversable.

CONVERSATION. *s.* Colloquy, converse, confabulation, communing; dull in conversation, illepid.

CONVERT. *v.* To convert to the same nature, to assimilate; to convert to private use, to impropriate, to appropriate. (See church.)

CONVERT. *s.* Proselyte.

CONVEX. *a.* (See glass and round.)

CONVEY. *v.* To delate; to convey with an armed force, to escort.

CONVEYANCE. *s.* Transmittal, transportance, vehicle, voiture; the mode of secret conveyance, subvection.

CONVEYING. *p.* Deferent; act of conveying, delation; act of conveying over, transmission, transvection; conveying or continuing of a trope or figure in rhetoric, through a succession of significations, metalepsis.

CONVEXITY. *s.* Gibbosity, gibbousness. (See glass and round.)

CONVULSION. *s.* Convulsion is either termed spastic, tonic, or clonic.

Spastic or tonic convulsion is that which does not alternate with relaxation.

Clonic, called also *Agitatorii* or *Motorii*, is, when the contractions are succeed-

..ed by a relaxation, but at the same time are repeated without the concurrence of the will, or the repetition of natural causes. Thirdly, Convulsions are called *spasms*, that are those preternatural contractions which are attended with great mobility of the system (Quincy); name given to medicines good against convulsions, antepileptics, antispasmodics.

COOL, *a.* Bowery, brusy, temperate, dispassionate, equanimous; cool vapour or gale, aura; cool and shady walks, bowers, &c. frescades; to walk in the cool air, to walk in fresco. (See cold)

COOLNESS. *s.* Fraicheur, fresco. . (See cool and cold.)

COPIER. *s.* Copiator, amanuensis, transcriber.

COPPER. *s.* Mixture of copper and gold, tambac, tambaqua; relating to copper, venereal, (old chym.)

COPPERY. *a.* Cupreous, eruginous, copperish.

COPULATE. *v.* To copulate as deer, to buck or rut; as swine, to brim; as ram and ewe, to blissom; as dog and bitch, to line or ligne; as foxes, to clicket; as birds, to tread.

COPULATING. *p.* The act of copulating backwards, retrocopulation.

COPY. *s.* Duplicate, impression, extype, apographon, extreat, exemplar, protocol, transcript, ectype; to copy deeds in a large and fair hand in a register, to engross; to copy over, to transcribe, to rescribe.

CORD. *s.* Braid, funicle; having many small cords or fibres, funicular.

CORDIAL. *s.* and *a.* Cordial made from the berry called kermes, alkermes; cordial, cardiack, cardiacal; names given to liquid or solid cordials, catholicon, elixir, bezoartics, roborantia, analeptics; compositions made with the intention of acting as. cordials, lætificantia. (See comforting.)

CORN. *s.* Repository of corn, bin; corn or grain in general, emblements; bearing corn, fructiferous, frugiferous; of or belonging to corn, frumentarious, frumentacious; corn to be ground, grist; corn chest, hutch; Indian corn, maize; mixed corn, as beans or pease with oats, wheat with rye, &c., mastlin, meslin, or miscellane; one who buys corn in one place and carries it to another, badger; an engrosser of corn to enhance its price, kidder.

CORNER. *s.* Quoin; the corner stones in a building, diatoni.

CORNERED. *a.* Angular, angulous,

CORNET. *s.* Cornet or standard-bearer, aquilifer.

CORPORAL. *s.* An officer in Italy under a corporal, lancepesade; corporal among the Turks, odadassa.

CORPORATION. *s.* Borough, burgh, fraternity; belonging to a corporation, municipal.

CORPSE. *s.* Having the appearance of a corpse, cadaverous; the custom of watching the corpse of a friend till burial, lichwake; the gate through which the corpse is carried to the grave, lich-gate.

CORPULENCY. *s.* Polysarchy. (See gross and grossness.)

CORRECT. *v.* To correct or whip, to firk, to chasten, to chastise, to discipline, to castigate, to reclaim, to venge.

CORRECTION. *s.* Emendation, castigation; house of correction, bridewell; incapable of correction, incorrigible.

CORRESPONDENT. *a.* Concordant, congruent, homotonous, equable. (See fit.)

CORRODING. *p.* Caustic, esurine; act of corroding, or biting, mordication. (See eating.)

CORROSIVE. *a.* Acrimonious; corrosive medicines, diæretics, phagedenics, caustics, escharotics. (See burning and eating.)

CORRUPT. *v.* To corrupt or bribe, to grease; to corrupt, to adulterate, to attaminate, to blend, to blight, to canker, to mosher, to contaminate, to vitiate, to defile, to fester, to rankle, to inquinate, to pervert, to taint, to sully, to seduce.

CORRUPT. *a.* Corrupt, naught, peccant, putrid, putredinous, vitious; corrupt matter from a sore, pus; consisting of such matter, purulent; corrupt dialect, cant, gibberish.

CORRUPTED. *p.* Embruted, gangrenous, morbid; that is not to be corrupted, imputrescible, unputrifiable, inviolable, or unviolable. (See rotten.)

CORRUPTING. *p.* Corrupting medicines, Phthartics, Septics, Septica.

CORRUPTION. *s.* Corruption or resolution of an organized body into principles; phthora, syderation, putrescence. (See rottenness); corruption of manners, depravity, pravity, vitiosity, enormity.

COSTIVE. *a.* To render costive, to constipate, to obstipate, to restringe, to astringe.

COSTIVENESS. *s.* Medicines which induce costiveness; astringents, stegnotics; costiveness is termed coprostacy, or obstipation.

COVER. *a.* To cover, as with clothes; to apparel, to mantle. (See dress); to cover, as with water, to deluge, to inundate. (See to drown); to cover with earth, to inhume, to inhumate. (See to bury); to cover or deceive, to hoodwink. (See to cheat); to cover or excuse, to palliate, to obduce. (See to excuse); to cover or inwrap, to envelope, to circumvest. (See to surround); to cover as a bird does her eggs, to incubate; to cover as with a fort, to ensconce, to enshield, to immask; to cover with leaves, to infoliate; to cover or plate over, to loricate; to cover over again with black, to redenigrate; to cover over with a delicate hue, as in the act of blushing, to suffuse.

COVER. *s.* Cover or plate, lamina; cover for wrapping a dead body, shroud; cover or pretence, stalking-horse. (See excuse.)

COVERED. *p.* Covered or concealed, miched, operculate; covered or clothed, y'clad.

COVERING. *p.* Integument, tegument, involucrum; covering or clothing, investient; covering or protecting, protective; covering to keep off the sun-beams, &c., awning; covering or bag containing a humour, cist, cista, cistus, cyst or cystus.

COVETOUS. *a.* Sordid, parsimonious, questuary, tenacious, avaricious, yare, philargyry; covetous wretch, huncks, micher, muck-worm.

COUGH. *s.* Medicines good in allaying a cough, bechics, bechica, pectorals; chincough, hic-cough, hooping-cough, pertussis, yux.

COUGHING. *p.* The act of discharging by cough, expectoration.

COUNCIL. *s.* The Turkish council, divan; any council or assembly of the people, folkmote, (Sax.); the council or court of the Lord Mayor and Aldermen of London, hustings; the supreme council of the Jews, sanhedrim or sanhedrin; the council chamber of the fallen angels, pandæmonium.

COUNSEL. *s.* Rede; (see advice); counsel or pleader, who, being bribed, absents himself as sick, such pretended sickness is termed argentangina. *i. e.* silver quincy, (Bailey.)

COUNSELLOR. *s.* Barrister; younger counsellor, puisne; privy counsellor, symmysta.

COUNTENANCE. *s.* Mein, phiz, aspect; sterness of countenance, torvity; horror of countenance, ghastliness.

COUNTERFEIT. *v.* To counterfeit, to falsify, to simulate, to fucate, to personate, to adulterate, to sophisticate; one who counterfeits, pseudo, simular. (See to corrupt.)

COUNTERFEIT. *a.* Ascititious or adsci-

titious, fictious or fictitious, spurious, supposititious, commentitious; counterfeit or copy, (not the original), ectype; counterfeit writing, plastography; counterfeit name, pseudonymous; counterfeit gems, amouses.

COUNTRY. *s.* Peculiar to one's own country, vernacular, endemial; of the same country, compatriote; relating to the same country, conterraneous; native or reared in a country, indigenous; born in the country, rurigene; to destroy or extirpate the people of a country, to depopulate, to dispeople; to encrease or decrease the population of a country, to populate, (Bailey); relating to the country, rural; country seat, vill or villa; the art of describing a tract of country, chorography; the art of laying down, or surveying a country, chorometry.

COURAGE. *s.* Metal, prowess. (See brave.)

COURAGEOUS. *a.* Dauntless, intrepid, magnanimous, valorous, virile; courageous by drink, pot-valiant. (See bravery.)

COURSE. *s.* Career, profluence; course, (order) series; astrological course or progressions of the sun, &c., profections; to change frequently the direction in a course, as a ship which is aukwardly steered, to laveer; course for the running of racehorses, hippodrome; the monthly courses are termed menses, emmenia, fluores, catamenia, gynæcia, menstrua, muliebria; medicines that excite the courses, emmenagogues, emmensgogics or menagogues; a difficulty in the flowing of them, dysmenorrhæa.

COURT. *s.* Any court of justice, assize, judicatory, tribunal; itinerant court of justice, eyre; court held by the Lord Mayor and Aldermen of London, hustings; meeting of grandees at court for paying their respects to the sovereign, levee, Fr.; the supreme court of the Jews, sanhedrim or sanhedrin; court instituted by Henry VII. and dissolved by Charles I. for punishing routs, riots, forgeries, &c. &c. which were not sufficiently provided for by the common law, star-chamber; the great hall or court of the fallen angels according to Milton, pandæmonium; of or belonging to a court, aulic, forensic, consistorial, presidial, foranequs; the clerk of court, actuary.

COURT-YARD. *s.* Barton.

COURTESY. *s.* Affability, comity, congee, obeisance, philanthropy. (See kindness, civil, and gay.)

COWARD. *s.* Coistril, craven, hilding, meacock, poltron or poltroon.

COWARDICE. *s.* Cowardliness, micropsychy, pusilanimity.

COWARDLY. *a.* Cowish, dastardly, murcid, recreant, timid. (See base.)

COW. *s.* Cows, kine ; sea-cow, thrichecus ; Saxon name for the month of May, in which season they milked their cows thrice a day, trimilchi ; name given to the new mode of inoculating for the small pox, from the matter being taken from the udder of a cow, vaccination ; it is also called the Jennerian method, from the name of its discoverer, Dr Jenners.

COXCOMB. *s.* Baccalare, jackanapes, princox or princock. (See fop.)

CRACK. *s.* Crack, or clift, scissure, chop, crevice, chasm, fissure, hiatus, apertion ; crack or noise, fragor, bounce. (See cleft.)

CRACKLING. *p.* The crackling noise which salt makes on being thrown into the fire, crepitation, decrepitation.

CRAFT. *s.* Ingeny, policy, ruse ; to use craft, to dodge.

CRAFTILY. *ad.* Speaking craftily, versutiloquent.

CRAFTINESS. *s.* Vafrity, callidity. (See cunning.)

CRAFTY. *a.* Subdolous, veteratorian, evasive, argute, callid colubrine, vaprous, vulpinary, Machiavelian, subtile or subtle ; crafty low fellow, lorel, proteus.

CRAGGY. *a.* Scopulous. (See Rough.)

CRAM. *v.* To cram into a writing with an intent to forge, to foist ; to cram or eat greedily, and to excess, to engorge. (See to eat.)

CRAMP. *v.* To cramp, to constrict. (See to confine.)

CRAMP. *s.* Spasm ; good in removing the cramp, antispasmodic ; afflicted with the cramp, spasmodic, spasmatic ; discourse concerning the cramp, spasmology ; cramp fish, torpedo. (See contraction.)

CRANE. *s.* Engine like a crane used by builders in raising stones, &c., catadrome.

CRAZINESS. *s.* Craziness from age, decrepitude, or decrepitness.

CRAZY. *a.* Frantic, moidered, puling, valetudinary. (See sickly and weak.)

CREATING *p.* All-creating, omnific.

CREATION. The creation of the world, cosmogany ; the six days work of creation, hexameron.

CREATOR. *s.* Of or belonging to a creator, demiurgical.

CREDIT. *s.* Credence, creed, reputation, vogue, creaunce ; a fellow deserving no credit, cataian ; not deserving credit, incredible, uncreditable.

CREDIBLE. *a.* Verisimilar, (See likely and probable.)

CREEP. *v.* To creep on the ground, to grovel ; to creep or cringe, to truckle.

CREEPING. *p.* Helical or helcical, reptitious ; a creeping in or on, obreption ; creeping up, scandent ; a creeping forth, ereptation.

CREPT. *p.* Crept in privately, arreptitious.

CRIME. *s.* Blot, demerit, malefaction ; petty crime, peccadillo ; an atrocious crime, piacle ; to charge with a crime, to endite ; or endict, indict or indite : free from crime, innoxious ; guilty of a crime, nocent ; to commit a crime, to perpetrate.

CRIMINAL. *a.* Atrocious, noxious, criminous, peccant, culpable. (See guilty) ; a criminal, malefactor, crackhemp, delinquent, culprit.

CRIMSON. *s.* Crimson colour, crimosin ; crimson or scarlet dye, coccinian.

CRISIS. *s.* Crisis or height, acme. (See height.)

CRITIC or CRITICK. *s.* Philologer, philologist, connoisseur ; critic who carries his remarks beyond reason, hypercritic.

CROCODILE. *s.* Crocodile of America, alligator ; name of a small animal of the rat kind, that destroys the eggs of the crocodile, ichneumon.

CROOKED. *p.* Curvated, flexuous, sinuous, kam, kimbo, recurvous, repandous, obuncous, bandyed, incurvated ; crooked as a scythe, falcated ; crooked as a hook, hamated.

CROOKED-BACKED. *a.* Gibbous, gibbose, humph-backed.

CROOKEDNESS *s.* Aduncity, arcuation, curvity, gibbosity, gibbousness, protuberancy.

CROP. *s.* The second crop of grass mown in autumn, aftermath, lattermath ; crop or stomach of a bird, choule, craw, gizzard, ingluvies.

CROP. *v.* To traverse.

CROSS. *a.* Litigious, curst, exceptious, froward, fractious, morose, perverse, retrograde, testy, waiward or wayward, inimical, repugnant, latrant, misadventured ; cross event, mishap ; lying or extending across, transverse.

CROSSING. *p.* Crossing or cutting, secant, intersecant, crucial ; the act of crossing a river or the sea, transfretation.

CROSSNESS. *s.* Crossness or peevishness, protervity, termagancy. (See peevishness.)

CROUD. *s.* To scruse, to bend, to huddle, to accloy. (See to press.)

CROWD. *s.* Confluence, frequence, concourse, group, prease. (See multitude.)

CROWDING. *p.* Act of crowding or stuffing, infarction, impaction. (See wedge.)

CROWN. *s.* Crown of glory, aureola ; crawn, tiar, or tiara, diadem, corona ; crown conferred by the Romans on those who first scaled the walls of a town, mural crown; to those who first boarded a ship, naval crown; formed like a crown, corrollated; the crown of the head, coryphe; having or being gifted with a crown made of laurel leaves, laurelled or laureated.

CRUEL. *a.* Barbarian, barbarous, bloody, bowelless, brutal, doghearted, ferine, ferocious, rapacious, butcherly, disnatured, fell, ruthless, salvage, savage, vindictive, gory, homicidal, incompassionate, inexorable, leonine, marble-hearted, novercal, relentless, remorseless, stern, truculent, torvous.

CRUELTY. *s.* Austerity, durity, immanity, inclemency, rigor, rigour, ferity.

CRUMBLED. *a.* That may be easily crumbled, friable, pulverable.

CRUMBLING. *p.* Act of crumbling, friation, pulverisation. (See powder.)

CRUSH. *v.* To mate, to enerve, to enervate, to infract, to pash, to perempt, to quash, to repress, to suppress, to sbend.

CRUSHING. *p.* Crushing or squeezing out, also trouble or affliction of any kind, thlipsis, or ecthlipsis; this last word is used when swelled eyes dart forth as it were sparks of light.

CRYSTALLINE. *a.* Hyaline. (See clear); the crystalline humour of the eye is termed crystalloides or glacialis.

CUCKHOLD. *s.* Cornute or cornuta.

CUCKHOLD. *v.* To cornute.

CUD. *s.* To chew the cud, to ruminate.

CUNNING. *a.* Dædalian, dædalin, dædal, political, shrewd, sleight, subdolous, callid, cautelous, colubrine, vulpinary, subtile, subtle; cunning trick, finesse, ruse; cunning person, reynard. (See crafty.)

CUP. *s.* Cup used in acts of devotion or worship chalice or calice; cup or bowl, also the concave inverted conical opening, into a volcano, crater; cup that has a spout for the convenience of decanting liquors, beaker; cup-bearer or butler, skinker.

CUP-BOARD. *s.* Buffet, armoire, Fr.

CUPPING-GLASS. *s.* Ventose, versicatory, cucurbitula.

CURB. *v.* To check, to restrain, (See check and blame.)

CURDLE. *v.* To coagulate, to quail, (Bailey); to curdle together, to concoagulate; curdled milk by the mixture of wine or beer, posset; the curdling of milk in the stomach into a substance like cheese, tyrosis.

CURE. *v.* To doctor, to lech.

CURE. *s.* Cure or relief, opitulation; affording a cure, remediate; those medicines which cure poison, or the bite of poison-

ous animals, theriaca or theriace; incapable of cure, insanable, irremediable, unremediable, remediless, immedicable.

CURED. *p.* That may be cured, sanable, remediable, medicable.

CURING. *p.* That part of physic which shews the method of curing diseases, therapeutics.

CURIOSITIES. *s.* Repository of curiosities, museum; collector of curiosities, vertuoso or virtuoso.

CURIOUS. *a.* Exquisite, prurient. (See eager.)

CURL. *v.* To crisp, to buckle, to ringlet.

CURL. *s.* The curls or ringlets of the hair of the head, of a beautiful woman, heart-breakers.

CURSE. *v.* To execrate, to imprecate, to beshrew, to blaspheme.

CURSE. *s.* Ban, anathema, imprecation, execration, interdiction, malediction, maranatha. (See ban.)

CURSED. *a.* Curst. (Johnson.)

CUSTOM *s.* Ure, guise, habit, assuetude, consuetude; grown into a custom, inveterate; discourse on customs and manners, ethology; custom or duty on goods, impost, hedagium; custom formerly paid in France on salt, gabel or gabelle; custom-house officer who oversees the waiters jerguer.

CUSTOMERS. *s.* One who stands to call in customers at a public sale, klicker.

CUT. *v.* To cut off, to abscind, to lop, to minish, to mutilate, to defalcate, to prescind, to proin, to prune, to rescind, to retrench; to cut off a limb, to amputate; to cut off the head, to decapitate, to decollate; to cut short, to drib, to truncate, to dock, to curtail; to cut in pieces, (to butcher) to excarnificate; to cut in small pieces, to fritter, to discind, to cantle, to carbonade; to cut into two, three, &c. to bisect, trisect, &c.; to cut obliquely, to decussate; to cut or cross, to intersect; to cut into hollows, to excavate; to cut out from, or away, to exect; to cut or separate, to incide, to gride; to cut up by the roots, to eradicate, to excind (see root); to cut again, to recoupe; to cut the stones from an animal, to geld, to castrate, to evirate, to eunuchate, to emasculate, to glib, to spay (this last word is only used in speaking of the castration of females); to cut or carve on, to insculp; to cut in and out, as the teeth of a saw, to indent; to cut, tear, or rend, to lancinate.

CUT. *s.* Not to be cut off, altered, or reversed, indefeasible, irreversible, indefesible, undefeasible; that cannot be cut or separated, insecable, insectile; that may be cut or divided, fissile, scissile, scissible; cut, (gash or cleft) cæsura, scissure (see cleft); cut or divided into two, three, &c. parts, bifid, trifid, &c.; cut or represntation, on copper, wood, &c. icon; the art of making wooden cuts or plates, lignography.

CUTTING. *p.* A cutting off, concision, recision, excision, elision; cutting one another, intersecant; act of cutting, scission; cutting or piercing, secant, trenchant; a cutting off any thing, eccope, ectome; a cutting open the womb or bowels, gastrotomy.

CYCLE. *s.* Cycle of the moon or lunar cycle, is a revolution of 19 years, so called, after the expiration of which all the lunations return to their former places in the calendar; that is, the new moons happen in the same months, and days of the month, hence the term, enneadecaterides.

CYPHERS. *s.* The art of secret writing, or the writing in cyphers, cryptography; a cypher consisting of one or more letters interwoven together, monogram; the manner of writing in cyphers, where the characters are interwoven in a variety of ways, polygraphy; cyphers or initial letters put for whole words, as the letters RSS., i. e. Regiæ Societatis Socius, are termed, sigles; cypher or *o* is called nullo, or zero.

D

DAILY. *a* and *ad.* Diurnal, ephemeral, quotidian; an account or journal of daily proceedings, diary.

DAINTIES. *s.* Cates, tit-bits, bons-bons, delicacies.

DAMAGE. *v.* To annoy, to damnify, to derogate, to disprofit, to disserve, to scath, to prejudice.

DAMAGE. *s.* Nocument, impierment, detriment.

DAMP. *v.* To irrorate, to humect, or humectate; to damp (or dispirit) to blank.

DAMP. *a.* Humid, dank, pluvial, pluvious.

DANCE. *v.* To skip, to gambol.

DANCE. *s.* Sort of antic dance when three persons hit one another on the breech, with one of their feet, pimpompet; an involuntary and convulsive dance or leaping, with which some maids are seized, before the eruption of the menses, St Vitus's dance, or chorea Sancti Viti, which see in Quincy's lexicon.

DANCING. *s.* One who practises the moorish dance, Morisco dancer; the art of dancing, tripudiation, saltation; of or belonging to dancing, saltatory, tripudiary; the art of rope-dancing, schoenobatica; the feigned inventress of dancing, Terpsichore; the act of dancing on a rope, funambulation; a rage for dancing, or more properly a kind of St Vitus's dance, tarantismus.

DANGEROUS. *a.* Climacteric, discriminous, hazardous, perilous, periculous, herculean, heretical, jeopardous, infective, insecure, parlous, unsecure; term used for all distempers which are not reckoned dangerous, acacos.

DARING. *a.* Adventurous, intrepid, undaunted, audacious, confident, hardy, malapert.

DARK. *a.* Sable, sombre, stygian, umbrageous, umbraical, umbrose, tenebricose, tenebrose, tenebrious, undiaphanous, Cimmerian, abstruse, enigmatical, hazy, rimy, funereal, opacous, opaque, immanifest, dingy, complex, inconspicuous, inevident, recondite, inscrutable, metaphysical, murky, mystic, tralatitious, metaphorical, nebulous, nebulose, nubilous, nubilose, obscure; half dark, semiopacous; dark like soot, fuliginous; dark colour, towards brown, olivaster.

DARK. *v.* To make or render dark, to obfuscate or offuscate; name given to all such bodies as give light in the dark, as the different phosphori, noctilucæ.

DARKEN. *v.* To eclipse, to infuscate, to intricate, to bedim, to obnubilate, to obnumbrate, to opacate.

DARKNESS. *s.* Caligation, obtenebration, dingyness; tending to darkness, dusk, duskish; great darkness (or obscurity) Cimmerian darkness, so called from the Cimmerii, a people in Scythia, who were environed with hills and woods.

DART. *v.* To ejaculate, to elaunce, to emit.

DART. *s.* Missile; bearing a dart, teliferous.

DARTED. *p.* That may be darted, jaculable.

DARTING. *p.* Act of darting missile weapons, jaculation; the act of darting through, trajection.

DASH. *v.* To inflict; to dash together, to collide; to dash in pieces, to elide, to allide; to dash against, to impinge.

DASH. *s.* Occursion, pash, rasure.

DASHING. *p.* The act of dashing to pieces, allision; a dashing or darting out, as light sometimes appears to do from inflamed eyes, ecthlipsis.

DATE. *v.* To date after the proper time, to postdate; to date before the proper time, to antedate. (See time.)

DATE. *s.* The period of reckoning from a date, epoch, era or æra; the famous date reckoned from, by the Arabians and Turks, who begin their accounts from the time that Mahomet was forced to make his escape from the city of Mecca to Medina, which was on Friday July 16. A. C. 622, begira.

DAUB. *v.* To bedaub, to grime, to hox, to infuscate; to daub over with paint, to infucate; to daub over with dirt, to moil, to bemire; to daub over with glutinous matter, to inviscate, to oint.

DAUBING. *p.* Act of daubing or plastering, oblimation. (See daub.)

DAY. *s.* That exists or lives but one day, hemerobious; one who turns day into night, lychnobite, diseases which last but one day, or are cured in one day, monohemerous; containing both a day and a night, noctidial; the space of 24 hours, or a day and night, nychthemeron; a fever or ague, the paroxysms of which return every 4th day, quartan; an ague which has two fits in three days, tertian; a fever which occurs every day, with intermissions, quotidian; any disease which occurs every third day, triduan; an ague which occurs every third day, tritæophyes, tritæophya, or tritæus; an extraordinary critical day, caused by the violence of a disease, intercedental or intercedent day; a day's work, char; a book in which the transactions of every day are registered, hemerologium; performed in a day, diurnal, ephemeral; day-book, diurnal, diary, journal; day inserted in leap-year, embolism, intercalary or intercalatory day; belonging to this day, hodiernal.

DAY-LIGHT. *s.* A distemper wherein the patient can only see in day-light, hemeralopia. (See candle-light.)

DAZZLING. *a.* Fulgent, fulgid, lucent. (See clear.)

DEACON. *s.* A Romish deacon, acolothist.

DEAD. *a.* Exanimate, amort, bloodless, defunct, inanimate, extinct; dead sleep, caros or carus, coma, lethargy; carriage for the dead, bier, hearse; dead appearance, cadaverous; dead body, carcase, corpse or corse; prayer or sacrifice for the dead, februation; an escutcheon for the dead, hatchment; the practice of watching the dead till buried, lich-wake; monuments for the dead, memorise, *L.*; coloured like a dead leaf, filemot or philomot, or more properly, feuille morte, *F.*; register of the dead, obituary; thirty masses said in thirty days for the dead, trental; song or verses in praise of the dead, threnody, epicedium, elegy; the bearer or bearers of the dead to the grave, clinicus, cliaici; receptacle for the remains of the dead, reliquary, shrine; vessel used for holding the ashes of the dead, urn; hymn which is sung to implore rest for the dead, requiem; covering for the dead, shroud; the state of the dead, supremity, hades, manes; dead or flat, as bad beer, vapid; divination by raising the ghosts of the dead, necromancy.

DEADEN. *v.* To obtund, to paralize, to impalsy, to torpify.

DEADLY *a.* Toxical, deleterious, fatal, mortiferous, pestiferous, lethiferous, lethal, deletery, fatiferous.

DEAFEN. *v.* To dorr. (See stupify.)

DEAFNESS. *s.* Surdity, cophosis, epicophosis; medicines which assist deafness, acoustics.

DEAL. *v.* To dole, to distribute, to dispense.

DEALER. *s.* Chafferer, dispensator; dealer in skins, fell-monger; dealing or trafficking, mercature.

DEATH. *s.* Consummation, perdition, quietus, decease, demise, dissolution, expiration, obit, exit; the death or crucifixion of our Saviour, deicide; a gentle and easy death, euthanasy; stoning to death, lapidation; tune sounded by huntsmen at the death of a deer, &c. mort; bringing death, mortiferous (see deadly); child born after the death of its father, posthumous child; work published after the death of its author, posthumous work; those persons who are taken off by violent deaths, biathanatoi; the punishment of pressing to death, formerly used to extort answers, *pain* or *peine forte et dure*, Fr.

DEBATE. *v.* To agitate, to canvass, to expostulate, to litigate, to contest, to moot.

DEBATING. *part.* Debating of law-suits, actitation, mooting.

DEBAUCHED. *a.* Dissolute, lecherous, libertine, deboist, deboyst, or deboished, (Shakespeare) profligate.

DEBAUCHEE. *s.* Leccator, lecher.

DEBAUCHERY. *s.* Abliguration, or, abligurition.

DEBAUCHING. *part.* The act of debauching women, thelyphthora.

DEBT. *s.* The owned remission of a debt, acceptilation, L. T.; the inability of paying debts, insolvency; to pay or lessen debts, to liquidate.

DEBTOR. *s.* A stone erected in the city of

Padua, resorted to by debtors, at which, if they openly declare their bankruptcy, are freed from prosecution, *lapis opprobrii*, i. e. the stone of reproach; house where debtors are first taken to, towards matters being accommodated with the creditors before being carried to jail, spunging-house.

DECANT. *v.* To elutriate. (See to strain.)

DECAY. *v.* To vade, to emaciate. (See lean.)

DECAY. *s.* Imbecility, decadency, ebb, declension, declination, decrement; not subject to decay, indefectible, undestroyable, indestructible. (See burnt.)

DECAYED. *a.* Decayed as a rotten bone, carious.

DECAYING. *part.* Decaying (or wasting) collabefaction, evanid, marcescent. (See fading.)

DECEIT. *s.* Artifice, duplicity, gullery, hypocrisy, leasing, mendacity, prevarication, pseudology, equivocation, rookery, simulation, circumvention; got by deceit, subreptitious, surreptitious.

DECEITFUL. *a.* Ambidextrous, collusive, designing, elusory, deceptious, fallacious, erroneous, jesuitical, illusive, insidious, punic, evasive, sophistical, subdolous, veteratorian, covenous; a deceitful argument, or false way of reasoning, paralogism; a deceitful person, Proteus, from Proteus the sea-god and prophet, who is fabled to have had the power of turning himself into any shape; very deceitful, pharmaical, prestigious, ambiloquent.

DECEITFULNESS. *s.* Prodition, cretism or criticism.

DECEIVE. *v.* To baffle to cajole, to countermine, to elude, to bambouzle, to befool, to crossbite, to flam, to jockey, to circumvent, to coneycatch, to coquet, to delude, to illude, to impose, to inveigle, to ludificate, to misadvise, to seduce, to supplant, to inescate, to bilk.

DECEIVER. *s.* Bubbler, cozener, cajoler, dissembler, canter, cogger, trickster.

DECEIVING. *part.* The act or art of deceiving or juggling, prestigiation.

DECENCY. *s.* Concinnity. (See fitness.)

DECENT. *a.* Coy, decorous, inhabitable or habitable.

DECEPTION. *s.* Hocus-pocus, juggle, imposture, inescation, ingannation, legerdemain. (See trick.)

DECK. *v.* To bedeck, to bedizen, to bedight, to betrim, to dizen, (See, to dress.)

DECLARATION. *s.* Predication, avowsal, enarration, enunciation, indiction; declaration made on oath, affidavit; declaration made before hand, prenunciation; a solemn declaration, protestation, asseveration.

DECLARED. *part.* That may be declared, predicable; that which is affirmed or declared, predicate. (See affirmation.)

DECLARING. *part.* A declaring, shewing, or indication, used generally of diseases, endeixis.

DECLINE. *v.* To decline a verb or noun, to inflect.

DECLINE. *s.* Declension, declination, ebb; decline or consumption, marasmus. (See consumption.)

DECOY. *s.* Duckoy. (Johnson.)

DECREE. *s.* Arret, hest, arbitration, arbitrament, arbitrage, edict, placit, audom.

DEDUCTION. *s.* Illation, consectary, corollary. (See inference.)

DEED. ... Achievement, covenant, feat; the first copy of a deed or writing protocol; any deed executed under the hand and seal of both parties, syngrapha.

DEEM. *v.* (See to judge, to think.)

DEEMED. *part.* Adeemed, putative.

DEEP. *a.* Profound, unemptiable, abysmal, internal, latent, intime (see secret); deep meditation is termed, a brown study; of a deep colour, not pale or faint, lush; deep brown colour, olivaster.

DEER. *s.* Pertaining to a deer, cervine; the branches of a deer's horns, antlers; the entrails of a deer, humbles, nombles, numbles; the lowest gut or rectum of the deer kind, inchipin; term used for the fat of the deer, snet; term used when a deer is so hard pursued that he foams at the mouth, embost, (hunting term); the place where deer harbour by day, lair or layer; the place where they lye to dry themselves, leer; tune or note blown by hunters at the death of the deer, mort or moot; term used for the crown of a deer's head, palmer; male deer which has cast his horns, pollard; term used for a lean deer, rascal; the track of a deer, slot; male fallow-deer, sorrel or sorel, dama; red male deer of 4 years old, staggard; young deer, fawn.

DEFAMATION. *s.* Obtrectation, detraction. (See censure and blame.)

DEFAME. *v.* To blemish, to detract, to distain, to debase, to infame, to vilify, to traduce, to calumniate.

DEFEAT. *v.* To foil, to frustrate, to baffle, to cajole, to countermine, to elude, to lurch, to vacate, to discomfit.

DEFECT. *s.* Inconclusiveness, inconsequence; that which serves to fill up a defect, suppletory; not subject to defect, indefectible. (See blemish and error.)

DEFENCE. *s.* Or security of a state or city, palladium; defence made in haste of barrels of earth, &c. barricado; defence or security incolumity muniment; proposed by way of defence, defensative.

DEFENCELESS. *a.* Immartial, indefensible. (See weak.)

DEFEND. *v.* To propugn, to espouse, to buckler; to enguard, to enshield, to defend against risk, to guaranty; to defend or fortify, to munite; to defend another's right, to patrocinate; to defend or protect in a holy place, to sanctuarise; to defend or shelter, to shroud; to defend from accusation, to vindicate.

DEFER. *v.* To adjourn, to postpone, to procrastinate, to protend, to protract. (See delay.)

DEFIANCE. *s.* Despite; in defiance of, maugre. (See contempt)

DEFILE. *v.* To intaminate, to contaminate, to vitiate, to conspurcate, to desecrate, to inquinate, to profane, to turpify.

DEFILEMENT. *s.* Defædation. (See base.)

DEFLOUR. *v.* To devirginate, to stuprate, to violate, to depucilate, to depudicate,

DEFLOURING. *part.* Act of deflowring, defloration, constupration, vitiation.

DEFORMED. *a.* Abnormous, haggard, ill-favoured, deform; term used for any ill-bred deformed wretch, Thersites.

DEFRAUD. *v.* To bilk, to cozen, to gull, to peculate or depeculate. (See to cheat.)

DEGRADE. *v.* To debase, to depose, to diminish, to embase, to imbrute. (See disgrace.)

DEGREE. *s.* Gradation ; to mark any scale with degrees, to graduate ; mathematical instrument for laying down degrees, protractor, graphometer; letter conferring a degree to act as phycisian, &c. diploma or dipsas ; one honoured with a degree, graduate ; of equal degree or rank, co-ordinate.

DEJECTED. *a.* Amort, chopfaln, chill, henpecked, hippish, hypochondriac.

DEJECTION. *s.* Prosternation, prostration ; dejection of the spirits, athymia. (See melancholy.)

DELAY. *v.* To adjourn, to hesitate, to postpone, to procrastinate, to protract, to retard, to suspend, to prorogue.

DELAY. *s.* Crastination, cunctation, dalliance, demur, endurance, lentor, prolongation, prorogation ; delay of punishment, reprieve, respite.

DELIBERATE. *v.* To pensitate. (See to consider.)

DELIGACY. *s.* Any delicacy, such as sweet meats, juncate.

DELICATE. *a.* Attic, cade, effeminate, femine, tid ; delicate morsels, tid-bits, bonbons, cates.

DELICIOUS. *a.* Ambrosial, ambrosian, tid. (See delicate.)

DELIGHT. *s.* Gratification, oblectation, solace, recreation. (See joy.)

DELIGHTFUL. *a.* Delectable, enchanting, delicious, elysian, chromatic, delightsome. (See charm.)

DELIVERANCE. *s.* Disencumbrance, acquittal, emancipation, enfranchisement, livery, rescue. (See to free.)

DELIVERY. *s.* Medicines which assist women in difficult delivery are called, ecbolica ; this term is also used for medicines which cause abortion.

DELVE. *v.* To pastinate.

DELUGE. *s.* Alluvion, cataclysm or cataclysmos ; existing before the deluge, antediluvian ; of or belonging to the deluge, diluvian. (See flood.)

DEMAND. *v.* To demand previously, to pre-require ; to demand often, to rogitate, to conflagitate. (See to ask.)

DEMAND. *s.* Challenge, exigence, postulate ; relating to a demand, petitory.

DEMONSTRATED. *part.* That cannot be demonstrated, indemonstrable or undemonstrable ; what is ocularly demonstrated, autoptical.

DEMONSTRATION. *s.* Demonstration is either,

I. *A priori,* or composition ; *i. e.* when in reasoning from principles, we pass, descending continually, till after many reasons made, we come at length to conclude that which was first intended.

II. *A posteriori,* or resolution, when contrariwise in reasoning, we pass from the last conclusion made by the premises, continually ascending, till we come to principles which are indemonstrable, and from their simplicity can suffer no further resolution.

III. *A fortiori,* is exemplified in VII. and XXI. Prop. 1st book of Euclid, and conveys the argument, that, if 100 is more than 10, *à fortiori,* it is more than one.

IV. *Apagogic, apagogical,* or by some termed, *reductio ad absurdum,* is that sort of demonstration, either logical or mathematical, that does not prove a thing directly, but shews the absurdity which arises from denying it : This is exemplified in the 14th Prop. of 1st Book, and 19th of the 3d Book of Euclid.

V. *Autoptical,* is what is seen, otherwise called, ocular demonstration.

VI. *Apodictical,* is a demonstration approaching to ocular. (See reasoning.)

DEN. *s.* Cave, antre, delve.

DENIAL. *s.* Disavowment, negation, denay, disaffirmance, obtension ; the denial of revealed religion, deism ; of a god, atheism.

DENIED. *part.* That cannot be denied, in-refragable, incontestible, or uncontestable. (See, to deny.)

DENY. v. To abnegate, to abstain, to disallow, to disavouch, to disown, to retract, to recuse, to renege, to resist.

DEPART. v. To depart from the subject in question, to digress; to depart to a distance, to elongate (see, to go and to leave); depart ye, avaunt, aroynt.

DEPARTURE. s. Decession, egression, exit, exodus, recess, obit.

DEPENDANT. s. correlative, fedary or federary, implicit, pendent, precarious, servile; any low dependant, minion, retainer, dependent.

DEPRIVE. v. To bereave, to despoil, to devest, or divest, to exauctorate.

DEPTH. s. Abyss, abysm, profundity. (See gulf.)

DEPUTE. v. To subrogate, to surrogate.

DEPUTE. s. Proxy, delegate, syndic; one who deputes another, constituent.

DERISION. s. Figure in rhetoric, when a person or thing is recommended by way of derision, diasyrmus, irony.

DESCENT. s. (Or succesive inheritance) hereditament, lineage; descent or slope, declination, declivity, proneness.

DESCRIPTION. s. Definition, diagraph; Description of the world, cosmography.

—— Of the seas, with their bays, gulphs, &c.	Hydrography.
—— Of pestilensial diseases.	Loimography.
—— Of particular places	Topography.
—— Of the pyramids.	Pyramidography.
—— Of gems.	Dactyliothogy.
—— Or treatise on opium	Meconology.
—— Of the little world, viz. man.	Microcosmography.
—— Of exceeding small objects.	Micrography.
—— Of fevers	Pyretology.
—— Of the entrails.	Splanchnology.
—— Of mechanics and other arts.	Technology.
—— Of fishes.	Ichthyology.
—— Of particular regions	Chorography.
—— Of animals in general	Zoography.
—— Of the sea.	Haliography.
—— Of the body of man, anatomically.	Anthropography, or anthroposophy.
—— By pictures or images.	Iconography.
—— Of ancient coins and medals.	Numismatography.
—— Of the heavens.	Ouranography.
Rhetorical description, so lively represented, that things seem as they were before our eyes.	Diatyposis.

A true and lively description of a person or thing. } Iconism.
(See discourse and treatise.)

DESCRIPTIVE. a. Chorographical.

DESERTER. s. Fugitive, hereslita, or bereslia, renegade or renegado.

DESIGN. s. Intent, drift, aim, counsel, purport, delineation (see purpose); the second design or intention, deuteroscopy.

DESIRE. v. To desiderate; to desire a thing earnestly, to efflagitate, or flagitate.

DESIRE. s. Ambition, ardour, eagerness, exoptation, monthsmind, avidity, ardour, eagerness, cupidity; the want or privation of desire, inappetence; moderate desire or wish, velleity; desire or aversion in brutes, instinct; expressive of desire, optative; an uncommon desire for women, mulierosity; sensual desire, philosarchy, voluptuousness, appetence or appetency.

DESIREABLE. a. Appetible.

DESIRED. part. Things or matters to be desired, desiderata; what is not to be desired or wished for, (as extreme old age,) inoptable.

DESK. s. Abacus, escroitore, or scrutoir.

DESPISE. v. To floccify, to misprize, to vilify, to debase, to defy, to contemn. (See neglect.)

DESTINIES. s. The destinies are,
Clotho, who bears a distaff.
Lachesis, who spins the thread of man's life, and
Atropos, who cuts it off.
These three are termed, Parcæ.

DESTROY. v. To abrogate, to abolish, to absorb, to absume, to dissolve, to erase, to everse or evert, to extirpate, to havoc, to bane, to cancel, to efface, to glide, to enecate, to jugulate, to infringe, to subvert, or subverse, to peremt, to rase or raze, to sap, to scath, to labefy, to lacerate, to landdam, to obliterate; to destroy buildings, to elapidate, to dilapidate. (See, to kill.)

DESTROYED. part. Easily destroyed or broken, fragile or frangible; that cannot be destroyed, indestructible, or undestroyable; that cannot be destroyed by fire, incombustible, incremable, asbestine.

DESTROYER. s. Destroyer of mankind, depopulator or populator. (See people.)

DESTROYING. part. The act of destroying, vastation, collabefaction.

DESTRUCTION. s. Homicide (Dryden) pest, eversion, excision, extirpation, extermination, havoc, devastation, doom, erasement, expunction, abolition, annihilation, bane, demolition, deperdition, desolation, perdition, privation, phthora, subversion, internecion; endeavouring

F 2

mutual destruction, internecine; destruction of mankind, depopulation or population. (Bailey.)

DESTRUCTIVE. *a.* Deleterious, exitial, exitious, fatal, lethiferous, malefick, or malefique, mortiferous, pernicious, pestiferous, scathful, deletory. (See deadly.)

DETECTING. *part.* Detecting or discovering, also not apt to fall, indiciduous or indeciduous. (Bailey.)

DETERMINATION. *s.* Decree, placit, arbitrement, arbitrage, resolve, verdict, laudum, arbitration; term given to such medicines as cause a determination of the humours of the body from one part to another, antispastics or antispasticons.

DETERMINED. *a.* Resolute, bent, stanch, statary.

DEVIATE. *v.* Totralineate. (See to wander.)

DEVIATING. *part.* Anomalous; deviating from a fixed rule, heteroclitical, heterodoxical.

DEVIATION. *s.* Evagation, aberration, tralineation

DEVIL. *s.* Cacodæmon, Abaddon, Lucifer, Deuse, Dragon, Elf, Imp, Barbason, Belial, Fiend, Fury, Apollyon; the devil is called by theologians, the Enemy; the devils, Lamiæ, Liliths; possessed with a devil, demoniacal; little devil, devilkin, half-devil, demi-devil; government which is so obnoxious as to resemble that of devils, demonocracy; worship of the devil, demonolatry; state of those who worship, out of fear of the devil, disidæmony or disidemony; the council-house of the devils, according to Milton, Pandæmonium.

DEVILISH. *a.* Demoniacal, diabolical, tartarean.

DEVOTE. *v.* To addict, to hallow, to dedicate.

DEVOTEE. *s.* Bigot, enthusiast.

DEVOTION. *s.* An indisposition to devotion, accidie.

DEVOTIONAL. *a.* Ascetic.

DEVOUR. *s.* To champ, to englut, to engorge, to flap-dragon, to glut, to gormandize, to lurch, to manducate, to raven. (See appetite.)

DEVOURING. *part.* Devouring or feeding on flesh - - - Carnivorous.

——— fish	- -	Piscivorous.
——— grass	- -	Graminivorous.
——— fruit,	- -	Frugivorous.
——— grain,	- -	Granivorous.
——— worms,	-	Vermivorous.
——— serpents,	-	Ophiophagous.
——— herbs,	-	Herbevorous.
——— vegetables in general.	}	Phytivorous.
——— mud,	-	Lutarious.
——— all things,		Omnivorous.

DEVOUT. *a.* Eremitical, heremitical, recluse.

DEW. *s.* The falling of dew, roration; producing dew, roriferous; full of dew, rorulent; the autumnal dew, scirona.

DEWY. *a.* Rorid, roscid, irriguous. (See moist.)

DEXTERITY. *s.* Expertness, address, legerity, adroitness; (see art) dexterity in dissections, or more generally, a dexterity in handling or manipulating, enchiresis or epicheresis. (Bailey.)

DIADEM. *s.* Tiar or tiara. (See crown.)

DIAL. *s.* Solarium, horodix, horologe; the pin or hand of a dial, gnomon; of or belonging to a dial, sciatherical, sciatheric; said of a sun-dial, when it is placed any way declining from the west or east, disorientated or disoccidentated.

DIALING. *s.* The art of dialing, gnomonics, sciagraphy or sciography, horography or horologiography.

DIALOGUE; *s* Interlocution, tete à tete.

DIAMETER. *s.* Dimetient (Bailey), half diameter, semi-diameter, radius; the shortest diameter of an elliptical orbit of a planet, diacentros; the longest diameter is termed, paracentros.

DICE. *s.* Term used at playing with a box and dice, to set a main, or throw a main; one who cheats at dice by slight of hand, palmer; divination by the casting of dice, cleromancy.

DICTIONARY. *s.* Dictionaries are, generally,

I. Of uncommon or obsolete words, and are termed, glossaries.

II. Of words of like meaning, and are named, synonymous.

III. Of new and affected words, and are termed, neological. Others are tactical, geographical, chymical, mathematical, &c. &c. as the case may be. Dictionary of arts and sciences, cyclopædia, encyclopædia; dictionary, lexicon; writer of dictionaries, lexicographer.

DIE. *s.* Dye, hue; to dye or tinge of a flesh colour, to incarnadine; to dye or flush as in blushing, to suffuse.

DIE. *v.* To die or expire, to die, to ghost; ready to die, moribund.

DIET. *s.* Fare, diæta; the diet prescribed to those in sickness, regimen; term used for a moderate diet, lessian diet (from Lessinis, the name of a famous physician who always recommended it to his patients.)

DIFFERENCE. *s.* Contest, discrimen, discrepancy, difference (quarrel) tiff; difference from an established rule, contraregular; difference in opinion, dissent;

accidental difference, modality; one who decides differences, umpire, moderator; difference from an established doctrine, particularly in matters of religion, heterodoxy.

DIFFERENT. *a.* Distinct, diverse; said of a mass composed of many different materials, farraginous, heterogeneous, heterogeneal; having different and opposite meanings, as the verb, to cleave, which signifies, to stick to, to hold together; and also to part asunder or divide, homonymous, ambiguous.

DIFFICULT. *a.* Abstruse, crabbed, arduous, cramp, difficil, obscure, laboriferous, herculean, transcendental, scrupose.

DIFFICULTY. *s.* Premunire, quandary, spinosity, intricacy, pectination; the solution of a difficulty, enucleation, enodation; an inexplicable difficulty, Gordian knot; Chaucer terms it dulcarnon, from a certain difficult and perplexing proposition solved by Pythagoras, on which he sacrificed an ox to the gods; to be in difficulty, to be in the suds, or to be at dulcarnon, as above.

DIFFICULTY of digestion   dyspepsy.
— In speaking   dysphony.
— In breathing   { dyspnoea or
                             dyspnoon.
— In making urine   { dysury, ischuria, ischury.
— In the administration of
   the laws, from their being ill ordered or conceived. } dysnomy.
— In keeping one's temper, dyspathy.
— An impatience or difficulty in suffering { dysphory.
— In accommodating the mind to contingencies } dysthymia.
— Or fault in sensation   dysesthesia.
— Of motion   dyscinesy.
— Of hearing   dysecoia.
— In the assimulating of the juices of the body } dyscracy.
— Term given to diseases which are cured with difficulty } dystherapeuta.
— Term given to ulcers which are difficult of cure } dysepulotica
— In bringing forth young   { dystochy, or dystochia.
— Of a matter or disease being brought to a crisis } dyscritos.
— An epithet given to such persons whose ulcers are difficult to heal } dyselchia or dyselches.
— Term used for those who vomit with difficulty } dysemeti.

DIFFICULTY of the flowing of the menses { dysmenorrheoth.
— In seeing objects distinctly dysopia.
— In swallowing   dysphagia.
— In the emission of semen { dyspermatismus.

DIGEST. *v.* To digest in the stomach, to concoct; to digest, (hawking term), to indue. (See to ripen.)

DIGESTED. *part.* Not digested, inconcocted, or unconcocted

DIGESTION. *s.* Coction, pepsis; medicine which promotes digestion, oxyporium, pepasticum; digestion which is too soon performed, predigestion; bad digestion, cacochylia, dyspepsia; good and easy one, eupepsy; slow digestion, bradypepsia or bradypepsy.

DIGGER. *s.* Pastinator; digger of graves, sexton.

DIGGING. *part.* Act of digging out of the earth, effusion; a digging up of a corpse after interment, exhumation, digging, fodient.

DIGNITY. *s.* Elevation, lordliness, amplitude, augustness. (See grand.)

DIGRESSION. *s.* Ecbasis. (See deviation.)

DILIGENCE. *s.* Notableness, notability, navity, impigrity, stirringness.

DILIGENT. *a.* Intent, intentive, vigilant, sedulous, assiduous, elaborate, observant, plodding; the diligent examination of a matter, excussion.

DIM. *a.* Caliginous, nebulous, nebulose, crepusculous, frouzy, blear.

DIMINISH. *v.* To abate, to abridge, to minorate, to mutilate. (See to lessen.)

DIMINUTION. *s.* Imminution, impairment; diminution in rhetoric, (i. e. when any thing is decreased beyond the exact truth) is called an hyperbole; thus, from Shakespeare, " he was so gaunt, the case of a flagellet was a mansion for him."

DIMNESS. *s.* Dimness of sight, caligation; dimness of sight attendant on old age, from too great flatness of the eyes, prisbytia or presbytae; one who is afflicted with dimness from too great a convexity of the eyes, myops; the disease is named myopia or catopsia.

DINING-ROOM. *s.* In a monastery where the friars or nuns eat together, refectory or refectuary.

DIOPTRICS. *s.* Anaclatics or anaclaticks.

DIRECT. *v.* To prescribe, to preside; to direct the man at the helm, to cun or cum. (See to order.)

DIRECT. *a.* The direct line from any missile weapon to the mark, is termed pointblank, (perhaps from point-blanc, Fr. i. e. the white mark, or bull's eye in the cen-

ve of the charges.)

DIRECTION. s. Lore, precipe, prescript; direction or advice; admonition, enjoinment. (See advice.)

DIRECTOR. s. Comptroller, mandator; those people that are directors to boats concerned in the herring fishery, who being placed on an eminence, point out how the shoal of herrings tend, are called conders.

DIRT. v. To befoul, to grime, to begrime, to sully, to daub.

DIRTY. a. Dingy, oozy, squalid; to make dirty by striking one leg or ankle against the other, to hox; dirty handkerchief, mackender; dirty woman, drab, drazel, malkin or maulkin, slattern.

DISAGREEMENT. s. Discord, discordance, discrepance, incoherency, incompatibleness, inconcurrency, inconciteness, inconsistency, indonsonancy, unconsonancy, disharmony.

DISAPPOINT. v. To balk, to frustrate, to fub, to lurch. (See to defeat.)

DISAPPROBATION. s. Improbation. (See censure and blame.)

DISAPPROVE. v. To improbate, to vituperate, to disallow. (See to censure, to blame.)

DISCHARGE. v. To acquit, to assoil, to assoilzie, to discard, to dismiss, to evacuate, to emit, to exudate, to manumit; to discharge from office, to exaucterate; to discharge a debt by paying a part, to compound; to discharge into the sea as a river, to disembogue; to discharge ordure, to eject, to mute.

DISCHARGE. s. Or issue in any part of the body, fontanel, seton; discharge of scurf from the head, furfuration; discharge of blood from any part of the body, hæmorrhage, or hæmorrhagia; inability to discharge debts, insolvency; term used in the Court of Exchequer for a full discharge or acquittance, quietus.

DISCIPLE. s. Sectator. (See follower.)

DISCIPLINE. s. Pedagogy.

DISCOVER. v. To perceive, to indicate, to betray, to bewray, to descry, to detect, to investigate; to discover at a distance, to ken.

DISCOVERING. part. The act of discovering to the view, retection; discovering or pointing out, indicant; discovering or detecting, indiciduous.

DISCOVERY. s. Apt to make discoveries, (treacherous) proditorious.

DISCOURAGE. v. To intimidate, to daunt, to dehort, to deter, to discountenance. (See fear and frighten.)

DISCOURSE. v. To converse, to dialogue,

to sermocinate. (See talk.)

DISCOURSE. s. Converse, discant, loquela, conference; discourse concerning the earth, geology; discourse of long continuance with many repetitions, diatribe, or diatriba, longiloquy; introduction to a discourse, exordium or proem; discourse concerning minute and sordid things, leptology; concerning the plague, limology; concerning trees, dendrology; vain and frivolous discourse, mateology; discourse concerning months, menology; little and trifling discourse, micrology; foolish discourse, morology; the heads of a discourse, syllabus; to interrupt one in his discourse, to obacerate; discourse consisting of two parts, dilogy; of three, trilogy; of four, tetralogy, &c. &c.; a moral discourse, tropology; introductory discourses are generally termed prolegomena; an argument containing the sum of a discourse, periocha; discourse or treatise on evil spirits, demonology; discourse full of superfluous words, perisology; the close of a discourse, peroration; a slowness in discourse or conversation, tardiloquy; the first part of a discourse or preface, protalogy; discourse concerning the mind or soul, psychology; concerning manners and customs, ethology; concerning fevers, pyretology; discourse to one's self, soliloquy; discourse by signs made with the fingers, dactylogy; concerning living animals, zoology; concerning the entrails of the human body, splanchnology, enterology; discourse on any subject, also the placing things in order, syntagma; concerning the veins, arteries, &c. angiology; concerning the human body, anatomically or otherwise, anthropology, or anthropometry; concerning thunder, brontology; concerning the quantity or dose of medicine to be taken at one time, dosilogy; concerning eruptive fevers, exanthematology; concerning diseases, nosology; concerning sentiment, gnomology; concerning flowers, anthology; concerning fishes, ichthyology. (See description and treatise.)

DISCUSS. v. To agitate, to eventilate, to ventilate. (See to examine.)

DISEASE. s. Account of the causes of diseases, etiology; the beginning or first attack of a disease is termed arche; the growth or progress, anabasis; the height of a disease, exacerbation, crisis or acme; and the declension of the distemper is called the paracme; a certain stage of the venereal disease, gonorrhea or blennorrhagia; the long continuance of any disease, inveteracy; description of pestilential diseases, loimography; term used for the sign or symptom of the loosening of a great disease, lytesis; the difficulty attending the bringing of some diseases to a crisis, dycrites; tending to disease, morbific; full of diseases; morbulent; state of disease, morbidity, morbidness, or morbosity; the change of one disease into another, or of its symptoms, metabole or methbasis; the seat or source of a disease, misera morbi; the previous symptoms of any disease are termed minnings; diseases which last but one day, or are cured in one day; are termed monohemerous diseases; producing diseases, nosopoetic; treatise concerning diseases, nosology; name given by physicians to such diseases as go beyond the common rule, nothi; description of the causes of diseases, pathology; charms used as preventive of disease, perismma, or perispta, (see charm); term sometimes given to medicines which are said to be good against all diseases, panacea, pancreatra, or panchresta; relapse into a disease, palindrome; the foreknowledge of diseases, prophasis; that part of physic which shews the method of curing diseases, therapeutics; that part of it which prevents or preserves from diseases, prophylactæce or prophylactics; term given to those diseases which are difficult of cure, dystherapeute; a primary or original disease, protopathy; the progress of a disease, diadoche; term used for such diseases as reign in the same place and time, sporadick; said of a disease when it proceeds or is generated by another, deuteropathy; diseases that affect a great many in the same country at once, or about the same time, enitemical, endemick, endemial, or epidemial diseases; those diseases that are common among all the people in the same or many countries, as the plague, small pox, &c. are called epidemical, epidemick; or generally, morbi pandemii; any disease which afflicts the patient for a long time, polychronios; such signs of a disease as are inseparable, designing the real nature and essence of it, (in contradistinction to symptomatic,) pathognomonick.

DISENTANGLE. v. To evolve, to unweave, (See loose, to clear, to free.)

DISGRACE. v. To eclipse, to infame, to shend, to dedecorate, to degrade, to discard, to misledit, to disparage, to displaise, to inodiate.

DISGRACE. s. Blot, obloquy, odium, opprobrium, deprivation, disrepute, stigma.

DISGRACED. a. Shent, stigmatised.

DISGRACEFUL. v. Ignoble, reputeless, scurrilous, ignominious, opprobrious, ludibrious. (See shameful.)

DISH. s. Terms used for any dish of meat of a high flavour acquired by long keeping, hogo or hogoo; any dish so altered by cooking that it can scarcely be known, kick-shaw. (Johnson.)

DISHONEST. a. Illegal, immoral, probrous, sinister. (See unjust.)

DISHONESTY. s. Improbity, turpitude. (See baseness.)

DISHONOUR. s. Disparagment, disrepute. (See disgrace.)

DISJOINT. v. To lux, to luxate.

DISJOINTED. part. Term used in surgery for the reduction of disjointed bones, mochlia; the state of being disjointed as a bone, euptoma.

DISLIKE. v. To abhor, to abominate, to improbate, to loathe or lothe, to disrelish.

DISLIKE. s. Disinclination, disgust, distaste, antipathy, disapprobation, disesteem, disfavour, mislike, nolition.

DISLODGE. v. To dislodge or rouse a beast of prey, to imprime, } (hunt. term.) to unharbour, }

DISMAL. a. Lurid, deplorable, dire, disastrous, doleful, dreary, feral, solitary, funereal, hersed, rueful, stygian, tenebrose, tenebricose, tenebrous.

DISMISS. v. To cashier, to degrade, to discard, to exauctorate, to reject.

DISMISSION. s. Demission. (See dismiss.)

DISOBEDIENCE. s. Incompliance, inconformity, unconformity, untractableness.

DISOBEDIENT. a. Immorigerous, repugnant.

DISORDER. v. To discompose, to distemper, to intumulate, to deray, to derange. (See to disturb.)

DISORDER. s. Broil, garboil, misrule; disorder occasioned by breach of law, anomy; disorder or irregularity of a disease, &c. ataxy.

DISORDERLY. a. Abnormous, inordinate, pell-mell, tumultuary. (See irregular.)

DISOWN. v. To abrogate, to disclaim, to renege, to renounce. (See to deny.)

DISPIRIT. v. To blank, to craven, to damp, to daunt, to dissinuate, to hyp. (See to discourage.)

DISPLAY. v. To blazon, to dispand; boasted display, venditation.

DISPOSITION. s. Posture, adjustment; the natural or preternatural disposition of the body, diathesis or diathesis; a certain disposition or application of a body to any thing near it, habitus; disposition of body accidentally contracted, but which by proper remedies may be removed, in contradistinction to the term habit, which is obtained by birth, &c.

schesis; that disposition of a natural body fitting it best to perform its functions,
idiocracy, or idiosyncrasy, (Quincy.)

DISPROPORTION. *s.* Asymmetry, imparity, inconcinnity. (See proportion.)

DISPROVE. *v.* To impugn, to refel, to refute, to confute.

DISPUTE. *v.* To altercate, to brawl, to
cavil, to expostulate, to fend, to argue, to
bicker. (See to censure.)

DISPUTE. *s* Obtension, tift, vitilitigation;
dispute about words, logomachy; relating to disputes, controversial, eristical,
disputative.

DISPUTED. *part.* That may be disputed,
problematical; that cannot be disputed
incontestable, incontestible, or uncontestable, incontrovertible, or uncontrovertible.

DISPUTATION. *s.* Any disputation or logical argument, dialexis; general term
for disputations, polemics.

DISPUTER. *s.* Disputant, polemic, quodli-
betarean.

DISPUTING. *part.* Captious, contesting,
cynical. (See peevish,)

DISQUIET. *v.* To exagitate. (See to reproach.)

DISSECT. *v.* To anatomise, to androtomise,
to zootomise.

DISSECTION. *s.* A peculiar readiness and
dexterity in dissection, enchiresis, or epichiresis; the dissection of the human body, anatomy, or androtomy.

DISSECTOR. *s.* Dissector of the human body, anatomist, androtomist; of the bodies of beasts, zootomist; of any animal,
anatomist.

DISSEMBLE. *v.* To assimulate, to sog.
(See to counterfeit.)

DISSOLVE. *v.* To colliquate, to fuse, to
liquify, to decompound or decompose, to
deliquate, to discandy, to resolve; aptness
to dissolve, liquescency; having the power to dissolve, resolutive.

DISSOLVED. *part.* The act of preparing
a substance, so as it may be more easily
dissolved, ceration or cerefaction, (old
chym.); that cannot be dissolved, indiscerptible, insoluble, unresolvable; that
may be dissolved, resoluble, liquable, so-
luble; any substance capable of being
melted or dissolved, liquamen.

DISSOLVING. *part.* Any dissolving liquor
is termed a menstruum.

DISSOLUTION. *s.* Resolution; the dissolution or corrosion of the solid parts of an
organised body, diabrosis.

DISTANCE. *s.* At a distance, aloof; an
interjection used as a word of abhorence,
by which any thing or person is wished
to be driven away or at a distance, avaunt,

the adverb aroynt is used in the same
way; distance, estrangement; equal distance, equi-distance; to see at a great
distance, to ken; the art of measuring
distances, longimetry; great distance of
time or place, longinquity; the art of
measuring at a distance, apomecometry;
instruments for measuring distances are
generally pantometers, theodilites, the
cross-staff, or Jacob's staff, which may be
either a fore-staff or back-staff; the art of
measuring distances by the fore or back-
staff, or by common staves, is called baculometry; the art of measuring distances and heights by piece-meal is termed
cultellation; the distance of a star or
planet from the ecliptic, curtation; the
distance of a planet's place from the sun,
reduced to the ecliptic, is termed the cur-
tate distance; the point of a planet's
greatest distance from the sun, aphelion;
the nearest distance, is perihelium or pe-
rihelion; term used for that part of the
heavens in which the sun or a planet is
at the greatest possible distance from the
earth, apogæon, apogeum, or apogee;
when at the nearest distance it is called
perigeum or perigee; the distance of any
place on the earth from the equator, or
of any star or planet from the ecliptic, is
called the latitude; the distance of any
place, east or west, from a first meridian,
and reckoned on the equator, or the distance of the sun or any luminary from the
first of Aries, reckoned on the ecliptic, is
termed longitude.

DISTEMPER. *s* See disease.

DISTILL. *v.* To distill twice with the
same materials, to cohobate.

DISTILLING. *part.* The art of distilling
is sometimes (though not accurately) called deliquium; the vessels generally used
for distilling are, alembics, or limbecs,
matrasses, retorts & cucurbites.

DISTINCT. *a.* Articulate, discrete, discre-
tive; distinct substance, personality,
hypostasis, (Johnson.)

DISTINCTION. *s.* Mark of distinction,
dignotion; a distinction, dividing, or separating, diastole.

DISTINCTNESS. *s.* Inconfusion or uncon-
fusion. (See clear.)

DISTINGUISH. *v.* To individuate, to discern; to distinguish by opposite qualities,
to contradistinguish.

DISTINGUISHING. *part.* Diagnostic, dis-
criminative.

DISTRACTED. *part.* Frenetic, lymphatic,
bestraught, insane, embroiled.

DISTRESS. *s.* Adversity, embarrassment,
exigence, indigence, infelicity, tribulation, indigency. (See need and grief.)

DISTRIBUTION. *s.* A distribution into equal parts, as is done in algebraic equations, by freeing them of fractions, isomeria; distribution of things, or the setting them in proper order, diacomesis; distribution, dole, dispensation. (See gift and leave.)

DISTURB. *v.* To alarm, to distemper, to embroil, to importune, to incommode, to commove, to discompose, to disquiet, to perturbate, to infest, to harrow, to perplex, to excite, to solicit, to turmoil, to agitate.

DISTURBANCE. *s.* Commotion, harrass, emotion, romage, turmoil, utis; disturbance during night, night-rule.

DISTURBED. *part.* Disturbed (or muddy) turbid; not to be disturbed, imperturbable.

DITCH. *s.* Fosse or foss, delve; ditch faced with a dike, so made as to be flush with the contiguous enclosures, and not seen till one is just on it, Aha! the act of encompassing with a ditch or trench, obvallation or circumvallation; to cleanse a ditch of mud, to fey; ditch filled with water round any fortified place, moat; a little ditch, scrobicle.

DIVE. *v.* To penetrate, to profound.

DIVER. *s.* Urinator.

DIVERS. *a.* Omnifarious, multifarious; of divers fashions, plurifarious.

DIVIDE. *v.* To fract, to intersect, to incide, to prescind, to sever; to divide justly, to apportion; to divide anatomically, to dissect, to anatomize, to androtomise, to zootomise; to divide, to distract, to distribute, to fritter, to dispart, to divaricate, to chap, to cleave, to compart, to discind; to divide into bands of 10, 100, &c., to decuriate, to centuriate, &c.

DIVIDED. *a.* Disjunct, partile; divided by furrows, sulcated; divided into two, bifidated, dichotomized, bipartile; into three, trifid, tripartile; into many small parts, multifidous, multipartile; divided or separated (as from the church) schismatic, schismatical; that may or can be divided, fissile, scissible, scissile; that cannot be divided, indiscerptible, insectile, intrenchant; that cannot be divided or torn, illacerable; any sum or quantity to be divided, dividend.

DIVIDING. *part.* A dividing asunder as by a deep cut, diacope; a dividing or separating, diastole; a dividing or separating generally used in surgery, by which parts morbidly or preternaturally concreted, are separated, diæresis; act of dividing, scission. (See, to cut.)

DIVINATION. *s.* Ariolation; divination by a wand or rod, rhabdomancy; by means of names, onomancy; by water in a bason, lecanomancy; by barley-meal, alphitomancy; by examining the entrails of beasts, &c. extispice or extispicium, aruspice or aruspicium; divination by means of mice, myomancy; the act or art of prophesying, foretelling, or divining, vaticination; divination performed by writing on the bark of a tree, stigonomancy; by dunghill cocks, alectryomancy; by meal or cakes, aleuromancy; by calling on the name of God, theomancy; of diseases by urine, uromancy; by arrows, belomancy; by numbers, arithmancy; by hatchets, axinomancy; by herbs and plants, botanomancy; by rings, dactyliomancy; by smoke, capnomancy; by looking in a mirror, catoptromancy; by the wrinkles and marks in the hands, chiromancy; by the casting of dice, cleromancy; by the calling up the ghosts of dead men, &c. necromancy; by a sieve or riddle, coscinomancy; by the belly, gastromancy; by fire, pyromancy; by walking in a circle, gyromancy; by observing certain circumstances attending sacred ceremonies, hieromancy or hieroscopy; by water, hydromancy; by the singing, flight, or feeding of birds, augury, ornithomancy; by a red hot iron, sederomancy; by casting of lots, sortilege; from any detached piece of verse, orthomancy or rhapsodomancy; divination or discovering of springs below ground, bletonism; by shadows, sciomancy.

DIVINE. *v.* To augur, to soothsay; the hazel rod cut in the shape of the letter Y, (by which it was pretended that one could divine where mines of gold and silver, &c. were to be found) is called *virgula divinatoria.*

DIVINE. *a.* Adorable, evangelical, superhuman, cherubic, theocratical; divine worship of the highest kind, latria; of the lowest kind, dulia.

DIVINELY. *ad.* Divinely inspired, entheastical.

DIVINER. *s.* Sort of chair in which the diviners or soothsayers at Rome sat when they took their observations, *sella solida*; for the diviners on the different subjects, see divination.

DIVINITY. The whole system of divinity, pantheology; of or belonging to divinity, theological.

DIVISION. *s.* Partition, precinct, purparty; division made of boards, bulkhead; of a country, canton; a division into halves, dimidiation, dichotomy; into three, &c. trisection, &c.

DIVORCE. *v.* To disespouse, to repudiate.

DIVORCEMENT. *s.* Term for the se-

G

lemnity, used by the ancient Romans, when a cake was parted between the divorced parties, diffareation.

DIZZINESS. *s.* Which produces a dimness of sight, scotomy ; medicines good against dizziness, dinica or dinnica.

DOCTOR. *s.* (See physician); quack doctors are termed, agyrtæ. (See quack.)

DOCTRINE. *s.* Lore, tenet ; any doctrine differing from the general opinion, heterodoxy ; soundness in opinion or doctrine, orthodoxy.

DOG. *s.* Dog-star, belonging to it, canicular ; of or belonging to the dog-kind, canine ; dog of a remarkably fierce nature, of the mastiff kind, hym; barking as a dog, latrant; to couple as dog and bitch, to ligne or line ; madness of a dog communicable by his bite, lyssa ; dog-keeper, feuterer ; the disease of having a voracious appetite like a dog, cynorexy or bulimy ; the madness occasioned by the bite of a dog, hydrophobia or cynanthropy, termed by some, aquæ pavor, from the dread of water consequent on the bite ; name given to one who has been unhappily bitten by a mad dog, cynodectos ; the eye-teeth or dog-teeth of animals, are called, cynodentes, or dentes canini, L. ; the place where fresh dogs are kept in readiness during a chace, relay ; a leader of dogs, veltrarius, L.; to unloose dogs after the chace, to unleash.

DOLEFUL. *a.* Lugubrious, funereal, funebral, funebrous (see dismal) ; doleful and lamentable music is termed, the Lydian mood, or Lydian strains. (Bailey.)

DOLT. *s.* Mooncalf, ninny, ninnyhammer, nizy or nisy, nincompoop, buzzard, cappochia, cuddy, jobbernowl, numskull.

DOMESTIC. *a.* Intestine, servile, menial.

DOMINION. *s.* Mastery, diction, domination, masterdom. (See power.)

DOOR. *s.* Instrument for forcing open doors, betty or bettie ; having double doors, biforous; little door, wicket, portal, postern; door-keeper, janitor, pylorus, ostiary.

DOSE. *s.* Dose or draught of any medicine, haust or haustus ; the taking of a dose of physic, propotisma ; discourse concerning the quantities of doses of medicine that ought to be taken at one time, dosilogy.

DOUBLE. *a.* Bifarious, bifold, binarious, binary, bimarian, bimarical, duplicate, amphibolous ; double-bellyed, digastric, geminous ; double (as twins) didymoi or dædymi ; having a double meaning, ambifarious ; the double meaning of a word, such as the verb, to egelidate, which signifies both to thaw and to freeze ; and the verb, to cleave, which signifies to adhere to, and also to part asunder, dilogy ;

a double meaning, as in several scriptural texts, dittology. (Bailey)

DOUBLING. *part.* Act of, ingemination, gemination, reduplication.

DOUBT. *v.* To bogle or bodge, to demur, to hesitate. (See delay.)

DOUBT. *s.* Dubiosity, dubiousness, hesitancy, jeopardy, query, quandary, suspense.

DOUBTFUL. *a.* Verecund, apocryphal, immanifest, precarious, pendulous, scrupulous, amphibological, amphibolous, ambiguous, enigmatical, equivocal; any doubtful expression, amphibology, or amphilogy ; any doubtful choice, dilemma ; universal doubt, scepticism, akepticism, pyrrhonism.

DOUBTFULNESS. *s.* Incertitude, ambiguity. (See doubt.)

DOVEHOUSE. *s.* Columbary.

DOWN. *s.* (Towards the ground) adown ; down (or fur) flix, flue ; down of plants, gossamer, lanugo ; bearing down, lanigerous; having soft and light down, pappous or pappose.

DOWNWARDS. *ad.* Act of looking downwards, despection, despiciency, prone, proneness or pronity.

DOWNY. *a.* Lanuginous.

DRAIN. *v.* To emulge. (See, to empty.)

DRAIN. *s.* Drain for water or filth, sough, suillage or sulliage.

DRANK. *preterite of the verb to drink.* That may be drank, potable, potulent.

DRAUGHT. *s.* (Or copy) ectype, apographon ; draught or ground-plot, ichnography ; draught (landscape) paisage ; the first draught of a picture, catagraph ; the first draught of a deed, protocol ; draught or sleepy dose, potion, haustus ; draught or drink taken before meat by way of a whet, propoma ; draught or act of drinking, potation.

DRAW. *v.* To delineate, to pourtray, to limn ; to draw to, to adduce ; to draw up as a curtain or sail, to furl ; to draw out the bowels, to gut, to eviscerate ; to draw out, to elongate, to exantlate ; to draw in with the air, to inhale ; to draw by force, to extort ; to draw over, to obduce ; to draw out or delay, to protract ; to draw out liquor from a vessel, as with a syphon, to deprome ; term given to medicines which draw, such as blisters, epispastics.

DRAW-BRIDGE. *s.* Portcullis or portcluse.

DRAWERS. *s.* A chest of drawers is sometimes called a nest of drawers ; chest of drawers with a door folding downwards adapted for writing, is named a scrutoir, scritore, scrutore or escritoir.

DRAWING. *s.* Drawing back, abducent ;

the act of drawing the will into action, elicitation; drawing up, attollent; the act of drawing out or unsheathing, evagination; a drawing out of liquor, &c. from a vessel, depromption.

DRAWN. *part.* Drawn off or estranged, alienate; drawn across cornerways, diagonal; clearly drawn or laid down, graphical or graphic; that may be drawn out, tractile, ductile; drawn away by stealth, abacted.

DREADFUL. *a.* Hideous, dire, effraible, grisly, horrent, horrible, stanchless, formidable, tremendous, terrific; very dreadful, formidolous, horrendous.

DREAM. *s.* Troubled with dreams, insomnious; the feigned god of dreams, Morpheus; an interpreter of dreams, oneirocritic; venereal dreams, oneirogmos.

DREAMING. *part.* A dreaming or slumbering, agripnia.

DREARINESS. *s.* Horror or horrour. (See gloomy.)

DREGS. *s.* Subsidence, fæces or feces, sediment, feculence, lees, mother, recrements, retriments, residuum, grout; dregs or encrusted matter on the inside of vessels, which have contained wine, argol or argal; dregs that are left after the straining of juices, magma; full of dregs, recrementitious, recremental, amurcous.

DRESS. *v.* To accoutre, to array, to caparison, to attire, to deck, to curry, to dight, to bedeck, to bedizen, to bedight, to invest, to betrim, to dizen, to equip, to perk, to pheeze, to preen, to prink, to proin, to prune, to habilitate; to dress, inelegantly, to mobble or moble.

DRESS. *s.* Vesture, apparel, habit, garb, investment, gaudery, guise, habiliment, attire; the dress with which the Spaniards clothe the Protestants at an *auto da fe,* when they censure them to the flames, sambenito, or sanbenito; the dress of any picture is called, drapery.

DRESSED. *part.* Kercheft, or kerchified, pranked or prankt, yclad, fangled; dressed in a gown, toged or togated; a being loosely dressed, discinct or dishabille.

DRESSING-ROOM. *s.* Tiring-room.

DRIED. *a.* Dried smoked fish, fumado; dried salted cod, haberdine.

DRIFT. *s.* Intent, nonce. (See design.)

DRINK. *s.* Beverage, potation; drink made of ale and roasted apples, lambswool; an American drink made from the roots of potatoes, mobby; drink of an exquisite taste, colour, and flavour, the feigned beverage of the gods, nectar; drink or draught before meats, propoma; given or inclined to drink, bibacious; an invitation to drink, bidale. (See liquor.)

For the origin of drinking healths, the following article, *Rowena,* is taken from the 30th edition of Bailey's Dictionary, printed at Glasgow in 1802.

"ROWENA, a beautiful daughter of "Hengistus, general of the Saxons, who "having the isle of Thanet given him by "king Vortigern, for assisting him against "the Picts and Scots, obtained as much "ground as he could encompass with an "ox-hide, to build a castle, which being "finished, he invited king Vortigern to "supper. After supper, Hengist calls for "his daughter Rowena, who, richly at- "tired, and with a graceful mein enters "with a golden bowl full of wine in her "hand, and drinks to king Vortigern in "the Saxon language, which is interpret- "ed, '*Be of health, Lord King;*' to which "he replied, '*Drink Health.*'

"This is the first health found in his- "tory, and claims the antiquity of more "than 1300 years. Vortigern, enamour- "ed with her beauty, married her, and "gave her and her father all Kent."

Name given by the monks to the best drink used in the monastery, karite; drink made of milk and ale, zythogala; Welsh name used for any kind of drink, meathe; rendered courageous by drink, pot-valiant; the proportion of meat, drink, &c. given to a soldier for a day, ration; a cooling drink made from raisins and barley, ptisan; fit for, to drink, poculent, potulent, potable; the old Danish custom of drinking, which was having a pin fixed on the side of a wooden cup, to drink exactly to the pin, or forfeit something, was termed, *ad pinnas bibere.* (Bailey.)

DRINK. *v.* To bouse, to quaff, to carouse; to drink at another's expence without invitation, to sponge or spunge; to drink one's health, to propine; to drink in or up, to imbibe; to drink cool and refreshing liquors, is termed, to drink *in fresco.*

DRINKER. *s.* Drinkers of water, aquæpotes; drinkers of wine, vinipotes.

DRINKING. *part.* A drinking-bout or drinking-match, carouse, potation, compotation; the art or property of sucking up, or drinking in, imbibition, absorption, sorbition; medicines good in excessive eating or drinking, acrapula or acraipula; drinking in, absorbent, bibulous; drinking companion, pot-companion; act of drinking together, potting. (See drunk.)

DRIVE. *v.* To elbow; to drive out by force, to ferret, to deforce, to dishabit; to drive away, to dispel, to disperse, to expel, to eject, to expulse, to exterminate, to extrude, to exulate; to drive with violence to foupe ; to drive or drift as a log of wood on the water, to hull ; to drive on, to goad, to impel ; to drive close together, to impact ; to drive by inches, to inch ; to drive in, to infix ; to drive or squander away, to profligate ; to drive forward, to propel ; to drive back, to repel, to repercuss, to repulse.

DRIVEN. *part.* Driven in, adacted ; driven on, actuated ; driven back, redacted ; driven together, serried.

DRIVER. *s.* Driver of asses, assignego. (See carriage and carter.)

DRIVING. *part.* Driving or forcing back, discutient ; the driving out or rejecting an argument as absurd, apodioxis (rhet.) ; the art or act of driving or guiding any carriage, aurigation ; the act of driving off, propulsion ; act of driving forward, pulsion.

DROLL. *v* To gleek, to sneer, to jibe.

DROLL. *a.* Jocose, jocular, comical, facetious, farcical, gestic, humorous, or humourous, queer.

DROLL. *s.* Banterer, mime. (See buffoon.)

DROLLERY. *s.* Buffoonery, mimiambus, dicacity. (See buffoonery.)

DROP. *v.* To extil, to drop gently into water, to dap ; to drop as small rain, to drizzle.

DROP. *s.* Gout ; little drop, droplet ; having the form of a small drop, guttulous ; the 1-20th part of a drop weight among chymists, karena ; hanging as drops, stirious.

DROOPING. *part.* Flaccid, limber. (See weak.)

DROPPING. *part.* As water, stillicidious, stillatitious.

DROPSICAL. *a.* Hydropical, hydropic.

DROPSY. *s.* A species of dropsy occasioned by the serous part of the blood spreading between the skin and the flesh, anasarca or catasarca, intercus or veternum ; sort of dropsy which makes the belly sound as a drum, tympany ; swelled by dropsy, edematose, or oedematous, or leucophlegmatous ; instrument used in drawing off water in a dropsy, tochar or trocar ; dropsy is either of the head, and is called,

		Hydrocephalum, or Hydrocephalus.
Of the chest,	-	Hydrothorax, or Hydrops Pectoris.
Of the belly,	-	Ascites.
Of the heart,	-	Hydrocardia.
Of the scrotum,	-	Hydrocele, or Hydrops Scroti.
Of the womb,	-	Hydrometra.
Of the ovaria,	-	Hydrometra ovarii.
Of the navel,	-	Hydromphalon, or Hydromphalos.

Of the eye,	-	Hydrophthalmia.
Of the knee,	-	Hydrops genu.
Encysted dropsy,		Hydrocistis.

One who is afflicted with a dropsy, is termed, asciticus or an hydropic ; general name for dropsy, hydrops. (Quincy.)

DROWN. *v.* To deluge, to indrench, to submerge or submerse, to immerse.

DROWNED. *part.* Demersed.

DROWSINESS. *s.* Somnolence, somnolency. (See sleep.)

DROWSY. *a.* Somniculous, gravedinous ; drowsy disease, veternus, lethargy ; drowsy person, mope or mopus.

DRUB. *v.* To curry, to lamm. (See beat.)

DRUDGE. *v.* To mail. (See, to toil, to labour.)

DRUDGE. *s.* Harmless drudge, lexicographer, plodder ; drudge in a kitchen, scullion.

DRUGGIST. *s.* Pharmacopolist, aromatopola ; drugster.

DRUGS. *s.* One who writes on drugs, pharmacologist.

DRUM. *s.* A particular beat of drum for soldiers to repair to their quarters, tatoo ; for a parley, chamade or shamade ; the kettle-drum is called, a tymbal.

DRUNK. *a.* Fap, timulent, maudlin, groggy, mellow ; half-drunk, semibousie ; to make one drunk, is termed, foxing him ; to make or render drunk, to inebriate, to intoxicate ; to make or render one half drunk, to muddle.

DRUNKARD. *s.* Bacchanalian, borachic, toper, vinipote.

DRUNKEN. *a.* Crapulous, crapulent, vinolent.

DRUNKENNESS. *s.* Ebriety, inebriety, intoxication, temulency, vinolency ; habitual drunkenness, ebriosity ; given or addicted to drunkenness, ebrious ; great drunkenness, perpotation, potting ; a stone which is pretended to be an antidote to drunkenness, dyonysias.

DRY. *v.* To exsiccate or exiccate, to parch, to torrify ; to dry with smoke, to blote ; to dry in the sun, to insolate.

DRY. *a.* Exsuccous or exuccous, jejune, arid, torrid ; dry and hot seasons (among physicians) inustion ; it is also used for the actual cautery ; dry and rough, squamose or squamous ; dry (poor) sterile, tabid ; the eating of dry meats, xerophagy.

DRYING. *part.* Act of drying, arefaction, torrefaction ; prepared for drying, cored ; drying up, desiccant, exsiccant or exiccant ; medicines destined for drying up sores, epulotics ; term used for any drying ointment, xeromyrum.

DRYNESS. *s.* Siccity ; causing dryness

siccific.

DUCK. *s.* Bringing forth ducks, anatiferous; young duck, moulter, duckling; the male of the wild duck, mallard; decoy duck is called, a stale bird.

DUCKING. *part.* Mersion. (See plunging.)

DUCKING-STOOL. *s.* Trebuck, tribucket, tumbrel.

DUEL. *s.* Combat, encounter, monomachy; the rules of duelling, duello; a place railed in, for beholding a combat or duel, steccado. (Span.)

DUG. *part.* Dug out of the earth, fossil or fossile.

DULL. *v.* To make dull, to disedge, to dose, to obtund, to hebetate.

DULL. *a.* Inert, obtuse, oscitant, sombre, torpent, tristful, hippish, hypochondriac, humdrum, dronish, inexpert or unexpert, insipid, doltish, barren, blockish, torpescent, torpid, unlustrous, phlegmatic, saturnine, semiopacous, undiaphaneus; dull (or cloudy) nebulous, nebulose, nubilous, nubilose; dull fellow, lobcock, mome, mope, mopus, booby, chuff.

DULNESS. *s.* Surdity, torpor, indocility; the goddess of dulness, Moria; dulness of hearing, dysecoia.

DULY. *ad.* Adequately, aright, equitably. (See fit.)

DUMB. *a.* Elinguid, obmutescent.

DUNCE. *s.* Blockead, buzzard, jobbernowl, dullard, jolthead, log, mome, nisy or nizy, oaf, wiseacre. (See dolt)

DUNG. *s.* Ordure; dung gathered for manure, compost; dung of a hare or sheep, crotels; of the deer kind, fumet; of a wolf, bear, or wild boar, lesses; of a fox, scumber; of any animal, dejecture, excrements, feces; full of dung, merdous.

DUNG. *v.* To dung as birds, to mute.

DUNGHILL. *s.* Misken or mixen, stercorary, tumbrel.

DUNGING. *part.* The dunging of any wild beast, fimashing.

DURABLE. *a.* Infrangible, livelong, perennial.

DURATION. *s.* Perpetuity, perennity, permanence, permansion, (see eternal); term used when any distemper has been of long duration, chronical.

DUSKY. *a.* Crepusculous, caliginous; a picture done in dusky shade, is said to be done in fresco. (See shady.)

DUST. *s.* Coom; to reduce into dust, to pulverize. (See powder.)

DUTIFUL. *a.* Allegiant, morigerous.

DUTY. *s.* Attendance, devoir, impose; the doing more than duty requires, supererogation; imposed as a duty, incumbent.

DWARF. *s.* Dapperling, dandiprat, minim, pigmy, pygmy, congeon, durgeon.

DWELL. *v.* To dwell with, to converse, to domiciliate, to hospitate; to dwell together as gregarious animals do, or mankind (in contempt) to kennel; to dwell in a place for a time, to sojourn.

DWELLING. *s.* Place of dwelling, bye, inhabitance, resiance; dwelling in the same place, cohabitant, commorant; private dwelling-house, libben.

DYING. *part.* Dying state, moribund; dying or vanishing, evanid. (See, to die.)

E

EAGER. *a.* Emphatical, intense, intensive, intent, lickerous, emulous, fervent, urgent, tare, prurient, strenuous, vehement, rapacious, voracious.

EAGERNESS. *s.* Salacity; eagerness acquired from a prosperous beginning, fleshment.

EAGLE. *s.* The stroke of an eagle in endeavouring to seize its prey, swoop; young eagle, eglet; the nest of an eagle, or any bird of prey, aerie or eyry. (See articles bird and hawk.)

EAR. *s.* The external ear, auricle; the second and third cavities of the ear, labyrinth; the almonds of the throat or ear, tonsils, amygdalæ; to buzz in the ear, to exsuffolate; to offend the ear, to regrate, —to grate; instrument used for cleansing the ear, melotes, specillum, or auriscalpium; instrument for injecting medicines into the ear, otenchytes; such medicines as are used in distempers of the ear, otica; an ear-pipe, or instrument for conducting of sound into the ear, outacousticon; a preternatural adhesion of the ears to the head, so as they are scarce distinguishable, coloboma; ear instruments for magnifying sound, microcoustics or otacoustics; pain in the ears or ear-ache, otalgia; to pull by the ears, to sowl.

EARLY. *a.* Too early, precocious, immature, premature, early, *ad.* betimes.

EARNEST. *a.* Vehement, wistful, eager, earnest,

EARNEST. *s.* In earnest; a good earnest

sequest, entreatance, flagitation, or efflagitation ; an earnest question, pusma ; to
obtain by earnest entreaty, to impetrate.

EARNESTNESS, *s.* Patheticalness, urgen-
cy. (See eagerness.)

EARTH. *s.* Any artificial sphere representing the earth, terella ; discourse concerning the earth, geology ; having the
same center as the earth, geocentric ;
what lies under the earth, subterraneous,
or subterranean ; the feigned goddess of
the earth, Tellus ; born or produced of the
earth, terrigenous ; of or belonging to the
earth, geotic ; the act of digging out of
the earth, effossion, exhumation ; made
of the earth, (clay,) fictile, or figulate ;
full of earth, terrulent ; the different
earths, according to the modern chemistry, are divided into calcareous or limy,
barytic or ponderous, magnesian, alumi-
nous, and siliceous or flinty ; an inquiry
into all the different qualities of earths,
geoscopy.

EARTHEN. *a.* Earthen ware of all kinds
is termed crockery.

EARTHLY. *a.* Terrene, terrestrial.

EARTHY. *a.* Terreous, terrestrious.

EASE. *v.* To mitigate, to relax, to alleviate, to asshage, to exonerate, to mollify.

EASE. *s.* Indolence, mund, vacation, glib-
ness, ataraxy, feriation ; state of, analgesia.

EASINESS. *s.* Of speech, facundity ; of
manner, affability.

EASING. *part.* Easing, redressive, assuaging, sedative, mollient, narcotic, peptic,
anodyne, demulcent.

EASY. *a.* Facile, pliant, flexible, lukewarm,
solute, pat, perspicuous, sedate, placid,
proclive ; easy of access, accostable ; easy conversation, confabulation ; easy
death, euthanasy or euthanasia ; easy-
minded, flexanimous.

EAST. *s.* Said of an east and west dial, when
it is turned from the due vertical plane,
disorientated. (See dial) ; blowing from
the east, etesian ; the north-east trade
wind in the Mediterranean, etesias ; relating to the east, exortive, levantine,
ortive ; the east wind, subsolanus, eurus.
(See wind ;) the East is one of the cardinal points of the compass:

EASTER. *s.* Easter - Eve, Parasceve ;
Christians in the second century who
maintained that Easter ought always
to be kept upon the fourteenth of the
moon of the first month, in conformity
to the custom of the Jews, Quartodeci-
mani ; the forty days between Easter and
holy Thursday, tesseracoste.

EASTERN. *a.* Levant, orient, ortive ; the
eastern part of a church, chancel.

EAT. *v.* To champ, to engorge, to manducate, to fare ; to eat away by degrees, to
corrode, to erode ; that may be eat, edible, esculent ; to eat greedily, to gormandize ; to eat at the same table, to intercommon ; to eat at another's cost without invitation, to spunge or sponge.

EATABLE. *a.* Esculent, mandible, edible.

EATER. Men-eaters, cannibals, anthropophagi ; great eaters are termed bori.

EATING. *part.* Edacious, esurine, corroding ; the act of eating through, exesion ;
act of eating or chewing, mastication ;
an eating less than usual, inedia ; eating
or corroding medicines, phagedenics, diæretics, or diæretica, ectillotica, ruptorys ;
eating room in a monastery, where the
friars or nuns eat together, refectory or
refectùary ; medicines good in cases of
over-eating, acrapula or acraipola.

An eating or living on dry meats,
xerophagy.

— Grass	graminivorous,
— Grain	granivorous.
— On flesh	carnivorous.
— Fish	piscivorous.
— Fruit	frugivorous.
— Worms	vermivorous.
— Herbs	herbivorous.
— Vegetables in general	phytivorous.
— Serpents	ophiophagous.
— Mud	lutarious.
— All things	omnivorous.

EBB. *v.* To ebb and flow as the sea, to estuate ; the strait or sea between Bœotia
and the Negropont, which is remarkable
for ebbing and flowing *seven* times in 24
hours, Euripus ; the recess or ebb of the
tide, ampotis.

ECHO. *s.* That science which explains the
nature and properties of echoes, catacous-
tics ; echo, resonance, or reboation.

EDGE. *s.* Brim, confine, cordon, frontier,
brow, labra, margin or margent, purlieu,
verge ; edge or ridge of a hill, ambe ; to
turn the edge (to blunt) to retund, to obtund, to hebetate. (See to blunt) ; the
edges of a roof which hang over the
walls, eaves.

EDGED. *a.* Or fringed, fimbriated. (See
border.)

EDICT. *s.* Placart, programma, rescript.

EDUCATE. *v.* To discipline, to nurture.
(See to teach.)

EDUCATION. *s.* The whole round of education or learning, encyclópedia or cyclopedia, or encyclopedy ; education begun late in life, opsimathy.

EEL. *s.* To fish for them with bait, to sniggle.

EFFECT. *s.* Consequent ; of no effect, ineffective, inefficacious ; causing effect, efficient ; to take effect, (L. T.) to inure ; goods or effects left by the dead, assets.

EFFEMINATE. *a.* Sybaritical, voluptuous. (See luxury.)

EFFORT. *s.* Heft, luctation ; any violent effort, impetus. (See attempt.)

EGG. *s.* The little speck in an impregnated egg which appears to leap before the chicken is hatched, is termed the *punctum saliens* ; the treddle of an egg, cicatricula ; unimpregnated eggs are called addle, or *ova xephyria* ; the white of an egg, glair or glaire, albumor, or albugo ; to sit upon eggs, to incubate ; consisting of or resembling eggs, ovarious ; the seat of the eggs in birds, &c. ovary, or ovarium ; formed like an egg, oviform ; animals that are produced from eggs in opposition to those that are produced alive at once, oviparous ; moulding on the cornice of a pillar representing a string of eggs, ovolo.

EJECTION. *s.* Of superfluities out of the body, apocrisis or apocrisia.

EIGHT. *a.* Eight-sided, octoedrical ; figure of eight sides, octogon. (See figure) ; happening every eight year, octennial ; the being eight years old, octogenary ; having eight petals or flower leaves, octopetalous ; belonging to the number eight, octonary ; one eight part, suboctive, or suboctuple. (See articles, one, two, three, &c.)

ELDERLY. *a.* Matronly ; elderly respectable man, gaffer, (O.) ; elderly woman, matron. (See old.)

ELDEST. *a.* Or first-born child, eigne.

ELEGANCE. *s.* Of manners, urbanity ; the want of elegance, inelegance.

ELEGANT. *a.* Courtlike, accomplished, beauteous, debonair. (See civil)

ELEPHANT. *s.* Behemoth, i. e. in the Hebrew language, " a wonderful creature;" some say it is the same with the Hippopotamus or Morse ; any tube or trunk in form of that of the Elephant's, proboscis.

ELEVEN. *a.* Eleven-sided figure, endecagon. (See figure) ; term used for a word having eleven syllabies, such as honorificabilitudinity, hendecasyllabon, (See articles one, two, three, &c.)

ELL. *s.* Ell measure, alnage ; ell auln, or alne.

ELM. *s.* The seed of the elm tree is called samara.

ELOQUENCE. *s.* Facundity ; full of, facundious ; the goddess of eloquence, suada.

ELOQUENT. *a.* Ciceronian ; not eloquent, ineloquent, infacund.

EMBALMER. *s.* Of dead bodies, pollinc-.

tor.

EMBASSY. *s.* Ambassage, embassage, ambassade, legation ; joint embassy, adlegation.

EMBLEM. *s.* Metaphor, hieroglyphic.

EMBOWEL. *v.* To eviscerate. (See bowel.)

EMBROIDER. *v.* To purfle.

EMERALD. *a.* Like an emerald, smaragdine.

EMINENT. *a.* Doughty, egregious, eximious, illustrious, signal.

EMPTINESS. *s.* Inanition, vacivity, vacaity.

EMPTY. *v.* To disembogue, to emulge, to evacuate, to egurgitate, to disgorge, to exantlate ; to empty water or other liquor with a laddle, to lade.

EMPTY. *a.* Addle, inane, flashy, flatulent, jejune, indigent, flatuous, frustraneous, raccha, lere, vacant, vacive, vacuous, ventose.

EMPTYING. *part.* Act of, vacuation, evacuation, depletion.

ENAMELLING. *part.* The art of enamelling with fire, encaustum, or encaustice.

ENCAMPING. *part.* The art of encamping an army, castramentation.

ENCHANTMENT. *s.* Conjuration, incantation, (See divination ;) dealing by enchantment, incantatory ; dealer in enchantments, saga ; act or power of breaking an inchantment, excantatation, or disenchantment.

ENCLOSE. *v.* To enmesh, to enwheel, to imbound, to immure, to enshrine, to invest, to bay, to impale, to encircle, to inclose.

ENCLOSURE. *s.* Immure, inclosure, purprise, mew, purlieu ; low walls of an enclosure, gison.

ENCOMPASSING. *part.* Circumambient, engirding, begirding, encircling.

ENCOUNTER. *s.* Hosting, tilt, tournament. (See combat.)

ENCOURAGE. *v.* To abet, to excite, to incite, to foment, to animate.

ENCOURAGEMENT. *s.* Incentive.

END. *s.* Expiration, termination, supremity, consummation, defunction, exigent, finis ; end or ruin, subversion ; the end of a plank which had been joined to another, or the club end of the stock of a musket, &c. but-end ; an unhappy end, catastrophe ; end is metaphorically termed, omega, being the last letter of the Greek alphabet ; chief end or purpose, crownet.

ENDEAVOUR. *v.* To essay, to assay, to aim. (See articles, aim, design, and guess.)

ENDEAVOUR. *s.* Luctation ; endeavour

or effort to expand, nitency.

ENDEAVOURING. *part.* Or attempting, molition, innitent.

ENDING. *part.* Desitive.

ENDLESS. *a.* Perpetual, eternal, immarcessible, indesinently, infinite, sempiternal.

ENDORSE. *v.* To indorse.

ENEMY. *s.* Adversary, fien'. antagonist, contendent, opponent; one who kills an enemy, hosticide; that part of fortification which teaches to attack an enemy with the greatest safety, and to most advantage, areotechtonics, or areotectonics.

ENFORCE. *v.* To inforce, to injoin or enjoin.

ENGAGE. *v.* To attract, to buckle, to encounter; to engage in an affair, to embark; to engage or pledge, to oppignorate.

ENGAGEMENT. *s.* Or fight, hosting; rencounter, skirmish. (See combat.); engagement or obligation, obstriction, sponsion.

ENGAGING. *part.* Alluring, appetible; to render or make engaging, to adonize.

ENGRAVE. *v.* To insculp, or to sculp.

ENGRAVER. *s.* On gems, lapidary; on stones in general, sculptor.

ENGRAVING. *part.* An engraving, cutting, or scarifying, encharaxis; an engraving or carving on plate, anaglyphice, or anaglyphic art; the art of engraving, tailledouce, toreutice, or the diagraphic art, or glyphice.

ENJOYMENT. *s.* Fruition, occupancy; one who is in the enjoyment of goods, possessions, &c. for a length of time, usucaptor, usufructuary.

ENLARGE. *v.* To exaggerate, to aggravate, to aggrandize, to bloat, to distend, to expatiate, to amplificate, to dilate, to descant; to enlarge or add a feather to a hawk's wing, to imp.

ENLIGHTEN. *v.* To enlighten with intermission, to flare.

ENQUIRER. *s.* A strict enquirer, indagator.

ENQUIRING. *part.* Inquiring; an enquiring after scissitation. (See inquiry.)

ENQUIRY. *s.* Strict enquiry, percontation.

ENRAGE. *v.* To enchafe, to envenom, to exasperate, to exulcerate, to incense. (See to provoke.)

ENRAGED. *part.* Hostile, indignant, infuriate, insensate, ireful, rabiate, rabid.

ENRICH. *v* (See gift.)

ENSIGN. *s.* A quilifer, gonfalon, or gonfanon.

ENSLAVE. *v.* To bethral, to inthral, to mancipate, to subjugate; to enslave or burden with soldiers, to dragoon.

ENTANGLE. *v.* To complicate, to elf, to emmesh, to illaqueate, to involve, to implicate, to inuncate, to shackle.

ENTANGLED. *part.* Implex, intricate. (See confused.)

ENTER. *v.* To enter upon, to inchoate. (See begin); to enter into, to penetrate, to immigrate.

ENTERING. *part.* Entering or coming in, introvenient. (See to come.)

ENTERTAIN. *v.* To convive, to regale, to junket.

ENTERTAINMENT. *s.* A noble entertainment or treat, regalio; private entertainment, junket, repasture; an entertainment given at funerals, arvil; entertainment of singing, music, &c. ridotto; any farcical entertainment, mommery; double entertainment given to students on holy days, gaudies.

ENTICE. *v.* To intice, to lure, to allure, to inveigle, to decoy. (See to deceive.)

ENTICEMENT. *s.* Inticement, lure, illective.

ENTICER. *s.* Inticer, siren, or syren.

ENTICING. *part.* Illecebrous, attractive, inticing.

ENTIRE. *a.* Intire, integral, plenary, solidungulous, (this last word is generally said of those beasts that have entire hoofs.)

ENTITLE. *v.* To entitle, or qualify, to habituate, to intitle.

ENTRAILS. *s.* Viscera, umbles, garbage, penetrails, offals; entrails of any beast, chawdron; of a deer, humbles, or nombles; divination by examining the entrails of sacrificed beasts, extispice or extispicium; discourse concerning the entrails, splanchnology.

ENTRANCE. *s.* Inchoation, inception, avenue, ingress, ingression; gradual entrance, illapse; entrance or introduction to a subject, proem; entrance or beginning, arche; secret or private entrance, subingression; entrance by force, intrusion, obtrusion. (See beginning.)

ENTREAT. *v.* To crave, to intreat, to implore, to invoke, to obsecrate.

ENTREATING. *part.* Suppliant, precatory, (Johnson.)

ENTREATY. *s.* Lathing, entreatance, obtestation, solicitation; to get by entreaty, to impetrate; an earnest entreaty, flagitation, or efflagitation; not to be moved by entreaty, inexorable.

ENVIOUS. *a.* Invidious, malign; an envious person is called a Zoilus.

ENVY. *v.* To emulate, to grunch, to malign, to pique. (See to grieve.)

EPOCHA. *s.* (See Æra.)

EQUAL. *v.* To attain, to paragon, to parallel.

EQUAL. *a.* Equable, equivalent, geminous, impartial, unpartial, homotonous, peregal ; having no equal, peerless, parlous ; equal order, co-ordinate ; equal weight, equiponderant, counterpoise, equipoise ; equal to, adequate ; equal quantity, ana ; equal with, coequal, compeer ; equal-angled, equiangular ; equal-sided, equilateral ; equal force or power, equipollent ; equal or indifferent, immaterial ; such figures as have equal circumferences or perimeters, are called isoperimetrical figures.

EQUALITY. *s.* Parity, equiformity, parallelism ; equality or indifference what way a matter goes, adiaphorous ; equality of laws, isonomy.

EQUALLED. *part.* Not to be equalled, peerless, parlous, unequalable.

EQUATION. *s.* The method of freeing an equation from fractions, isomeria ; equations that have but one root, in contradistinction to quadratic equations that have two, and cubic that have three, are called lateral equations. (See algebra.)

EQUIP. *v.* To accoutre, to indue. (See to dress.)

EQUIVOCAL. *a.* Ambiguous, jesuitical, homonymous ; words of equivocal signification, homonymia.

ERECT. *a.* Perpendicular, normal.

ERROR. *s.* Aberrance, errour, illusion, defect ; full of errors, erroneous ; liable to errors, fallible, peccable ; exemption from error, inerrability, infallibility ; error in chronology, either in reckoning under or over the period when events happened, metachronism, or parachronism ; when reckoning before the proper time, it is called prochronism or antichronism.

ESCAPE. *v.* To elude, to evade, to evitate, to evite. (See avoid) ; to escape privately, to elope.

ESCAPE. *s.* Avolation, elusion, goby.

ESCAPED. *part.* Not to be escaped, inevitable, or unevitable.

ESSAY. *s.* Bout, proffer, tentative, tractate, assay.

ESSENCE. *s.* The essence or active principle by which medicines operate, hæcceity.

ESTABLISH. *v.* To affear, to authorize, to confirm. (See to confirm.)

ESTATE. *s.* Domain, hereditament.

ESTEEM. *v.* To addeem, to deem. (See to reckon.)

ESTEEM. *s.* Cordiality, vogue, existimation.

ETERNAL. *s.* Uncreate, sempiternal, eviternal. (See duration.)

EVE. *s.* The eve before a holiday, vigil

Easter-eve, parasceve.

EVEN. *v.* To make even, to librate, to equilibrate. (See to balance.)

EVEN. *a.* Adequate, equanimous, dispassionate, flush, horizontal, or horisontal, reciprocal.

EVENING. *s.* Late in the evening, serotine ; close of the evening, cockshut ; relating to the evening, vespertine ; the evening star, Vesper or Hesperus ; evening prayers, vespers ; to wax towards the evening, to advesperate.

EVENNESS. *s.* Equability, levelness, placity, rectity, rectitude ; evenness of mind, equanimity.

EVER. *ad.* Ere, eternal, perpetual ; for ever, indesinently.

EVERLASTING. *a.* Sempiternal, uncreate, eviternal. (See duration.)

EVIDENCE. *s.* Attestation, avouch, eviction, probation ; evidence or clearness of expression, enargia.

EVIDENT. *a.* Apparent, confest, indubious, indubitable, indubitate, luculent. (See clear) ; an evident proposition is called an apodexis or axiom.

EVIL. *s.* The king's evil, struma, scrophula or scrofula ; such medicines as are good against it, antistrumatics ; to wish or call down evil, to imprecate ; to cast out evil spirits, to exorcise ; term used for the joy felt by some at the misfortunes or evils befalling their neighbours, epicharikaky. (See bad.)

EUNUCHS. *s.* Semimares ; term used in Turkey for a white eunuch, ichoglan ; Capon is used (in ridicule,) for an eunuch.

EWE. *s.* Old ewe, croan, gimmer ; the act of generation between a ewe and a ram, blissoming.

EXACT. *a.* Circumstantial, pat, precise, quaint, rigid, terse, graphical ; not exact, inaccurate, or unaccurate.

EXACTNESS. *s.* Accuracy, nicety ; exactness or nicety in behaviour, punctilio ; want of exactness, imprecision.

EXALT. *v.* To extol, to aggrandize, to dignify, to elate, to elevate, to promove.

EXAMINATION. *s.* Recognition, assay, disquisition, examen ; an examination by torture, anacrisis ; a thorough examination, pervestigation, scrutiny, excussion.

EXAMINE. *v.* To ventilate, to peruse, to pose, to pry, to reconnoitre, to speculate, to essay or assay, to eventilate, to perpend, to agitate, to canvass, to collate, to discuss ; to examine by question, to interrogate ; to examine again, to recognize, to revise, to traverse ; to examine nicely, to scan, to trutinate ; to examine into, to animadvert, to explorate or ex

H

plore.

EXAMINED. *part.* One who is examined, examinate.

EXAMINER. *s.* Examinator, indagator.

EXAMPLE. *s* Ensample, exemplar, model, specimen, sample, instance, precedent, or president, paradigm.

EXCELLENCY. *s.* Excellency above another thing, transcendency, precellency.

EXCELLENT. *a.* Peerless, primal, prime, passid, celestial, exquisite, eximious, incomparable ; excellent above all others, pre-eminent ; that may be more excellent (or overcome,) superable.

EXCEPTION. *s,* Exclusion, proviso, salvo, purview.

EXCESS. *s.* Intemperance, saturity, satiety.

EXCESSIVE. *a.* Nimious. (See great.)

EXCHANGE. *v.* To exchange one piece of land for another, to excambion ; to exchange, to barter, to commute, to truck, to permute, to scourse, to scoss, to swop or swap, to chop.

EXCHANGE. *s.* Burse ; counter-exchange, swop or swap, permutation ; exchange of prisoners, cartel ; exchange of place or abode, intermigration ; the mutual exchange of place, translocation ; exchange or change where merchants meet, excambium.

EXCHANGED. *part.* That cannot be exchanged, incommutable. (See to change.)

EXCHEQUER. *s.* Hanaper.

EXCLAMATION. *s.* By way of conclusion to a subject, although not clearly connected with the words foregoing, epiphonema.

EXCOMMUNICATE. *v.* To interdict, to abgregate, to accurse, to anathematise.

EXCOMMUNICATION. *s.* The highest degree of, maranatha.

EXCREMENTS. *s.* Fœces. (See dregs) ; the first excrements of a child from resembling the colour of opium or poppy, are called meconium ; the act or faculty of voiding excrements, diachoresis.

EXCURSION. *s.* Evagation. (See to ramble.)

EXCUSE. *v.* To dispense, to exculpate, to forceve, to palliate, to recuse, to apologize.

EXCUSE. *s.* Advocacy, or advocation, colour or color, evasion, prophasis, salvo, proviso, subterfuge, tergiversation.

EXECUTE. *v.* To syndicate. (See censure.)

EXECUTIONER. *s.* Ketch, nubbing cove, Jack-Ketch.

EXEMPTION. (See freedom.)

EXERCISES. *s.* Relating to strong exercises, gymnastic, gymnic ; a place where exercises and games are performed, palaster ; that part of physic which preserves health by exercises, gymnastics.

EXHAUST. *v.* To exantlate. (See to empty.)

EXHAUSTED. *part.* Not to be exhausted, unemptiable.

EXHORTATION. *s.* Admonition, hortation, hortative, protrepticon.

EXISTENCE. *s.* Not to be brought into existence, ingenerable, ungenerable.

EXISTING. *part.* At the same time, co-existing, contemporaneous, or cotemporaneous ; the state of not existing together, inco-existence ; things capable of existing together are termed compossible ; and when the contrary, incompossible.

EXPEL. *v.* To expulse. (See to drive ; to expel by ecclesiastical authority, to anathematise. (See to excommunicate.)

EXPELLING. *part.* An expelling or driving out an argument as absurd, apodioxis.

EXPENSE. *s.* Free of all expense, impensible, gratis L.

EXPENSIVE. *a.* Prodigal, sumptuous, dapatical, opiparous.

EXPERIMENT. *s.* Essay or assay ; any experiment performed in such a satisfactory manner as to point out and determine the most rational way of proceeding in search of the matter sought, is called the *experimentum crucis,*

EXPERT *a.* Dædalian or dædalin. (See cunning.)

EXPERTNESS. *s.* The want of, inaptitude or unaptness. (See dull.)

EXPLAIN. *v.* To decipher, to solve, to resolve, to construe, to define, to delucidate, to elucidate, to expound, to illustrate ; tending to explain, explicative ; to explain by notes, to postil ; to explain previously, to premise.

EXPLAINED. *part.* What cannot be explained, inenodable, inexplicable.

EXPLANATION. *s.* Exposition, interpretation, definition, dilucidation, ecclaircissement, elucidation ; explanation or key, clavis ; by means of notes, glossing ; of a difficulty, enodation or enucleation ; a more particular explanation of what was mentioned before, epexegesis.

EXPLANATORY. *a.* Exegetical, expository, illustrative (See to explain.)

EXPLOIT. *s.* Achievement, chivalry. (See attempt.)

EXPRESS. *v.* To enunciate, to articulate. (See to declare.)

EXPRESS. *a.* Explicit, categorical, peremptory.

EXPRESSED. *part.* That may be expressed or spoken, effable.

EXPRESSING. *part.* A concise mode of expressing ones self, brachylogy. (See word.)

EXPRESSION. *s.* Clearness of expression, enargia.

EXTEND. *v.* To dilate, to distend, to imp, to propagate; to extend or jut out, to protrude, to prolapse; to extend as a line of coast, to trend; to extend at the same time or place, to co-extend.

EXTENDED. *part.* Jacent; excended between, interjacent.

EXTENT. *s.* Marjoration, amplitude, expansion, latitude.

EXTRACTING. *part.* The art of extracting any hurtful substances out of the body, exæresis, exærisis, or exhæresis.

EXTRAORDINARY. *a.* The being very eminent or extraordinary in good or bad, superlation. (See great)

EXTRAVAGANT. *a.* Exorbitant, excessive, nepotal, nepotine, prodigal, impendious, voluptuous; extravagant joy, gairishness; extravagance in living, inabstinence.

EYE. *v.* (Or view), to pink or pinker.

EYE. *s.* A certain oblique and arch cast of the eye, leer; a glance or wink of the eye, oeilliad, oeliad, or oeilaid; what attracts the eye in allusion to the north polar star, cynosure; known or depending on the eye, ocular; relating to the eye, opthalmia; having eyes, oculate; one who cures distempered eyes, oculist;

having one eye, monocular, monocoloms; having two, &c. binocular, &c. —— many multocular; having little eyes, also a disease in them, microphthalmy; a person who has but one eye, monops or arimaspe; one who sees only with one eye, monoptic; the humours of the eye are termed, 1st,

The vitreous or hyaloides.
aqueous or hydatoides.
crystalline or crystalloides, or glacialis.

which is by some termed the lens; blearedness of the eyes, lippitude; a disease of the eyes, causing the patient to sleep with them open, lagopthalmy, or blepharoptosis; a bloody and inflamed appearance within the eyelids, stiony, stion, or crithe; wateryness of the eyes, delacrymation; an unnatural protuberance of the eyes, as if they were ready to start out of their sockets, ecpiesmos; extravasation of blood on the eye, commonly called bloodshot, hæmatops or hyposphagma; a particular affection of the eye, which makes objects appear to shake as if one was on horseback, hippus; a preternatural growing together of the eyelids, coloboma; a certain liquid for strengthening the eyes, lynceus, or collyrium; any dry application for sore eyes, xerocollyrium; having one eye, mopeeyed. See further in treatises on the eye.

F

FABLE. *s.* System or explanation of fables, mythology; the moral of a fable, epimythium.

FABULOUS. *a.* Legendary, rabbinical.

FACE. *v.* To confront. (See compare and oppose.)

FACE. *s.* Phiz, jole or jowl, muns; having an ugly face, hatchet-faced; one who judges by the face, physiognomist or physiognomer; side view of the face, profile; lying with the face upwards, supine; with the face downwards, prone; to lye with the face upwards, to resupinate; mask for the face, visard or vizard; one having sharp nostrils, hollow eyes, low temples, the forehead dry and wrinkled, and withall a pale and livid complexion, is said to have a *facies hippocratica*, or Hippocrates's face; the face of the sun or planet, disk.

FADE. *v.* To vade. (See decay.)

FADING. *part.* Deciduous, marescent, transitory. (See decaying.)

FAIL. *v.* To recoil, to flinch, to shrink.

FAILURE. *s.* Defection, deficiency, delinquency; incapable of failure, infallible.

FAGOT. *s.* Bevin, billet, (See firewood and fuel.)

FAINT. *s.* Debile, evanid, lank; faint colour, pallid; faint sketch, adumbration; ready to faint, qualmish.

FAINTHEARTED. *a.* Dastardly; fainthearted fellow, dastard, meacock; faintheartedness, micropsychy. (See cowardice.)

FAINTING. *part.* Deliquium, lypothymia, lipopsychy, syncope, apsychy; medicines which suddenly raise the spirits in faintings, psychagogica.

FAIR. *a.* Frank, ingenuous, candid, evenhanded, equitable, imprejudicate, logical, impartial, or unpartial; seemingly fair and honest, plausible; fair (not cloudy,) enubilous, or innubilous. (See clear.)

FAIRS. *s.* Relating to them, emporetic or emporetical.

FAIRY. *s.* Hobgoblin, ouphe, pigwidgeon. (See spirit.)

FAITH. *s.* Fey, creaunce, confidence; one destitute of faith, nullifidian; one who holds that faith alone is sufficient for salvation, solifidian; the greatest height of faith, plerophory.

FAITHFUL. *a.* Retentive, liege, allegiant.

FAITHLESS. *a.* Disloyal, infidel, punic; faithless person, cataian. (See treacherous.)

FALL. *v.* To fall upon, to alight; to fall together, to collapse; to fall or strike against, to impinge; to fall out, to betide; to fall by succession, to devolve; to fall slowly, to dribble, to drizzle; to fall away, to dwindle; to let fall in a careless manner, to lob; to fall down in adoration, to prostrate; to fall back, to recede, to relapse; to fall under, to succumb or succomb; that falls out of its place, prociduous; ready to fall off, succiduous; not liable to fall off, indeciduous.

FALL. *s.* Lapse, decadency; sudden fall, illapse; sort of machine like an umbrella, contrived in breaking a fall in descending from great heights, parachute; done after the fall of man, sublapsary.

FALLING. *part.* Cadent; a falling down, casure, delapsion; a falling off or away, decidence; falling as leaves in autumn, deciduous; the falling down of any thing from its place, procidence; the falling sickness, epilepsy; it is also called *morbus, herculeus,* or *caducus,* from the violence of its attacks.

FALSE. *a.* Adulterated, unplausible, or implausible, adscititious, or ascititious, ambidextrous, deceptious, calumnious, defamatory, erroneous, heretical, hypocritical, juggling, parricidal, parracidious, perfidious, pseudo, punic, recreant, romantic, spurious, insidious, supposititious; a false accuser, or carrier of little faults, sycophant; false argument, sophism, elench, pseudomenos; false shew, feint; false optics or deception, heteroptics; false shew, illusion; one who inserts false passages from an author, interpolator; false glory, pseudodoxy.

false messenger   pseudangelist.
— apostle   pseudoapostle.
— brother   pseudoadelphus.
— doctor or quack   pseudomedicus.
— named   pseudonymous.
— writing   pseudography.
name of a fountain in Sicily wherein all

written false oaths were said to sink, Acadina.

FALSEHOOD. *s.* Flam, falsity, mendacity, pseudology, erroneousness, fiction, leasing; the forging of falsehoods, cretism, or creticism; those who boast of slander and falsehood, abydocomists.

FALTERING. *a.* Act of faltering or nodding, titubation.

FAME. *s.* Celebrity, conspicuousness, eudoxy.

FAMILY. *s.* Blood, clan, stirp, descent, lineage, meiny, descendants; account of the different branches of a family, genealogy, pedigree. (See birth.)

FAMOUS. *a.* Illustrious, signal, celebrious, eximious; to render or make famous, to celebrate, to carol; made famous, famosed.

FAN. *v.* To ventilate. (See to blow.)

FANCIFUL. *a.* Capricious, imaginative, chimerical, fantastic.

FANCY. *s.* Fantasy, freak, humor or humour, ingenium, caprice, chimera, crotchet; heat or warmth of fancy, enthusiasm.

FANNING. *p.* The act of fanning, flabellation.

FARCE. *s.* Farce or interlude, exodium.

FAREWELL. *s.* Adieu, F.; farewell or sending away, propempticon; a bidding farewell, valediction; farewell speech, apobapterion.

FARM. *v.* To farm out, to demise, (Bailey.)

FARM. *s.* Barton, grange; consisting of, farms, predial.

FARFETCHED. *a.* Catachrestical. (See abuse.)

FARRIER. *s.* Leech, veterinarius; farrier's instrument for bleeding cattle, phlen.e.

FASHION. *s.* Vogue, mode; according to the fashion, a la mode; having many fashions, multimodus.

FAST. *a.* Fleet, glib, pellmell. (See quick.)

FASTEN. *v.* To affix, to instop, to belay, to brace, to clinch, to confix, to coss, to cramp, to infix; to fasten or catch with a hook, to inuncate.

FAT. *a.* Pinguid, adipal, adipose, carnose, corpulent, obese, fatkidneyed, unctuous, pursy, queasy; fat boy, fub; fat wench, blowze; fat man in ridicule, porpus or porpoise, (Entick); fat short woman, pundle, squab, dowdy, ronion; bread socked in fat, brewis; the fat of the caul, &c. sevum; the fat of swine, lard, saim; the fat of the deer kind, snet; to grow fat, to batten, to impinguate,

FATAL. *a.* Climacteric, exitial, gory, lethiferous, malign, mortiferous. (See deadly.)

FATE. *s.* Doom, ure. (See destiny.)

FATHER. *s.* Abba, gaffer; the murder or murderer of a father, parracide; one who kills his father or mother, parenticide; to take or occupy after one's father, to patrissate; the state of privation of a father or mother, orbate.

FATIGUE. *v.* To fatigate, to defatigate, to bag, to harrass, to surbate.

FATIGUE. *s.* Lassitude; a medicine which relieves fatigue, myracopinm, or acopon. (See weariness.)

FATIGUED. *part.* Fatigued; not to be fatigued, indefatigable, or infatigable..

FATTEN. *v.* To batten, to carnify, to impinguate; place where hogs are kept to fatten, franks. (See fat.)

FAULT. *s.* Delinquency, deviation, erroneousness, frustration, malefaction; petty fault, peccadillo; heinous fault, piacle; to find fault with, to carp; a finding fault with or chiding, correption, vituperation; fault-finder, momus.

FAULTLESS. *a.* Inculpable, unculpable. (See blameless.)

FAULTY. *a.* Defective, vitiable, faultily.

FAVOUR. *s.* Favor, behalf, benefaction; tending to gain favour, insinuant; act of catching at favour, captation; to get into favour, to ingratiate; to steal into favour, to insinuate.

FAVOURABLE. *a.* Propitious, favonian. (See kind, mild, tender.)

FAVOURER. *s.* Adherent, fautor.

FAVOURITE. *s.* Minion.

FAWNER. *s.* Coaxer, parasite, pickthank. (See flatterer.)

FAWNING. *part.* Adulatory, servile; fawning behaviour, pollaver.

FEAR. *v.* To apprehend, to boggle or bodge, to intimidate.

FEAR. *s.* Tremor, affright, consternation, dismay; fear without cause, panic; causing fear, terrific (See terror); a kind of melancholy wherein the patient is assailed with groundless fear, panophobia; state of those who worship out of fear, disidæmony or disidemony; fear or aversion to cold things, psychrophoby; fear of, or aversion to water, hydrophobia, *aquæ pavor.*

FEARFUL. *a.* Diffident, timid, timorous, tremulous, trepid, formidolous.

FEARFULNESS. *ad.* Meticulosity.

FEARLESS. *a.* Dauntless, unaffrighted, intrepid, dreadless.

FEAST. *v.* To convene, to regale; to feast privately, to junket.

FEAST. *s.* Repasture, festival, jubilee, banquet, epulation, carousal; relating to a feast, epulary; a feast held in popish countries from twelfth-day till Lent, Carnaval or Carnival; feasts of love and cha-

rity held among the primitive Christians, agapæ; feast or supper given at funerals, arvil; the person whom one (who has been invited to a feast) carries along with him, umbra, L.; the feasts and sacrifices of the Greeks, called the feasts of sober men, nephalia.

FEATHER. *s.* Fulness of feathers, plumosity; covered with feathers, plumous, plumigerous, aligerous: such fowls as are furnished with feathers on the feet, as owls, &c. plumipedes; deprived of feathers (bare) deplumated, callow, implume, unfledged; to drop or shed feathers, to moult, to mue or mew.

FEEBLE. *a.* Debile, imbecile, impotent. (See weak.)

FEE. Fees of a prison, carcelage; fee exacted by a person's fellow prisoners on his commitment, garnish; fee of office, perquisite; fee given to a barrister to prevent him from pleading for the adverse party, is called a retainer, or retaining fee; settlement in fee, infeoffment; grant in fee, infeodation. to unite to the fee, to infeoff. } L. T.

FEED. *v.* To fare, to foster, to cherish; to feed or live on spoil, to forage; to feed full, to batten; to feed on twigs or sprouts as cattle, to browse.

FEEDING. *part.*

Feeding on flesh	-	Carnivorous.
—— fish	-	Piscivorous.
—— grass	-	Graminivorous.
—— fruit,	-	Frugivorous.
—— grain,	-	Granivorous.
—— worms,		Vermivorous.
—— serpents,		Ophiophagous.
—— herbs,		Herbivorous.
—— vegetables in general.	}	Phytivorous.
—— mud,	-	Lutarious.
—— all things,		Omnivorous.

The manner or state of feeding, or being fed, nutrication.

FEEL. *v.* To feel in the dark, to poke, to grope; to feel compassion, to relent; to feel or try the depth of a wound, to probe.

FEELER. *s.* The feelers of insects, &c. are called, antennæ.

FEELING. *part.* Patheticalness, pathos, sympathy; the act of feeling, aisthesis.

FEET. *s.* Having two feet, bipedal.
—— three, tripedal.
—— four, &c. quadripedal, &c.
—— many, multipedal.

Any thing supported by three feet, trivet or tripod; to tie the feet together, to hopple; the point opposite the Zenith, immediately under our feet, Nadir; a stamping or noise made by the feet, supplosion; bath for the feet, pediluvium; gout in the feet, podagra; the extent of three feet, &c. in any direction, tripedal, &c.; placed under the feet, suppedaneous; fowls having feathered feet, plumipedes; having feet as ducks or water fowl, palmipede; animal with many feet, polypus; those animals that have entire feet, are termed, solipedous, or solidunguious animals.

FEIGN. v. To assimulate, to personate, to simulate, to dissemble. (See pretend.)

FEIGNED. part. Commentitious, hypothetical. (See hypocritical.)

FELLOWSHIP. s. Sodality, communion; fellowship at table, commensality.

FELT. part. That may be felt, palpable, tactile.

FEMALE. s. Of a buck, rabbit, or hare, doe; such animals or plants as have both male and female parts together, are termed, hermaphroditical or androgynous; half female, will-gill, (used in derision.)

FEN. s. Bog, marish, marsh, morass; a fen which shakes below one's feet, quagmire.

FENCE. v. To empale; to fence off, to parry.

FENCE. s. Sepiment, staccado, diathyrum, palisade or palisado; low fence, gison; low fence or ditch, sunk so as not to be perceived till you are just on it, which, from the surprise it causes, is termed, aha! or, haha!

FENCING. part. A thrust or push in fencing, longe or allonge; piece of stuffed leather used in fencing, plastron or plastran.

FENNY. a. Marish, quaggy, uliginous, moorish, wearish.

FERMENT. v. To mantle.

FERMENTATION. s. Zymosis; instrument for measuring different degrees of fermentation, zymosimeter.

FERRY. s. Traject. (See frith.)

FESTIVAL. s. (See feast.)

FETCH. s Stratagem, artifice, tergiversation. (See trick.)

FETTER. v. To garnish, to gyve, to immanacle, to manacle, to shackle. (See chain.)

FEVER. s. Medicines good against fever, anti-febriles. febrifuge, pyretics, alexipharmics, alexiterics; relating to fevers, febrile; that species of burning and raging fevers peculiar to sailors, wherein they imagine the sea to be green fields, and will throw themselves into it, if not restrained, calenture, (Quincy); slow and continued fever, generally ending in consumption, hectic; discourse concerning fevers, pyretology; concerning eruptive fevers, exanthematology; fever that generally seizes women in childbed the 4th day after delivery, lacteal fever, or milk

fever; continual fever wherein the outward parts are cool, and the inward parts burn, lipyria or lypiria, causon, or causus; spots which appear in putrid fevers, petechiæ; fever that declines daily, is termed, a paracmastical fever; spotted and flatulent fever, pemphigodes or pemphingodes; terrible fever, wherein the patient is troubled with dreadful imaginations, phricodes; a putrid fever which grows continually stronger, epacmastic fever; the interval between the paroxisms of a fever, epiparoxism; fever in which the patient is almost melted with moisture, elodes; fever incident to women in childbed, puerperous or puerperal, fever; restlessness usually accompanying the cold fits of an intermittent fever, pandiculation; a standing up of the hair from fright, as is the case in quartan fevers, horripilation. (For a greater variety of fevers, see treatises on the subject.)

FEWNESS. s. Paucity. (See small and smallness.)

FIBRE. s. An exceeding small fibre, fibrilla, filament; having small fibres, funicular.

FICKLE. a. Variant, versatile, inconstant, unconstant.

FICKLENESS. s. Instability, or unstability, lubricity, mutability. (See change.)

FIDDLE. s. Fiddle of three strings, rebec or rebeck.

FIDDLER. s. Crowder.

FIELD. s. To the field, afield; relating to the fields or grounds, agrarian.

FIERCE. a. Fell, furious, impetuous, ardent, breme, ferocious, ravenous, rapacious, predacious; fierce look, truculent.

FIERCENESS. s. Ferocity, ferity. (See cruel.)

FIFTH. a. One fifth part of any thing, subquintuple.

FIFTY. a. Captain or ruler of fifty men, pentecontarch; man of fifty years of age, cinquater or cincater.

FIGS. s. Resembling them, caricous.

FIGHT. s. Fray, rencounter, skirmish; fight with swords, digladiation; single combat or fight with sword, pistol, &c. duel; that part of fortification which teaches how to fight an enemy to the best advantage, areotectonics; rules prescribed for fighting duels, duello; close fight, half-sword; mock-fight, joust or just; sea fight, or the representation of it, naumachy; given or inclined to fight, pugnaceous; a fight on horseback, hippomachy, (see battle and combat); the feigned fight of the giants against the gods, gigantomachy or theomachy; fighting of cocks, or cock-fighting, alectryo-

FIG [67] FIG

machy; the feigned fight or battle between the pigmies and the cranes, pygmæageranomachy; fight or battle with a shadow, sciomachy.

FIGHTER. *s.* Pugil, pugilist; fighter or sword-player, scrimer, gladiator.

FIGURATIVE. *a.* Allegorical, metaphorical, tralatitious.

FIGURE. *s.* The art of foretelling by figures drawn on the earth, geomancy; such geometrical figures as have equal circumferences or perimeters, are called, isoperimetrical figures; any rectangular figure, orthogon; the circumference of any figure, perimeter or periphery, this last word is mostly applied to curvilinear bodies or planes; any figure of three angles, trigon or triquetra; figure having an obtuse angle, amblygon; the art of measuring figures standing on their bases, epipedometry; the base of a geometrical figure, bedra; the art of making or casting figures in moulds, also the art of making the moulds themselves, is called the proplastic art; proplasm or proplasma is sometimes used for a mould, wherein any metal or soft matter which will afterwards grow hard, is cast; a type or figure drawn of the world, typocosmy; any figure raised from a block of wood or stone, *relievo*, and is distinguished into *alto relievo*, when much raised from the surface, and *basso relievo*, when little raised; when one half of the figure rises from the plane, i. e. when the body of a figure seems cut in two, and one half is clapped on a ground, it is called *demy relievo*; when in a basso relievo there are some parts that stand clear out detached from the rest, the work is called a *demi-bosse*; if a work is insulate on all sides, it is called a figure *in relievo*, or a round imbossment, such are *statues*, *acroteria* or *acroteres*, &c.; any thing, (generally precious stones) that has figures of heads engraved on them, so as to rise above the ground, *intaglio*; the art of making hollow or concave figures in metals, &c., diaglyphice; geometrical figures are either rectilinear or curvilinear, plane or solid.

Planes Rectilinear are,

Triangles, or trilateral figures, and are either, right-angled, acute, obtuse, or oblique, scalenous, isosceles or equilateral.

Quadrilateral; such are squares, oblongs, rhombi, rhomboids, and parallelograms; all other four-sided figures are called; trapezia or trapezioids.

Planes Curvilinear are,

Circles, and their segments, and ellipses, vulgarly called ovals.

Solids Rectilinear are,

Pyramids, or figures bounded by triangles, the base being either a square, triangle or polygon.

Prisms or *Prismoids;* are solids bounded by several parallelograms; the bases may be either polygons, parallelograms or triangles, equal and parallel; hence prisms are generated by the continual addition of these figures as their bases.

Parallelopipeds, are solids contained under six parallelograms, the opposite sides of which are equal and parallel; parallelopipeds are also prisms, the ends of which are equal parallelograms; parallelopipeds are generated by the motion or continual addition of a square, oblong, rhombus or rhomboid. Euclid, B. XI. Prop. 29, 30, 31.

Parallelopleuron is a solid generated from a trapezium, the two opposite sides of which are parallel, but the remaining two are not parallel.

The five regular or Platonic bodies are, viz.

I. The *Tetrahedron* or *Tetraedron,* contained by four equal and equilateral triangles.

II. The *Cube* or *Hexagon* is a solid contained by six equal squares.

III. The *Octahedron* is contained by eight equal and equilateral triangles.

IV. The *Dodecahedron* is contained by twelve equal pentagons which are equilateral and equiangular.

V. The *Icosahedron* is a solid figure contained by twenty equal and equilateral triangles.

Solids Curvilinear are,

Cylinders, which are solid figures described by the revolution of a right-angled parallelogram, about one of its sides, which remains fixed; or they may be generated by the continual addition of circles, each equal to the base of the cylinder.

Note, whether the bases be ellipses or circles, the figure is still a cylinder. (Greg. Prac. Geom. p. 112.)

Cones are solid figures described by the revolution of a right-angled triangle about one of the sides containing the right angle, which side remains fixed. If the fixed side be equal to the other side containing the right angle, the cone is called right-angled; if it be less than the other side, an obtuse angled; and if greater, an acute angled cone.

Spheres, are solids described by the revolution of a half-circle about its diameter, which remains fixed.

Spheroids are solids generated by the entire rotation of a semi-ellipsis about its axis.

Prolate Spheroid is a solid produced by the revolution of a semi-ellipsis about its longest diameter.

Oblate Spheroid is that solid figure produced by the revolution of a semi-ellipsis about its shortest diameter.

Besides the above, there may be plane figures of any number of sides, viz.

The Tetragon of four equal sides and angles.

— Pentagon of five —
— Hexagon of six —
— Heptagon of seven —
— Octagon of eight —
— Enneagon of nine —
— Decagon of ten ——
— { Undecagon } of eleven ——
  { Hendecagon }
  { Endecagon }
— Dodecagon of twelve ——
        &c. &c. &c.

All figures having more than four or five sides, are called polygons or multilateral figures; that branch of perspective by which any figure (viz. the human face) is so delineated in a square, &c. as to produce a deformed representation, but if viewed at a distance and point, it shall appear formous, and shew a true copy of the original; this art is called, anamorphosis or the anamorphous art.

The square, &c. containing the deformed representation, is called, the *craticular ectype;* the space containing the true representation, is called, the *craticular prototype.*

FILING. *part.* The act of, limation; the filings of any metal, limature.

FILL. *v.* To replenish, to satiate, to saturate; to fill up, to eke, to englut, to impregnate, or impregn.

FILLED. *part.* Filled, or charged with, fraught; completely filled, replete.

FILLET. *s.* (See bandage.)

FILLING. *part. p.* Filling up, complemental; act of filling up, impletion; the act of filling up with clay or mortar, lorication; of filling up chinks, obstipation.

FILM. *s.* Flake, pellicle.

FILTH. *s.* Mulloc, ordure, recrement. (See dregs.)

FILTHINESS. *s.* Coenosity, fedity, squalor; filthiness (or baseness) turpitude.

FILTHY. *a.* Excremental, sinewed, carnal, fuliginous, sordid, squalid, verminous; the act of making filthy, defœdation.

FIN. *s.* Such fishes as have soft fins with bones, but not pointed, are termed malacopterygious fishes: those having hard and bony fins, are called, osteopterygious.

FINAL. *a.* Decisory, decretory, peremptory, ultimate; final sentence or award, laudum; final part or conclusion, perclose; final purpose, goal, crownet; final answer, ultimatum.

FIND. *v.* To find out, to deprehend, to decry, to detect, to reconnoitre; to evestigate; to find or supply, to suppeditate.

FINE. *v.* To sconce, to amerce, to mulct; to render fine, to subtiliate.

FINE. *a.* Elegant, palacious, epic, garish or gairish, gim, gimmy, gorgeous, kerchiefed, or kerchieft, nitid, limpid, luculent, meracious, modish, topping, transpicuous, gent, quaint, subtile or subtle, tenuous, tenuious; fine (delicate) tid; fine or soft, mellow; fine (bright) orient; fine (of good flavour, said of wine) racy.

FINE. *s.* Person to whom a fine is acknowledged, cognisee; the person who passes a fine, cognisor; that cannot be expiated by fine, inemendable; acquired by fine, multatitious; fine in use among the Saxons, which was paid *nine times* over, as a compensation for great crimes, triniumgeld. (Bailey.)

FINERY. *s.* Gaudery, pageantry. (See show.)

FINGERS. *s.* Discourse by signs made by the fingers, dactylogy; of or belonging to the fingers, digital; contempt shewn by the snapping and pointing of the fingers, fico (Ital.); art of numbering on the fingers, dactylonomy; as much of any powder, &c. as may be taken up with three fingers, dragmis.

FINISH. *v.* To absolve, to accomplish, to achieve, to consummate. (See end.)

FIRE. *s.* To set on fire, to accend, to ignite or ignify; divination by fire, pyromancy; incantatory lines written on a building, said to prevent it from fire, arse-verse; not consumable by fire, asbestine, incremable; ready to take fire, combustible; a general fire or conflagration, empyrosis; a trial by fire and water, ordeal, or ordael; of which there were by the ordalian law, abrogated by king John, four kinds, viz.

Ordeal by Combat, when the person accused of murder was obliged to fight the next relation, &c. of the person deceased.

Ordeal by Fire, was when the party accused, undertook to prove his or her innocence by walking blindfold and barefoot between nine red-hot plough-shares, laid at unequal distances one from another, or by holding a red-hot iron in his or her hand.

Ordeal by Cold Water, was the being bound and thrown into a river or pond, like the trial of witches.

Ordeal by Hot Water, was by putting the hands and feet into scalding water.

The state of being on fire, incension; power of resisting fire, incombustibility; flash of fire, leam; god of fire, Vulcan, Mulciber; the art of making fire-works, pyrotechnics or pyrotechny; fire works in general, are termed, pyroboli; an animal fabled to have the power of living in fire, salamander; one whose department it is to look after the fire in a brew-house, &c. stoaker; containing fire, igneous; producing fire, igniferous; flowing with fire, ignifluous; ingendered in the fire, iguigenous; having power over fire, ignipotent; vomiting fire, as a volcano, ignivomous; fire - raiser, incendiary; firestone, pyrites.

FIREWOOD. *s.* Faggots, bevins, bavins, billets, &c. (See fuel.)

FIRM. *a.* Stable, compact, congregate, consistent, findy, immutable, indissoluble, inflexible, infrangible, resolute, sclerotic, solidungulous, spiss, stanch, undaunted, unrebated; firm, (lasting) perdurable; firm, or (obstinate) pertinacious.

FIRMNESS. *s.* Durity, insisture, confidence; firmness (strength) brawniness; want of firmness of mind, irresolution. (See strength.)

FIRST. *a.* Initial, prior, antecedent, previous, primal, prime, pristine, primordial or primordiate; the first inhabitants of a country, aborigenes or autochtones; the first-born child, eigne; the first of a dissertation, genesis; first fruits, premices, annates; relating to first-fruits, primitial; first or chief, premier; such as was at first, primeval; first of the kind, primigenial, primigeneous; first-born, primogenial; first copy of any writing, protocol; first martyr, protomartyr; at first, erst; in the first place, imprimis, *L.*

FISH. *s.* The head of a fish, jole or jowl; to fish with a rod, to angle; dam to catch fish in, by means of wheels in a river, butrock; well in a ship for keeping fish alive, cauf; dried or smoked fish, fumado; the pickle fish are kept in, garum; the doctrine of the nature of fishes, ichthyology; to fish by means of bladders, to hux; pond for young fish, nurse-pond; to preserve or fry fish in oil, to marinate; name of a remarkable fish in the Mediterranean, furnished with membranes resembling oars and sails, by which means it actually makes way on the surface of the water, but strikes the whole and sinks on being surprised, nautilus, i. e. a little mariner; term used for such fishes as have soft fins, with bones, but not pointed, malacopterygious; for those that have hard

and bony fins, osteopterygious; those who bring fish from the sea-coast, to sell in the inland parts, ripiers; the liberty or privilege to catch fish, piscary or piscany; any little fish, piscicle; of or belonging to a fish-pond, or where fish are generally caught, piscinal; living on fish, piscivorous; any place in a river made for catching fish, perceptura; full, or abounding in fish, piscuient; cuttle or ink-fish, so called from the ancients writing with the liquor it discharges, sepia; to fish for eels with a bait, to sniggle; fish-pond, vivary; name of a fish, which, when alive, benumbs the hands on being even touched with a stick, torpedo; name of a fish of the eel kind found in the South-American Seas, 22 feet long, that is capable of killing a man by an electrical shock, gymnotus electricus; sort of barbed spear to strike fish with, tren; term for such fish as leave the rivers at a certain season, and go into the sea, but afterwards return into the rivers, such as the salmon, anadromous; name given to those who live solely on fish, ichthyophagi; name of a narcotic plant used to intoxicate fish with, *coculus indicus*, hence also called; *baccæ piscatoriæ.*

FISHER. *s.* The directors of the fishers of herrings, who are stationed on an eminence to observe how the shoal tends, conders; the bird named kingsfisher, famed for the calm and serene weather which prevails during its incubation, halcyon or ispida, hence the phrase, "halcyon days;" fishers of oysters, dredgers.

FISHING. *part.* Books or treatises on fishes and fishing, balientics; name for unlawful fishing-nets, kidles.

FISTULA. *s.* The operation of cutting for a fistula, syringotomia or syringotomy.

FIT. *v.* To accommodate, to adapt, to adjust, to fay, to attemper, to besort, to coincide, to fadge, to habilitate; to quadrate, to tally; to fit up, to equip; to fit with fetters; to garnish.

FIT. *a.* Acceptable, adviseable, applicable, behoveable, compatible, competible, competent, expedient, apposite, consonant, equitable, inservient, subservient, apt, concinnous, condign, congruous, equi-necessary, idoneous, matchable, meet, opportune, pat, pertinent, semblative, valid, relevant; more fit, fitter, (Perry, Entick) most fit, fitlest; fit for being eat, edible; fit (disorder) or trance, gyre or gire; the irregularity of a fit, ataxy; fit of drunkenness, cups; those fits or spasms to which women are mostly subject, hysteria or hysterics (see convulsion); the height of a fit which returns at certain

I

times, paroxysm or paroxism ; sudden fit of sickness, qualm ; moved by fits and starts; subsultive or subsultory ; a double fit in a fever, epiparoxism.

FITNESS. *s.* Aptness, aptitude, allowableness, capability, concinnity, congruity, correspondence, decorum, disposition, pertinence, pertinency, tempestivity ; the fitness of the bones, discernible in their articulation, paragoge or paragogue ; the fitness or aptitude of the parts of an organised body, symbolism, symbole, or etiphoria (see body); the want of fitness, inexpedience, inexpediency, unexpedience.

FITTING. *part.* The fitting of parts, coaptation, adaptation, adaption, harmony ; not fitting, incongruous, misbecoming, unbecoming, unsuitable, indecorous.

FIVE. *a.* Consisting of the number five, quinary ; five-sided figure, pentagon ; having five sides and angles, pentagonal, pentaedrous ; any engine with five pullies, pentapast ; a building in which there are five rows of columns, pentastyle ; verse of five feet, pentameter ; noun that has only five cases, pentaptote or pentaptoton; the first five books of the Bible, written by Moses, Pentateuch ; any five-stringed instrument, pentachord ; having five petals, pentapetalous ; having or bearing five leaves, quinquefoliated ; stanza in a poem, consisting of five verses, pentastich ; a medicine consisting of five-ingredients, pentepharmacon ; consisting of five articles, quinquarticular ; lasting or happening in five years, quinquennial ; five fold, quintuple ; cloven into five, quinquefid; consisting of five parts, quinquepartile ; any composition of five ingredients, diapente ; five ounces or inches, quincunx, this word is also used for a plantation of trees, disposed originally in a square consisting of five trees, one at each corner, and a fifth in the middle, which disposition repeated again and again forms a regular grove, wood; or wilderness ; formed like a quincunx, quincuncial ; having five angles or corners, quinqueangled or quinquangular ; having a seed vessel divided into five partitions, quinquecapsular; a sequence of five cards of the same colour at the game of piquet, quint.

FIX. *v.* To ascertain, to assign, to confirm, to confix, to covenant; to define, to prescribe; to stint, to appoint; to fix or fasten, to clinch ; to fix in, to infix; to fix in, as one shoot in another, to ingraff or ingraft; to fix or strengthen, to insinew; to fix or bind the arms, to pinion; to fix or compose feathers as birds do, to preen ; to fix

or take root, to radicate ; to fix or limit, to scant ; to fix with stakes, to palisade.

FIXED. *part.* Combinate, determinate, immutable, inalienable, inevitable, unevitable, unconvertible, inconvertible, indefeasible or undefeasible, irreversible ; fixed or bent upon, intent ; fixed (applied to a particular part of the body) topical ; that cannot be fixed, indeterminable or undeterminable, undeterminate or indeterminate; moveless, resolute, stable, statary.

FLAG. *s.* Royal flag, labarum ; flag, banner, guidon. pavilion ; small flag, bandroll, pennon, pennant; pendant.

FLAMBEAU. *s.* Lead or tede.

FLAME. *s.* Accention or accension, empyrosis ; consisting of flames, flammeous ; vomiting flames, flamivomous ; the vital flame of animals, biolychnium.

FLASH. *s.* Flash of light, coruscation, leam.

FLASHING. *part.* Coruscant. (See bright.)

FLAT. *a.* Discous, insipid, obtuse, procumbent, prolate ; flat-nosed, camoys; flatleaved, planipetalous ; flat as dead beer, vapid.

FLATTER. *v.* To cajole, to daub, to fawn, to glaver, to gloze, to cant, to coax, to wheedle, to pollaver, to soothe ; to flatter (submit) to knuckle.

FLATTERER. *s.* Courtdresser, parasite, pickthank, plume-striker, gnatho.

FLATTERING. *p.* Courtly, dedicatory, sycophantic.

FLATTERY. *s.* Complaisance, adulation, blandishment, compliment.

FLAVOUR *s.* Any dish of high flavour, hogo or hogoo.

FLAX. *s.* To beat flax, to hatchel or hitchel ; the refuse of flax, hurds ; a weight of flax about 112 lbs., kirtle ; bearing flax, linigerous.

FLEA. *s.* Lop ; abounding with fleas, pulicose, pulicous.

FLEECE. *v.* To flecce or comb, to curry, to pheese.

FLESH. *s.* Of or belonging to flesh, carnous, carneous ; to generate flesh, to carnify ; to deprive of flesh, to discarnate, to emaciate, to excarnate; act or process of the regeneration of flesh in an ulcer, granulation ; growth of bad or proud flesh, hypersarcosis ; to breed or cover with flesh, to incarn ; a die of a flesh colour, incarnadine ; to clothe or invest with flesh or corporeal substance, to incarnate ; living on flesh, carnivorous; medicines which fill up wounds with flesh, sarcotics, incarnatives or plerotics, anacollemata ; the flesh of beasts taken in hunting, venison ; eating of, or feeding on flesh, sarcophagy ; coffins of stone, anciently in use which had the property of speedily consuming the flesh, sarcophagus, or sarcophagum; the breeding of flesh, sarcosis; the preternatural growth of flesh on any part of the body, generally called an excrescence, ecsarcoma; one who has that just proportion of flesh, which constitutes strength and symmetry of body, eusarcos.

FLESHY. *a.* Brawny, corpulent; fleshy excresence on any part of the body, sarcoma; general term for the fleshy parts of the body, myscles; that part of anatomy which treats of the fleshy parts, sarcology.

FLIGHT. *s.* Of steps, gradatory, gradual; flight of birds, or where they are kept, volery or volary.

FLINT. *s.* Silex, *L.*; of or belonging to flint, silicious.

FLOAT. *v.* To buoy, to hull.

FLOATING. *p.* Fluctuant; floating at random, adrift; the act of floating above, superfluitance; floating above, superfluitant.

FLOCK. *s.* Of birds, bevy, covey; a separation from the flock, disgregation or abgregation; going in flocks, gregarious; flock of pheasants, nide or nye.

FLOOD. *s.* Deluge, fresh or freshet, inundation, alluvion, (see deluge); flood interposed or flowing between two or more parts, interluency.

FLOOR. *v.* To floor with boards, to contabulate.

FLOORING. *part.* Contignation, entablature, entablement.

FLOUR. *s.* Consisting of fine flour, siligeneous.

FLOURISHING. *p.* Verdant, vernant, virent. (See green.)

FLOW. *s.* Aptness to flow, diffluence or diffluency; an eloquent flow of language, elocution; to flow gently and silently, to glide; what flows under, subterfluous; the strait between Bœotia and the Negropont, which flows and ebbs *seven times* in twenty-four hours, Euripus.

FLOWER. *s.* Description or collection of flowers, anthology; having flower leaves or petals, corollated; shooting in the form of flowers, efflorescent; relating to flowers, floral, florulent; flower wore as an ornament in the head-dresses of women, egrette; border of flowers, wreath; festoon; composed of flowers, flosculous; flowers in branches, garlands, chaplets, wreaths; the gathering of flowers in May-day, maying; verb, to may; bunch of flowers, posie, nosegay; any plant which bears but one flower, monanthus, two, &c. dianthus, &c.; flower garden, parterre; the flower leaves of plants,

shrubs, &c. petals; an extravagant fondness for curious flowers, anthomania; flower-border, floroun, or more properly, fleuron, *F.*; the opening and shutting of flowers, particularly of the class syogenesia, at certain times of the day, is called, *horologium floræ.*

Flowers (courses) emmenia, menses, catamenia, menstrua, muliebria.

FLOWING. *part.* To any part, affluent, exuberant; the flowing of water, &c. interluency (Johnson); the act of flowing, manation; flowing round or about, circumfluent, diffluent; flowing down, defluous; flowing into, influent; act of flowing into, influx; act of flowing out, emanation, efflux, effluxion or effluvium; the flowing and ebbing of the sea, estuation; flowing between, interfluent, interfluous; a flowing between, intermeation; a flowing or overflowing, alluvion (see deluge); the act of flowing against, abundation; flowing forward, profluent; flowing backward, refluent; a flowing out, as water out of a spring, scatebrosity, scaturience.

FLUID. *s.* The science of weighing fluids, hydrostatics; half fluid, semi-fluid.

FLUTTER. *v.* To stammer, to maffle, to palpitate. (See stammering.)

FLUX. *s.* Diarrhœa, lientery, profluvium, (see Quincy's Lexicon, art. Diarrhœa.) flux attended with a great discharge of mucus, leucorrhœis; flux attended with blood, dysentery.

FLY. To fly against, in argument, to eschew, to resist, to oppose, to oppone, to oppugn; to fly off, to evaporate; to fly upon or over, to involate; to fly or shift from place to place, to demigrate; to fly back, to result, to resile; to fly high, as eagles, to soar; to fly down, or away, to devolate.

FLY. *s.* The Spanish or French fly used as a vesicatory, cantharides; the best and largest are brought from Italy, (Quincy); the name of an American fly which shines in the night so brightly, that persons may see to travel, read, and write by the light of it, cucuyos.

FLYING. *part.* Fugitive, volant; flying, (changeable) volatile, vplatic; flying asunder, dissilition; the art of flying away, avolation, or evolation; the quality of flying away, fugacity, volatility; the flying off in fumes, effumability; flying about like vapour, lambent; the act of flying, volitation; the act of flying over or athwart, tranation; a flying beyond, transvolation; flying as with full sails, velivolant; act of flying to, advolation, advolition; flying high, as eagles do, soaring, alivolant.

FOAM. *v.* To spume, to despumate.

FOE. *s.* Adversary, emissary, fiend, opponent. (See enemy.)

FOETUS. *s.* The anatomical dissection of the fœtus, embryotomy; marks on the fœtus induced by the imagination of the mother, nævi; membrane sometimes covering the head of the fœtus, sillyhow, by some termed, vitta; surgical instrument for drawing the fœtus out of the womb, embryulcus or ungula.

FOG. *s.* Haze, rime, exhalation.

FOGGY. *a.* Misly, drizzly, hazy, rimy.

FOISTED. *part.* (Put in the place of something else) subdititious. (See forge.)

FOLD. *v.* To corrugate, to duplicate, to envelope or invelope, to furl, to implicate, to involve, to complicate; to fold round about, to obvolve.

FOLD. *s.* Plicature, plication.

FOLLOW. *v.* To cleave, to dangle, to ensue, to follow consequently, to result; to follow after or search out, to evestigate. (See search.)

FOLLOWED. *part.* Followed with a bad intention, dogged; that cannot be followed, insectable.

FOLLOWER. *s.* Adherent, disciple, sectator.

FOLLOWING. *part.* Posterior; following necessarily, consectaneous; following or attendant on a matter, sequacious, sequent, subsecutive; a following, assectation; not following necessarily, inconsequent.

FOLLY. *s.* Insipience, irrationality, levity, pageantry, fatuity, frenzy, impertinence, or impertinency, indiscretion, puerility, stolidity, temerity, insulsity; folly approaching to madness, paraphrosyne; the feigned goddess of folly, Moria.

FOMENT. *v.* To foment or rub any painful part, to embrocate.

FOMENTATION. *s.* Malagma, cataplasma, or diaplasma, this last word is generally used for a fomentation over the whole body, such as the warm bath.

FOND. *a.* Fain, notional, observant, maternal, amorous; fond-man, meacock.

FONDLE. *v.* To bill, to cocker.

FONDLER. *s.* Dallier, pratler, dandler.

FONDLING. *s.* Nest-cock.

FONDNESS. *s.* Addiction, affection, dalliance, dottage; fondness for nephews, nepotism.

FOOD. *s.* Diæta, *L.*; aliment, forage, commons, fare, nutriment, prog, provender, viands; fit for food, esculent, edible; provider of food, purveyor, caterer or cateress; nice food, cates, tit-bits, bonbons; relating to food, cibarious; want of food in the stomach, inanition; handful of food, luncheon, lunch; food taken between meals, nunchion; double allowance of food given to students on holy days, gaudies; food for cattle from trees, shrubs, &c. boscage.

FOOL. *s.* Turlurn, buzzard, capochia, changeling, driveller, fopdoodle, ignoramus, mooncalf, nizy, nidget, noodle, oaf, nincompoop, ninnyhammer, dolt, jobbernowl. (See simpleton)

FOOLISH. *a.* Incautious, uncautious, undiscreet, (see folly) insensate, insulse, mawmish, absonant, absonous, farcical, bardous, inept; foolish fellow, wiseacre, ignaro; foolish and trifling discourse, morology, liplabour, lipwisdom, tillyvalley or tillyfally; to render foolish, to stultify.

FOOLISHNESS. *s.* Fatuity, insipiency, desipience.

FOOT. *s.* On foot, a-foot; little foot, pedicule or pedicle; consisting of a foot and one half, semipedal or sesquipedal (Bailey) consisting of half a foot, semipedal (Johnson); to tread under foot, to deculcate or conculcate; of, or belonging to a foot, pedal; going on foot, pedestrial, pedestrian, pedestrious, pedaneous; belonging to the muscle spread over the sole of the foot, plantary; name for what is applied as medicines to the sole of the foot, suppedanea or supplantalia; placed under foot, suppedaneous; the foot of a statue, &c. pedestal.

FOOT-GUARDS. *s.* Of the grand Seignior, consisting of 300 men, armed with bows and arrows, solachs.

FOOTMAN, } *s.* Pedes, skip-kennel, varlet, valet, *Fr.*

FOOT-BOY. }

FOOTED. *a.* Web-footed as water-fowl, palmipede. (See feet.)

FOOTSTEPS. *s.* Or traces, vestiges, *Fr.*

FOP. *s.* Baccalare, coxcomb, fribble, macaroni, beau, milksop, popinjay.

FOPPISH. *a.* Apish, finical, quaint.

FORAGE. *s.* Of or belonging to, pabular.

FORBEAR. *v.* To abstain. (See to deny.)

FORBEARANCE. *s.* Connivance, respite; long forbearance, longanimity. (See to suffer.)

FORBID. *v.* To forfend, to hush, to inhibit to interdict, to prohibit.

FORBIDDING. *p.* A forbidding, vetation; veto, *L.*

FORCE. *v.* To compel, to necessitate, to force asunder any thing, also to separate husband and wife, to divorce; to force or tear in two, to dilacerate; to force down farther, to detrude; to force below water, &c. to drench; to force through, to efforce; to force off or away, to expulse, to expel; to lessen in force or effect, to invalidate; to force open, to wrench, to ranch; to force up from the stomach, to retch; to force or commit a rape, to stuprate.

FORCE. s. Cogency, dint, compulsion, energy, pithiness, validity, vigor; force or power, puissance, vehemence; having equal force, equipollent, equivalent; getting or acquiring by force, extorsive; by force, perforce; the force of habit, inurement; violent force, orgasm, impetus; communicated force, impulse; force of language so as to move the passions, patheticalness; possessing a greater force, prepotency; force tending from the centre, centrifugal; to the centre, centripetal; open force or violence, rapine.

FORCED. part. Forced interpretation, detortion, catachresis; forced out of the proper vessels, as blood sometimes is, extravasated; forced back, redacted.

FORCIBLE. a. Coercive, energetic, emphatic, puissant, vive; forcible (weighty) ponderous.

FOREBODE. v. To ominate, to prognosticate, to soothsay, to portend, to presage, to predict, to vaticinate. (See foretell.)

FOREBODING. p. Auspicial; foreboding from the impression of one's own mind, thyromancy.

FOREIGN. a. Peregrine, remote, adscititious, ascititious, advectitious, extraneous, extrinsic, barbaric, exterraneous, alien, exotic; foreign trader, mercantant.

FOREIGNER. s. Alien, allophylus.

FOREKNOWING. part. Prescious, prescient.

FOREKNOWLEDGE. s. Prenotion; the foreknowledge of diseases, prophasis.

FORERUNNER. s. Harbinger, precursor, prodromus, antecursor.

FORERUNNING. p. Procatarctic, as the precatarctic cause of a disease.

FORESIGHT. s. Caution, forecast, previdence, prospicience; the want of foresight, improvidence.

FORESKIN. s. Prepuce, epagogium; to cut off the foreskin, to circumcise.

FOREST. s. Full of forests, saltuose.

FORESTAL. v. To regrate.

FORESTALLING. p. Abrochment.

FORETASTE. s. Antepast, prelibation.

FORESTER. s. Saltuary.

FORETELL. v. To abode, to prognosticate, to divine, to ominate, to predict, to vaticinate, to anticipate, to prenunciate, to foretoken, to foreshow, to presage, to betoken. (See, to divine.)

FORETELLER. s. Predictor, soothsayer. (See diviner and fortuneteller.)

FORETELLING. p. Fatidical; foretelling by the casting of stones, lithomancy; from the impressions of one's mind, thyomancy; by the manner one laughs, geloscopy.

FORFEIT. v. To confiscate. (See to seize.)

FORFEITURE. s. Deodand. (See fine.)

FORGE. v. To fabricate, to falsify; to forge or fashion on an anvil, to stithy.

FORGED. p. (Not true) pseudo, subditious, supposititious.

FORGERY. s. To insert by forgery, to foist.

FORGETFULNESS. s. Lethe, oblivion, amnesty; causing forgetfulness, oblivial, oblivious.

FORGIVE. v. To absolve, to forgeve, to remit. (See pardon.)

FORGIVEN. p. Not to be forgiven, irremissible; that may be forgiven, veniable, or venial, ignoscible.

FORGIVING. p. A forgiving or pardoning, condonation.

FORLORN HOPE. a. Those men who are put upon the most desperate services, and who in all probability must fall, are called enfans perdues. (Military term.)

FORM. v. To compose, to construct, to dispose, to efform, to configure, to extruct; to form into a mass, to concrete; to form into a ball, to conglomerate, to glomerate; to form into one body, to incorporate, to incorpse; to form before hand, to preform.

FORM. s. Reglement; form or representation of a thing, icon; belonging to a form, modal; prescribed form, formula; having many forms, multiform; having different forms, variform; nice form, or ceremony, punctilio.

FORMAL. a. Modal, stiff, budge, ceremonial, ceremonious, incommunicative, inconversable, or unconversable, uncommunicative, prim, precise, primitive, prudish, ritual.

FORMED. p. That may be formed, mouldable; half formed, semiformed, demiformed.

FORMER. a. Ancient, anterior, or anterior, prior.

FORMERLY. ad. Aforetime, erst, quondam, L. ci-devant, F.

FORNICATION. s. Michation or moechation, palliardise.

FORSAKE. v. To abandon, to desert, to secede.

FORSAKEN. a. Derelict, lorn, forlorn, destitute; forsaken by a mistress, lasslorn.

FORT. s. Little fort, fortillage, fortin, muniment.

FORTIFICATION. s. muniment, munition, bulwark; the act of scaling the walls of a fortification, escalade; that part of fortification which teaches how to attack an enemy with the greatest advantage, areotectonics.

FORTIFY. *v.* To empale, to munite. (See strengthen.)

FORTRESS. *s.* Block-house, citadel.

FORTUNE. *s.* To impair a fortune by clandestine means for the purposes of hurting the heir, to imbecile.

FORTUNE-TELLER. *s.* Conjurer, soothsayer, fatiloquist, diviner, geomancer; of or belonging to a fortuneteller, genethliacal.

FORWARD. *v.* To adjute, or adjuvate, to promote. (See to aid.)

FORWARD. *a.* (Keen,) sanguine; importunately forward, officious.

FOUL. *v.* To inquinate, to besmear, to bemire, to daub.

FOUL. *a.* Lutulent, turbid, rubiginous, sordid, eruginous, feculent, dingy, verminous, squalid; foul (or drossy) scorious.

FOULNESS. *s.* Mucoseness, mucosity, solure, fedity.

FOUND. *p.* Goods or money found and unclaimed, inventiones, L. T.; what is found, repertitious.

FOUNDATION. *s.* Basis, substruction.

FOUNDLING. *s.* Repertitius, L.

FOUR. *a.* The number four, quaternion, quaternary, quaternity, tetras; cloven into four, quadrifid; divided into four, quadripartite; consisting of four years, tetraeterid; happening once every four years, quadrennial; having four sides, quadrilateral; vessel with four oars on a side, quadrireme; word of four syllables, quadrisyllable, tetrasyllable; consisting of four ways or turnings, quadrivial; having four feet, quadrupedal; consisting or written in four different languages, tetraglottic; consisting of four leaves as some plants, tetraphyllous, tetrapetulous, quadriphyllous; discourse consisting of four parts, tetralogy; stanza having four verses, or lines, tetrastitch; a noun of only four cases, tetraptote, or, tetraptoton; the government and jurisdiction of four provinces, tetrarchy, or tetrarchate; bearing four seeds, tetraspermous; any composition consisting of four ingredients, diatessaron.

FOURFOLD. *a.* Quadruple.

FOURTH. *a.* One fourth part, subquadruple.

FOWL. *s.* The stomach of a fowl, different terms for; craw, choule, crop, ingluvies, gizzard; such fowls as have feathered feet are termed plumipedes; those which have webbed toes are termed palmipedes; dealer in fowls, poulterer; young fowl, pullet.

FOWLING. *p.* Or bird-catching, art of,

aucupation.

FOX. *s.* Reynard; young fox, vixen; company of foxes, skulk, (hunt. term); cant phrase used among huntsmen for the tail of a fox, holywater sprinkle; name used by hunters for the dung of a fox, scumber; the noise made by foxes at the rutting season, clicketing.

FRACTION. *s.* The method of freeing an equation from fractions, Isomeria.

FRAGMENT. *s.* Cantlets, orts, mammock; any part or fragment cut off, frustum; fragments collected from books, analecta, analects, cento.

FRAGRANT. *a.* Aromatic, balmy, odoriferous, odorous, odorate.

FRAIL. *a.* Brittle, fallible, fragile, peccable.

FRAME. *s.* Made of beams and boards joined together, contignation.

FRANCE. *s.* Relating to France, Gallican.

FRANKINCENSE. *s.* The act of fuming with, thurification; bearing or yielding frankincense, thuriferous.

FRANKNESS. *s.* Apertness. (See plainness and freedom.)

FRAUD. *s.* Deception, elusion, barratry, circumvention; obtained by fraud, surreptitious.

FRAUDULENT. *a.* Collusive, covenous, delusive, crafty, illusory, surreptitious; fraudulent agreement, covin.

FREAK. *s.* Caprice, vagary. (See frolick.)

FRECKLE. *s.* Freckles arising from sunburning, ephelis.

FRECKLED. *a.* Lentiginous.

FRECKLEDNESS. *s.* Nevosity.

FREE. *v.* To exempt, to exonerate, to disembroil; to set free, to manumit, to abjugate, to absolve, to acquit, to disenthral, to emancipate, to denizen, to enfranchize, to franchise, to extricate; to strip or free of covering, to divest or devest; to free or separate good from bad, to garble.

FREE. *a.* Frank, allodial, liberal, vacant, communicable; free or voluntary, ultroneous; free (liberal), munificent; free (easy of access), accostable; set free, also gay, solute; name given to freestone as it is taken out of the quarry, ashlar.

FREEDOM. *s.* Latitude, manumission, affranchisement, franchise, denization, immunity, indult, or indulto, disencumbrance; privation of freedom, disfranchisement; freedom or exemption from punishment, impunity; mutual freedom in the exercise of religion, intercommunity; freedom of will or action, spontaniety; a liberty or freedom of speech, parrhesia.

FREEZE. *v.* To congeal, to glaciate, to sgelidate.

FRENCH. *s* Relating to them, Gallican.

FREIGHT. *s.* The freight of passengers in a ship, navilage.

FREQUENT. *a.* Crebrous.

FREQUENTNESS. *s.* Crebritude.

FRESH. *a.* Mustulent; fresh or recent, neoterick, or neoteric; a growing fresh, raw, or sore again, as wounds, recrudescent; stream of fresh water, freshet; to walk in the fresh air, to walk *in fresco.*

FRESHNESS. *s.* Fraicheur F.; freshness or newness, novity.

FRET. *v.* To chafe, to disquiet, to enchafe, to exulcerate, to corrode, to foment, to repine, to erode

FRETFUL. *a.* Splenetic, testy. (See peevish.)

FRIAR. *s.* The parlour in a monastery where the friars meet for conversation, locutory.

FRIEND. *s.* Gaffer, ally, belamie, conciliator, counsellor; secret friend, privado; pretended friend, mouth-friend.

FRIENDLY. *a.* Amicable, benign; friendly (easy of access), accostable; friendly salutation, belaccoile, F.

FRIENDSHIP. *s.* Amity, accordance. (See agreement); friendship at table, commensality; pretended show of friendship, semblance.

FRIGHT. *v.* To haze, to intimidate, to affright, to deter, to fray, to gallow, to ghast, to appal, to hare.

FRIGHT. *s.* Sudden fright, occasioned by, pitapat, palpitation; fright, consternation, or stupor, occasioned by an external accident, ecplexis; fright without cause, panic; the standing up of the hair through fright, as in quartan fevers, horriplation.

FRIGHTFUL. *a.* Effraible, faxed, formidable, ghastly, grisly, hideous, horrible, (See dreadful); any frightful object, bugbear, manducus. (See spirit.)

FRINGED. *p.* Fimbriated.

FRISK. *v.* To gambol. (See frolic.)

FRISKING. *p.* Capering; act of, saltation.

FRISKY. *a.* Coltish, rampant.

FRITH. *s.* Estuary, fret.

FROG. *s.* Paddock, porwigle, tana.

FROLIC. *s.* Gambol, vagary, caper, curvet, freak; disposed for frolics, waggish.

FRONT. *s.* In the front, afore, infront; front of an army, van, avantguard.

FRONTIER. *s.* Of or belonging to a frontier, limitaneous.

FROST. *s.* Rime, pruina.

FROTH. *v.* To despumate; to raise froth as a ship under way, to spoom.

FROTH. *s.* Made up of soap and water, lather; froth, spume, achne.

FROWARDNESS. *s.* Protervity.

FROZEN. *a.* Frorne, congealed, frore, glacial; that may be frozen, gelable; water frozen in the act of dropping, icicle.

FRUGAL. *a.* Chary, economical, or oeconomical, parsimonious, provident.

FRUGALITY. *s.* Parcity.

FRUIT. *s.* Bearing fruit, fetiferous, frugiferous, fructiferous; to gather fruit, to vindemiate; not bearing, or incapable of bearing fruit, infrugiferous; dry husks of fruit, murk; those fruits which contain only one kernal or seed, monopyrenous; the goddess of fruits, Pomona; term used for all kinds of shell fruits, acrodrya; first fruits, annates, premices, premitiæ; of or belonging to first fruits, primitial.

FRUITFUL. *a.* Fecund, prolific, fructuous, teemful, feracious, fertile, generative, prolifick, prolifical, foetiferous; to make fruitful, to enwomb, to impregn, or impregnate, to improlificate.

FRUITFULNESS. *s.* Uberty.

FRUSTRATE. *v.* To balk, to circumduct. (See to defeat.)

FRY. *v.* To fry fish in oil, to marinate.

FUDDLE. *v.* To boose

FUDDLED. *p.* Temulent, fap.

FUEL. *s.* Nutriment, pabulum; sort of compound fuel made of the dross of coals and earth, &c., hot-shoots.

FULFILL. *v.* To accomplish, to effectuate. (See to finish.)

FULL. *a.* Inundant, convictive, diffuse, distinct, exuberant, flush, copious, beetle-browed, comprehensive, conclusive, exigetical, explanatory, expository, fecund, fraught, protuberant, replete; full number, complement; very full, enunciative; full of small shoots or shrubs, frutescent; fall state, impletion; full state of body, plethora, or plethory; invested with full power, plenipotent; full of earth, terrulent; full of sand, sabulous; full of thought, cogitabund.

FULLER. *s.* Fuller's earth, smectis; a plant of singular use in raising the nap upon woollen cloth, called Fuller's thistle teasel.

FULLY. *ad.* Plenarily.

FULNESS. *s.* Plenitude, satiety, repletion, saturity, chariness, cloyment, impletion, infarction, constipation; fulness of humours, plethora, or plethory; one who holds the doctrine of universal fulness, plenist.

FUME. *v.* To evaporate, to fumigate, to suffumigate; to fume or grow angry, to chafe.

FUME. *s.* Exhalation; act of passing into fume, vaporation; a flying off in fumes, effumability.

FUNDAMENT. *s.* Nock, podex ; sort of solid medicine introduced into the fundament to produce a stool, suppository ; term used for one whose fundament is not perforated, atretus ; the fundament of a beast, tuel.

FUNERAL. *s.* Funeral poem, elegy, epicedium; a pompous funeral monument, mausoleum ; gate of a church through which funerals pass, lichgate ; funeral ditty sung by one person, menody ; funeral rites, exequies, obsequies ; supper formerly given at funerals, arvil supper ; song of lamentation at or after a funeral, threnody ; funeral pile, pyre ; belonging to a funeral pile, rogal.

FUNERAL. *a.* Funereal.

FUNNEL. *s.* Shaped like a funnel, infundibuliform.

FUR. *s.* Flix, flue.

FURIOUS. *a.* Breme, brainish, desperate, boisterous, outrageous, pallmail, phrenetic, splenic, impetuous.

FURNISH. *v.* To accoutre, to equip, to indue, to suppeditate.

FURNITURE. *s.* Garniture, apparatus ; to deprive of furniture, to disgarnish.

FURROWED. *ad.* Sulcated ; having furrowed stalks, pandurated.

FURTHER. *v.* To adjute, or adjuvate. (See to aid.)

FURY. *s.* Ire, phrenitis, chafe, desperateness, ferocity, incensement ; done with great fury, precipitance, transport, or transportation ; fury, barbason, hag ; the furies are, Megaras, Alecto, and Tisiphone; they are also called Eumenides or Diræ.

FUTURITY. *s.* Past existence ; an approaching to futurity, futurition.

G

GAIETY. *s.* Galliardise, glee, hilarity, pleasantry. (See mirth and joy.)

GAILY. *ad.* Jocundly, airily, bonnily, cheerily. (See gay.)

GAIN. *v.* To achieve, to attain, to earn.

GAIN. *s.* Lucre, vantage, emolument ; bringing gain, lucrative, lucriforous, lucrous.

GAINED. *p.* (What is gained) acquist or acquest.

GALE. *s.* Gentle gale, aura, loomgale, breeze, or breese.

GALL. *s.* Bile, choler ; flowing with gall, fellifluous.

GALLANT. *a.* Amorist, amoroso, cicisbeo, leman, belamour.

GALLEY. *s.* Having three, &c. tiers of oars on a side, trireme, quadrireme, &c.

GALLERY. *s.* Outside gallery, balcony, corridor ; projecting gallery, miradore ; uncovered gallery, paradrome, or peridromis.

GALLON. *s.* The measure of one half gallon, semicongius.

GALLOP. *s.* Hand gallop, Canterbury gallop ; a full gallop, tantivy ; short and pressed gallop, *terra à terra.*

GALLOWAY. *s.* Garran.

GALLOWS. *s.* Belonging to the gallows, patibulary.

GAME. *s.* He who has lost the game, sitting out, and giving another his place, levelcoil ; tune at the death of game (among hunters), mort ; the illegal killing of game, poaching ; any place where games

and exercises are performed, palaster ; games at tennis, hand-ball, and such like, sphærachamy.

GAMESOME. *a.* Ludescent, lusory, lusorious.

GANG. *s.* Junto, cabal, cabala.

GANYMEDE. *s.* Ingle, pathic, catamite, bardac. (See boy.)

GAOL. *s.* Goal, jail ; fees paid, or money exacted by fellow prisoners on commitment to gaol, garnish.

GAP. *s.* Chasm, chink, hiatus, apertion, fissure. (See clift.)

GAPING. *p.* Act of gaping, hiation.

GARDEN. *s.* Belonging to gardens, hortulan ; of, or belonging to a kitchen garden, olitory ; flower garden, parterre.

GARGLING *v.* Or washing of the throat or mouth, diaclysma.

GARLANDS. *s.* Bays, laurels, chaplets, coronals.

GARMENTS. *s.* Habiliments, attire, investment, vesture, palliament.

GARNISH. *v.* Or to adorn round about, to circumvest. (See, to adorn.)

GARRET. *s.* Room above a garret, cockloft.

GARRISON. *s.* Belonging to a garrison, presidial.

GASH. *s.* Or cut, cæsura. (See cut.)

GATE. *s.* Gate of a church-yard, through which funerals pass, lich-gate ; small back-gate, postern, pseudethyrum ; gate, portal ; keeper of a gate, pylorus ; female keeper of a gate, portress ; sort of gate or bridge, occasionally let down or raised, port-cullice.

GATHER. v. To deduce, to levy, to muster; to gather or form in an abscess, to imposthumate; to gather up treasure, to thesaurise; to gather fruit, to vendemiate; gather into a ball, to conglomerate, to glomerate.

GATHERED. p. Collectitious, excerpt, gleaned.

GATHERING. p. Gathering together of people unlawfully, parasynaxis, conventicle; a delirious fumbling wherein the patient seems to be gathering something from the bed-cloaths, it is generally a fatal symptom, and is termed carpologia.

GAUDY. a. Flashy, garish, gairish, meretricious.

GAUGING. s. Stereometry.

GAY. a. Airy, bonny, blithe, boon, cavalier, debonnair, facetious, finical, flippant, genial, gent, gim, gimmy, gleeful, jant, jaunty, juvenile, modish, lusory, jocund, jolly, jovial, joyous, lusorious, nitid, solute, sportive, vivacious; gay brisk man, galliard.

GELD. v. To castrate, to evirate, to eunuchate, to emasculate, to glib, to spay.

GELDED. p. Mutilous. (See cut and maim.)

GEMS. s. Counterfeit gems, amouses; dealer in gems, lapidary; treatise on gems and medals, dactyleotheca.

GENDERS. s. Of double genders, androgynous, hermaphrodital.

GENERAL. a. Oecumenical, pandemic, topical, appellative, epidemical, exceptless; the most general and universal conception of things, transcendentals; general form, formula; general rule, poris.n; general disease, morbus, pandemius.

GENERALISE. v. To common place.

GENERATED. p. Procreated, begot, propagated; what cannot be generated, ingenerable.

GENERATION. s. The parts of generation, physis, genitals; generation or clan, stirp, sept; generation of the gods, theogony; succeeding generation, posterity, progeny; that sort of generation which is effected by the contact of parts, without intromission, adosculation; act of generation between a ram and ewe, blissoming; between animals in general, coition.

GENERATIVE. a. Prolifical, prolific.

GENEVA. s. Gin, tityré.

GENIUS. Ingeny.

GENTLE. a. Bland, clement, flexile, flexible, mansuete, meek, placid, pacific, pigeon-livered; gentle gale, aura; gentle

death, euthanasy.

GENUINE. a. Authentic, extradictionary, intrinsic, intrinsical, legitimate; not genuine, suppositious.

GEOMETRY. s. Pantometry, stereometry.

GHOST. s. Mormo, spectre; ghosts, manducci, apparitions, larvæ, phantoms, lemures, manes.

GHOST. (Holy) s. Paraclete; heretics in the 12th century, who denied the divinity of the Holy Ghost, Macedonians; heretics who held Melchizedeck to be the Holy Ghost, Melchizedechians; heretics in the 3d century, who affirmed that the Holy Ghost was Christ's sister, Elcesaitæ; Christian heretics who held that God himself, along with the Holy Ghost, suffered with the Son, Patripassians; a term used among divines signifying a Being of the same substance or essence with God and Christ, such as the Holy Ghost, homoousion.

GIANT. s. Colossus, gargantua; like a giant, gigantic; the supposed giant who had one large eye in his forehead, Polypheme; the feigned battle of the giants and the gods, theomachy, gigantomachy.

GIBE. s. Quib, quip, sarcasm. (See reproach.)

GIDDINESS. s. Dinus, vertigo, fugitiveness, incogitancy, inconsiderateness; giddiness, or swimming in the head, scotomy.

GIDDY. a. Highty-tighty, janty, jaunty, inadvertant, incautious, puerile, rantipole, vertiginous, unchary.

GIFT. s. Almsdeed, boon, collation, donation, largess, gratuity, endowment, indowment, corban, dole, doron, gratification, sportule, sportula, passade, passado; gift or fee of office, perquisite; liberal and extravagant gift, erogation; gift left at death to a church, &c. mortuary; gifts which are sent, in place of those granted on the spot, missives; relating to gifts munerary; one who gifts, donor.

GIFTED. a. Doted.

GILDING. p. Act of gilding with gold, deauration, inauration; gilding with silver, inargentation.

GIMCRACK. s. Conundrum, trangram.

GIN. s. (Snare) Laqueus.

GIN. s. (Liquor) Geneva, tityré.

GIRDED p. Succinct, begirded, engirded.

GIRDLE. s. Baldric, cestus, cincture, perizoma, diazoma.

GIRL. s. (Different terms for), Blowze, coquette, filly, flirt, grissette, maypole, hoiden, mappet, mopsy; wanton girl, parnel, tomboy, giglet; name of an herb which steeped in drink is said to make a woman conceive a girl, thelygonum.

K

GIVE. v. To adjudge, to attribute, to confer, to dispose, to distribute, to impart, to vouchsafe ; to give up, to cede ; give in marriage, to betroth ; give notice, to cund ; to give up to punishment, or destruction, to devote ; give up or yield, to succumb ; give up by inches, to inch ; give up or relinquish as highly wicked, to reprobate ; give bark, to remit.

GIVING. p. Act of, largition ; a giving or doing more than is required, supererogation.

GLAD. a. Fain, joyous ; to make glad, to letificate, to elate, to elevate, to exhilirate ; a making glad, letifical.

GLANCE. s. Glance of the eye, oeilliad, oeliad, oeilaid ; to glance over or touch upon in discourse, to perstringe.

GLANDS. s. Treatise on the glands, adenography.

GLARE. s. Glare of light, coruscation.

GLASS. s. Belonging to glass, vitreous, vitreal ; to change into glass, to vitrify, to vitrificate ; convex or concave glass used in telescopes, lens ; cupping glass, vesicatory, cucurbitula, ventose ; optical glass for viewing objects which do not lye directly before the eye, polemoscope ; spy-glass, perspicil ; mathematical glass for shewing the different colours by, prism ; glass which shews the same object many times repeated, polyscope ; glass with which distant objects are viewed, telescope ; glass so fitted that like the eye of an animal it may be turned many ways, and is used in making experiments in darkened rooms, scioptic, or scioptric glass ; glass for viewing the body of the sun, helioscope ; glass used in catching larks, daring glass ; glass which is convex on one side, and concave on the other, meniscus, convexo concave, or concavo-convex ; glass which is convex on both sides, omphaloptic ; glass which is concave on both sides, concavo-concave ; glass which is plain on the one side, and hollow on the other, planoconcave ; glass which is plane on the one side and raised on the other, planoconvex ; weather glass, baroscope, barometer, aeroscope, manometer; weather glass is sometimes termed the Torricellian tube, or experiment, from Torricelli, or Torricellius, the inventor ; perspective glass, having two sights, so as both eyes may see at once, binocle, or binocular glass; glass for viewing minute objects with, engyscope, microscope ; vessel in which glass utensils are washed in, montet, monteth, monteith ; drinking glass filled to the brim, bumper, brimmer.

GLASSY. a. Hyaline glassy humour of the eye, vitreous humour, hyaloides.

GLAZIER. s. Glazier's diamond, emeril, emrod, emry.

GLEANED. p. Collectitious; what is gleaned, excerption.

GLEANING. p. Gleaning of corn, spicelegy.

GLIMMER. v. To flare. (See to glitter.)

GLIMMERING. p. Dawning, crepusculous.

GLIDING. p. Gliding over as a pale flame, lambent.

GLITTER. v. To effulge, to glisten, to glister.

GLITTERING. p. Coruscant, effulgent, gorgeous, lucent, lucid ; act of glittering, emication.

GLOBE. s. Formed like a glob, globated ; small globe, globule, spherule ; half globe, semiglobe, hemisphere.

GLOOMY. a. Dolesome, feral, glum, hersed, sombre, infestive, lurid, murky, nubilous, obscure, tenebricose, tenebrose, tenebreus, tristful.

GLORY. s. Crown of glory, aureola ; false glory, pseudodox ; vain glory, kenedoxy, G.

GLOSS. v. To comment, to gloze.

GLOSS. s. Or polish, politure.

GLUE. v. To glue together, to agglutinate, to conglutinate.

GLUE. s. Like glue, glutinous, viscid, viscous ; the fish from which a fine kind of glue is made, anciently substituted for glass, isinglas fish ; glue made from a bull's hide, taurocolla ; from fish, particularly from isinglass fish, ichthyocolla ; glue made for the joining of wood, &c. xylocolla ; for the cementing of stones, lithocolla.

GLUT. s. Or excess, saturity, satiety.

GLUTTON. s. Cormorant, gulch, gulchin, gargantua. (See appetite and greediness.)

GLUTTONY. s. Bulimy, alogy, adephagia, adephagy, eligurition, obligurition, gulosity, lurcation, polyphagy, cynorexy.

GNASHING. p. Gnashing of the teeth, frement, or bryamus.

GNAWING. p. Mordecant, mordacious ; gnawing round about, arrosion.

GO. v. To go round or about, to circumambulate ; go fast, to hie ; go off, to abscond ; go beyond, to transcend ; go backward, to retrograde ; to go before, to precede, to antecede ; go at large, to go a shack.

GOAL. s. Gaol, jail ; fee paid, or money exacted on commitment to goal, garnish.

GOAT. s. Goat-feeted, capripede ; stuff made of goat's hair, mohair ; animal produced between a she goat and a ram, musimon, umber ; one of the feasts of Bacchus, in which goats were eaten alive, omophagia; herd or company of goats, trip.

GOD. s. God, as being the first former of all things, Protoplast; God, the Almighty, the Deity, the Divinity, the Eternal, Jehovah, the Omnipotent, the Supreme, Ubiquitary, Elohim, Tetragrammaton; God among the Chinese, Xangti; doctrine of one god, monotheism; god-making, apotheosis, deification; doctrine of two opposite gods, ditheism; of many, polytheism; God's self existence, autotheism; of or belonging to God, or a Creator, demiurgical; Christian heretics who held that God the Father and the Holy Ghost suffered as well as the Son, Patripassions; heretics that appeared in Egypt A. D. 359, who held that God had the form of man, Anthropomorphites; half-god, demigod; one who believes in only one God, unitarian; the feigned generation of the gods, theogony; the feigned fight of the gods and giants, theomachy, gigantomachy; the fighting against, or attempting to resist God, theomagical; belonging to, or regarding the wisdom of God, theomagical; a form of giving glory to God, doxology; that brings forth a god, an epithet applied to the Virgin Mary, deiparous; the power of working miracles by means of prayer to God, theurgy; divinition by calling on the name of God, theomancy; one God in three persons, Trinity; doctrine of three distinct Gods in the trinity, tritheism; term applied to God to express the unity of the Godhead in a trinity of persons, Triune; term used among divines signifying a Being of the same substance or essence with God himself, homoousion.

GOING. p. Going out, act of, egression, exodus, ecbasis; going round about, circumition; going by, or passing by, preterition; going before, previous, prior, antecedent; going back, retrocession, retrogradation, retrogression; the act of going from place to place, adition. (Johnson.)

GOLD. s. Producing or bringing gold, auriferous; gilding with gold, deauration, inauration; metal composed of gold and copper, tambac, tambaqua; gold-refiner's name for a caract, siliqua; gold in mass, bullion; writing with gold, aurigraphy.

GOLDEN NUMBER. a. Enneadecaterides. (See cycle.)

GONE. p. And past, preterlapsed,

GOOD. a. Good cheer, dapatical; good state of the body, euchrasy, euchymy; good-natured, mansuette; good name, eudoxy, euphemism; speaking good and

holy things, sanctiloquent.

GOODNESS. s. Lover of goodness, philogathus.

GOODS. s. Goods found and unclaimed, waif; goods in pack, bale; place for landing goods, wharf, hithe; goods floating on the sea, flotson; goods from a shipwreck, jetsam, orjetson; goods thrown overboard when in danger of shipwreck, lagan; goods whereof immediate sale and profit may be made, manual goods; goods in the disposal of the wife, paraphernalia; goods sent over sea at the risk of a creditor, trajectitious goods.

GOVERNESS. s. Governante, moderatrix, tutoress.

GOVERNMENT, s. Dition, gubernation; government of a city or town, police; art of government, polity; bad government, misgovernment.

Governments may be either

Theocratic	in which God himself governs.
Eirenarchic	peaceable government,
Stratocratic	military government.
Aristocratic	government by the nobles.
Oligarchic	where a few principal persons govern.
Democratic	where the common people govern.
Monarchic } Dynastic }	kingly government.
Timocratic	where the richest individuals have rule.
Autocratic	where the state is governed by one having absolute and despotic power.
Dulocratic	where servants and slaves domineer.
Ethnarthic	termed a principality.
Heptarchic	or government of seven kings, as that of the Saxon kings in England.
Hierarchic	sacred government.
Republic, } Republican }	termed a commonwealth.
Optimatic	where the commonwealth is governed by nobles.
Utopian	immaculate government.
Ochlocratic, } Polygarchic }	where the multitude have rule.
Dinarchic, } Duarchic }	where the government is in the hands of two persons.
Triarchic	in the hands of three.

Gynæcocratic where women have the management, and in ridicule termed petticoat government.

Demonocratic where the government is so obnoxious as to resemble that of devils.

GOVERNOR. *s.* Toparch, dynastic, prefect; governor anciently in seaport towns, especially in London, portreve, or portgreve; governor or principal of a college, magnificus, gymnasiarch.

GOUT. *s.* Gout in the hip, sciatica, ichias.
— in the knee, gonagra.
— in the shoulder, omagra.
— in the feet, podagra.
— in the hands, chiragra.
— in the jaw, siagonagra.
— in the back, rhachisagra.
the wandering gout is termed arthritis planetica, or arthritis vaga; medicines good against the gout, antiarthritics, antipodagrica.

GOUTY. *a.* Arthritic, podagrical; goaty swelling in the ancles, talaria.

GRACE. *s.* Grace with beauty, pulchritude.
The graces are, Aglaia, Euphrosyne, and Thalia, feigned as being the goddesses of elegance, friendship, and handsome conversation.

GRACEFUL. *a.* Graceful flow of words, euphony.

GRACEFULNESS. *s.* Chroma; gracefulness of speech, charientismus.

GRADUAL. *a.* Gradual entrance, illapse.

GRAFT. *v.* To inoculate.

GRAFT. *s.* Scion, imp; grafts for striking into the clifts of trees, enthemata.

GRAFTED. *p.* Insitive. (See branch.)

GRAFTING *p.* Act of grafting, insition, ablactation.

GRAIN. *s.* Grain or produce of the ground, emblements; belonging to grain, frumentarious, frumentacious; bearing grain, graniferous; eating or living on grain, granivorous; abounding in grain, polypyrenous; having three grains or kernels, tricoccous; having four, quadricoccous, &c.; resembling grains, granulary; small grain or particle, granule; the weight of four grains among jewellers, but 24 among gold-refiners, carat.

GRAMMAR. *s.* To resolve a sentence according to the rules of grammar, to parse; speech or sentence contrary to the rules of grammar, solecism.
Grammar consists of four parts, viz.

Orthography { Teaches how words ought to be written, the true pronunciation of which is called orthoepy.

Etymology, Teaches their derivation.

Prosody, { The quantity and accent of syllables.

Syntax, { The due construction of words.

GRAMMARIAN. *s.* Humanist, philologer, philologist.

GRAND. *a.* August, palaceous, splendid, pompous, magnific; quality of being grand, magnality; grand of mein, portly; Grand Seignior's title, paudishaw; his foot guards, salachs, capiagi; palace where his women are kept, seraglio.

GRANT. *v.* To admit, to impart, to concede, to deign, to vouchsafe.

GRANT. *s.* Concession, donation, largess, indult, indulto, proviso, purview; grant in fee, infoedation; one to whom a grant is made, grantee.

GRAPES. *s.* Formed like a bunch of grapes, botryoid; bearing grapes, uviferous.

GRASS. *s.* Last crop of grass, eddish, edish; full of, or abounding in grass, gramineal, gramineous, herbose, herbulent; living on grass, graminivorous, phytivorous, herbivorous.

GRAVE. *a.* Demur, glum, matronal, bas, catonian, saturnine; affectedly grave, prudish.

GRAVELLY. *a.* Calculous, sabulous, scrupose; gravelly concretion which breeds in the bodies of animal, psammos.

GRAY. *a.* Roan, grizzle, liard, grey.

GRAVITY. *s.* The property directly opposite to gravity, levitation, or levity; relating to the center of gravity, centrobarycal.

GRAZE. *v.* Graze cattle by the week, to agist; graze or touch lightly upon, to perstringe.

GREASY. *a.* Adipose, gourdy, oleaginous, oleose, oleous, pinguid, queasy, unctuous; grease or fat of swine, saim; the black grease of carriage wheels, gome.

GREAT. *a.* Burly, dread, huge, elephantine, formidable, tremendous, enormous, herculean, vast, immense, immane, infinite, swinging, multipotent; very great, omnipotent, nimious; the quality of being great, magnifical, magnality, maximity.

GREATNESS. *s.* Amplitude, intensity; personal greatness, immediacy; greatness of soul, megalopsychy.

GREECE. *s.* Belonging or relating to Greece, hellenistic, hellenistical.

GREEDINESS. *s.* Avidity, edacity, adephagy, adephagis, gulosity, ligurition.

GREEDILY. *ad.* Feeding greedily, depascent.

GREEDY. *a.* Avaricious, avidulous, carnivorous, gormandizing, insatiate, insatiable, licherous, licorous, mercenary, rapacious, voracious, ravenous, questuary, envious.

GREEN. *a.* Of a light green colour, glaucous; green, vernant, virent, verdant; the general green appearance of the fields in spring, verdure, verdárous; green like grass, gramineal, gramineous; green like leeks, porraceous; green like an emerald, smaragdine; ever-green, sempervirent; green sickness, chlorosis, icterus, malacia, pica.

GREY. *a.* Roan, liard, grizzle, gray.

GRIEF. *s.* Dolor, anguish, heartache, egritude, penance, res'piscence, sollicito, contriteness; mutual grief, condolence, condoleance; that apathy, or state of mind on which grief never acts, dedolency; uncommon or extreme grief, pregravation; sort of sleepy potion which allays care and grief, nepenthe.

GRIEVE. *v.* To discomfort, to dole, to repine, to wail, to bewail.

GRIND. *v.* (See to bruize.)

GRITTY. *a.* Calculous, sabulous, tophaceous, scrupose. (See gravelly.)

GROGGY. *a.* Boosy, tap, maudlin.

GROIN. *s.* Swelling in the groin, generally from venereal infection, bubo; species of rupture when the intestines fall into the groin, bubonocele; belonging or relating to the groin, inguinal.

GROOM. *s.* Chief groom, equerry. (See horse.) groom of the bed-chamber to the Grand Seignior, capi-aga.

GROSS. *a.* Burly, burley, adipal, corpulent, crass, palpable, pursy, spiss, terrene, terrestrial.

GROSSNESS. *s.* Spissitude, crassitude, obeseness, obesity; grossness of body, polysarchy.

GROVE. *s.* Hoult, holt, barrow, boscade; relating to, or abounding in groves, nemoral, nemorose, nemorous.

GROUND. *s.* Ground after one crop has been taken off, etch; beam of timber laid next the ground in a building, grunsel, groundsel; lying under ground, subterraneous, subterranean; ground-plot, or draught of a building *in plano*, ichnography; small piece of ground inclosed with a hedge, pickle, pightel, pingle; the art and method of enriching ground by labour, emponema; belonging to the art of improving and manuring the ground, geoponical; term used of ground when the owner does not feed it with his own stock, but takes other cattle to graze, to gise the ground.

GROUNDS. *s.* (Dregs) fæces. (See dregs.)

GROWING. *p.* Growing together, accretion, aggeneration; a growing less, decrescent; growing near wells, fontige-nous; growing out under another, subnascent; growing together of the eyelids, lips, &c or the adhesion of the ears to the head preternaturally, coloboma.

GROWTH. *s.* One of full growth and age, adult; preternatural growth on any plant or animal, supercrescence.

GRUB UP. *v.* To assart. (See root.)

GRUDGE. *v.* To grunch.

GRUDGE. *s.* odium, pique, enmity.

GRUNT. *v.* To grunt as a boar at rutting-time, to fream.

GUARD. *s.* Defensive, escort; private soldier on guard, sentinel, sentry; the foot-guards of the Grand Seignior, capiagi, salachs; night guard performed by a whole army, when there is apprehension of danger, biovag, bihovac.

GUARDING. *p.* Guarding or surrounding, stipation, tutelar, tutelary; guarding or preventive, prophylactic.

GUESS. *v.* To conjecture, to divine, to preominate, to presage, to prognosticate.

GUIDE. *s.* Guide in Italy to travellers, veturino.

GUIDING *p.* The guiding or driving any carriage, aurigation.

GUESSING. *p.* Guessing from an idea impressed on one's mind, thymomancy. (See divination.)

GUILTY. *a.* Criminous, culpable, nocent, nocive, nocuous, noxious, peccaminous, peccant.

GULF or GULPH. *s.* Abyss, abysm, gurge, sinus, syrtis; full of gulphs, voraginous.

GUMS. *s.* Relating to the gums, gingival; swelling of the gums, paradontis; itching of the gums, when children breed teeth, odaximus.

GUN. *s.* Gun or musket, carabine; bore of a gun, gunchase; the firing of guns, displosion; act of driving nails into the touchhole of guns, to render them useless, spiking; stopper for the mouth or muzzle of great guns, tampion, tamkin, tompion, tomkin; bundle of rags, &c. put over the powder and ball in a gun, to prevent the charge from shifting forwards, wad, wadding; the two projecting semicircular pieces of metal on the top of some great guns, resembling handles, maniglions; the projecting pieces of metal on which a great gun rests on its carriage, trunnions. (See cannon.)

GUNNER. *s.* Gunner's term for a train of powder rolled up in a pitched cloth, saucisse; method used by gunners for blowing a spike out of the touchhole of a great gun, by a train laid from the muzzle of the piece, uncloying.

GUT. *v.* To eviscerate, to exenterate, to viscerate.

GUTS. *s.* Entrails, intestines, viscera, garbage, offals, humbles; the small guts, chitterlings, ilia; the lowest gut in the deer kind, inchipin; membrane enveloping the guts, mesentery, peritoneum; twisting of the guts, vermiculation, mulligrubs; rumbling of the guts, borborygmus; the vermicular or spiral motion of the guts, which tends to void the excrements, peristaltic motion; discourse concerning the guts, spanchnology.

GUTTER. *s.* Small gutter, rindle.

H

HABIT. *s.* Increment, apparel, consuetude, practice, guise, vesture, investment, habitude, ure; habit or constitution of the body, schesis, hexis; that part of physic which teaches how to acquire a good habit of body, evectica; good habit of body, euchrasy or euchymy; an ill habit of body, cachexy or cachexia, intemperies.

HABITABLE. *a.* Inhabitable; this word means also not habitable, (Bailey.)

HABITATION. *s.* Biding, bye, inhabitance.

HABITUAL. *a.* Hectic.

HACK. *v.* To carbonade, to gride.

HAG. *s.* Beldam, lamia.

HAIL. *s.* Abounding in, grandinose or grandinous.

HAIR. *s.* Set with strong hairs, setaceous; resembling hair, capillaceous, capillary, cilicious; deprived of hair, depilous; having the hair in a disordered state, dishevelled; to mat or entangle the hair, to elf; term given for the hair of a beautiful woman, when hanging in ringlets on the breast and shoulders, heart-breakers; curl of hair, ringlet; having short hair (bald) peeled; a falling off of the hair from any part of the body, phalacrotis, or phalacrosis, defluvium; when the hair of the eye-lids grows inwards, and is troublesome to the eyes, phalangosis, this word also means a double or triple row of the eye-lashes (Quincy); medicines which have the effect of eradicating hairs, are called, ectilotica; disease of the hair when it splits at the ends, dichophyia; ointment to take away hairs, smith, depilatory; act of cutting or shaving the hair, tonsure; lock of hair, tuz or tuzz; hair hanging down loosely, tresses; fracture of a bone, so small as to resemble a hair, trichysmus; term used for any plant having leaves like hair, trichophyllon; term used for a double row of hair on the eye-lids, distichia; an ingredient of a composition, to take off hair, without the trouble of shaving, rusma (for a particular account of this, see Quincy's Lexicon); thread or stuff made o goat or camel's hair, mohair; disease which makes the hair to fall off, ophiasis, alopecia or alopechy; the standing up of the hair of the head through terror, as is the case in quartan fevers, horripilation; (see Quartana Continua, Quincy); instrument called tweezers, used in pulling out hairs, acantabolus.

HAIRINESS. *s.* Pilosity.

HAIRY. *a.* Faxed, hirsute, crinated, crinigerous, crinosed, villose, vellous, hispid, shagged, shaggy.

HALBERD or HALBARD. *s.* Partisan.

HALF. *s.* Mediety, moiety, demi, semi, subduple or subduplicate; half-drunk, semi-bousie; half a circle, semicircle; half of the circumference, semicircumference; half burnt, semiustulate, or semicombust; half a gallon, semicongius; half conspicuous, semiconspicuous; half round, semiannular; half bath, in which the patient sits only up to the middle, semicubium; half diameter, semidiameter, called also the radius; half transparent, semidiaphanous; half formed, semiformed; half a globe, semiglobular; formed like a half moon, semilunar; half males, i. e. eunuchs, semimares; belonging somewhat to the sea, semimarine; half dark, semiopacous; consisting of a foot and a half, semipedal; half a line (in poetry) hemistic; belonging to half a sphere, semispherical; half a sphere, hemisphere; half an ounce, 'semis' or semissis; half a tone, semitone or hemitone; containing three halves, sesquialteral; containing three half feet, sesquipedal.

HALL. *s.* Large hall or church, basilic; hall among the Turks and Persians, in which their court of justice is held, divan; lofty spacious hall, salon or saloon.

HALT. *v.* To claudicate.

HALTER. *s.* Laqueus.

HALVED. *p.* Bifidated.

HAMMER. *v.* To malleate; to work or bray with a hammer, to tudiculate.

HAMMER. *s.* A large hammer used by smiths, sledge; capable of bearing the hammer, malleable.

HANDS. *s.* Divination by the wrinkles and marks on the hands, chiromancy, palmistry; seated on the right hand, dextral; on the left, sinister or sinistrous; the hand or pen of a dial, gnomon; having long hands, longimanous; slight of hand practised by jugglers, legerdemain; chains for the hands, manacles; coarse and large hands, mutton fists; done by the hand, manual; guidance by the hand, manuduction; holding by the hand, manutention; hand whose beauty no phrase can express, is termed, a phraseless hand; using both hands, ambidextrous; the gout in the hand, chiragra; a talking by signs made with the hands, chirology; the state of being left-handed, scævity, sinister; small quantity taken up in the hand, pugil.

HANDICRAFT. *s.* Manualist, artisan.

HANDFUL. *s.* Maniple.

HANDLE. *v.* To palm.

HANDLE. *s.* Haft or heft; handle of a sword, hilt; having handles, ansated.

HANDKERCHIEF. *s.* Dirty handkerchief, muckender.

HANDLING. *p.* Frequent handling or feeling, attrectation; handling or manual operation, in opposition to mere theory, manipulation.

HANDSEL. *s.* Earnest money.

HANDSOME. *a.* To make handsome, to adonize; handsome, beauteous, bonny; a handsome ordering or disposing of things, eutaxy.

HANG. *v.* To hang on, to append; to hang from, to depend; hang over, to impend; to hang over or delay, to suspend; proverbial expression, signifying to hang a man first, and judge him afterwards, Lidford-law.

HANGING. *p.* Pendent, pendulous, pendable; the state of hanging over, impendence; hanging (suspended) pensil or pensile; hanging downwards, proclive; hanging down as icicles, stirious.

HANGER. *s.* A hanger on, trencher fly, parasite.

HANGMAN. *s.* Ketch, Jack-ketch, nubbing cove. (Cant word); hangman, or executioner in an army, provost.

HANNIBAL. *s.* Name of the feigned deity worshipped by the ancient Romans, who frighted Hannibal from Rome, Rediculu

HAPPEN. *v.* To bechance, to befal, to befortune, to betide, to continge.

HAPPINESS. *s.* Auspiciousness, beatitude, weal, faustitude.

HAPPY. *a.* Beatific, halcyon; to make happy, to imparadise.

HARANGUE. *s.* Declamation; the harangue of a general to his soldiers, allocution.

HARASS. *v.* To harrow, to jade, to infest, to surbate, to pester.

HARBOUR. *v.* To nestle, to shroud.

HARBOUR. *s.* Haven; having no harbours, importuous.

HARD. *a.* (Difficult) abstruse, difficil, perplexed; hard (firm) sclerotic, findy, fodient; hard, (knotty) geniculated, nodose, nodous; hard as adamant, adamantian; hard (not to be pierced) impervious, impenetrable; a collection of matter forming a hard and round body, conglobation; hard as iron, ferreous; hard (gritty) sabulous, tophaceous; hard (frozen) frore, frorne, glaciated; hard (burdensome or oppressive) onerose, onerous; hard as bone, osseous; hard as stone, petrescent; hard (cruel) remorseless; hard (flinty) silicious; hard as a mass of horn, solidungulous; hard (scaly) squamose, squamous; hard-hearted, marble-hearted, obdurate.

HARDEN. *v.* To indurate, to congeal, to glaciate, to insinew; to harden by long continuance, to inveterate.

HARDENED. *p.* Impenitent, obdurate.

HARDNESS. *s.* Brawniness, callosity, durity, impenetrability, imperviousness, imporosity; having the hardness or properties of adamant, adamantine; hardness or calosity of the joints, epiporoma; hardness of the skin, induced by much labour, as on the palm of the hands, &c. tylus.

HARE. *s.* Belonging to a hare, leporine, leporean; cant name for a hare, puss; the tail of a hare, scut; young hare, leveret; to take out the bowels of a hare, to hulk; to trace the steps of a hare (among sportsmen) to prick; the passing of a hare through a hedge, is termed by huntsmen, musing; term used for a cleft in the lip of some people resembling that of the hare, *labia, leporino.*

HARLOT. *s.* Leman (from l'aiman, *Fr.*) lupanatrix.

HARM. *s.* Annoyance, nocument.

HARMLESS. *a.* Blameless, innocuous, innoxious, offenceless, undisobliging.

HARMONIOUS. *a.* Melodious, rythmical.

HARMONY. *s.* Accord, concert, amity, numerosity, symmetry, symphony.

HARNESS. *s.* Complete harness, panoply; harness for a horse, ephippium.

HARNESSING. *p.* Act of, lorication.

HARP. *s.* Belonging to one, lyric or lyrical; poet who writes songs to the harp, lyric; musician who plays upon the harp, lyrist.

HARPSICHORD. *s.* The keys of organs and harpsichords, tastatura.

HARROWING. *p.* The art of harrowing or breaking of clods, occation.

HARSH *a.* Absonous or absonant, incongruous, discordant, dissonant, immusical or unmusical, grating; harsh or rough to the palate, acerb, austere; harsh or rough as some plants, asperous; sounding harsh, halsening; harsh (noisy) streperous; harsh (void of tenderness) inclement, stern; harsh (not pleasant to the ear) inharmonious or unharmonious, scabrous.

HARSHNESS. *s.* Tetricity.

HARVEST. *s.* Ingathering; harvest-supper, medsyppe; of or belonging to harvest, messorious.

HASTE. *s.* Hastiness, expedience, immaturity, pernicity, precipitance or precipitancy, rapture; great haste (hunting phrase) tivy, contracted from tantivy; done with haste, noise, and irregularity, tumultuary; done with too much haste, immaturely.

HASTEN. *v.* To accelerate, to hie, to dispatch or despatch, to maturate, to precipitate, to properate, or approperate.

HASTILY. *ad.* Apace.

HASTY. *a.* Abrupt, cursory, ejaculatory, festinate, heady; indeliberate or undeliterate, unpremeditated, precipitate, precipitous; too hasty, subitaneous, temerareous, immature, premature, preproperous.

HAT. *s.* Covered as with a hat, galericulate, pileated; the stuff which hats are made of, felt; hats made of Spanish wool, vigone or vigogne.

HATCH. *v.* To incubate.

HATCH. *s.* Brood, covey, bevy.

HATCHET. *s.* Bill; divination by hatchets, axinomancy.

HATE. *v.* To abhor, to absonate, to disdain, to lothe, or loathe.

HATEFUL. *a.* Abominable, accursed, confounded, odible, execrable, nauseous, odious, repudious, hainous or heinous.

HATRED. *s.* Animosity, detestation, enmity, aversion, hostility, despitefulness, feud, odium, ire, malevolence, mislike, inveteracy, invidiousness, malignity, rancor or rancour; hatred to mankind, aphilanthrophy or misanthropy.

HAUGHTY. *a.* Imperious, luciferian, misproud, arrogant, elate, fastidious, assuming, cavalier, orgillous, supercilious, uppish; a very haughty person, lordan, or lordant; using a haughty stile of language, grandiloquous.

To haul up quickly by means of 'ithout the assistance of a pulley,

HAVOC. *s.* Carnage, internecion.

HAUTBOY. *s.* Piva.

HAWK. *s.* To purge a hawk, to enseam; young hawk just taken from the nest, eyas or ias hawk; hawk trained for sport, falcon; the art of training of hawks, falconry; name of a small sort of bastard hawk, kestrel; to eke or add a feather to the wing of a hawk, to imp; method of enticing hawks to return to the hand, leure; rise or ascent of a hawk, mounty; the male of the sparrow hawk, musket; name for an old stanch hawk, make hawk; to pinion the wings of a hawk, to mayl; place where hawks are kept, mew; to dung as hawks, to mute; the hard breathing of a hawk (term in falconry) pantas or pantais; name for a hawk of the falcon or game kind, peregrine; the toes of a hawk, petty singlers; sort of disease which attacks the foot of a hawk, pinne; term used of a hawk when he seizes his quarry, and pulls the feathers, hair, &c. of its body, pluming; when a hawk dresses or sets its feathers in order, it is said to proin or preen; any fowl, &c. flown at, and killed by a hawk, is called its quarry; to recover a hawk to the fist, to rabate; hawk that is wild and coy, is called a ramage hawk; gravel given to a hawk to assist digestion, rangle; male hawks are named, jerkins or tiercelets; name given among falconers to the first year of every hawk, soreage; hood put upon a hawk when first drawn, rufterhood; a nest of hawks, ayry or aerie; the pinion of a hawk's wing, sircel; term in falconry for a hawk which has not as yet cast her first feathers, sore hawk; the stroke or dash of a hawk on its prey, swoop; silver rings round the legs of a hawk, with the owner's name engraven on them, varvels or verveles.

HAZARD. *s.* Adventure, jeopardy, periclitation.

HAZARDOUS. *a.* Insecure or unsecure, periculous, perilous.

HAZY. *a.* Nebulous, nebulose. (See cloudy)

HEAD. *s.* Head or height of a disease, &c. acme; heads of a subject, epitome; belonging to the head, cephalic; the top of the head, coryphe; of or belonging to the top of the head, coronal; the head, costard, pate; scurf on the head, dandriff or dandruff, furfur; discharge of scurff from the head, furfuration; giddiness in the head, dinus; knot of ribband, worn on the head, favor, favour, fontange; feigned monster with many heads, hydra; dropsy in the head, hydrocephalus; head of a salmon, jowl; baldness of the head, madarosis; the point of the heavens right over the head, zenith; head (in contempt) noddle, pate, sconce; the cutting off the head, obtruncation; belonging to the hind part of the head, occipital; to the fore part, sincipital; to hold up the head with an affected air, to perk; head of a ship, prore, prow; an operation formerly performed for relieving inflammation in the eyes, which consisted in an incision being made across the fore part of the head, from one temple to the other, peri-scyphismus; heads of a discourse, sylla-bus; a membrane covering the head of the fœtus, or new-born infant, betoken-ing happiness, sillyhow; name given to that part of the amnios which sticks to an infant's head when new born, vitta; the preternatural adhesion of the ears to the head, so as to be scarcely distinguishable, coloboma; one who has a remarkably large head, macrocephalus.

HEADACH. s. Cephalalgy, cephalæa, ce-phalopony or homonopagia.

HEADLAND s, Promontory, cape, neeze, ness.

HEADLESS. a. (Without ruler.) Acepha-lous.

HEADSTRONG. a. Pervicacious, temera-rious, refractory, restiff, restive, resty, si-nistrous.

HEADY. a. Passionate man, hotspur.

HEAL. v. To cicatrize, to doctor, to lech.

HEALED. a. Mark of a healed wound, es-char; that cannot be healed, immedi-cable; that may be healed, medicable, sanable.

HEALING. p. Epulotic.

HEALTH. s. One who being sick, is soon restored to health and strength, euanas-phaltos; health, invalescence, sanity; good state of health, valetude; the act of drinking one's health, is called, brindice; return to health, convalescence; that de-viation from a certain standard or weight and bulk, which a person cannot admit of, without falling into disease, is termed, by physicians, the Latitude of Health; art of preserving health, diateretics; bring-ing or conducing to health, salutiferous; that part of medicine which preserves health by exercise, gymnastics; that part of physic which gives rules for the pre-servation of health, synteretics; one who is always anxious about his health, vale-tudinarian; that part of physic which shows the way of living fit for old men, in order to preserve their health, geronto-comy; that part of physic which teaches the way of preserving health, Hygiena; and is divided by some into three parts, viz. prophylactic, synteretic, and analep-tic; what tends to preserve health, hygi-

astic; that particular temperament of body which constitutes good health, hy-giea. (For the origin of drinking healths, see Drink.)

HEALTHY. a. Chopping, crank, laudable, salubrious, salutary, salutiferous, sane; the healthy state of any animal body, ulome-lia.

HEAP. v. To heap together, to accumulate, to acervate, to coacervate, to cumulate, to congest, to coagment, to exaggerate, to aggravate, to gove, to aggerate.

HEAP. s. Amassment, cluster; heap or ac-cumulation of arguments, sorites; con-fused heap, a farrago, a macaronic.

HEAPED. p. Heaped up, aggested; matter heaped up, (obstruction) oppilation.

HEARING. p. Medicines to help hearing, also the term for the doctrine of sounds, acoustics; instruments to help hearing by magnifying the sound, microcoustics or otacoustics; difficulty or dulness of hear-ing, dysecoia.

HEARKENING. p. Or listening, ausculta-tion.

HEART. s, Or inner part of any thing, core; the dilatation of the heart is termed, dia-stole or dyastole; contraction of it, is termed, systole; membrane that surrounds the heart, pericardium; heart, liver, and lights, pluck, (Johnson); palpitation of the heart, palmos; the faculty or power of knowing the heart, cardiagnostic; to fix in the heart, to incardiate.

HEARTBURN. s. Cardialgia.

HEAT. v. To Chafe; to effervesce, to calify.

HEAT. s. Esture, excandescence, ardency, ardour, broil, fervor, fervidness; great heat, calidity; boiling by heat, exestu-ation, or exestication; instrument for measuring extreme degrees of heat, pyro-meter; shining from heat, gleening; in-creasing heat, incalescence; heat (fury) incensement; suffocating heat, pother; great heat of the weather, sultriness; gentle heat, tepidity, tepor; instrument for measuring heat and cold, psychrome-ter, thermometer, thermoscope; instru-ment for measuring different degrees of heat or caloric, calorimeter; term given to the natural heat of animals, biolych-nium; what decreases heat, refrigerant; heat (anxiety with confidence) sanguine-ness, sanguinity; in a heat or passion, fumingly; that innate heat supposed to be produced in a child in the womb, ther-mon-emphyton; heat raised to ignition, ustion; medicines which cause heat, ther-mantics; that natural heat which is mea-sured or perceived by the pulse, thermo-metron.

L

HEATHEN. *a.* and *s.* Of or belonging to the heathen, ethnic.

HEATING. *p.* Calorific.

HEAVEN. *s* The highest heaven empyreum ; the heavens, expanse, firmament ; a configuration of the heavens taken at the hour of birth, horoscope ; description of the heavens, ouranography ; contemplation or viewing of the heavens, uranoscopy.

HEAVENLY. Ethereal, ethereous, supernal, beatific, celestial, divine, empyreal, supramundane.

HEAVINESS. *s.* Hebitude, lentitude, lentor ; heaviness or grief, dolor ; heaviness, (dullness) indocility, surdity ; heaviness (drowsiness) somnolence or somnolency.

HEAVY. *a* Fatkidneyed, blockish, doltish, clumsy, cumberous, obtuse, inert, oscitant, loutish, gravid, burley, massy or massive, spiss, torpid ; heavy (sorrowful) dampy ; heavy (sleepy) lethargic ; heavy (burdensome) onerose, pressitant, ponderous, onerous ; heavy, (cloudy) nubiferous ; heavy, (dull) saturnine, phlegmatic ; heavy (gross) pursy ; heavy, (procreant) teemful ; heavy, (lazy) desideose, desidious ; heavy, (sad) tristful ; to make heavy, to degravate ; the line a heavy body is supposed to descend in, without acceleration, is called, an isochronal line.

HEBREW. *a.* Of or belonging to the Hebrew tongue, Ebraick or Ebraical ; one versed in Hebrew, Hebraist, Hebrecian.

HECTOR. *v.* To brustle, to crackle.

HECTOR. *s.* Brave, huffer, bravo.

HEDGE. *s.* Sepiment ; small piece of ground inclosed with a hedge, pickle, pightel, or pingle.

HEEDFUL. *a.* Attent, attentive, vigilant.

HEEDLESS. *a.* Reckless, incautious, inconsiderate, incurious, indolent, listless, perfunctory, temerarious, uncautious.

HEELS. *s.* Sore heels occasioned by cold, kibes or chilblains ; to kick with the heel, to recalcitrate : heels over head, arseversy or arsy-versy.

HEIGHT. *s.* Celsitude, altitude, ascendant, (Temple) elevation, eminence, excelsity ; great height, superlation ; height of stature, procerity ; the art of measuring heights, altimetry ; instrument for measuring heights, pantometer ; the art of measuring heights and distances by piecemeal, cultellation ; the measuring of heights by means of staves, baculometry ; the height of a disease, acme, crisis, exacerbation ; the height of a play is called the counter-turn. (For the instruments used in taking the angles in measuring of heights and distances, see angles.)

HEINOUS. *a.* Hainous, atrocious, nefandous, nefarious ; any heinous crime is called a piacle.

HEIR. *s.* Joint heir, co-heir.

HELL. *s.* Abyss or abysm, Gehenna (Hebrew), Manes (Lat.), Pandæmonium ; Tophet, (used allegorically as being the name of the valley where the Ammonites sacrificed their children) ; hell is also called Avernus by the poets ; the border of hell is named, Limbo ; poetical name for one of the rivers in hell, Acheron or Acheruns, Gr. ; of or belonging to that river, Acherontic ; the feigned judges in hell are, Rhadamanthus, Æacus, and Minos.

HELLISH. *a.* Stygian, infernal, tartarean.

HELMET. *s.* Morion or murrion ; covered as with a helmet, galeated.

HELP. *v.* To abet, to adjute or adjuvate, to conduce, to rede, to assist.

HELP. *s.* Adjument, adminicle, subvention, succour, opitulation ; united help, coadjuvancy ; bringing help, opiferous.

HELPER. *s.* Adjutant, coadjutor, concurrence, myrmidon, paranymph.

HELPING. *p.* Accessory, auxiliary, subservient, collateral, subsidiary, inservient, relevant.

HELPLESS. *a.* Aidless, forlorn ; in a helpless situation, lurch.

HEMP. *s.* Comb for dressing hemp, hitchel or hatchel ; refuse of hemp, hurds.

HERALD. *s.* Pursuivant.

HERBAGE. *s.* Term for, agistment ; divination by herbs and plants, botonomancy ; of, or belonging to herbs, botanical, herbaceous ; eating or devouring herbs, herbivorous.

HERDS. *s.* Going in herds, gregarious ; herd of colts, rag ; of goats, trip.

HEREDITARY. *a.* Gentilitious, endemical.

HERETIC. *s.* Infidel ; chief heretic, heresiarch.

HERITAGE. *s.* Cleromancy.

HERMAPHRODITAL. *a.* Androgynous.

HERMAPHRODITE. *s.* Andria.

HERMIT. *s.* Anchorite, solitaire, F. solitary, ascetic, eremite ; female hermit, hermitess.

HERO. *s.* Champion ; of or belonging to a hero, agonistic or agonistical.

HERON. *s.* Place where herons or herns breed, hernshaw, hernery.

HERRINGS. *s.* The quantity of 500 herrings is called a mease.

HETERODOX. *a.* Unorthodox.

HICCUP. *s.* Singultus or syngultus.

HID. *p.* Covert ; state of lying hid, latinancy ; lying hid, latinant.

HIDDEN. *a.* Abstruse, cryptic, enigmatical, inscrutable, latent, occult, sepilible, talismantic, cryptical ; hidden or masked, visored, private.

HIDE. *v.* To hide, to abscond, to skulk, to ensconce, to obduce, to disguise, to envelope, to enwomb, to hoodwink, to immask, to inhumate or inhume ; hide (cloud over) to obumbrate.

HIDEOUS. *a.* Grisly, horrent, horrible, horrid ; to render or make hideous, to bemonster.

HIDING. *p.* That has the power of hiding, abdative.

HIGH. *a.* Aerial, eminent, arduous, celestial, presumptuous, orgillous, uppish ; high raised or pointed, copatain ; high and bombastic language, fustian.

HIGHEST. Meridional, supreme.

HIGHNESS. *s.* (Height) celsitude. (See height.)

HILL. *s.* Little hill, hilloc, hommoc, monticle ; born on the hills, montigenous ; wandering on the hills, montivagant ; hill or high land jutting into the sea, promontory ; ridge or edge of a hill, ambe ; full of hills, tumulose.

HINDER. *v.* To embar, to blockade, to counteract, to debar, to let, to incommode, to infringe, to inhibit, to preclude, to prohibit, to retard, to obviate ; what hinders, prevenient.

HINDERANCE. *s.* Retardation, intercision, cumbrance, detention, embargo, impediment ; cause of hindrance, interpellation, let, obstacle, intercipient.

HINDERING. *p.* Quality of hindering, obstruent.

HINT. *v.* To hint at, to allude, to insinuate, to suggest.

HINT. *s.* Memoir, caveat, moniment, allusion, cue, inkling, inuendo, item, admonition, advice.

HIRE. *v.* To hire out, to ablocate or oblocate ; to hire or bribe, to retain, to hire out for vile purposes, to prostitute.

HIRE. *s.* Fare, bribe ; hire given to a guide, guidage ; a letting out to hire, location.

HIRED. *p.* Conductitious ; hired murderer, bravo ; that cannot be hired out, illocable.

HIRELING. *a.* Mercenary.

HISS. *v.* To explode, to decry ; to hiss off the stage, &c., to exsibilate.

HISSING. *p.* Sibilant.

HISTORIAN. *s.* Historiographer.

HISTORY. *s.* The history of family descendants, genealogy, pedigree ; the secret history of one or more persons, anecdote ; history of events, chronicle ; to record in history, to historify ; the science of computing time since the creation, &c. for the establishment of true dates in history, chronology ; any short history, nar-

ration, or narrative ; a lover of history, philo-historicus.

HIT. *v.* To hit at a mark, to collimate, to hurtle ; to hit or wound, to inflict ; to hit, (in fencing), to butt.

HOARINESS. *s.* Or mouldiness, vinew.

HOARSE. *a.* Guttural, streperous.

HOARSENESS. *s.* Raucity, asaphy.

HOARY. *a.* Finewed, liard, roan, mucid.

HOBGOBLINS. *s* Lemures.

HOG. *s.* A hog dressed whole, barbecue ; hog's lard, saim.

HOG-STYE. *s.* Frank.

HOLD. *v.* To occupate ; to hold together, to cleave, to clinch, to hend ; to hold in a string as dogs, to leash ; to hold out or contend, to obtend ; to hold out or stretch out, to protend ; the act of laying hold of, prehensile ; hold (support) retinacle.

HOLDING. *p* The act of holding or keeping off, abstension ; the act of holding or keeping a holiday, feriation ; holding fast, tenacious.

HOLE. *s.* Cranny, dell, foramen, aperture, sinus, terebration ; the making of holes, (as rabbits, &c. do,) burrowing ; to drive out from holes, to ferret ; full of lurking holes, latebrous ; full of holes, multicavous or multiforous ; hole made by a punch, pertusion ; hole made by a very small instrument, puncture ; bored with holes, pertused ; breathing hole, spiracle, suspiral ; to make a hole through any thing, to transforate.

HOLINESS. *s.* Sanctimony, sanctitude, sanctity.

HOLLOW. *v.* To dint, to excavate, to tubulate.

HOLLOW. *a.* Vacuous, cavernous, cavous, dishing ; hollow in the inside, concave ; on both sides, concavo-concave ; hollow on one side, and raised on the other, concavo-convex ; hollow on one side, and plain on the other, plano-concave (see glass) ; hollow between hills, dingle ; any hollow or cavity, lisne ; hollow made with any tool, grove or groove ; hollowed like a tile, imbricated ; made hollow, incavated or excavated.

HOLLOWED. *a.* Hollowed (as a furrow) sulcated.

HOLY. *a.* Hymnic, devotional, immaculate ; writer of sacred or holy things, hagiographer ; speaking holy things, santiloquent.

HOLY GHOST. *s.* Paraclete ; heretics in the 11th century who denied the divinity of the Holy Ghost, Macedonians ; heretics who held Melchisedeck to be the Holy Ghost, Melchizedecians.

HOME. *s.* One who never was from home, nest-cock.

HOMELY. *a.* Villatick.

HONEST. *a.* Incorrupt, uncorrupt, unequivocal, impartial, or unpartial ; seemingly honest and fair, plausible ; not honest, uningenuous.

HONEY. *s.* Liquor made from honey and water, hydromel, mead, metheglen ; producing honey, melliferous, mellific ; act of making honey, mellification ; consistof, mellean, melleous ; flowing with, mellifluent, or mellifluous ; of the same kind or nature as honey, melligenous ; any juice or liquor boiled up to the consistence of honey, mellago ; the time or season of taking honey out of hives, mellation ; wine mingled with honey, mellitism, or mellitismus ; wine mingled and boiled up with honey, mulse ; vinegar boiled up with honey, oxymel ; drink made of honey, &c. sometimes taken before meals, propoma ; formed like a honey comb, fav form.

HONOUR. *v.* To dignify, to revere ; to honour with a degree, to graduate.

HONOUR. *s.* Honor, eminence, ennoblement, laud, reputation ; the love of honour, philotomy ; ladies of honour, palasins.

HONOURABLENESS. *s.* Honorificabilitudinity, (Bailey) ; this is the only word in the English language that can be called an Hendecasyllabon. (See words.)

HOODED. *a.* Cuculated, galeated, kerchiefed, kerchieft.

HOOF. *s.* The hollow of an animals hoof, particularly of the horse, frog ; deprived of the hoof, exungulated ; having an entire hoof, (not cloven), solidungulous, solipedous, or solipedal.

HOOK. *v,* To enunciate.

HOOK. *s.* Crotch, tach or tache ; hook or grappling iron used in sea fights, grapnel ; hook used by clothiers for stretching clothes on, tenterhook ; iron hook used in securing large fishes, gaff ; hook for drawing a dead child out of the womb, uncus, or ungula ; hook for cutting pease, meak.

HOOKED. *p.* Hamated, aquiline, falcated,

HOOPED. *p.* Hooped petticoat formerly worn by ladies, fardingale, from *Vertue garde,* F.

HOPE. *v.* To dispensate, to affiance.

HOPE. *s.* Affiance, reliance ; term used for the forlorn hope of an army, *les enfans perdus d'une armée.*

HOPED. *p.* That may be hoped for, sperable.

HOPELESS. *a.* (State of distress or want,) dead lift ; hopeless deplorable, despairful; hopeless state, despondence, or despondency.

HOPPER *s.* Hopper of a mill, tremella, er, trementa.

HORNED. *a.* Cornuted ; general name for horned cattle, rotherbeasts ; horns of a buck, attire ; to cast the horns, to mew ; having one horn, unicornus ; having two horns, bicornous ; three, &c. as some sheep, tricornous, &c. ; bearing horns, cornigerous ; belonging to the class of animals which have horns, cornigenous ; horn of plenty, cornucopia ; horn of the moon, cusp ; little horn, cornicle ; horned mooney, cornuted ; broad horned beasts, platycerotes ; the horns or feelers of insects, antennæ ; those animals which have their horns turned backwards and forwards again, as rams, are termed reciprocicornous.

HORNS. *s.* Having horns like bulls, tauricornous.

HORNY. *a.* Corneous, corniculated.

HORRIBLE. *a.* Atrocious, inexpiable, nefandous, nefarious, horrendous, dire, grisly, plaguy, tremendous.

HORRID. *a.* Effraiable, faxed, hainous, heinous, ghastly, mortiferous, sightless, vellose, villous ; any living object which has a horrid appearance, gorgon, in allusion to the three daughters of Phorcus and Cete, viz. Euryale, Medusa, and Stheno, who had only one eye among them.

HORROR. *s.* Direness ; horror of countenance, ghastliness ; causing horror, horrific.

HORSE. *s.* The little horny excrescence on the inside of a horse's knee, osselets ; superb dress for a horse, caparison ; covering for a horse, housing ; horse troops, cavalry ; a leap from one horse to another, desulture ; keeper of the horse to the king, equerry ; horse that draws between the shafts of a carriage, fillerhorse ; a horse under 14 hands high is called a galloway, garran, or hobby, (Johnson) ; the fabulous monster of half man half horse, Hippocentaur ; the feigned winged horse of Milton, hippogriff, pegasus ; horse soldier in Ireland, hobbler ; place for lodging of horses, hostry ; dealer in horses, jockey ; horse doctor, leech ; spare horse, leer horse ; person who takes care of horses at stabling, ostler, from hotelier, F. an inn-keeper, or from oatstealer, Grose's Vulg. Dict. ; horse trained for ladies, palfrey, or palfry; dull bad horse, malt horse ; curb, to keep down a horse's head, martingale ; names for the river horse, (a large amphibious animal found about the Nile), hippopotamus, morse; the act or art of training a horse, or place where trained, manege, F. ; the goddess of Horses, hippona ; the prancing and leaping of a mettled horse, pannade, salts ; horse hired for travelling post-hackney, horse that goes easy, pad-nag ; the exercise of vaulting the wooden horse, laying only one hand over the pommel of the saddle, pomada ; horses placed at different distances on a road to relieve others, relay ; said of a horse when he pushes backwards in the draught, &c. restive, resty, or restiff; sort of poultice for horses, remolade ; a particular gait or tread made by a horse in going sideways round a centre, volt ; sort of bit or curb used for horses, scatch ; place for the running of race horses, hippodrome ; bridle which crosses the nose of a horse, snaffle ; place where oats are kept for horses, avery ; horse harness of any kind, ephippium ; horse made use of for the purpose of getting near game, stalking horse ; officer in the king's stables who provides oats for the horses, avenor ; horse which has not been gelded, stoat or stallion ; an inclosed place where horses are run for prizes, catadrome ; horse for carrying necessaries on a journey, sumpter-horse; those employed in carrying camp-cullinary apparatus, &c. bat-horses ; the horse which draws between the shafts of a carriage, thiller horse ; the act of ambling in a horse, tolutation ; horse that hath two white feet, one on either side, is called a traversed horse ; name for a horse's yard, byental ; leathern cover for a horse's tail, trousequeue, F. ; horse-doctor, hirer, or courser, veterinarius ; one who lets out horses, and also acts as a guide to travellers, veturino ; Turkish light horse, the avant-guard of the Grand Seignior's army, acangii ; a particular leap in which a maneged horse appears to throw out his hind feet, showing the shoes, balotade ; the name of the famous horse of Alexander the Great, from its head resembling that of an ox, Bucephalus ; a worn out worthless horse, harridan ; four pronged iron instrument thrown in the way of an enemy's horse to lame them, caltrops ; the famous poison or love-doze used by the ancients, which is said to have been procured from the forehead of a young horse or mare, hippomanes.

HORSEBACK. *s.* Procession on horseback, cavalcade ; on horseback, equestrian, cock-horse ; block by which one mounts on horseback, jossing-block ; a contest on horseback, hippomachy ; such disorders as are incident to much riding on horseback, hippuris ; a particular affection of the eyes which makes objects shake as if one were on horseback, hippus.

HORSEMAN. *s.* Light horseman, pricker ; horseman completely armed, cataphract ; horseman -cavalier, chevalier; horse-ra-

cer, courser ; inferior horsemen who serve in the Grand Seignior's court, ulufagi.

HOSPITAL. *s.* For those who are suspected of the plague, lazaretto, pest-house ; hospital for poor sick people, nosocomium ; for poor old people, gerontocomium.

HOSPITALITY. *s.* Philoxeny, xenodochy.

HOT. *a,* (Bitter) acrid ; hot, (burnt up) arid, adusted, callid, epispastic, fervent, ardent, fervid, furious, phrenetic ; growing hot by fermentation, incalescent ; hot and dry seasons, inustion ; very hot or irascible, splenic ; hot, (anxious) prurient ; hot as in summer, sultry ; hot, vehement, scorching, torrid ; hot (burning), ustorious ; hot as a tumour, phlegmonous ; hot baths, thermæ.

HOUGH. *v.* To hamstring, to subnervate.

HOUND. *s.* Small hound with which hares are hunted, beagle ; blood hound, limer, or leamer ; three hounds are termed a leash, (hunt. term) ; a kennel of hounds, mute ; reward given to hounds after having taken the game, quarry ; a recalling of hounds from a wrong scent, recheat ; hounds kept ready to be cast off during a chace, relay ; leader of hounds or dogs of chace, veltrarius.

HOUR. *s.* Any instrument for shewing the hour of the day or night, watch, horodix, or horologe; the art of discovering it by a shadow, sciagraphy ; an account of the hours or time, horography ; the art of measuring time by hours, horometry.

HOURLY. *a.* Horal, horary.

HOUSE. *s.* Domicile, messuage ; private dwelling-house, libben ; small and mean house, cot ; term for the servants or domestics of a house, meiny ; house where debtors are taken to, towards matters being accommodated with the creditor before being carried to jail, spunging-house ; incantatory lines written on a house to prevent it from burning, arseverse ; woman hired in, occasionally to do the drudgery work of a house, char-woman.

HOUSE OF OFFICE. *s.* Jakes, boghouse ; house of correction, bridewell, panopticon.

HOUSEBREAKER. *s.* Effracter, L. T. milken, cant.

HOUSEBREAKING. *s.* Burglary ; instrument used in housebreaking, bettee or betty.

HOUSEHOLD. *a.* Household gods, lares ; household servants, meiny.

HOUSEWIFE. *s.* Huswife.

HOWLING. *p.* Howling, or yelling, ululable ; howling like a dog, ululation.

HUGE. *a.* Immense, nimious, swinging, (See great.)

HUMAN. *a.* More than human, superhuman.

HUMANITY. *s.* Or courtesy, philanthropy.

HUMBLE. *v.* To abase, to condescend, to depress, to subjugate, to subdue.

HUMBLE. *s.* Meek, profound.

HUMMING. *p.* Term in ornithology for the humming bird, being the smallest of the feathered tribe, tomineso.

HUMOUR. *s.* Collection of humours in any part of the body, congestion ; thin sharp humours arising from ulcers, ichor ; medicines which dilute viscous humours, leptuntics ; the ripening of preternatural humours, pepasmos ; the act or mode of forcing humours from one part of the body to a contrary, is called revulsion.

HUMOUR. *s.* (Freak) humor, cue, fantasy.

HUNDRED. *p.* Cent ; contraction of centum, L. centenary ; the space of a hundred years, century ; the number of five hundred herrings, mease ; captain or commander of an hundred soldiers, centurion.

HUNGER. *s.* To kill by hunger, to famish ; the utmost distress of hunger, limoctonia, limologia, or limomachia ; to allay hunger, to exaturate.

HUNGRY. *a.* Voracious, esurient, jejune, meagre.

HUNT. *v.* To hunt, to course ; to hunt after, to evestigate. (See to search.)

HUNTER. *s.* Female hunter, huntress.

HUNTING. *p.* Laws regarding hunting are called leash laws ; relating to hunting, venatic ; act of hunting, venation, venery ; books or treatises on hunting, cynegetics

HUNTSMAN. *s.* Venator ; huntsman on horseback, pricker ; a certain note that a huntsman winds on his horn, mot.

HURRICANE. *s.* Typhon, hermitan ; partial hurricane or whirlwind, tornado, or turnado.

HURRY. *v.* To precipitate, to accoil ; to hurry with fear, to hare.

HURRY. *s.* Flurry, precipitance ; done in a hurry, festinate.

HURT. *v.* To grate, to vulnerate, to contuse, to cruciate, to violate, to damnify, to disserve, to embase, to endamage, to excruciate, to impair, to injure, to malign, to regrate, to scath.

HURT. *s.* Annoyance, detriment, disaster, disprofit, lesion, tort, bane, nocument, prejudice ; that may be hurt, violable ; that cannot be hurt, intrenchant, inviolable, or unviolable ; not hurt, inviolate ; hurt done to any part of the body, oblesion.

HURTFUL. *a.* Offenceful, injurious, lethiferous, malefic, nocent, nocive, nocuous, noxious.

HUSBAND. *s.* Consort, lord ; fit for a husband, lapidable ; desirous of a husband, virose ; pertaining to a husband, marital ; the state of having one husband, monogamy ; two at once, bigamy ; three at once, trigamy ; severals, polygamy, (Bailey.)

HUSBANDMAN. *s.* Ruricolist.

HUSBANDRY. *s.* Agriculture ; term for all the kinds of implements used in husbandry, gainage.

HUSKS. *s.* Dry husks of fruit, murk.

HUSKY. *a.* Siliculose, siliquose, siliquous, furfuraceous, paleous.

HUT. *s.* Cell, cot, cottage, hovel.

HYDROMETER. *s.* Names given to it, aquapoise, areometer.

HYPOCRITE. *s.* Dissembler, tartuff.

HYPOCRISY. *s.* Dissimulation, simulation, pharasaism.

HYPOCRITICAL. *a.* Pharasaical.

I & J

I, too frequently repeated, either in writing or speaking, egotism, or iotacism.

JACK. *s.* Jack of all trades, alpheg, factotum.

JACK-DAW. *s.* Lupus, monedula.

JAGGED. *a.* Barbed, dentated, fimbriated, incised, crenated, lacinated, laciniated.

JAIL. *s.* Gaol or goal ; fees exacted on commitment to jail, garnish.

JAVELIN. *s.* Or spear, hasta.

JAUMBS. *s.* Or sideposts, parastades, (Architecture).

JAUNDICE. *s.* Icterus ; afflicted with the jaundice, icteric or icterical ; name of a bird which, when looked upon by one who has the jaundice, cures the person and dies itself, loriot ; name of a medicine made from urine, said to cure the jaundice, rebisola.

JAW. *s.* Mazard, chop, mandible, maxilla ; the holes or sockets of the jaws in which the teeth are set, præsepia, alveoli ; gout in the jaw, siagonagra ; of or belonging to the jaw, maxillary.

JAWBONE. s. Jawbone of a whale, menker.

ICE. s. To turn into ice, to conglaciate. (See to freeze.)

ICICLE. s. Resembling an icicle, stalactical; hanging as an icicle, stirious.

ICY. a. Glacial.

IDEA. s. Fantasy, impulse, perception; previous idea, presension.

IDIOT. s. Changeling, cappochia, driveller, mooncalf, oaf, disard; idiot, is termed an insolated person by Lavater.

IDLE. a. To settle, to fribble, to lounge, to saunter.

IDLE. s. Idle rambler, male or female, gadder; idle fellow, growt-head, lubbard, or lubber, lungis.

IDLE. a. Inadvertent, ocious, remiss, indolent, lag, lazing, lither, supine, vacant desideose, mawmish, desidious; idle science, mateotechny.

IDLENESS. s. Inapplication.

IDLER. s. Doodle, driveller, drone.

JEER. v. To frump, to snub, to gibe, or gybe, to glike.

JELLY. s. Formed into a jelly, gelatine, gelatinous; jelly made from gristle, galreda.

JERUSALEM. s. Of or belonging to it, Hierosolomitan.

JEST. v. To jest, to gibe, to jeer.

JEST. s. Low jest, conundrum, trangram, quib, or quip; writer of jests, mimiographer.

JESTING. p. Jesting and satirical speeches, maker of, terræfilius. (See university.)

JESUS CHRIST. s. Sect. A. C. 71, who denied the divinity of Jesus Christ, and rejected all the Gospels but St Matthew's, Ebionites, so called from their ringleader Ebion; the reign of Jesus Christ on earth 1000 years, millenium; one who maintains the above, Millenarian; heretics led by one Marcion a stoic, who denied that Jesus was the Son of God, hence called Marcionists; heretics in the 4th century who denied the incarnation, &c. of our Saviour, Procliniatæ; ceremony performed in the Church of Rome on Wednesday, Thursday, and Friday before Easter, in representation of the agony of Jesus Christ, and darkness in the garden, tenebræ, or tenebres; name given to the napkin of St Veronica, on which the papists pretend the face of Jesus Christ is represented, Vernicle.

JEWELS. s. Of or belonging to jewels, gemmary, gemmenous; term used of jewels when they appear natural, or not factitious, naif; jewel-house, gemmary.

IGNORANCE. s. Nescience, rudity, inscience; pretended ignorance, connivance.

IGNORANT. a. Countrified, charlatanical, illiterate; ignorant of, miscognizant, L. T.; to be ignorant of, to ignore; ignorant fellow, ignaro, ignoramus.

ILL. a. (Sick) clinical; forboding ill, portentous. (See bad.)

IMAGE. v. To effigiate.

IMAGE. s. Effigy, icon, simulacre; breaker or demolisher of images, also a name given to those of the Greek Emperors of Constantinople who discouraged the worship of images, iconoclast; that branch of perspective by which the image or representation of any figure is so delineated in a square, &c. as to produce a deformed representation of the original; but if viewed at a certain distance and point, it shall appear formous, and show a true copy of the original, is called anamorphosis, or the anamorphous art; the square, &c. containing the deformed image, is called the *Craticular Ectype*; the space containing the true representation, is called the *Craticular Prototype*.

IMAGINARY. a. Notional, utopian, chimerical, commentitious.

IMAGINATION. s. Phantom; heat of imagination, enthusiasm; weakness or derangement of the imagination, moria, paraphrosyne.

IMAGINE. v. To imagine without just grounds, to surmise; to imagine before hand, to presurmise.

IMITATE. v. To imp, to ape, to mime or mimic, to emulate; man or woman who imitates, imitator, imitatrix.

IMITATION. s. Mimesis; of or belonging to imitation, imitary, imitative.

IMMEDIATE. a. Incontinent, instantaneous, presentaneous.

IMMENSE. a. Huge, infinite, interminable, interminate, nimious.

IMMODESTY. s. Impudicity, lusciousness, obscenity.

IMMORTALITY. s. Athanasy, or Athanasia.

IMMOVEABLE. a. Inflexible, unmoveable.

IMMUSICAL. a. Unmusical, inharmonious, unharmonious.

IMPARTIAL. a. Unpartial, imprejudicate, unprejudicate.

IMPASSABLE. a. Invious, unpassible.

IMPEDIMENT. s. Barricado, remora.

IMPENETRABLE. a. Adamantean.

IMPERFECT. a. Inadequate, undecisive.

IMPERFECTION. s. Blur, defect, deficiency, immaturity; what serves to fill up imperfections, suppletory.

IMPERTINENT. a. Pragmatical; a word

formerly used when any thing said was rejected as trifling or impertinent, tilly-valley, or tillfally, (Shakes.)

IMPLANTED. *p.* Ingenite, insitive, infixed.

IMPORTANT. *a.* Consequential, essential, material, moliminous, momentous, ponderous; not important, importless, immaterial, unimportant.

IMPOSE. *v.* To impose upon, to bam; to bamboozle, to mountebank, to beguile, to cully, to gull.

IMPOSED. *p.* One easily imposed upon, geck.

IMPOSSIBLE. *a.* Impracticable, unattainable, infeasible, unfeasible, unpracticable.

IMPOSSIBILITY. *s.* The impossibility of existing together, incompossibility.

IMPOSTURE. *s.* Juggle, ingannation.

IMPOTENT. *a.* Impotent persons are termed, anaphrodisiaci.

IMPRACTICABLE. *a.* Infeasible, unfeasible.

IMPREGNATE. *v.* To impregnate, to improlificate, to ingravidate.

IMPRISON. *v.* To coop, to incarcerate, to immure, to pen, to prison, to mew. (See prison.)

IMPRISONMENT. *s.* Durance, duresse, prisonment.

IMPROBABLE. *a.* Implausible, romantic.

IMPROPER. *a.* Immaculate, (Johnson) inapposite, incompetent, inexpedient, illicit, impolitic, unexpedient; improper behaviour, indecorum, indecorousness.

IMPROVE. *v.* To meliorate, to rectify, to edify; to improve by labour, to elaborate.

IMPROVEMENT. *s.* Melioration, meliority, proficiency.

IMPRUDENT. *a.* Impolitic, indiscreet, undiscreet.

IMPUDENCE. *s.* Effrontery, front.

IMPUDENT. *a.* Malapert, procacious, audacious, brazen, confident, frontless.

INABILITY. *s.* Impuissance, impotence, incompetency, inadequateness, insufficiency, disability, unsufficiency.

INACTIVE. *a.* Inergetical; inactive, (sitting much), sedentary.

INACTIVITY. *s.* Inapplication, torpidness, torpitude, torpor, unactivity.

INANIMATE. *v.* To animate, to vivificate.

INATTENTION. *s.* Inadvertence, ablepsy.

INATTENTIVE. *a.* Inconsiderate, incurious, indolent, unattentive.

INBORN. *a.* Ingenerated, innate, inge-

).. *n.* Ingenerated, innate, ingenite.

.IOUS. *a.* Indiscreet, uncautious,

unchary, undiscreet.

INCENSE. *s.* Thymiama.

INCENDIARY. *s.* Bouteseu.

INCH. *s.* 1-12th part of an inch, line.

INCHANTMENT. *s.* Or enchantment used by magicians when they pretend to drive away diseases, præstigiæ.

INCIVILITY. *s.* Incomity, uncivility, unpoliteness.

INCLINATION. *s.* Bent, bias, proneness, pronity, propension, propensity, fantasy; earnest inclination, months mind.

INCLINED. *p.* Inclined or disposed, affectioned; not inclined, inapt, or unapt; inclined, or sloping, prone, proclive, propense.

INCLINING. *p.* Inclinatory, deviating, proclive, proclivous.

INCLOSE. *v.* To circumscribe, to embale, to enclose, to enwheel, to immure, to inshrine, to invest.

INCLOSURE. *s.* Enclosure, purprise, mew, purlieu; low wall of an inclosure, gison.

INCOMPLETE. *a.* Immature, uncomplete.

INCOMPREHENSIBLE. *a.* Acataleptic, uncomprehensible.

INCONCEIVABLE. *a.* Unconceivable.

INCONSCIONABLE. *a.* Unconscionable.

INCONSISTENT. *a.* Incoherent, incongruous, incompatible, inconsonant or unconsonant.

INCONSTANCY. *s.* Instability, levity, mutability.

INCONSTANT. *a.* Volatic, unconstant.

INCONVENIENT. *a.* Incommodious, inexpedient, unexpedient, inopportune.

INCORPOREAL. *a.* Asomatous.

INCREASE. *v.* To encrease, to ascervate, to exasperate, to traduce, to augment, to eke, to enhance.

INCREASE. *s.* Accretion, exaggeration, additament, aggravation, increment, majoration, propagation.

INCREASING. *p.* Increasing, progressive, superadvenient; increasing, or having an increasing quality, auctive (obsolete); increasing heat, incalescence.

INCREDIBLE. *a.* Legendary.

INDEPENDENT. *a.* Allodial, autocratic.

INDETERMINATE. *a.* Indeterminate as to time, aorist, G. indeterminate, undeterminate.

INDEX. *s.* An index to the Scriptures, which shows in how many texts any word occurs, concordance; index, or pin of a dial representing the earth's axis, gnomon; index to a book, elenchus. (Bailey.)

INDICATION. *s.* Indication of a disease, showing what is to be done, endeixis.

INDIFFERENT. *a.* Ajapherus as adiaphorous, listless, luke-warm.

INDIRECT. *a.* Collateral; an indirect demonstration, apagogical demonstration.

INDISPOSITION. *s.* An indisposition to devotion, accidie.

INDIVISIBLE. *a.* Matter or thing, according to Euler, &c. monad, or monade.

INDOLENT. *a.* Indolent person, bedpresser; supine indolence, analgesia.

INDORSE. *v.* To endorse.

INDULGE. *v.* To cocker, to gratify.

INDUSTRIOUS. *a.* Sedulous; industrious in contriving, plodding.

INDUSTRIOUSNESS. *s.* Gnavity.

INDUSTRY: *s.* Notableness, notability.

INEQUALITY. *s.* Imparity, imparility, unequality.

INEXCUSABLE. *a.* Unapologetical.

INEXPRESSIBLE. *a.* Ineffable, inenarrable, unexpressible.

INFAMY. *s.* Reproach, stigma, brand, opprobrium, probrosity.

INFANT. *s.* The art of weaning an infant, ablactation; the murder or murderer of an infant, infanticide; of or belonging to infants, infantile; infant baptism, pœdobaptism; sucking infants are called suberes, or nefrendes, in contradistinction to exuberes, who are those that are already weaned; sleepy song used for infants, lullaby; infants just born are termed neophytes; that part of the amnion which sometimes sticks to the head of the new born infant, vitta.

INFEASIBLE. *a.* Unfeasible.

INFECT. *v.* To infect, to invenom, to envenom, to impoison, to empoison, to taint; liable to infect, infectious, or infective.

INFECTIOUS. *a.* Malign, virulent, contagious.

INFER. *v.* To ratiocinate. (See reason.)

INFERENCE. *s.* Connotation, consectary, corollary, illation, implication.

INFERIOR. *a.* Subordinate.

INFERIOR. *s.* Underling, understrapper.

INFERNAL. *a.* Tartarean; most infernal, nethermost.

INFERRED. *p.* That may be inferred, inductive, illative, inferible.

INFERTILE. *a.* Unfertile. (See barren.)

INFINITE. *a.* Illimitable, immense, unlimitable.

INFIRM. *a.* Valetudinary.

INFLAMMATORY. *a.* Phlegmonous.

INFLAMMABLE. *a.* The inflammable part of a body, according to the old chemistry, phlogiston.

INFLAME. *v.* To inflame with love, to enamour.

INFLAMER. *s.* Incensor.

INFLUENCE. *s.* Auspice, energy, prevailment, prevalence, predominancy.

INFORM. *v.* To apprize, to certify, to cund; to inform by hint, to suggest.

INFOLD. *v.* To implicate, to imply.

INFORMATION. *s.* Monition, indoctrination; one who gives information, informant.

INFORMER. *s.* Delator, sycophant.

INGLE. *s.* Pathic, catamite, ganymede.

INGRAFT. *v.* To ingraff, to ineye, to inoculate.

INGRAFTED. *p.* Budded, insitive.

INGRAFTING. *p.* The art of, insition; one of the methods used in ingrafting, ablactation.

INGRAIN. *v.* To ingrain with dirt, to begrime.

INHABITANTS. *s.* The original inhabitants of a country, aborigines, or autochtones; an inhabitant of the caves of the earth, troglodyte; an inhabitant of a town, oppidan; the inhabitants of the globe are termed by geographers, either ascii, amphiscii, heteroscii, and periscii, (see shadow); or 1st, *Periœci,* who are those inhabitants of the earth who live under the same parallel of latitude, but opposite semicircles of the meridian. 2d, *Antœci,* who are those inhabitants that dwell under the same semicircle of the meridian, but in different parallels of latitude, the one being just as far north as the other are south of the equator. 3d, *Antipodes,* who live feet to feet, or diametrically opposite to each other; Pope Gregory the VI. excommunicated all those who believed the existence of the antipodes.

INHABITED. *p.* Place not fit to be inhabited, inhabitable, or uninhabitable, (Johnson.)

INHERITANCE. *s.* Hereditament; joint inheritance, parcenery.

INJECTION. *s.* Clyster, immission, enema, lotion, (Quincy); instrument for injecting liquors into the womb, metrenchyta.

INJUNCTION. *s.* Hest, impose, imposition, intermination.

INJURE. *v.* To aggrieve, to blast, to damnify, to derogate, to disadvantage, to disaster, to disprofit, to disserve, to endamage, to impair, to malign, to ranch, to to violate, to vulnerate.

INJURIOUS. *a.* Affrontive.

INJURY. *s.* Oblesion, scathness, supercherry, tort, annoyance, disservice, impairment, prejudice.

INK. *s.* Ink balls used by printers, pompets; ink-fish, sepia; equipage of ink, pens, sealing wax, &c. standish; certain liquids, such as vinegar, alkalies, urine, &c. which when written with, as common ink, *are invisible,* yet when applied to the fire, or passed over with a certain chemical solution, *do appear,* and may be read

M

distinctly, are called sympathetic inks.

INKY. *a.* Atramentous.

INLAID. *a.* Inlaid work, or chequer work, vermiculated work.

INLAY. *v.* To vermiculate.

INNER. *a.* Interior, interiour, internal.

INNOCENCE. *s.* Acacy.

INNOCENT. *a.* Blameless, innocuous, innoxious, offenceless.

INOFFENSIVE. *a.* Innocuous, undisobliging, unoffensive.

INQUIETUDE. *s.* The act of walking about through inquietude of mind, deambulation.

INQUIRE. *v.* To inquire into, to pry, to query, to scrutinize.

INQUIRER. *s.* Strict inquirer, indagator, scrutator, scrutineer.

INQUIRY. *s.* Inquest, interrogatory; vain inquiry, mateology; proceeding by enquiry, zetetick; making inquiry, inquisitive, inquirent; strict inquiry, pervestigation, scrutiny, anacrisis; previous inquiry, precognition. (See enquiry).

INROLLED. *p.* Or registered, ascriptitious.

INSCRIPTION. *s.* On medals, &c. legend; inscription on a pillar, stellography, memento, moniment, (Spenser).

INSECT. *s.* The noise or scream made by an insect, fritinancy; like an insect, insectile; writer on insects, insectologer; living on insects, insectivorous.

INSENSIBILITY. *s.* Apathy, callosity.

INSENSIBLE. *a.* State of being insensible, passivity.

INSERT. *v.* To interlard; to insert a bud, to ineye.

INSERTED. *p.* Inserted between, intercalary, or intercalar.

INSIDE. *a.* Inside view, introspection; hollow inside, concavity.

INSIPID. *a.* Ingustable, intastable, untastable.

INSNARE. *v.* To illaqueate.

INSOCIABLE. *a.* Incommunicative, inconversable, uncommunicative, unconversable.

INSOCIABLENESS. *s.* Unsociableness, incomity.

INSOLENCE. *s.* Surquedry.

INSOLENT. *a.* Contemptuous, lordly, dominative, imperious, presumptuous.

INSPIRED. *p.* Entheastical, enthusiastical; inspired writer, hagiographer.

INSTANCE. *s.* An instance or example of something said or done, paradigm.

INSTANT. *a.* Immediate, proximate; instant effect, instantaniety; instant, trice.

INSTIL. *v.* To inculcate, to insinuate.

INSTRUCT. *v.* To dictate, to discipline, to inculcate, to indoctrinate, to initiate.

INSTRUCTED. *p.* (Learned) erudite.

INSTRUCTION. *s.* Tuition, document, edification, erudition, indoctrination, lore, monition, parenesis; incapable of instruction, indocible or indocile; instruction begun late in life, opsimathy.

INSTRUCTIVE. *a.* A short instructive sentence, gnoma.

INSTRUMENTS. *s.* Implements, utensils, apparatus, equipage.

INSUFFERABLE. *a.* Intolerable, insupportable, or unsupportable, unsufferable.

INSULT. *s.* Flout, indignity.

INSULT. *v.* To fig.

INSURMOUNTABLE. *a.* Insuperable, insurmountable.

INTELLECT. *s.* Quickness of, acumen.

INTELLECTUAL. *a.* Intelligential.

INTEMPERANCE. *s.* Inabstinence; intemperance from prodigality, asotia.

INTEND. *v.* To destinate, to purport.

INTENT. *a.* Attent, attentive, intensive, nonce; the second intention (or purpose) deuteroscopy.

INTER. *v.* To inhumate or inhume, to tumulate.

INTERCEPT. *v.* To interclude, to interlope.

INTERCESSOR. *s.* Paraclete.

INTEREST. *s.* Compound interest, anatocism; usurious interest, feneration; interest paid for money, usance.

INTERPRETER. *s.* Latimer, truckman.

INTERROGATION. *s.* Or question, erotema.

INTERRUPT. *v.* To interrupt one in his discourse, to obacerate.

INTERRUPTION. *s.* Interruption of any natural evacuation, apolepsia.

INTERVAL. *s.* Interval between the paroxysms of a fever, dialemma.

INTESTINES. *s.* Discourse concerning the intestines of the human body, splanchnology. (See guts)

INTIMATE. *a.* Intimate acquaintance, skainsmate.

INTOXICATED. *a.* Temulent.

INTREATY. *s.* A lathing; intreaty or invocation, deesis; easy of intreaty, impetrable. (See entreaty.)

INTRICATE. *a.* Dædalian, Gordian, implex, labyrinthian, amfractuous or anfractuous; certain intricate arguments (in logic) ceratine arguments.

INTRIGUE. *s.* Intreague, affair, amour, cabal.

INTRIGUE. *v.* To chamber.

INTRODUCTION. *s.* Introduction to a discourse, exordium, preamble, proem; introduction to an office, inauguration; introduction, induction; pertaining to an introduction, isagogical; to speak of by the way of introduction, to premise; introduction to a play, prologue.

INTRODUCTORY. *a.* Preparatory, preliminary, preludious, prelusive; introductory discourses, prolegomena.

INTRUST. *v.* To delegate, to consign.

INVARIABLE. *a.* Immutable, inflexible, unvariable.

INVECTIVES. *s.* Invectives of Demosthenes, against Philip king of Macedon, were called, Philippics; hence any bitter saying now bears the same name.

INVENT. *v.* To excogitate; she who invents, inventress.

INVENTION. *s,* Figment, fiction, device, excogitation.

INVITE. *v.* To attract; serving to invite, invitatory.

INUNDATION. *s.* Cataclysm; of, or belonging to the general inundation, deluvian.

INWARD. *a.* Interior, interiour, internal, intestine, intime, intrinsic; inward passage, indraught.

JOB. *s.* Job or day's work, char.

JOG. *s.* Succussion or succussation.

JOIN. *v.* To accouple, to ally, to adapt, to fay, to hive, to inosculate, to involve, to annex, to chime, to cement, to attack, to complicate, to imp; to join to, to adjoin; to join together, to adjugate, to league, to co-join, to collapse, to combine, to to compact, to concorporate, to connect, to conjugate, to appendicate, to connex, to consociate, to consolidate, to consort; to join together with planks or boards, to contabulate; to join close together, to pan (Bailey); to join over again, to reconjoin.

JOINED. *p.* Conjunct, continuous; not joined, incompact, incontiguous.

JOINING. *p.* Concomitant; joining to, accessory; joining or touching, attiguous; the act of joining, synthesis, syzygia; the joining of two rivers, &c. confluence; act of joining, contaction; a joining together, syndesmos.

JOINT. *s.* Commissure, flexion or flexure, juncture; of or relating to joints, arthritic or arthritical, articular; to put out of joint, to lux or luxate, to dislocate, to eluxate; hardness or tophaceous concretion on the joints, epiporoma; liquor formed between the joints for lubricating them, synovia; of or belonging to the knee-joints of beasts, suffraginous,

JOINTED. *p.* Geniculated.

JOLLITY. *s.* In high mirth and jollity, cock-a-hoop.

JOLLY. *a.* Epulary.

JOLT. *s.* Succussion or succussation.

JOVIAL. *a.* Symposiac.

JOURNAL. *s.* Adversaria, ephemeris, diary, diurnal, itinerary, hæmerologium

JOURNEY. *s.* Account kept of a journey, itinerary; provisions for a journey, viaticum; of, or belonging to a journey, viatic

JOY. *s.* Feriation, glee; excessive joy, extacy, exultance or exultation, jovisaunce or joyance; to wish one joy, to gratulate or congratulate; singing for joy, jubilant; joy felt at the misfortunes of others, epicharikaky.

JOYFUL. *a.* Joyous.

JOYFULLY. *ad.* Jocundly.

JOYFULNESS. *s.* Festivity, gairishness, hilarity.

IRISH. *a.* Irish foot soldier, kern; Irish horse soldier, hobbler; of, or belonging to the Irish people, Hibernian.

IRON. *s.* Impregnated with iron, chalybeate; consisting of iron, ferreous, ferruginous; of or belonging to iron, martial (O. C.) to unite bars of iron by means of heat, to weld; the scales which fly off from red-hot iron in the act of hammering, battitura; divination by means of red-hot iron, sederomancy; water in which hot iron hath been quenched, apobamma or *aqua fabrorum*; the first forge in the iron mills, blomary.

IRONICALLY. *ad.* A figure in rhetoric, when a person or thing is commended ironically, is called, diasyrmus.

IRONY. *s.* Irony or dissimulation, accismus.

IRREGULATE. *v.* To render or make irregular.

IRREGULAR. *a.* Anomalous, Gothic, heteroclitical, incondite, immethodical, informal, informous, abnormous, difform, enormous, erratic, preternatural, romantic, tumulose, ununiform.

IRREGULARITY. *s.* Diformity, inordinancy, inordination, intemperance, misgovernment; the irregularity of a fit or any disease, ataxy.

ISLAND. *s.* Belonging to an island, insular; full of islands, insulous.

ISLETS. *s.* Islets formed by the shifting of tides or streams, alluvia.

ISSUE *s.* (Offspring) progeny, stirp; issue or discharge opened in the body, fontanel, seton, rowel,

ITCH. *s.* Itch in cattle, dogs, &c. mange; tending to the itch, pruriginous; itching (curious) prurient.

ITCHY. *a.* Troubled with the itch, impetiginous (see scab) prurigenous, scabious.

ITEM. *ad.* Inkling, innuendo. (See hint.)

JUDGE. *v.* To adjudge, to animadvert, to criticise, to deem, to doom, to opine, to syndicate; to judge before hand, to prejudge, to prejudicate.

JUDGE. *s.* Judge or critic in matters of taste, connoisseur; not cognizable by a judge, injudicable; the twelve Judges of England are, the Lord Chief Justice and Judges of the Court of King's Bench, the Lord Chief Justice of the Court

M 2

of Common Pleas, and the Lord Chief Baron and the other Barons of the Court of Exchequer ; younger or inferior judges in courts of law, are termed, puisne judges; the feigned judges of hell are, Rhadamanthus, Æacus, and Minos.

JUDGMENT. *s.* Verdict, censure, discernment, ingenium; to give judgment between two, to dijudicate; of or belonging to judgment, judicatory ; a failing in the judgment or understanding, moria; those heretics in the 4th century, who denied the general judgment, procliniatæ ; delay of the execution of a judgment in criminal affairs, respite ; judgment-seat tribunal ; judgment or sentence, crisis ; the decisive judgment or opinion pronounced by an arbiter, laudum.

JUDICIAL. *a.* Pretorian.

JUGGLER. *s.* Juggler or cheat, hicciusdoccius, hocus-pocus.

JUGGLING. *p.* Act of juggling, prestigiation.

JUICE. *s.* Void of juice, exsuccous, or exuccous; juice of fruits boiled and inspissated by sugar, apochylisma or succago; fault in the assimilation of the juices of an organized body, dyscracy.

JUICINESS. *s.* Succpsity, succulency, foison or foizon.

JUMPING. *p.* Act of jumping, saltation.

JUNCTION. *s.* The act of the junction of two against one, syncratism.

IVORY. *s.* Of or belonging to ivory, eburnean.

JURY. *s.* To swear in a jury, to empannel; decision of the jury, verdict.

JURYMAN. *s.* Juror.

JUST. *a.* Adequate, impartial, unpartial, imprejudicate, even-handed, attic, condign, conscionable, equitable, inculpable, unculpable, irreprehensible, underogatory ; most just, fitliest. (Entick.)

JUSTICE. *s.* Impartiality, equity ; court of justice, judicatory ; a justice of the peace, irenarch.

JUSTIFICATION. *s.* Avowry.

JUSTIFY. *v.* To vindicate, to approve, to deraign, to exculpate, to verify, to avow, to authorise.

JUSTNESS. *s.* Propriety, vicety.

JUT. *v.* To jut out, to beetle, to bulge, to elbow, to project, to prolapse, to protrude.

IVY. *s.* Producing ivy, hederaceous ; ivy, alehoof ; made of, or like ivy, hederal, hederose.

K

KEEN. *a.* Poignant, piquant, pungent, acumenated, parlous, apprehensive, eager, invective, peracute, intensive, sagacious, keen (sharp-sighted) perspicacious, keen (ill-natured) sarcastic ; keen, (sharp) trenchant.

KEEP. *v.* To keep off, to fend, to enguard ; to keep back, to detain ; to keep at a distance, to estrange ; to keep up, to prop; to keep in, to restrain or retain.

KEEPER. *s.* Keeper of asses, assinego ; keeper of a gate, pylorus.

KEEPING. *p.* The art of keeping off, absteption or abstention ; the act of keeping a woman, concubinage.

KENNEL. *s.* Kennel of hounds, mute.

KEPT. *p.* That cannot be kept under, insuppressible.

KERNEL. *s.* Nucleus ; having three kernels, tricoccous; such fruit as contains one kernel, is called, monopyrenous.

KEY. *s.* Clavis; the act of shutting up by key or bolt, obseration , keys of organs or harpsichords, tastatura.

KICK. *v* To spurn; to kick backwards with the heel, to recalcitrate.

KIDNEYS. *s.* The operation of cutting or opening the kidneys, nephrotomy ; kidney bean, phaseolus.

KILL. *v.* To butcher, to dispatch, to enecate, to eventerate, to jugulate, to excarnificate, to immolate, to laniate, to landdam, to peremt, to trucidate, to contrucidate ; to kill by hunger, to famish ; one who kills an enemy, hosticide ; one who kills father or mother, parenticide. (See murder.)

KILLED. *p.* Killed or cut off before, precidaneous.

KILLING. *p.* Act of killing, necation, occision, peremption, trucidation, grassation, interfection ; the act of killing beasts for sacrifice, mactation; the accidental killing of a man, chance-medley.

KILN or KILL. *s.* Oast, ost, oust.

KIND. *a.* Obsequious, propitious, affable, affectionate, liberal, maternal, matronly, amicable, beneficent, benign, boon, bounteous, brotherly, compassionate, complaisant, courteous, duteous ; kind or courteous person, philanthropos.

Possessing many kinds, multifarious;

multigenerous; containing all kinds, omnifarious, omnigenous; bearing many kinds, multiferous; kind (order) predicament; of the same kind, congenerous, congenite; of another kind, extragenous or extragene- ous, heterogeneal or heterogeneous; one of a particular turn or kind, kidney.

KINDLE. *v.* To accend, to ignite, to ignify; to gliscere; to kindle again, to relume, to relumine.

KINDLING. *p.* Act of incension, accension.

KINDNESS. *s.* Benevolence, civility; kindness to strangers, philoxeny, xenodochy.

KINDRED. *s.* Affinity, cognation; belonging to kindred, connate.

KING. *s.* Potentate; king or grand negus of Abyssinia, Presterjohn; vested in the king, monarchical; to play the king, to monarchise; rights peculiar to a king, prerogatives; he who governs in the absence of a king, inter-rex, regent; the murder or murderer of a king, regicide; the race of Greek kings, successors of Alexander the Great, Seleucidæ; deputeking, viceroy; the king's assent to a private bill in Parliament, is, in French, thus: " *Soit fait droit comme il est desiré.*"

KINGLY. *a.* Basilical, regal, monarchal, or monarchical.

KINGS-FISHER. *s.* Ispida, halcyon. (Ornith.)

KISS. *v.* To kiss heartily, to exosculate.

KISS. *a.* Buss, pash, inosculation; act of saluting by a kiss, deosculation, adosculation, osculation, suaviation.

KITCHEN-DRUDGE. *s.* Scullion; belonging to the kitchen, culinary; of or belonging to a kitchen-garden, olitory.

KITE. *s.* Puttoc; of, or belonging to a kite, milvine.

KNAPSACK. *s.* Knapsack for a soldier holding his victuals, &c. in, gardeviante, haversack.

KNAVE. *s.* Ambidexter, caitiff, cozener, scelerate.

KNAVISH. *a.* Caitiff, light-fingered.

KNEAD. *v.* To malaxate.

KNEE. *s.* The whirlbone on the top of the knee, mola, patella, scutum, or os scutiforme; of, or belonging to the knee-joint of a beast, suffraginous.

KNEEL. *v.* To kneel down in adoration, to prostrate.

KNEELING. *p.* Particularly at devotion; genuflection,

KNICK-KNACK. *s.* Jiggumbob.

KNIFE. *s.* Wood knife, parazon; knife used by surgeons, with which wounds in the thorax are widened, scolopomacherion; cant phrase for a combat with knives, sinck and snee.

KNIT. *v.* To connex.

KNIT. *p.* That may be knit, nexible.

KNOB. *s.* Exuberance, extumescence.

KNOBBED. *a.* Clavated.

KNOCK. *v.* To dash or knock out, to elide.

KNOCK. *s.* Percussion.

KNOT. *s.* Articulation, boss, braid, brede; the marriage-knot, nouse; running knot, noose; separation or loosening a knot, enodation; knot of ribbands put on a hat, &c. favor or favour, fontange; full of knots, nodose, nodous; to tie a double knot, to renodate; knot which cannot be unloosened, irrenodable.

KNOTTED. *a.* Geniculated.

KNOTTY. *a.* Nodose, nodous, sclerotic, tuberose, tuberous.

KNOW. *v.* To ken, to con, to perceive.

KNOWING. *p.* Discerning, intelligent, sapient.

KNOWLEDGE. *s.* Erudition, ken, privity, cognition, comprehension, perception, sapience; circle of knowledge, cyclopœdia or encyclopœdia; certain knowledge, assurance; done with knowledge (not by accident) imperate; having much knowlede, multicious; want of knowledge, nescience; infinite knowledge, omniscience, pansophy; perfect knowledge, perspiscience; previous knowledge, precognition, prension; knowledge of future events, prescience; the most general knowledge of things, trancendentals; certain heretics who condemned all manner of inquisition after knowledge, as being of no use to them, from whom God only required good actions, gnostimachi; the knowledge of many arts and sciences, polymathy; smatterer in any kind of knowledge or learning, sciolist.

KNOWN. *p.* Confest, notorious; not known, obscure; that may be known, perceptible; to become known, to transpire; things or matters necessary to be previously known, præcognita L.; to make known, to disclose, to reveal, to promulgate, to promulge.

KNUCKLES. *s.* To beat with the knuckles, to knub, or knubble.

L

LABORIOUS. *a.* Operose, arduous; laborious person, plodder.

LABOUR. *s.* Labor; produced with much labour, elaborate; labour for the same end, co-operation; cessation from labour, feriation; done or made without much labour, illaborate; of or belonging to beasts of labour, jumentarious; capable of enduring labour, laboriferous; one who hates labour, misoponis; labour performed with difficulty and danger, herculean; relief from labour, respiration; to labour very hard, to turmoil, to allaborate; method of enriching the soil, by labour, emponema.

LABOURER. *s.* Labourer employed in the army to undermine forts, &c. pioneer; labourer who bears a hod, hodman.

LACE. *s.* Braid; gold and silver lace, orris.

LADDER. *s.* Ascending like a ladder, climacterical.

LADIES. *s.* Ladies of honour, palasins.

LAID. *p.* Clearly laid down or drawn, graphic or graphical; laid (placed) posited.

LAKE. *s.* Lough or loch, meer or mere; bounded by a lake, meered.

LAMB. *s.* Tame lamb, corset; little lamb, lambkin, yeanling; lamb weaned and brought up by the hand, cade lamb, cosset.

LAME *a.* Mutilated, mutilous.

LAMENT. *v.* To wail, to bemoan, to bewail; to lament together, to complore.

LAMENTABLE. *a.* Deplorable, feral, lachrymable; doleful and lamentable music, Lydian mood. (Bailey.)

LAMENTATION. *s.* Ejulation; making great lamentation, plorabund.

LAMP. *s.* Lucern; lamp for burning on the altar of a chapel, luminare.

LAMPOON. *s.* Pasquil, pasquin, pasquinade.

LANCE. *s.* Headed like a lance, lanciolated; to lance or open, to scarify.

LANDS. *s.* Lands pertaining to the church, glebe; of or belonging to lands, agrarian; one put out of his lands, disseisee; name or term used of land after one crop has been taken off, etch; land recovered from the sea, is termed innings; land worn out by tillage, fream; neck of land joining a peninsula to the main-land, isthmus; term used of a ship, when she has just got out of sight of land, landlay'd; that can live both on land and in water,

amphibious; composed of land and water, terraqueous; lands, houses, &c. premises; high land or head land, promontory; land-marks set up by the ancients, representing men and women, thermes; to exchange one piece of land for another, to excambion; the art of measuring land, geodesia.

LANDING. *p.* Place of landing of goods, hithe, wharff.

LANDLADY. Hostess.

LANDLORD. *s.* Host.

LANDSCAPE. *s.* Paisage.

LANGUAGE. *s* Diction, lingo; impurity of language, barbarousness; flow of language with eloquence, elocution; person skilled in different languages, linguist; written in many languages, polyglot; rude and mean language, ribaldry, scurrility; language of the Welsh is called the Cymraegan tongue; the rudiments of any language, accidence; the peculiar language used in the Apocrypha and New Testament, is called, hellenistical language; term used by M. Demaimieux for his method of representing ideas by symbols, *and not words*, which symbols may be read and understood by six persons at the same time, each of whom speak a different language, and cannot converse with each other, pasigraphy; M. Demaimieux denominates an *universal* language founded on the above, pasilaly.

LANGUID. *a.* Lank, lithe, lithsome.

LANK. *a.* Macilent.

LANGUOR. *s.* Imbecility, lassitude.

LAP. *s.* Of, or belonging to the lap, gremial.

LAPIDARY. *a.* Lithoglyphic.

LAPPING. *p.* (Licking) lambative, lambitive; the act of lapping, lambition.

LARGE. *a.* Expansive, ample, capacious, chopping, elephantine, gigantic, gourdy, copious, immense, pinguid, swinging; small part of a large sum, driblet; vastly large, enormous, huge, immane, infinite; one who has a remarkably large head, macrocephalous; large bellyed, abdominous.

LARGENESS. *s.* Amplitude, gravidity, latitude.

LASHING. *p.* Act of, flagellation.

LAST. *v.* To dure or endure.

LAST. *a.* The last, or final part or conclusion, perclose; the last purpose, &c. ultimate; last but one, penult; the last stage, state, or consequence, ultimity.

LAST. *s.* Dernier, lag, etch.

LASTING. *p.* Amaranthine, durable, dureful, indissoluble, livelong, perdurable; permanent; any lasting distemper, chronical; not lasting, dureless.

LATE. *a.* (Modern) neoteric; visit paid late at night, couchee; late in the evening, seratine, vespertine.

LATIN. *a.* One skilled in, Latinist.

LAUDANUM. *s.* Nepenthe.

LAUGH. *v.* To cackle, to giggle; to laugh with scorn, to scoff; one who never laughs, agelastic; prediction by the manner one laughs, geloscopy.

LAUGHING. *p.* Gleeful; act of laughing to scorn, irrision.

LAUGHTER. *s.* Exciting laughter, risible; involuntary laughter, *risus sardonius*, i. e. sardonic or sardonian laughter, so named from the herb sardonia, which is said to produce this effect; involuntary and convulsive laughter, sardiasis; foolish and incessant laughter, is called Abderian laughter, from Democritus the Abderite, who was a great laugher; an epithet for the four middle fore teeth, because they are seen in laughter, gelasinos.

LAVISH. *a.* Effuse, prodigal, profuse.

LAVISHNESS. *s.* Prodigence, prodigality.

LAUREL-TREE. *s.* Bay; crowned with laurel, laureate, laurelled.

LAW. *s.* One who is engaged in a law-suit, litigant; to make laws, to legislate; constitution or set of good laws, eunomy; done out of the ordinary course of law, extrajudicial, anomy; the Irish law or law of Ireland, is termed, the Brehone law; one who is consulted in cases of law, juris-consult; the science of law, jurisprudence; professor of civil law, jurist, civilian; done against law, illegal; to enjoin as a law, toimpose; equality of laws, isonomy; a difficulty of administering the laws from their being ill conceived, dysnomy; not agreeable to laws, preterlegal; the making or giving of laws, legiferous; wager or bet upon the issue of a point of law, laygager; the time during which a law-suit is depending, litispendence; to exercise in law pleadings, to moot; the oracle of doubtful questions in the Mahometan law, mufti; writer of the law, nomographer; to proclaim a law for the dissolution of a former, to abrogate; the law of recompense, which rendereth one good or evil turn for another, lex talionis; summary explanation of law titles, and the subject matter of them, paratitla; law made ancient'y in France, preventing

the succession of females to the crown, Salique law; the act of debating lawsuits, actitation; law made among the Romans for dividing the lands got by conquest among the common soldiers, Agrarian law; a contradiction between two laws, antinomy; living according to one's own law, autonomy; severe punishments for slight offences are termed, Draco's laws, from Draco, legislator at Athens, famed for severity.

LAWFULNESS. *s.* Allowableness, legitimacy, legality.

LAW-MAKER. *s.* Thesmothete, nomotheta, legislator.

LAWYER. *s.* Civilian, jurist; Irish lawyer, Brehone; lawers or pleaders of causes, are called, causidica.

LAY. *v.* To lay down as a pledge or security, to depone; to lay up, to deposite, to intreasure, to stow; to lay up treasure, to thesaurise; to lay out money, to disburse or dispurse; to lay on, to inflict, to impose; to lay flat (fall down) to prostrate.

LAYER. *s.* Stratum; the act of laying layer upon layer, stratification.

LAZINESS. *s.* Indolence, pigritude, torpor, torpitude, accidie.

LAZY. *a.* Indolent, lither, murcid, retchless, desidiose, desidious; lazy fellow, grouthead, lounger, lubbard or lubber, loord, lungis, micher; lazy and very haughty person, lordan or lordant.

LEAD. *s.* Old name given to white lead, ceruse, psimmytheon or psimmythium; red lead, minium; lead and silver as found in their native mixture, plumbagine; one who works in lead, plumber.

LEADER. *s.* Chieftain, demagogue, premier.

LEADING. *p.* (Principal or chief) especial, inductive; the act of leading back, retroduction.

LEAF. *s.* Large leaf used for that of a ledger, folio, (see book); any plant which springs from the seed, with only one leaf, monocotyledon or monophyllon.

LEAGUE. *s.* Conjunction, alliance, combination, confederacy; relating to a league, federal.

LEAN. *v.* To make lean, to emaciate, to macerate; lean, gaunt, meager, haggard, marcid, macilent, tabid.

LEANING. *p.* The ancient posture of leaning at meals, accubation; fitted to a leaning posture, discubitory; the act of leaning at meat, discumbency; the act of leaning or lying, recubation, recumbency.

LEANNESS. *s.* Marcor, marcidity, macritude.

LEAP-YEAR. s. Bissextile or intercallary; the adding of a day to the year as in leap-year, embolism; leap from one thing to another, transilience; leap, croupade, curvet, gambol; a skip or leap from one horse to another, desulture; sort of leap in which the heels are over the head, summersault or summerset.

LEAPING. p. Salient, saltant; of or belonging to leaping, saltatory; the state or quality of leaping back, resiliency or resilition; a leaping up, subsultive; the act of leaping upon any thing, supersaliency, insulture.

LEARNED. a. Erudite, intelligent, literate, profound; self learned, automath; learned men, literati.

LEARNER. s. Neophyte, novice, tyro, inceptor.

LEARNING. p. Leer, literature, lore; a lover and promoter of learning, philomath, Mecænas; love of learning, philomathy; learning begun late in life, opsimathy; man of worth and learning, tanquam; the whole round of learning, cyclopedia, encyclopedy.

LEASE. s. Demise; one who takes a lease of another, lessee; one who grants a lease to another, lessor.

LEATHER. s. Name of fine Spanish leather, cordwain, or more properly corduvan, from Cordova, a town in Spain; kind of leather much used by bookbinders, prepared from the skin of a goat, marroquin, vulgarly called morocco; resembling leather, coriacious; Prussian leather, pruce; name of a shrub, a species of rhus, used by curriers in dressing of leather, sumach, or sumack; straps or thongs of leather, laines; the tanning of leather, alutation; piece of stuffed leather used in fencing, plastron or plastran; sort of fine and soft leather prepared from the skin of the shamois or Chamois goat, shammoy or shammy; to dress leather, to taw.

LEATHERN. a. Bottles made of hogs skins, wherein wines are brought from the tops of the mountains in Spain, borachios; leathern bag for carrying clothes in, portmanteau.

LEAVE. a. To abdicate; to leave off, to absist; to leave, to shun, to bequeath; to leave behind, to cote, to distance; to leave by will, to devise; to leave as pledge, to oppignorate, or impignorate; to leave or withdraw, to secede.

LEAVE. s. Congee, dispensation, furlough; granting leave, permissive; a taking leave, valediction.

LEAVEN. s. Zuma or Zymoma.

LEAVES. s. Leaves or flowers of plants, petals; having one leaf as some plants, which are just come above the ground, monophyllous; having two, diphyllous, or bipetalous; having three, tripetalous, triphyllous; having four leaves, quadriphyllous; having five, pentapetalous; consisting of four leaves, tetrapetalous; having many leaves, polypetalous; having flat leaves, planipetalous; having leaves like hair, trichophyllous; bunch or row of leaves, feuillage, or foliage; coloured as a dead leaf, filemot, feuillmort, (corrupted philemot); consisting of leaves, foliaceous; full of, or bearing leaves, frondose; to cover or spread with leaves, to infoliate; having broad leaves, latifolious; leaves which come forth in the spring, vernous; to beat into thin leaves, to foliate; to insert blank leaves, to interleave.

LECTURE s. Prelection; the lectures of Aristotle in the more nice and difficult parts of philosophy, to which only friends and scholars were admitted, were termed Acroatics; and those which any one had liberty to hear, were termed Exoterics; lecture or admonition given in bed by a wife to her husband, is termed a thoral or curtain-lecture.

LEECH. s. Sanguisuga.

LEES. s. Argal or argol, fæces, or feces, feculence, sediment, mother.

LEFT-HANDED. a. Sinister; the state of being left-handed, scœvity.

LEG. s. Of or belonging to the leg, crural; the leg of a horse, gambrel; swelled in the legs, gourdy; fetters for the legs, gyves; of or belonging to the calf of the leg, sural; having the legs bowed outwards, baker-legged; a person who has the legs bent outward, blæsus, G.; having legs of equal length, as isosceles, triangles, equicrural.

LEDGER. s. Ledger.

LEEK. s. Porret; of or belonging to leeks, porraceous.

LEGACY. s. Bequest; that may be left by legacy, legable; one to whom a legacy is left, legatory, or legatee.

LEGER. s. Ledger.

LENGTH. s. Or tallness, procerity; the art of measuring lengths, longimetry; length or distance from a fixed meridian, longitude; three, &c. feet in length, breadth, or depth, tripedal, quadripedal, &c.; instrument for measuring lengths, heights, &c. pantometer.

LENGTHEN. v. To eke, to elongate, to prolong, to protract.

LENGTHENED. p. To make a slow and lengthened noise, to intone.

LENT. s. The time of Lent, tesseracoste; of or belonging to Lent, quadragesimal.

LENTILS. s. Decoction made from lentils,

phacoptissana.

LEPARD. *s.* Pard, pardle, libbard.

LEPER. *s.* Lazar.

LESSEN. *v.* To abate, to debase, to dequantitate, to derogate, to detract, to diminish, to disadvantage, to rebate, to subordinate, to dispraise, to disquantity, to dwindle, to extenuate, to palliate, to degrade, to impair, to minish, to disparage, to minorate, to retrench, to mitigate, to alleviate, to mutilate.

LESSENING. *p.* Declension, degradation; lessening, (softening), paregoric, mollient, emollient; not lessening or under valuing, underogatory.

LESSON. *s.* Lore, prælection.

LETHARGY. *s.* Caros, coma; for the particular distinction, see Quincy under these heads.

LET. *v.* To demise, to impede; to let in, to intromit.

LETTER. *s.* Advice or notice by letter, aviso; letter, epistle; letter sent by one bishop to another in favour of a third party, demissory letter, (see Bishop;) small letter or card, billet; letters bound up in leaves which the Roman generals sent to the senate, when their contents were announcing victory and conquest, laureated letters; what is written after a letter, &c. is finished, postscript; of or belonging to letters or letter-carrier, tabellarious; cypher of two or more letters interwoven, monogram; any single letter of the alphabet, gramma; transposition of the letters of the alphabet, as in the word amor, which admits of twenty-three different ways of arrangement, viz. mora, oram, roma, &c. is called an anagram.

LEVEL. *v.* To complanate, to complane, to librate; to level at a mark, to collimate; any level place, estrade; on a level, aflat; level, flush, horizontal.

LEVER. *s.* Vectis; lever which has the point of support or fulcrum placed between the power and the weight to be raised, such as the wheel, windlass, capstan, crane, &c. are called heterodromous levers; lever which has the weight between the power and the fulcrum, such as the rudders or helms of ships, and the oars of boats, are called homodromous levers.

LEWD. *a.* Lubric, lubricous, deboist, lecherous, libidinous, meretricious, dissolute, impious, lascivious, naughty, riggish, salacious, vitious; lewd woman bona-roba.

LEWDNESS. *s.* Lubricity, lush, impudicity, obscenity, incontinence, lasciviousness, pravity, profligacy.

LIAR. *s.* Losel, lier, lyer.

LIBEL. *s.* Lampoon, pasquil, pasquin, pasquinade.

LIBERAL. *a.* Munificent, ample, impendious, bounteous, polydore; not liberal, uningenious.

LIBERTY. *s.* Discretion; to set at liberty, to abjugate, to disencarcerate; one set at liberty, libertine; heretics in the 2d century, who maintained that Christians were at liberty to do what they pleased, Lampetians; the goddess of liberty, Muta; granting liberty, permissive; liberty or freedom of speech, parrhesia; lover of liberty, phileleutheros.

LIBRARY. *s.* One who has the care of a library, librarian.

LICE. *s.* Infected with, pedicular, pediculous; name of a plant called staves acre, from its property of destroying lice, phtheiroctonon.

LICENCE. *s.* One authorised by licence, licentiate.

LICK. *v.* Lick over, to lech.

LICKED. *p.* Any medicine to be licked up by the tongue, eclegma, lambative, or lambitive, linctus.

LICKING. *p.* Lambent; act of, lambition.

LID. *s.* The preternatural growing together of the lids of the eyes, coloboma.

LIE. *v.* To lie flat, to prostrate; to lie at table after the manner of the ancients, to accumb; to lie hid, to latitate; to lie on a bed, to lig; to lie close, to nestle; to lie concealed, to skulk; to lie in wait flat upon the belly, to lie *perdue*; to lie in a particular direction as a coast, to trend.

LIE. *s.* (Mixture of water and the ashes of certain plants,) lye, lixivium; impregnated with lies, lixivial, lixivious, lixiviate.

LIE. *v.* To cog, to falsify.

LIE. *s.* Fiction, figment, flam, mendacity, pseudology; the act of telling lies, leasing; telling lies, mendaciloquent; the act of forging lies, of which the inhabitants of Crete were so notorious, cretism, or cheticism.

LIFE. *s.* (Vigour) mettle, vivency; the state of a single life, celibacy; length of life, longevity; the gay or early part of life, May; life, or natural heat of animals, biolychnium; life which is quite unsuitable to a certain age, as if the pulse &c. of a child was like that of a man, heterorythmus, (see pulse); the love of life, philopsychy; a return to life, revection, resuscitation; renewal or recovery of life, reviviscency; those organs which immediately concern life, vitals.

LIFELESS. *a.* Exanimate, dejected, depressed, inanimate.

N

privative; loss of teeth, dedentition.

LOST. *a.* Forlorn, lorn, irremediable, unremediable, moidered, pendulous; that cannot be lost, inamissible or inamissable; lost, loscable.

LOT. *s.* Ballot; the act of choosing by lot the place of them that were before refused, subsortition; divination by the casting of lots, cleromancy.

LOUD. *a.* Boisterous, brawling, mobbish, obstreperous, canorous, sonorous, streperous; vociferous; loud and shrill noise, clangour.

LOUSY. *a.* Pediculac, pediculous; the lousy disease, phithiriasis. (See lice.)

LOVE. *v.* To revere; to make love, to honey; to love to excess, to dote; to inflame with love, to enamour; to charm or cause love, to philter.

LOVE. *s.* The want of love to mankind, aphilanthropy; love intrigue, amour; too much addicted to the love of women, mulierose; the love of honour, philotimy; self-love, philanty; the love of life, philopsychy; love of the flesh (voluptuousness) philosarchy; love of learning, philomathy; the love of parents towards children, philostorgy; love abstracted from sensual gratification, Platonic love; a love potion, pepire; love dose used by the ancients, hippomanes; exciting love, aphrodisiacal; relating to love, venereal; a mad and violent love-passion, aphrodisia, phrenitis.

LOVE-LETTER. *s.* Billet-doux.

LOVER. *s.* Courtier, inamorato, paramour; lover of mankind, philanthropist; lover of one's brethren, philadelpus; lover of goodness, philagathus; lover of money, philargyry; lover of liberty, phileleutheros; lover of chemistry, philochymist; lover of history, philohistoricus; lover of languages, philologer; lover of learning or the mathematics, philomath; lover and encourager of arts, philotechnus; lover of the fair sex, agapet; that sort of melancholy to which lovers are subject, erotomania.

LOVING. *p.* The act of loving, dilection.

LOW. *a.* Neap, pidling, plebeian, popular, proletarious, putid, sordid, abject, acephalous, hedge-born, base, triobolar, trivial, menial, servile, mobbish, suppliant; low (deep-seated) profound; low (earthy) terrene; terrestrial; low wall of an enclosure, gison; low jests, buffoonery; low wretch, fustilarian; any low production in writing, Grub-street, hedgenote, (Gay;) low in spirits, hippish, hypochondriac; low or faint, lypothymous; low speech of no value, micrology.

LOWER. *a.* Puisne.

LOWING. *a.* Lowing or bellowing, mugient.

LOWNESS. *s.* Lowness of spirits, depression, dejection, hyp, hypochondria; lowness (meanness) veraility.

LOYAL. *a.* Allegiant.

LOYALTY. *s.* Fealty, realty.

LOZENGE. *s.* Rhombus; medical lozenges are called, trochisks or trochisci.

LUCK. *s.* Good luck, faustity.

LUCKINESS. *s.* Faustitude.

LUCKY. *a.* Lucky hit, windfall.

LUMP. *s.* Fet. (See bit.)

LUMPY. *a.* Grumous.

LUNGS. *s.* Lights; a division of the lungs or liver, lobe; inflammation of the lungs, peripneumony; of or belonging to the lungs, pulmonary, pulmonick; medicines good for all distempers in the lungs, penidium.

LURK. *v.* To lurch, to latitate, to skulk.

LURKING. *p.* Act of lurking or lying hid, latinancy; lurking, latinant; full of lurking holes, latebrous.

LUST. *s.* Cupidity, list, venery, urigo, concupiscence; medicines which incite to lust, aphrodisiacs, philters.

LUSTFUL. *a.* Lascivious, lecherous, libidinous, ruttish, carnal, concupiscent, salacious, venereous; lustful person, lewdster, hircosus (see age); not lustful, uncarnate, unlibidinous.

LUSTING. *p.* Lusting after a man, virose.

LUSTRE. *s.* Brightness, brilliancy, eclat, effulgence, irradiation, nitency, politure, refulgence, resplendence, resplendency, sheen, splendour or splendor; wanting lustre, unlustrous.

LUSTY. *a.* Nervous, nervy.

LUTE. *v.* To loricate.

LUTING. *p.* Luting (among chymists) lorication.

LUXURIOUS. *a.* Nepotal, nepotine, sybaritical, voluptuous.

LUXURIOUSNESS. *s.* Philosarchy.

LUXURY. *s.* Lush, lux; one given to luxury, voluptuary.

LYE. *s.* Lye or mixture of water and the ashes of certain plants, lie or lixivium; impregnated with lyes, lixivial, lixivious, lixiviate.

LYING. *p.* Lying between, interjacent, intermedial, intermediate; lying round about, circumjacent; lying down, act of, cubation, decumbence, decumbency; act of lying on the ground, humicubation; lying at length, jacent; act of lying on, incumbency; lying hid, latinant, miching; lying down, procumbent, recumbency; lying or resting on somethingelse, superincumbent; lying near to, attiguous, adjacent.

LYING. *p.* (Telling falsehoods) mendacilo- quent; act of lying, mentition, mendacity.

LYING-IN. *p.* (Child-bearing) puerpereus, puerperal.

M

MACHINES. *s.* One who professes the con- struction of machines, mechanician; of or belonging to a machine, machinal; little machines or active atoms, machinu- læ (among physicians.)

MACHINERY. *s.* Enginery.

MAD. *a.* Furious, bestraught, delirious, lymphatic, fanatical, frantic, infuriate, in- sane, moonstruck, outrageous, phrenetic, rabiate, rabid, rabious, turbulent, insen- sate; mad state, dementation; to be in a mad state, to dwaule.

MADMAN. *s.* Lymphatic, desperado, bed- lamite, frenetic, lunatic, maniac.

MADNESS. *s.* Debacchation, dementation, distraction, phrenzy, insania, frenzy, lu- nacy, rabies, phrenetis, paraphrenesis; mad- ness occasioned by the bite of a dog, &c. producing a dread of water, hydrophobia, pantophobia or cynanthropia; madness occasioned by the bite of wolves, wherein the patient leaves his home and wanders among the tombs till day-break, lycan- thropy, by some called, cynanthropy; madness proceeding from the bite of any poisonous creature, but particularly that of a mad dog, lyssa; madness, or extra- vagant fondness for curious flowers, an- thomania; madness without fever, mania; madness produced by administering hip- pomanes, hippomania (see mare); a par- ticular kind of madness in which the pa- tient is furiously irritated, and endea- vours to lay violent hands upon himself, antaneasmus or anteneasinum (see melan- choly); fit of madness, lune; full or pos- sessed with madness, furibund.

MAGAZINE. *s.* (Storehouse) promptuary, reconditory.

MAGGOT. *s.* The first change of a maggot, aurelia, chrysalis.

MAGIC. *s.* Incantation, necromancy, con- juration. (See divination.)

MAGICAL. *a.* Incantatory, talismantic; magical tricks practised, by those who pretend to drive away diseases, prestigiæ.

MAGNANIMITY. *s.* Megalopsychy.

MAGNETISM. *s.* Magnetism, or the power of attraction, alliciency.

MAGNIFICENT. *a.* August, sumptuous, palaceous, pompous, polydore, regifical; vainly magnificent, tumorous.

MAID. *s.* Old maid, grissette; fond name given to a young maid, pigsney; maid servant, misking-frow, (Bailey); maiden lady, spinster.

MAIL. *s.* Coat of mail, hauberk; the act of harnessing or covering with a coat of mail, lorication.

MAIM. *v.* To mutilate, to vulnerate.

MAIMED. *p.* Mutilated, mutilous, defec- tive, truncated.

MAINTAIN. *v.* To desponsate, to espouse; maintain (justify) to vindicate.

MAINTENANCE. *s.* Sustentation, susten- ance; separate maintenance, alimony.

MAKE. *s.* Make or structure, compacture, compagination, constitution.

MALE. *a.* & *s.* Masculine; male child, ma- niken; half males, will-jills, semimares; such animals or plants as have male and female parts in the same individual, are termed, hermaphroditical or androgynous.

MALICE. *s.* Despite, dudgeon, enmity; malitisioty; extreme malice, rancour or rancor; secret malice, heartburning; dis- position void of malice, acacy.

MALICIOUS *a.* Invidious, vindicative, vin- dictive, vengeful, virulent, wreakful; very malicious, implacable, inexorable.

MALIGNANT. *a.* Invidious, rancorous.

MALIGNITY. *s.* pravity, virulence, viru- lency.

MAN. *s.* Microcosm (i. e. little world); little man, manikin, homunculus; man aged 50 years, cincater or cinquater; man in general, earthling; man of plea- sure, agapet; fabulous monster, half man half horse, hippocentaur; plant having roots resembling the privities of a man, mandrakes; effeminate man, milksop; man-hater, misanthrope, misanthropist, or aphilanthropist; description of man, microcosmography; fabulous monsters, having the upper parts like a man, and the body like an ass, onocentaurs; ana- tomical description of the human body, or man, anthropography; the considering of a man anatomically, anthropometria; the knowledge of the nature of man, an- throposophy; man-eaters, cannibals, an- thropophagi; done after the fall of man, sublapsary.

MANAGEMENT. *s.* Gubernation, mana- gery; good management, economy; skil- ful management, manœuvre; bad management, mal-administration, misgovernment.

MANAGER. *s.* Mediator, negotiator, presider, procurator.

MANGINESS. *s.* Psora.

MANHOOD. *s.* The period when a youth puts on the appearance of manhood, hebe; manhood, puberty, virility; to deprive of manhood, to evirate. (See, to cut.)

MANIFOLD. *a.* Multiplicious, multitudinous

MANKIND. *s.* The hatred of mankind, misanthropy or aphilanthropy; hater of mankind, misanthropist, aphilanthropist; lover of mankind, philanthropist.

MANLY. *a.* Virile, virose; to make or render manly, to masculate.

MANNER *s.* Guise, mein; discourse concerning manners and customs, ethology.

MANSLAUGHTER. *s.* Chancemedley.

MANUFACTURER. *s.* Artificer, opificer, artisan or artizan.

MANURE. *s.* Compost, (See dung.)

MAPS. *s.* The art of planning and designing maps, mappery

MARBLE. *s.* Covered with marble, marmorated; of or belonging to marble, marmorean, marmoreous.

MARE. *s.* Offspring of a mare and a bull, jumart; Spanish or Barbary mares are called, jennets; the noted poison or lovedose used by the ancients, obtained from the forehead of a young mare or horse, hippomanes.

NIGHT MARE. *s.* Incubus, ephialtes, succubus, o' succuba.

MARGIN. *s.* Margent.

MARGINAL. *a.* Marginal note, gloss, postil

MARINERS. *s.* Mariner's compass, *pyxis nautica.*

MARK *v.* To betoken, to dint, to distinguish; to mark with degrees, to graduate.

MARK. *s.* To hit a mark, to collimate; mark, attribute, boundary, butt, characteristic, vestige, criterion, indication, liniament, symptom, cynosure; any mark of infamy, stigma; brown, black, or livid marks under the skin, from extravasated blood, by means of a bruise, ecchymoma, ecchymosis.

MARKET. *s.* Mart, mercat; of or belonging to markets, emporetic, emporetical, mercative, nundinal, nundinary, foraneous; clerk of the market, zygostates; of or belonging to such office, zygostatic; market-place, empory.

MARRIAGE. *s.* Of or belonging to marriage, conjugal, marital. relating to marriage, hymeneal or hymenian, jugal, connubial; of or belonging to marriage, nuptial, sponsal; relation by marriage, affinity; heretics who condemned marriage, Severians; marriage constituted by eating of bread together, confarriation; the marriage-feast, bridal; marriagesong, epithalamium; to engage for marriage, to espouse, to betroth; the first month after marriage, honeymoon; the god of marriage, Hymen; sort of temporary marriage among the Mahometans, kabin; a second marriage, deuterogamy; the marriage knot, nouse (Crashaw); the marriage of *one* wife only, monogamy; one who disallows a second marriage, monogamist; a very singular law, instituted by Eugenius king of Scotland, regarding marriage, marchet, (for an account of which see Bailey); hater of marriage, misogamist.

MARRIAGEABLE. *a.* Viripotent, lapidable, nubile.

MARRIED. *p.* Covert, mated; the state of not being married, celibacy; the being married to two wives at once, digamy, or bigamy.

MARROW. *s.* Dish of marrow and grated bread, moile (in cookery); to take out the marrow, to emedullate.

MARRY. *v.* To consort, to desponsate, to espouse.

MARRYING. *p.* A fine levied by the Romans for not marrying, uxorium.

MARSH. *s.* Marish, morass.

MARSHY. *a.* Boggy wearish.

MARTYRS. *s.* Register of, martyrology; the first witness or martyr who suffered death in testimony of the truth, as Abel in the Old Testament, and St Stephen in the New, protomartyr.

MASK. *v.* To mumm.

MASK. *s.* (Pretence) stalking horse; wearing a mask, larvated; mask entertainment, mommery; mask for the face, visard.

MASKING. *p.* (In brewing) moacks.

MASS. *s.* Aggregate, compound, congregation; mass of dung prepared for manure, compost, ; mass of small bodies, congeries, concrement; to join in one mass, to incorporate.

MASSACRE. *s.* Carnage, internecion. (See murder.)

MASTER. *s.* Gaffer; of or belonging to a master or teacher, didascalic, or didactic.

MASTERLY. *a.* Stile of language, ciceronian.

MAT. *v.* Or entangle the hair, to elf.

MATCH. *v.* To compeer, to mate.

MATCH. *s.* Lunt; match or wooden pipe rammed into a bomb for the purpose of making it explode, fusee ; match fixed at the end of a staff for firing cannon, linstoc.

MATERIALS. *s.* Formed of different materials, farraginous.

MATHEMATICS. *s.* Mathesis; those compendious notes or characters in mathematics by which are represented the sums, differences, or rectangles of several quantities are termed ligatures ; lover of mathematics, philomath ; physician who performs cures upon mathematical principles, Iatromathematic.

MATRIMONIAL. *a.* Connubial, nuptial, hymeneal.

MATRIMONY. *s.* Hater of, misogamist.

MATTER. *s.* To gather matter, to beal, to suppurate ; that happy modfiication of matter composing an animal body, which qualifies it to be able to perform acts proper to it, entelechia. (See synchronism and euphoria, Bailey) ; the difficulty attending the bringing any matter or a disease to a crisis, dyscritos ; of the same matter or essence, commaterial ; void of matter, immateriate, incorporal ; matter (the original chaos), hyle ; composed of matter in general, materiate, materiated ; matter of a sore, pus, or pyon, tabum ; matter or pus gathered in an abscess, imposthume ; matter in a wound which is not tainted by any infection, is called laudable matter ; consisting or composed of matter, or pus, purulent ; the running of thin corrupt matter from a sore, sanious, sanies ; the progressive ripening of matter or pus, sympepsis.

MAW. *s.* The maw of an animal, abomasus.

MAXIM. *s.* Adage, aphorism, dictate, institute, protasis.

MAYOR. *s.* The ancient name of the Mayor of London, portgreve, or portreve.

MAZE. *s.* Mizmaze.

MEADOW. *s.* Mead, savanna.

MEAL. *s.* (Diet) refection ; divination by meal or cakes, aleuromancy ; divination by barley meal, alphitomancy ; to work meal into dough, to knead ; of or belonging to meal, pollinarious, farinaceous ; coarse meal, pollard, grout.

MEAN. *a.* Abject, ignominious, avaricious, base, bunting, caitiff, disingenuous, doggerel, contemptible, crestless, grovelling henpecked, cuckoldy, dastardly, doltish, flimsy, mercenary, mobbish, illiberal, inelegant, servile, menial, paltry, paultry, peaking, penurious, plebeian, prolitarious, putid, sordid, reputeless, servile, roynish, triobolar, trivial, venal ; mean fellow, craven, cullion, hilding, fustilarian, tomboy, grovelier, ribald, garlic eater ; mean cowardly man, meacock ;

mean rascal, taterdemallion, scroyle, skipjack or skipkennel ; mean dirty woman, drazel, drab ; mean born, hedge-born ; mean house, dog-hole, hovel ; mean trifling thing, fingle-fangle ; mean author, garreteer, grubstreet ; mean ravenous wretch, harpy, hunks ; of mean birth, ignoble ; mean artifice, malversation ; mean speech of little value, micrology ; mean (little or trifling) minute ; mean and rude language, ribaldry.

MEANING. *p.* Received meaning of a word, &c. acceptation ; to alter from the original meaning, to detort ; equal in meaning, equivalent.

MEANING. *s.* Import, intent, drift ; having double meanings, ambifarous, ambiguous ; the double meaning of words, such as the verbs, to cleave, to egelidate, &c. dilogy.

MEANNESS. *s.* Curship, degeneracy, vility ; meanness of spirit, pusillanimity, recreancy, vernility, micropsychy.

MEASLES. *s.* Morbilli ; measles or such like eruptions, exanthemata.

MEASURES. *s.* Tables of measure where the denominations are generally known, such as money, weights, &c. in contradistinction to such as have multifarious denominations, geodetical tables; name given by Mr Locke to the 1-10th part of a line, a line being 1-10th of an inch, and an inch being 1-10th of a philosophical foot, which is equal to the half of a pendulum vibrating seconds in latitude 45 °, Gry ; that divisor which measures a sum exactly without a remainder, aliquot ; reducible to sum measure, commensurable ; skilled in the knowledge of weights and measures, oedastic.

MEASURED. *p.* That cannot be measured, immeasurable, immensurable, unmeasurable, incommensurate.

MEASUREMENT. *s.* Admeasurement.

MEASURING. *p.* The act of measuring, mensuration ; the measuring distances or land, longimetry. (See mensuration) ; the art of measuring heights and distances by staves, baculometry ; the art of measuring plane surfaces, planimetry ; the art of measuring objects at a distance, apomecometry ; the art or science of measuring the contents of solid bodies, stereometry ; measuring of triangles, trigonometry ; the art of ascertaining the number of men in an army, &c. by forming them into a geometrical figure, stratarithmetry ; the art of measuring heights and distances by piece meal, cultellation ; the art of measuring figures standing on their bases, epipedometry ; the art of measuring a country or ground, choronometry, geometry.

MEAT. *s.* The act of feeding on one kind of meat, monophagie ; the rank smell of meat, fumette ; place or receptacle for butcher meat, larder ; proportion of meat and forage given to a soldier for a day, ration ; dressed meats, viands ; remains of meat not eaten at table, offals. (Arbuthnot.)

MECHANIC. *a.* Mechanic powers are the balance, lever, wheel, wedge, screw, and pulley ; contrary to the laws of mechanics, immechanical.

MECHANIC. *s.* Mechanician, craftsman.

MEDALS. *s.* Treatise on gems and medals, dactyliotheca ; the space next within the edge or circumference of a medal, on which the motto is written, exergue, or exergum ; the words round the edges of a medal, legend ; large medal, medallion ; the description of ancient coins and medals, numismatographia.

MEDICINE. *s.* The art of medicine is divided into five branches. 1st, Physiology, which considers nature with respect to the cure of diseases, particularly the human body, its parts, structure, health, life, functions, and economy. 2d, Pathology, which treats of the nature, differences, causes, effects, &c. of diseases, and is sometimes confounded with Nosology. 3d. Semeiotica, which treats of the signs of health and sickness. 4th, Hygiena, which teaches the preservation of health. 5th, Therapeutica, which respects the prescription of medicines, or the method of cure, (Quincy) ; writer on medicine, pharmacologist ; universal medicine, catholicon, diacatholicon, panacea, pancrestos, or panchrestos ; medicine not yet made public, nostrum ; place where medicines are prepared, dispensary ; treatise concerning the art of preparing medicines, pharmacology ; the art of compounding medicines, pharmaceutice ; that part of chemistry which treats of the preparation of medicines, pharmachochymia ; dispensary or collection of medicines, pharmacopoeia ; maker or compounder of medicines, pharmacopoeius ; general name for any medicine, pharmocum : student of medicine, philiatros ; abounding with medicines, polypharmacal ; general name for such ingredients as give medicines a good scent, hedysmata ; that active principle in medicines by which they operate, hæcceity ; the art of medicine is called, *Ars Machaonia.*

MEDITATE. *v.* To contemplate, to speculate. (See study.)

MEDITATION. *s.* Deep meditation, brown study ; previous meditation, precogitation.

MEDLEY. *s.* Medley of dishes, ambigu.

MEEK. *a.* Mansuete, pigeon-livered. (See gentle.

MEET. *v.* To advene, to coincide, to congregate, to conjugate, to obviate, to shrine.

MEET. *a.* Advisable, idoneous.

MEETING. *s.* Conjunction, convention, conventicle, encounter, occursion, parasynaxis, concourse, resort, rencounter ; place of meeting, rendezvous, rendevous ; the meeting of rays, corradiation ; a meeting in a point, incidence ; meetings, dissolving them upon foreknowledge or conjecture of their ill success, obnunciation.

MELANCHOLY. *a.* Discomfort, dolefulness, hyp, dump ; melancholy induced by groundless fear, panophobia ; melancholy or depression of spirits, athymia ; afflicted with melancholy, atrabilarian, hypochondriac, or hypochondriacal, langorous, pensive, saturnine, tristful ; the first approaches or symptoms of melancholy, when the individual begins to dislike company and conversation, aphilanthropy ; melancholy madness occasioned by the bite of a dog, wherein the victim imitates their actions, cynanthropy ; when the patient is afflicted with the dread of water, hydrophobia. (See madness) ; term used for that sort of melancholy to which lovers are subject, erotomania ; the third degree of melancholy (according to Wedelius) is called exanthropia.

MELT. *v.* To colliquate, to deliquate, to discandy, to dissolve, to liquate, to liquify, to fuse ; to melt as a candle set in a current of air, to sweal, or swale ; to melt with compassion, to relent ; having power to melt, dissolvent ; aptness to melt, liquescency.

MELTED. *p.* Illiquated, molten ; that may be melted, fusible, liquable, resoluble ; in a melted state, fusion ; general name for such things as may be melted, liquamen ; pot generally made of ground bones, &c. and sometimes of the carbure of iron, in which metals are melted, crucible ; the preparing any substance so as it may be melted, ceration, cerefaction.

MELTING. *p.* The act of melting mixed bodies by fire, eliquation ; the act of melting, liquefaction, illiquation ; melting state, liquescent ; the melting of ores, smelting ; this is also called the docimastic art.

MEMORY. *s.* Out of memory, immemorial ; any thing done to perpetuate the memory of an action, &c. monumental ; of or belonging to the memory, memorative; that hath a good memory, memorious; done by memory, memoriter, L.; precepts or rules to help the memory, mnemonics; the art of memory, mnemosyne; medicines which restore the memory, anamnetics, or anamnestics.

MEN. *s.* The seven wise men of Greece were Bias, Chilo, Cleobulus, Periander, Pittacus, Solon, and Thales; that part of physic which shews the way of living, fit for old men, gerontocomy; hospital for poor old men, gerontocomium; men eaters, cannibals, anthropophagi; effeminate men are termed, androgynæ.

MEND. *v.* To meliorate, to sarcinate, to vamp.

MENDED. *p.* That may be mended, corrigible, mendable; that cannot be mended, inemendable.

MENSURATION. *s.* Of heights and distances, longimetry; mensuration of boards, glass, pavement, &c. planometry; mensuration of timber, stone, and all solid bodies, usually called gauging, stereometry; mensuration of land, geodæsia. (See measuring).

MENTIONED. *p.* Not to be mentioned, (horribly heinous) nefandous.

MERCHANDIZE. *s.* Or goods carried over sea at the risk of a creditor, is termed trajectitious merchandize; of or belonging to merchandize, emporetic, or emporetical.

MERCILESS. *a.* Bowelless, ruthless.

MERCIFUL. *a.* Clement, merciable, propitious.

MERCURY. *s.* Stilbon, G. (i. e. glittering) the planet Mercury is so called, because it twinkles more than the rest of the planets; of or belonging to mercury or quicksilver, hydrargyral.

MERCY. *s.* Lenitude, lenity, pitifulness, ruth; the mercy-seat, propitiatory.

MERIDIAN. *s.* Orthographic projection of the sphere upon the plane of the meridian, analemma; when any luminary is on the meridian, it is said to culminate.

MERRIMENT. *s.* Jocundity, disport, galliardise, glee, jocoseness, jocularity, jovialness, pleasantry; noisy merriment, revel.

MERRY. *a.* Facetious, fain, gleeful, humorous, or humourous, sportive, jocose, jocular, jocund, blithe, jolly, jovial, joyous, burlesque, comical, vivid, boon, boosy, waggish, ludicrous; Merry Adrew, buffoon, jack-pudding, kicksboe, saltimbanco, harlequin; merry fellow, grig; to make or render merry, to exhilarate; the state of not being merry, unjoyous; of or belonging to merry making, symposiac.

MESS-MATE. *s.* Skainsmate, trencher-mate.

MESSENGER. *s.* Nuncio, internuncio, apparitor, bum-bailiff, catchpole, harbinger; false messenger, pseudangelist; one who is his own messenger, autangelist.

METALS. *s.* The art of refining metals by the cupel, affinage; small mass of metal, linget, ingot; the art of working metals, metallurgy; base metal of any kind, ochimy, ochomy, or ockamy; mould for casting metals in, plasm; the art of making concave figures in metals, diaglyphice.

METHOD. *s.* Practice, reglement, disposition; done without method, erratic, immethodical; method among mathematicians is of four kinds, viz. 1st, Analytical, or resolution. 2d, Poristical, which determines when and by what means, and how many different ways, a problem may be resolved. 3d, Synthetical, or composition, opposed to analytical. 4th, Zetetick, or algebraical.

MICE. *s.* Divination by means of mice, myomancy; the name of an herb said to be fatal to mice, myophonon.

MIDDLE. *s.* Centre, medium, medial, median, mediate; middle point of any solid, centrum; of or belonging to the middle, mediastine; middle state, medeity, mediocrity.

MIDRIFF. *s.* Diaphragm, diazoma.

MIDWIFE. *s.* Medewife, i. e. a woman of worth or merit, (Bailey); to act the part of a midwife, to obstetricate.

MIDWIFERY. *s.* Of or belonging to midwifery, obstetric, or obstetrical.

MIDWIVES. *s.* Umbilisecæ, L.

MIGHT. *s.* Enforce, potency, efficacy, vigor.

MIGHTY. *a.* Dread, valid; mighty in wisdom, sapientipotent.

MILD. *a.* Placid, affable, bland, clement, epicerastic, lenient, mansuete, meek, pacated, pigeon-livered.

MILDNESS. *s.* Lenitude, lenity, lithness.

MILE. *s.* The 1-8th part of a mile, furlong; measure at sea of one mile, a knot; of three miles, league.

MILITARY. *a.* Military art, military tactics; Saxon term for military men, or those worthy of bearing arms, firdwrithi.

MILITIA. *s.* Milice.

MILK. *s.* The first milk of a cow, &c. after the production of its young, biesting, colustrum; to milk out, to emulge; wheat boiled in milk, furmenty, or frumenty; milk-house, lactary; giving milk, lactant, lactation; milk cow, milch cow; that which makes or produces milk, lactifical, lactescent; milk curdled by staleness, loppermilk; milk curdled with

O

beef or wine, posset; posset made of milk and ale, zythogala; the liquor obtained by steeping the stomach of a calf in warm water, with which milk is curdled, runnet; the extension of the breasts by too much milk, sparganosis; the Saxon name for the month of May when they milked their cows thrice a day, trimilchi; that aptitude of secerning the milk in the breasts, is termed the galactopletic faculty.

MILKY. *a.* The milky way, galaxy, *via lactea,* L.; a milky juice, particularly of barley, boiled until it be so soft as to pass through a strainer, cremor; milky fever that comes on childbed-women about the fourth day after delivery, lacteal fever; milky, lacteous, lacteal.

MILL. *s.* Myle, G.; the hopper of a mill, tremella, or trementa; of or belonging to a mill, molar, molendarious; mill for forcing water, forcier.

MIMIC. *v.* To ape, to belie.

MIMIC. *s.* Mime, or mimer.

MIND. *s.* To put in mind, to prompt; to mind, (care for) to reck; to call to mind, to bethink; weakness of mind, insipience; difficulty or weakness of mind in accommodating itself to contingencies, dysthymia; one of a particular turn of mind, genio; the immediate perception of the mind without ratiocination, intuition; greatness of mind, magnanimity; of or belonging to the mind, mental; a change of mind or opinion, metanoia; a cheerfulness of mind, ecthymosis; an account or treatise of the soul or mind, psychology; having an easy and unsteady mind, flexanimous; a walking about through inquietude of mind, deambulation; term used by Aristotle to express the human mind, entelechia.

MINE. *s.* Entrance into a mine, adit; hazle rod in the shape of the letter Y, which being cut according to the time of the planetary aspect, and held by the two forked ends, some pretend will discover mines; this rod is hence called *virgula, divinatoria,* (Bailey); mine charged for the purpose of blowing up, fougade.

MINGLE. *v.* To mingle, to attemper, to commix, to compound, to immix.

MINGLED. *p.* Liard, roan, promiscuous; the body mingled with another, admixture; that may be mingled, miscible, permiscible.

MINISTER. *s.* Pastor, cleic, ecclesiastic; first minister of state, premier.

MINUET. *s.* Menuet, passepied, F.

MINUTENESS. *s.* Parvity, parvitude. (See smallness.)

MIRACLES. *s.* Any art that performs, or

seems to perform, miracles, thaumaturgics; the power of working miracles by means of prayer to God, theurgy.

MIRACULOUS. *a.* Supernatural, preternatural.

MIRROUR. *s.* Speculum; divination by looking in a mirrour, catoptromancy.

MIRTH. *s.* Comicalness, festivity, galliardise, glee, hilarity, jocundity; the want of mirth, injocundity; in high mirth, cockahoop.

MIRY. *s.* Lutulent, sloppy.

MISCARRIAGE. *s.* Abortion, or abortment, ectrosis, aborsement, exambloma, or examblosis; medicines that cause miscarriages, anblotics, ecbolica, or ectrotica; miscarriage procured by art or violence, abactus.

MISCHIEF. *s.* Pest, tort, bane, detriment; promoter of mischief, make-bate; full of mischief, baleful.

MISCHIEVOUS. *a.* Malefic, or malefique, nocent, nocive, offenceful; very mischievous, pernicious, tortuous.

MISER. *s.* Curmudgeon, hunks, pinchfist, pinchpenny, recreant, snudge.

MISERABLE. *a.* Unblest. (See unhappy.)

MISERABLY. *ad.* Elengelic.

MISERY. *s.* Bale, calamity, dole, infelicity; misery is allegorically called Pandora's box, which is feigned to have contained all sorts of evils, with hope at the bottom.

MISFORTUNE. *s.* Pandora's box, disaster, mishap, stound; joy felt by some at the misfortunes of others, epicharikaky.

MISS. *s.* Or mistress, damisella. (See mistress.)

MISSION. *s.* Ambassage, ambassade; to send upon a mission, to ablegate; joint mission, adlegation.

MIST. *s.* Exhalation, haze, rime.

MISTAKE. *s.* Hallucination, misprise, peccadillo, erroneousness, liable to mistake, fallible; exemption from mistake, inerrability, unerrableness, infallibility.

MISTAKEN. *p.* That may be mistaken, mistakable.

MISTRESS. *s.* Concubine, gammer, leman, damisella.

MISTY. *a.* Nebulous, nebulose.

MIX. *v.* To mix metals with others of a harder nature, as silver is mixed with a proportion of copper, to allay, to alloy; to mix, to involve, to malaxate, to hive; to immingle, to incorporate, to interlard, to blend, to confound, to confuse, to interweave, to pleach, to braid, to plight.

MIXED. *p.* Chaotic, miscellaneous, motley, or motly, adulterated; that may be mixed, miscible; incapable of being mixed, immiscible, immixable, incommiscible.

MIXING. *p.* A mixing or tying together, alligation; a thorough mixing, permixtion, or permixion; act of mixing, permistion, or permixtion.

MIXTURE. *s.* Medley, mixtion, migma, mistion, composition; mixture or folding together, complication; mixture of oats and barley, dredge; any odd mixture, farrago; the compound resulting from the mixture of two or more substances, which compound is something very different from either of the simples, *tertium quid*, L.

MOAN. *s.* Ejulation, mone.

MOANING. *p.* Querimonious.

MOB. *s.* Or crowd, frequence, concourse, mobile, mobility.

MOCK. *v.* Mock at, to fleer, to leer, to flout, to frump, to illude, to ludificate.

MOCK. *s.* Mock fight on horseback, just; mock fight or assault, feint, joust; mock moon, paraselene.

MOCKERY. *s.* Derision, flout, illusion, irony.

MOCKING. *p.* Act of mocking, irrision, subsannation.

MODE. *s.* Relating to a mode, vogue, modal.

MODEL. *s.* Module, paragon, proplasm.

MODERATE. *v.* To contemper, to mitigate, to alleviate.

MODERATE. *a.* Abstemious, abstinent, dispassionate, moderable, temperate; moderate diet, Lession diet (of Lessinus a famous physician.)

MODERATION. *s.* Mediocrity, medeity.

MODERN. *a.* Neoteric.

MODEST. *a.* Bashful, coy, discreet, pudious, verecund; woman affectedly modest, prude; not modest, immodest.

MOIST. *a.* Dank, humid, humific, pluvial, pluvious, rorid, subriguous, uliginous, uvid.

MOISTEN. *v.* To humidate, to bedew, to imbrue, to irrigate, to irrorate, to malaxate, to humect, to humectate.

MOISTENING. *p.* Act of moistening, madefaction, rigation, insuccation.

MOISTNESS. *s.* Maddidity, succosity, succulency.

MOISTURE. *s.* Instrument to measure the quantity of moisture in the air, hygrometer, hygroscope, (Johnson), hydroscope (Bailey); the art of determining the weight of mixture in the air, hygrostatics; rottenness from too much moisture, spargefaction, mydesis; the want of moisture, siccity.

MOLE. *s.* (Animal), molewarp, mouldwarp, or moulwarp, talpa, topinaria; mole (false conception,) molacarnea, (Anat.); mole or mark on the body, nœvus.

MOMENT. *s.* Lasting for a moment, momentally, momentary, momentaneous; in a moment, trice.

MONASTERY. *s.* Cloister; parlour in a monastery, where the friars meet for discourse, locutory.

MONASTIC. *a.* Monastic life, monachism.

MONEY. *s.* Mammon, moneta, pelf; money unpaid though due, arrears; to lay out money, to disburse; alloy of money, lega; one who doats on money, mammonist; one who raises money on loan for others, money scrivener; of or belonging to money, nummary, nummular, pecuniary, pecunious; money to the amount of 100,000l. Sterling, plum; fulness of money, pecuniosity; lover of money, philargyry; money tables, where the denominations are generally known in contradistinction to numbers which have multifarious denominators, geodetical tables.

MONGREL. *a.* Mongrel or mangrel animals, are such as the offspring of a bull and mare, jumart; of a lion and camel, leucrocuta; of a horse and she-ass, or an ass and mare, mule; of a ram and she-goat, musimon, such in general are called, hybrida.

MONK. *s.* Conventual.

MONKEY. *s.* Of or belonging to a monkey, cercopithecan; monkey, homunculus.

MONKISH. *a.* Monachal.

MONSTERS. *s.* Bearing or bringing monsters, ostentiferous; monster, prodigy.

MONSTROUS. *a.* Portentous, prodigious, teratical.

MONTH. *s.* Register or account of what is done in a month, menology; the first day of every month among the ancient Romans, calends; child that dies within a month after birth, is called, chrisom; the four kinds of lunar months are, the periodical, or the interval marked by the return of the moon to the first point of Aries, which is of 27 days, 7 hours, 43 minutes, 5 seconds; the sidereal or term of its return to a given fixed star, of 27 days 7 hours, 43 minutes, 12 seconds; the synodical, or term of its return to the sun of 29 days, 12 hours, 44 minutes, 3 seconds; and the anomalistical, or term in which it returns to its apogee of 27 days, 13 hours, 18 minutes, 34 seconds (see year); happening once a month, menstrual.

MONUMENT. *s.* Cenotaph; temporary monument set over a grave, hearse; a pompous funeral monument, mausoleum; verses, &c. cut on stone monuments, lapidary verses; monuments, memoriæ, L.

MOON. *s.* The face of the moon, disk; the period betwixt old and new moon, inter-

O 2

lunar, or interlunary; relating to the moon, lunar or lunary; formed like a half moon, lunated; one revolution of the moon round the earth, lunation; any thing shaped like a moon, lune; little moon, meniscus; resembling the moon, moony; new moon, novilunium, neomenia; relating to full moon, plenilunary; of or belonging to that space of time in which the moon performs one revolution, dracontic; the different appearances or positions of the moon, phases; the slight appearance of full moon which happens sometimes on the 2d or 3d day of her age, penumbra; mock moon, paraselene; the appearance of new moon a day later, by means of the lunar equations, proemptosis; those Christians in the 2d century who maintained that Easter ought always to be kept upon the 14th day of the moon of the first month, quarto decimani; half moon, semilune or demilune; moon (in the Heath. Myth.) Selene; description of the moon, selenography; situated under the moon, sublunary; of or belonging to the course of the moon, synodical; full moon, panselene (Harris); cycle of the moon, being a revolution of 19 years, enneadecaterides (see cycle); said of the moon when in the first or last quarter, falcated, bifurcated; said of the moon when her enlightened part appears bunched out or convex, which happens while she moves between her quadratures in her opposition to the sun, gibbous; the period of time when the moon does not appear, interlunium; those spaces of time or periods where the sun and moon, or two remarkable points in their orbits, such as the apogee, the nodes, &c. being supposed to set out from the same point in the heavens, would meet there again, are termed, the lunisolar periods. (Bossut.)

MOP. *s.* Mop used for cleaning the floor of an oven, scovel.

MORAL. *a.* Ethick, tropological; moral of a fable, epimythium; moral reflection, epiphonema.

MORALITY. *s.* Treating of morality, ethological.

MORNING. *s.* Matin; of or belonging to the morning, matutine; morning prayers, matins; of or belonging to morning prayers, matutinal.

MOROSE. *a.* Chuffy, agelastic.

MOROSENESS. *s.* Cynical.

MORSEL. *s.* Sippet; delicate morsel, titbit, bons-bons, F. bonner-bouche.

MORTAL. *a.* Exititious, exitial, fatal, feral, lethal, fatiferous. (See deadly.)

MORTAR. *s.* Small mortar to grind colours in, molliner; the act of pounding in a mortar, pestillation, pistillation, trituration; mortar for throwing small bombs or shells, hobit.

MORTIFICATION. *s.* Gangrene, necrosis, sphacelus or aposphacelis.

MORTIFY. *v.* To chasten, to chastise; to mortify or harrass with corporal hardships, to macerate, to sphacelate.

MOSES. *s.* The first five books of the bible written by Moses, Pentateuch.

MOSS. *s.* Full of moss, muscose; sort of greenish moss found on human skulls, said to have medicinal virtues, usnea; the clearing of trees from moss, emuscation.

MOTHER. *s.* Gammer, dam; common mother, commere; one who kills his mother, parenticide, matricide; of or belonging to a mother, maternal.

MOTION. *s.* To put in motion, to exagitate, to excite, to incite; communicated motion, impulse; devoid of motion, inert; the motion of a body in a right line, lation; motion, motation; causing motion, motary; difficulty or defect in voluntary motion, dyscinesy or dyscinesia; the motion backwards of a piece of ordnance on being discharged, recoil; the doctrine of rotatory motion, trochilics or trochilice; remaining without motion as stagnant water, restagnant; having the power of motion to another place, locomotive, locomotion; motion or petition in a court of law, emparlance.

MOTIVE. *s.* Incentive, incitation, inducement, incitement.

MOTTO. *s.* A device, a short sentence; motto on a ring, posy or posey.

MOVE. *v.* To actuate, to agitate, to bestir, to budge, to emmove; to move as the embryo in the womb, to quob; an inability to move, dyscinesy or dyscinesia.

MOVEABLE. *a.* Motable, mobile; moveable property, chattel; moveable by entreaty, exorable.

MOVED. *p.* That cannot be moved, moveless.

MOVER. *s.* Movent, motor.

MOVING. *p.* Pendulous, motory, ambulatory; the power of moving, motivity; self-moving, automatical, automatous; moving slowly, tardigrade, or tardigradous.

MOULD. *s.* Matrice, matrix, proplasm; mould for metals, plasm; the art of making moulds for casting figures, proplastice; moulds (among chymists) made of iron of different forms, into which melted metals are poured, lingots or lingets; that may be formed in a mould, mouldable.

MOULDY. *a.* Finewed, foisty, fusty, mucid, vinnewed, emucid.

MOULTING. *p.* Moulting or casting feathers, &c. defluvium.

MOUNT. *s.* Barrow.

MOUNTAINS. *s.* Little mountains, monticles; full of little mountains, monticulous; born on the mountains, montigenous; wandering on the mountains, montivagant; burning mountain, volcano. ..

MOUNTEBANK. *s.* Charlatan, empiric, medicaster, saltimbanco.

MOURNFUL. *a.* Elegiac, funereal, lugubrious, rueful, tragic, tragical, funebral, funebrous; mournful song, threnody; mournful ditty, dirge.

MOURNING. *p.* Well-known tree used as an emblem of mourning, cypress (Shakes); causing mourning, luctiferous; mourning querimonious, querulous.

MOUSE. *s.* Little mouse, musculus; shrewmouse, ranny.

MOUTH. *s.* Mouth or arm of the sea, estuary the mouth of a river, lade, ostiary, estuary; mouth or opening, orifice; mouth of a vein, artery, &c. stoma; what is put into the mouth to hinder speech, gag; a washing or gargling the mouth, diaclysma, gargarism; told by word of mouth, oral; the canal leading from the mouth to the stomach, oesophagus; to stop one's mouth before he has quite told his tale, to obacerate; wry mouth, mop.

MOUTHFUL. *s.* Gobbet.

MUCH. *a.* Too much, nimious; the state of being too much, nimiety.

MUD. *s.* Sediment; to cleanse from mud, to fey; full of mud, limous or limose; like, or of the colour of mud, luturious.

MUDDINESS *s.* Feculence, coenosity.

MUDDY. *a.* Oazy, oozy, turbid, uliginous.

MULTIPLICATION. *s* Multiplication of numbers, once, twice, thrice, &c. into themselves, producing their squares, cubes, biquadrates, &c. involution; the numbers by which any multiplication is produced, are termed, factors.

MULTIPLIED. *p.* Multiplied by the same number or multiplier, equimultiple; number given to be multiplied, multiplicand.

MULTIPLY. *v.* To multiplicate.

MULTITUDE. *s.* Confluence, meiny, populace.

MUNGREL. *s.* Mongrel.

MURDER. *v.* To assassinate, to jugulate, to kill.

MURDER. *s.* Carnage, butchery, massacre, havoc, murther; the murder or murderer of our blessed Saviour, deicide; of a father, parricide; of a mother, matricide; of a parent, parenticide; of a son or daughter, infanticide; of a brother, fratricide; of a sister, sororicide; of a king,

regicide; of a bishop, episcopicide; of a prophet or poet, vaticide; of a stranger, hospiticide; of an enemy, hosticide; self-murderer, suicide. (See, to kill.)

MURDERER. *s.* Murderer for hire, bravo, occiser.

MURDERING. *p.* Act of, interfection; murdering with aggravated circumstances of cruelty, trucidation.

MURDEROUS. *a.* Gory, homicidal.

MURMUR. *v.* To growl, to maunder, to susurrate.

To repeat murmurs, to remurmur; murmur, susurration

MUSCLE. *s.* The doctrine of the muscles of the human body, myology myography; the dissecting of the muscles, myotomy. (See sarcology.)

MUSE. *v.* To brood, to meditate.

MUSES. *s.* The muses are nine, viz: *Calliope,* the muse of eloquence and heroic poetry; *Clio,* who presides over history; *Erato,* over love and poetry; *Euterpe,* over music; *Melpomene,* over tragedy; *Polyphymnia,* over rhetoric; *Terpsichore,* over music and dancing; *Thalia,* one of the graces, and the muse of comedy and lyric poetry; and *Urania,* who presides over astronomy.

MUSHROOM. *s.* Morilee, truffile, shampinion, from champignion, F.

MUSIC. *s.* Fitted to music, dittied; music or musician, gleek (Shakesp.); papal church music, motets, motetto or motetti, these motetti are composed with much art and ingenuity, some of them for one, two, three, four, or more voices, and very often accompanied with several instruments (Bailey); pieces of divine music frequently made use of in the Roman church, messa; music performed in the night by lovers, at the windows or doors of their mistresses, serenade; concert of music performed in the midst of the night, or morning early, in the open air, serenata.

MUSICAL. *a.* Harmonic, harmonious, melodious, canorous, numerous, rythmical; to render musical, to melodise; musical composition of two parts, duetti or duetto; of three, trio, &c.; a musical assembly or entertainment, ridotto, opera.

MUSICIAN. *s.* Gleek, tweedledumtweedledee; company of musicians, minstrelsey; musicians who go about at night or morning to entertain others with their music, waits.

MUSING. *p.* Overcome by or with musing, bemused.

MUSTER. *s.* The place where soldiers are mustered and paid, diribitory.

MUSTY. *a.* Vinnewed, finewed, froazy, mucid, rancid.

MUTTER. v. To murmur, to mussitate, to strepitate.

MUTUAL. a. Reciprocal, commutual; mutual assistance, coadjument; mutual cause, concause.

MYSTERIES. s. An interpreter of mysteries, mystagogue.

MYSTERIOUS. a. Acataleptic, cabalistical, inexplicable, inscrutable, occult, anagogical. (See hidden).

N

NAILS. s. Fangs, talons; a skinny appendage sometimes at the root of a nail, agnail; term or cant phrase used among gunners for spiking or driving in iron nails into the touch-hole of cannon, poisoning.

NAKED. a. Callow; naked, (unfledged) pinfeathered; to make naked, to denude or denudate, to divest; naked picture, nudity; act of making naked, nudation; to strip naked, to connudate. (See bald.)

NAME. v. To indigitate, to clepe, to nominate; to name first, to prenominate.

NAME. s. To call by name, to nuncupate; name, appellation; good name, eudoxy, euphemism; having the same name, cognominal; having two names, binominous; consisting of three names, trinomial; having four, &c. quadrinomial; having many names, polynomial, multinomial; list or roll of names, matricula; primitive or radical names are called, impositious names; predicting by names, onomantic, onomantical; the art of, is called, onomatechny; names derived from one's ancestors, patronymics; name added to the sirname on account of some great action, agnomen; relating to fictitious names, pseudonymous; something added to a name, suraddition (Johnson); having the name only, nominal, titular, titulary.

NAMED. p. Behight, benempt, ycleped.

NAMELESS. a. Anonymous.

NAP. s. Nap taken in the afternoon, zest.

NAPIER. s. Baron Napier's method of computing by rods or bones, rhabdology.

NARROW. a. Incapacious, strait; narrow passage, enfilade; the act of making narrow, angustation. (See, to contract.)

NASTINESS. s. Mulloc, ordure, squalor, feuity.

NASTY. a. Eruginous, excremental, fetid, mucid, noisome, squalid, verminous, frouzy; nasty smell, fetor.

NATIONS. s. Peculiar to nations or countries, gentilitious, endemial, endemical, endemic or endemick; nation or country, leod.

NATIVE. a. Indigenous, ingenite, natal, pandemic.

NATIVITIES. s. Astrological table for calculating them, speculum; artificial method of rectifying them, trutina hermetis (astrology.)

NATURAL. a. Genial, ingenite, innate, intrinsic, intrinsical; natural to a country, indigenous, vernacular; collector of natural curiosities, vertuoso or virtuoso; not natural, insitive, preternatural.

NATURE. s. Physis (Bailey); the nature of any thing, essence; of the same nature, connaturality; unlike in nature, heterogeneal, heterogeneous; similar in nature, homogeneal or homogeneous; the doctrine of the constitution of the works of nature, physiology; any thing apparently above the ordinary course of nature, supernatural; differing from the ordinary course of nature, preternatural; term used for the peculiar mode that nature takes to build and produce things in the order that is most agreeable to their property, plasticnature, or architectonic nature.

NAVAL. a. Naval management or manoeuvering, naval tactics.

NAVEL. s. A starting or protuberance of the navel, or dropsy of the navel, exomphalos; navel-string, funicle, laqueus; rupture of the navel, omphalocele; a flatulent rupture of the navel, pneumatomphalus; a stony substance sometimes bunching out of the navel, poromphalon; a fleshy excrescence of the navel, sarcomphalum; of or belonging to the navel, umbilical; formed without a navel, (as Adam and Eve must have been,) anomphalos; and thus they are represented in all drawings and paintings, (Quincy); any thing applied to the navel when it starts, epomphalum; a swelling of the navel, turgid with blood, hæmatomphalocele; name of a species of swine in America, said to have its navel placed on its back, javaris.

NAVIGATION. s. The art of navigation, histiodromia.

NEAR. ad. a. Adjacent, circumjacent, proximate, proxime; near (sparing) parsimonious; near related, affined.

NEARNESS. s. Confinity, impendence,

propinquity, proximity, vicinage, vicinity.

NEAR. *a.* Near-sighted, purblind, porblind.

NEAT. *a.* Elegant, gimm, gimmy, meracious, nitid, quaint, terse, natty, tidy, feateous, dexterous.

NEB. *s.* Nib.

NECESSARY. *a.* Essential, requisite; quite necessary, indispensible or indispensable; necessary before hand, pre-requisite ; equally necessary, equinecessary.

NECESSITY. *s.* Enforcement, compulsion, exigence.

NECK. *s.* Of or belonging to the neck, cervical; pain in the neck accompanied with stiffness, crick; neck of a bird, juke; joint of the neck, or region about the first vertebra of the back, nape, nucha; medicine tied round the neck as a charm against diseases, periamma or periapta ; chain or collar of jewels worn round the neck, carcanet.

NEEDLESS. *a.* Supervacaneous.

NEGLECT. *v.* To contemn. (See despise.)

NEGLECT. *s.* Default, disregard, misprision, omission, omittance, pretermission.

NEGLIGENCE. *s.* Inadvertence, oscitancy, oscitation, recklessness.

NEGLIGENT. *a.* Perfunctory, reckless, improvident, supine.

NEIGHBOUR. *s.* Gaffer, gammer ; a country neighbour, geburus; of or belonging to neighbours, vicinal.

NEIGHBOURHOOD. *s.* Vicinage, vicinity, environs; the being in the neighbourhood, adjacency.

NEIGHBOURING. *a.* Conterminous, adjacent.

NEPHEW. *s.* A fondness or affection for nephews, nepotism.

NERVES. *s.* Of or belonging to the nerves, neuretic; description or discourse concerning the nerves, neurology ; remedies against the diseases of the nerves, neurotics ; a section or cutting of the nerves, neurotomy. (See neurotomy.)

NEST. *s.* Nest of a bird of prey, serie or eyry; nest of snails, escargatoire; the art of building nests, nidification ; the time of remaining in the nest, nidulation; nest of caterpillars, pucker.

NET. *s.* To catch in a net, to enmesh, to mesh ; the meshes of nets are called mocks or mokes; unlawful fishing-nets, kidles ; formed of net-work, meshy ; short nets used by fowlers for taking pheasants alive, Hay's pocket (from the inventor) ; made in form of a net, reticular, retiform ; small net, reticula, reticle; net rete. *L.* ; large fishing net generally used in rivers, seam, sean, or seine ; net used in catching partridges, tunnel.

NETTLES. *s.* Full of nettles, urticose.

NEUTRAL. *a.* Adiaphorous, or adiaphorous.

NEUTRALITY. *s.* Adiaphory.

NEWS. *s.* False news, mistidings; to tell or shew ill news, to obnunciate ; new (fresh) mustulent, virent ; new (modern) neoteric, recent ; new (outlandish) peregrine.

NEWNESS. *s.* Novity.

NEXT. *a.* Next to, immediate, instant, proximate, proxime ; the state of being placed next to, juxtaposition.

NIB. *s.* Neb.

NICE. *a.* Delicate, fastidious, quaint, precise, prim, finical, gustful, fragrant, lickerish, mellow, scrutinous, tid ; over nice, prude, scrupulous ; nice, proud dame, minniken ; nice food, cates.

NICETY. *s.* Accuracy, chariness, criticalness, vicety, exquisiteness, quillet; nicety of behaviour, punctilio ; trifling nicety, quidity.

NIGGARD. *s.* Churl, curmudgeon, hunks. (See miser.)

NIGHT. *s.* Importing the beginning of night, acronycal ; this term is applied to the stars, of which the rising and setting is called acronycal, when they either appear above, or sink below the horizon at sun set ; to wax toward night, to advesperate ; an attack made during the night by soldiers, with their shirts over their apparel, in order to be known to each other, camisade, or camisado ; act of watching all the night, excubation ; night mare, incubus, succubus, succuba, ephialtes; one who turns night into day, lychnobite ; any disturbance in the night, night rule ; turning towards night, nightward ; containing both a night and day, noctidial ; consisting of two nights, binoctial ; of three, &c. trinoctial, &c. ; bringing or causing night, noctiferous ; an account of business transacted in the night, noctuary ; night walking, noctambulation ; wandering in the night, noctivagant ; act or state of lying out all night, pernoctation ; one entire night and day, nychthemeron ; a night guard performed by the whole army when there is any apprehension of danger, biovag, or bihovac ; name given to those who see by night, or according to others, to those who cannot see by night, nyctalops ; this distemper is called nyctalopia. (See candle light.

NIGHTINGALE. *s.* (Ornith), luscinia, philomel.

NIMBLE. *a.* Active, yare, alipede, quiver, agile, fleet, flippant, lithe, lithesome; volant, voluble.

NIMBLENESS. *s.* Legerity. (See lightness.)

NIMBLY. *ad.* Adroitly, featly. (See light.)

NINE. *a.* The number of nine, ennead; relating to the number nine, enneatical, novenary; of nine days continuance, novendial; of nine years continuance, novennial; every ninth year of ones life is called an enneatical year, or climacterical year. (See year and articles one, two, three, &c.

NIP. *v.* To vellicate. (See to pinch.)

NIPPLES. *s.* Of the breast, papillæ, teats; little swellings like nipples, which sometimes break out in the night time, perinyctides; the red circles round the nipples of the breasts, halo.

NOBILITY. *s.* The nobility, or the government of the state by nobles, optimacy, (Johnson) (Bailey.)

NOBLE. *a.* Intrepid, doughty, dread, ingenuous, magnanimous, magnific, epic, equestrian, illustrious, palacious, peerless, topping, unparagoned; the body of nobles, optimacy.

NOBLENESS. *s.* Of birth, eugeny.

NODDING. *p.* Act of, nutation, titubation.

NOISE. *s.* Garboil, boation, bombilation, misrule, racket, rixation, bounce, brabble, bruit, churm, or churme, clatter, clutter, utis, fragor; confused and hideous noise, tintamar; noise and pursuit after a robber, &c. hue and cry; any place of noise, beargarden; hoarse noise, raucity; the making a noise like snorting, rhonchisonant; making a small and skreaking noise, stridulous; making noise by stamping with the feet, suppiosion; noise occasioned by fired gunpowder, explosion, detonation; noise or scream made by an insect, fritinancy; to make a noise like thunder, to fulminate; to make a slow and protracted noise, to intone; to raise up noise, to deray; to make a loud noise by the voice, to vociferate; to noise abroad, to verbigerate; to stupify with noise, to dorr; crackling noise as salt makes on being thrown in the fire, crepitation, or decrepitation.

NOISY. *a.* Garrulous, highty-tighty, hurly-burly, mobbish, obstreperous, streperous, tumultuary, tumultuous, termagant; noisy fellow, belwether, blusterer, bully.

NONPLUSSED. *p.* When one is nonplussed, he is said to be at *Dulcarnon,* from an intricate proposition so named by Pythagoras, on the discovery of which he sacrificed an ox to the gods, (Bailey.)

NOON. *s.* The act of sleeping at noon, meridiation; done or performed before noon antemeridian or A. M.; done after noon, post meridian or P. M.; of or belonging to noon, meridional.

NORTH. *a.* North wind, Septentrio; name given in Italy and the Mediterranean to the north wind, tramontane; the north or polar star, Cynosure; instrument for measuring the motion of the north star about the pole, nocturlabe; relating to the north artic, boreal, cæsias, hyperborean, septentrional; to tend towards the north, as the needle in the mariner's compass, to septentrionate; north, is one of the cardinal points of the compass.

NORTHERN. *a.* Arctic, boreal, cæcias, hyperborean, septentrional.

NOSE. *s.* Neese; relating to the nose, nasal; having a flattened nose, camoys, (from Camus, F.); mucus from the nose, myxa; full of snot from the nose, mucculent; having a nose of a horny substance, as some insects, nasicornous; a fleshy excrescence which sometimes grows in the nose, polypus, sarcoma; one who has a flat snub nose, simous; the name of a famous surgeon who was said to have made a new nose to one of his patients out of the piece of another man's flesh, Tagliacotius, or Taliacotius.

NOSEGAY. *s.* Posy, posey.

NOSTRIL. *s.* Medicines which are to be put up the nostrils, nasalia; syringe for injecting up the nostrils, rhinenchites, or enchyta.

NOTABLE. *a.* Eximious.

NOTARY. *s.* Of or belonging to a notary notorial; chief notary, prothonotary,

NOTCH *s.* Indentation, cæsura. (See cut).

NOTCHED. *a.* Crenated, dentated, lacinated, laciniated.

NOTE. *s.* Annotation, indication, comment, gloss, postil; to write notes, to comment; one who makes notes upon an author, scholiast; explanation by notes, glossing.

NOTICE. *s.* Notice by letter, aviso; to give notice, to cund, to promulgate; public notice given of any thing, ban; notice, (or hint) memento; worthy of notice, observable, regardable; previous notice, premonition, premonishment.

NOTION. *s.* Conception, perception; previous notion, preopinion, prescension; an imperfect notion or suspicion, surmise.

NOTWITHSTANDING. *ad.* Maugre, nathless, nevertheless.

NOUNS. *s.* Nouns of one case, monoptote, monoptoton; of two cases, diptote, diptoton; of three, triptote, triptoton; of four, tetraptote, tetraptoton; of five, pentaptote, pentaptoton; of six, hexaptote, hexaptaton; noun that is not declined with cases, aptoton; such nouns as vary from the common forms of declension are termed heteroclite.

NOURISH. *v.* To nourish or cherish, to refocillate, to focillate.

NOURISHED. *p.* The being nourished together, connutritious.

NOURISHING. *p.* Alible, nutritive.

NOURISHMENT. *s.* Aliture, aliment, nutriment, introsumption; the due nourishment of an organized body, eutrophy; the want of nourishment, atrophy, cacotrophy. (See Consumption); what does not afford nourishment, inalimental; victuals which afford good nourishment, euchylos.

NUMBER. *s.* Divination by numbers, arithmancy; the science of numbers, algorithms; one skilled in numbers, numerist; numbers multiplied by the same quantity, equimultiples; having the same number as another, equinumerant; being above the number, supernumerary; the greater number in voting, majority; the lesser, minority; the golden number,

enneadecaterides. (See Cycle); number which contains another twice, thrice &c. without a remainder, multiple; number which divides another into two parts, bipartient; into three, tripartient; four, &c. quadripartient, &c.; number given to be multiplied, multiplicand; a numbering one by one, dinumeration, enumeration; the act of numbering on or by the fingers, dactylonomy; the art of numbering an army or body of men, by throwing them into a geometrical figure, stratorithmetry.

NUN. *s.* Conventual, minchin.

NURSE. *v.* To cherish, to foster, to nousel, to noursle, to nurture.

NURSE. *s.* Matron, fosterdam; nurse or physician who attends bed-rid patients, clinicus; nurse's sleepy song, lullaby.

NURSERY. *s.* Of snails, escargatoire.

NUTS. *s.* Producing or bearing nuts, nuciferous.

NUTRITION. *s.* A disproportionate nutrition when one part of the body is nourished more or less than another, alogotrophy.

O

OAK. *s.* The fruit of, acorn, mast; of or belonging to the oak, roborean; strong as the oak, robusteous; a finer sort of oak, or oak artificially prepared, wainscot.

OATH. *s.* The tendering or taking of an oath, adjuration; bound by oath, conjured; relating to an oath, juratory; the act of binding or securing by an oath, objuration; an inducing of one to give a false oath, subornation; fountain in Sicily wherein all written false oaths are said to sink, Acadina; the act of taking a solemn oath, dejeration.

OATS. *s.* Officer in the king's stables who provides oats for the horses, avenor; place where the oats are kept, avery.

OBEDIENCE. *s.* Homage, morigeration, sequacity; relating to obedience, obediential.

OBEDIENT. *a.* Buxom, (Milton), morigerous, allegiant, obsequious, compliant, obsequible.

OBJECTION. *s.* The anticipation of an objection, prolepsis.

OBLIGATION *s* Obstruction, sponsion; an involuntary obligation, mancipation.

OBLIGED. *p.* Beholden, bounden, fain.

OBSCURE. *v.* To bedim, to intricate, to blear, to obfuscate, to obnubilate, to opacate.

OBSCURE. *a.* Complex, abstruse, immanifest, inevident, mystic, cimmerian; obscure (dim) caliginous; obscure, (lowborn), hedge-born.

OBSERVATION. *s.* Animadversion; previous observations, prolegomena; an useful observation or short sentence, gnoma.

OBSTACLE. *s.* Let, remora. (See hinderance.)

OBSTINACY. *s.* Headiness, inflexibility, inflexibleness.

OBSTINATE. *a.* Impersuasible, inconvincible, inveterate, opinionative, contumacious, unpersuadible, pertinacious, perverse, petulent, pervicacious, positive, fefractory, restiff, restive, tenacious.

OBSTRUCT. *v.* To blench, to contravert, to impede, to intercept. (See to hinder.)

P

OBSTRUCTING. *p.* Obstruent, obstupefactive, oppilative.

OBSTRUCTION. *s.* Barricado, intercision, obstacle, let ; obstruction in the
circulation of the juices of an organized
body, immeability, infarction, constipation ; cause of obstruction, intercipient ;
obstruction of the natural perspiration,
adiapneustia ; all medicines which are
good in removing obstructions, ecphrac-
tics ; to open obstructions, to deoppilate.

OBTAIN. *v.* By earnest entreaty, to impetrate.

OBTAINED. *p.* That may be obtained, impetrable : obtained by fraud, subreptitious, surreptitious.

OBTAINING. *p.* An obtaining or acquiring, assecation.

OBTUSE. *a.* Obtuse angled, Amblygonial.

OCULAR. *a.* Ocular demonstration, au-
topsy.

ODD *a.* Legendary, incredible, inform,
inordinate, unordinary, antic, equivocal,
ambiguous, gothic, grotesque, humorsome, mawkish, mystic, petulant, versatile, uncouth, preposterous, promiscuous,
quaint, queer, ununiform.

ODDNESS. *s.* Inordinancy, inordination.

ODIOUS. *a.* Abhorrent, invidious, loathful,
odible, hainous, or heinous ; to render
odious, to inodiate.

OFFENCE. *s.* Misfeasance, maleaction, deviation ; exemption from all offence, impeccability.

OFFEND. *v.* To disoblige, to grate, to
pique, to regrate.

OFFENSIVE. *a.* Fetid, fulsome, nauseous,
obscene, mephitical, noisome, noxious,
obnoxious, putid ; offensive to the smell,
putredinous, putrid ; whatever is offensive to a neighbourhood, nuisance.

OFFER. *v.* To proffer, to tend, to propound ;
to offer op as a sacrifice, to immolate ; to
offer as a reason, to obtend.

OFFERED. *p.* The thing offered, offer-
tory.

OFFERING. *s.* A whole burnt offering, holocaust ; offering made to a god or goddess, incense, oblation.

OFFERINGS. *s.* Obventions. (Law term.)

OFFICE. *s.* Function, ministration ; fee of
office, perquisite ; to discharge from office, to exauctorate.

OFFSPRING. *s.* Posterity, progeny, (See
articles, Brood, Breed, and Mongrel;) offspring or shoot, imp ; a beautiful offspring, callipædia.

OFTEN. *ad.* Or frequent, crebrous.

OIL. *s.* The fæces or grumous part of oil,
amorge ; holy oil or ointment, chrism ;
of the nature of oil, oleaginous ; rock oil,

petroleum, naphtha, maltha, pissasphal-
tum or pisselæum ; name of a sovereign
oil used in many diseases, polychreston,
(Bailey) ; such oils as are obtained by
distillation, in opposition to those which
are got by expression, are called stillatitious.

OILY. *a.* Adipose, oleaginous, oleose, oleous,
unctuous.

OINTMENT. *s.* Liniment, unction, unguent ; drying ointment, Xeromyrum ;
an universal fomentation or ointment,
diaplasma.

OLD. *a.* (Common) trite, stale, finewed, inveterate, superannuated ; very old, fangless ;
the act of trimming up old things, mangonism ; place where old clothes are vamped
up and sold, frippery ; old worn-out animal, gib or gibbe ; old worn-out cat, gibcat
or grimalkin ; name of contempt for an
old maid, grissette ; old rope, junk ; old
soldier, veteran ; the state of growing
old, senescence ; belonging to or consequent on old age, senile ; the Greek version of the Old Testament, Septuagint ;
very old, grandevous ; a vigorous old age,
agerasy ; that part of physic which shows
the way of living fit for old men, gerontocomy ; an hospital for poor old men,
gerontocomium ; term used by Galen for
the period of life when a person begins to
grow old, paracmasticos ; old people who
have lost their teeth, are called, nefrendes.

OMBRE. *s.* To play at ombre, to punt.

OMEN. *s.* Bodement, portent ; of or belonging to omens, auspicial.

ONE. *a.* The numbering one by one, dinumeration ; containing one and one half
more, as 9 contains 6 and ⅔ more, sesqui-
alter or sesquialteral ; producing one
at a birth, uniparous ; two at a birth,
biparous, &c. ; done by one voice,
univocal ; one-stringed instrument, mo-
nochord, monocordo, monorchordo ; one-
leafed plant, monocotyledon, monophyllon ; person with one eye, monoculus ;
funeral ditty sung by one person, monody ;
diseases which last but one day, or are
cured in one day, monohemerous ; act of
feeding on one kind of meat, monophagic ;
animal who sees with one eye only, monoptic ; noun which has but one case,
monoptoton, monoptote ; one-kernel'd
fruit, monopyrenous ; man who has but
one testicle, monorchis ; epigram or any
composition consisting of one verse, mo-
nostichon, monestick ; word of one syllable, monosyllable ; doctrine of one God,
Monotheism ; having but one tone, monotony. (See Two, Three, Four, &c.
and article Eye.)

ONLY. *ad.* Dernier ; real and only, extra-dictionary.

ONSET. *s.* Assault ; sudden onset, orgasm.

OOZE. *v.* To transmeate.

OOZING. *p.* Act of oozing through, permeation.

OPEN. *v.* To deobstruct, to disafforest, to evolve, to disclose, to expand, to reclude, to relax, to diffuse ; to open up the belly, to eventerate ; to open obstructions, to deoppilate.

OPEN. *a.* Accostable, apert, apparent, confest; open (not reserved) communicable, candid, downright ; open (artless) faunic, frank, explicit, ingenuous ; open (babbling) leaky; open like a net, meshy, reticulated ; open to view, obvious; open as an expanded flower, patulous ; open to the wind, or that may be blown thro', perflable ; the act of laying open, patefaction.

OPENING. *p.* Deobstruent, deoppilative, diarrhœtic, aperient ; an opening or breach, chink, cleft, orifice, sinus, hiatus, aperture ; opening or cut, incisure, cæsura; lawn or opening in a wood, glade ; an opening or proposal, overture.

OPERA. *s.* Ridotto.

OPINION. *s.* Verdict, existimation ; stiffness in opinion, tenacity (see Obstinacy); difference in opinion, dissent, heterodoxy; a change of mind or opinion, metanoia ; opinion formed before hand, preconceit ; opinion or principle, tenet, sometimes wrote tenent ; the final opinion and sentence pronounced by an arbiter, laudum.

OPIUM. *s.* Treatise concerning opium, mecanology, opeology.

OPPOSE. *v.* To combat, to confront, to contradict, to contrast, to contravent, to cope, to contend, to encounter, to obtend, to oppugn, to militate, to obviate, to oppone, to pose, to recuse, to resist.

OPPOSED. *p.* That may be opposed, refragable.

OPPOSITE. *a.* Hostile, afront, diverse, contrarious, repugnant ; the opposite or contrary (in geometry) converse ; opposite weight, counterbalance, counterpoise; opposites or contraries, antithets.

OPPOSITION. *s.* Renitency, contrariety, contrariness, contravention, controversy, co-rivalry, discord, enmity, impediment, oppugnancy ; opposition in argument, obtension; opposition of one thing to another, antithesis; opposition (casual meeting) rencounter.

OPPRESS. *v.* To extort, to gripe, to subdue, to aggrieve, to injure ; to oppress with soldiers, to dragoon ; to oppress or load, to onerate.

OPTICS. *s.* False optics, heteroptics.

ORABLE. *s.* Oracle of all doubtful ques-

tions in the Mahometan law, mufti.

ORDER. *v.* To order, to prescribe ; order, (to trim) to preen, to proin ; to order, to regulate ; to put in order, to adjust ; to order or arrange, to array ; to order (for the purpose of purchase) to bespeak ; to order (or lay out) to dispose.

ORDER. *s.* Appointment, commission, decree, dictate, enjoinment, impose, insisture, injunction, mandate ; order (or edict) placart, manifesto ; order (march) procession ; repealed order, countermand ; order (command) hest, behest, bidding ; without order, erratic, pell-mell ; done out of order, informal ; regular order, gradation, series ; the act of setting things in order, diascosmesis ; the chief of a sacred order, hierarch. The Orders in Architecture are five: The Tuscan, Doric, Ionick, Corinthian, and Composite.

ORDERED. *p.* Prescript.

ORDERING. *p.* Ordering or commanding, imperative ; an ordering or arranging of things in a handsome manner, eutaxy.

ORDERLY. *a.* The disposing or placing of things in an orderly manner, syntagma.

ORES. *s.* The melting and assaying of ores, smelting ; called also the docimastic art.

ORGAN. *s.* (Musical instrument) which plays by the means of water, hydraulus ; the keys of organs, harpsichords, &c. tastatura.

ORGANS. *s.* Not furnished with, or void of organs, inorganical, unorganised.

ORIGIN. *s.* Of the same origin ; congenerous, congenite.

ORIGINAL. *a.* Fundamental, prime, primal, primeval, primogenial, primigenious, primitial, primordial, primordiate, pristine, queer; original of a copy, prototype, protoplast, archetype ; an original writing, autography ; original copy, protocol ; true copy of an original, estreate; an original disease or affection, protopathy ; a primitive or original word, prototypon, etymon ; the original inhabitants of a country, Aborigines or Autochtones.

ORNAMENT. *s.* Embellishment, exornation, gaudery, garnish ; to deprive of ornament, to disgarnish.

OVEN. *s.* Mop used for cleansing an oven, scovel.

OVERBALANCE. *v.* To preponder, or preponderate.

OVERCOME. *v.* To conquer, to vanquish, to foil, to prevail, to debellate; that may be overcome, vincible, exuperable, superable.

OVERPLUS. *s.* Surplus, surplusage.

OVERSET. *v.* Liable to be overset, crank.

OVERSIGHT. *s.* Hallucination, misprision.

OVERTHROW. *v.* To everse, to evert, to raze.

OVERTHROW. *s.* Subversion.

OUTCRY. *s.* Clamour, ejulation, exclamation.

OUTLINE. *s.* Outline of a picture, contour; sort of thin transparent stuff, to trace the outlines of a picture through, tammy.

OUTLIVE. *v.* To supervive, to survive.

OUTWARD. *a.* Extraneous, extrinsic.

OUTWEIGH. *v.* To preponder or preponderate.

OWL. *s.* The horned owl, asio; to cry as an owl, to hoot; owls and other nightly ill-foreboding birds are called, lich-fowls.

OXEN. *s.* Oxen, bulls and cows are called beeves, neat.

OYSTERS. *s.* Broiled oysters, escalop; the oyster (term in ichthyology) ostrea; that part of the sea where oysters spawn, cultch (Bailey); fishers of oysters, dredgers.

P

PACIFIED. *p.* That may be pacified, mulcible.

PACIFY. *v.* To appease, to pacate.

PACK. *v.* To pack up, to embale.

PACK. *s.* Pack of goods, bale, fardel.

PACK-HORSE. *s.* Sumpter-horse.

PAD. *s.* Pad on which a woman sits when on horseback, pillion.

PAGAN. *s.* Ethnic, infidel, painim.

PAIN. *v.* To ache, to cruciate, to excruciate, to agonize.

PAIN. *s.* Dolor, ailment, anguish, torsion; pain in the head, megrim, cephalalgia, or cephalopony; medicines which assuage pains, paregorics, antalgicks, opiates, anodynes; general name for pains in any part of the body, tormina; as *tormina ventris*, the gripes, or *tormina post partum*, the after-pains of women; an insensibility of pain, dedolency, (See Easing and Comforting); incapable of suffering pain, impassible.

PAINFUL. *a.* Darting, homefelt, penile; painful or laborious, laboriferous; a growing painful again, recrudescent.

PAINT. *v.* To depict, to emblaze, to fard, to limn, to fucate, to impaint, to infucate, to pourtray or portray.

PAINTER. *s.* Limner; painter on paper or parchment, alluminor; coarse and low painter, dauber; painter's staff to lean on, mastic, or maul-stick; painter's board for holding his colours, palette; painter's frame or support for holding the picture, easel; of or belonging to, or produced by a painter, pictorial; painter's statue or figure, which when dressed may be placed in different natural attitudes, layman; painter or writer of trifling and base things, rhyparographer.

PAINTING. *p.* A painting or drawing on large paper, cartoon; painting with colours mixed with glue or size instead of oil, is called, painting in distemper; a particular way of painting in fresco, by preparing a black ground on which was placed a white plaister, is called scratchwork (Bailey): the laying the ground colour under the colour wanted, sublition; the art of painting is called, the diagraphic art; term used in painting when an object is represented endways, giving it an appearance of shortness, foreshortening; the art of painting, painture, F.

PAIR. *s.* Brace, doublet, gemini.

PALACE. *s.* Palatium, L. derived from mount Palatine, on which stood the royal mansion-house in Rome.

PALE. *a.* Lurid, pallid, ghastly, sallow; pale as a sick virgin, maid-pale.

PALES. *s.* The act of enclosing ground with pales, palification; pales set up as an enclosure or defence, palisade or palisado; pale or fence, staccado.

PALPITATION. *s.* The palpitation of the heart and arteries, palmos.

PALSY. *v.* To impalsy, to torpify.

PALSY. *s.* One afflicted with the palsy, paralytic; palsy which seizes all parts of the body below the head, paraplegia; palsy on one side only, hemiplegia or hemiplexia; palsy in some parts only of one side, is termed, a paralysis.

PALTRY. *a.* Paultry, piteous; paltry wretch, runnion.

PANGS. *s.* Anguish, dolor. (See Grief.)

PANT. *v.* To palpitate, to quappe.

PANTING. *p.* Act of, anhelation.

PAP. *s.* Of or belonging to the paps, mamillary; having paps, mammeated.

PAPER. *s.* Blank piece of paper to be filled up with such conditions as the person to whom it is sent, thinks proper, *carte blanche*, F.; waste or blotting paper, maculature; a sort of paper used by the ancients in drawing a first draught of any thing, which could afterwards be rubbed out, palimpseston; a flag or rush used by the ancients, which they substituted for paper, papyrus; paper which was set apart by the ancients for religious purposes only, hieratic paper.

PARADE. *s.* Bravado, fanfaronade, venditation.

PARALLELS. *s.* Parallels of altitude are termed, almacanters, almacanteras, or almicanthars.

PARCH. *v.* To adure, to torrify.

PARCHED. *p.* Adusted, arid, torrid.

PARCHING. *p.* The act of parching or drying up, adustion.

PARDON. *v.* To absolve, to remit, to forzeve.

PARDON. *s.* Absolution, remission, amnesty, condonation; capable of pardon, ignoscible; of or belonging to a pardon, absolvatory.

PARDONABLE. *a.* Veniable, venial, ignoscible.

PARDONED. *p.* That cannot be pardoned, irremissible.

PARENTS. *s.* The privation or loss of parents or children, orbation.

PARISH. *s.* Of or belonging to a parish, parochial; parish burdens, scot and lot.

PARK. *s.* Park or warren where living animals are kept, vivary.

PARLEY. *s.* Name of a particular beat of drum for a parley, shamade or chamade.

PARLIAMENT. *s.* The king's assent to a bill in parliament runs thus: " *Soit fait droit comme il est desiré.*"

PARLOUR. *s.* Dining-room or *parlour,* zeta, G.

PARSON. *s.* Cleic, pastor, rum.

PART. *v.* To fract, to dissever, to garble, to compart; to part asunder, to sever, to cleave.

PART. *s.* Fet, impartance, quota, scot; an infinitely small part, differential; parts, purtenances or appurtenances; the similarity or likeness of parts in an organized body, homoeomery or homoeomeria.

PARTICLES *s.* Atoms or atomys, minima; poisonous particles, or atoms, miasma or miasm; particles emanating from bodies, effluvia or effluvium.

PARTNER. *s.* Consociate, associate, fedary or federary, colleague, confederate, puefellow; partner (generally used in an ill sense) accomplice.

PARTRIDGES. *s.* The season of going to the haunts of partridges early in the morning or evening, to listen to the calling of the cock partridge, is called juekking-time; name of a certain sort of net for catching partridges, tunnel.

PARTY. *s.* Faction, junto; leader of a party, demagogue, partizan or partisan.

PASS. *v.* To elapse, to pass over, to per-

vade; to pass through, to permeate; to pass through as water, to transmeate; to pass into, to immigrate; to pass from place to place, to transmigrate.

PASS. *s.* Narrow pass, defile; pass (in fencing) allonge; pass, transit.

PASSAGE. *s.* Duct, gullet, indraught, exit, exodus; the act of opening a passage, apertion; narrow passage, enfilade; passage between, intercurrence, passage of water, lade; passage or freight, naulage; admitting a passage, pervious; passage of any planet just by, or under any fixed star, transit; passage over (ferry) traject; passage or removal, transition.

PASSED. *p.* That cannot be passed, invious, immeable; that cannot be passed through, impertransible, impervious; that may be passed through, permeable.

PASSING. *p.* The passing the summer in any place as birds of passage do, estivation; passing or flowing between, interfluent, intercurrent; the act of passing or flowing between, intermeation; not passing from one to another, intransitive; the passing or changing from one thing to another, either in the curative indications or the symptoms of a distemper, metabasis or metabole; passing by or omission, preterition, pretermission; the passing by or beyond assigned limits, transcursion; a passing over or crossing the sea, transfretation; passing away (fading) transitory.

PASSION. *s.* Ire, chafe, emotion, fervour, fume; the being void of passion, apathy; seized with passion, impassioned; one who provokes the passions, incensor; what moves the passions, pathos; passion, affection, or disorder, pathema; passion of long continuance, eipathy; an aptness to such passions of the mind, as bring on real distempers, excandescency.

PASSIONATE. *a.* Splenetive, vehement; passionate man, Hotspur.

PASSIVE. *a.* Adiaphorous or adiaphorous.

PAST. *p.* Aforetime, preterlapsed; soon past or over, transient.

PASTURE. *s.* Pasture-ground, mead, savanna.

PATCHING. *p.* The act of patching together, consarcination.

PATIENCE. *s.* Endurance; the want of patience, intolerance; having great patience, longanimity.

PATTERN. *s.* Ensample, exemplar, model, mirrer or mirrour, proplasm, paradigm, parragon, apographum; the art of making patterns or moulds for casting, &c. proplastice.

PAVE. *v.* To stratuminate.

PAVEMENT. *s.* Pavement of stepping

stones, sarn.

PAUSE. *v.* To hesitate, to muse, to respite.

PAUSE. *s.* Intermission.

PAWN. *v.* To impawn, to impignorate, to oppignorate.

PAWN. *s.* Pawn or mortgage, antichresis, deposit; pawn-broker's shop or booth, lombar-house.

PAWNING. *p.* Act of pawning, pignoration.

PAY. *v.* To discharge, to defray, to liquidate, to dispurse; to pay one's reckoning, to escot; to keep in pay, to retain; to pay back, to retribute, to renumerate, to requite; the ability to pay debts, solvency; the inability, insolvency.

PEACE. *s.* Indisturbance, undisturbance, mund, requiem, tranquillity; bringing peace, pacal; promoter of peace, gownsman: peacebreaker, perturbator.

PEACEABLE. *a.* Pacific, pacal; peaceable government, eirenarchy; peaceable times, halcyon-days.

PEACEFUL. *a.* Halcyon, pacific.

PEARL. *s.* Margarita (Nat. Hist.); that brings forth or produces pearls, margaritiferous; mother of pearl, nacre.

PECULIAR. *a.* Peculiar to a place or country, endemial; peculiar temper or disposition, idiosyncracy.

PEDANT. *s.* Grammaticaster, pedagogue.

PEDLAR. *s.* Pedler, huckster, hucksterer, badger.

PEEL. *v.* To peel off, to exfoliate, to excorticate; to peel off the bark from trees, &c. to deliberate.

PEEVISH. *a.* Exceptious, froward, fractious, frampold, humorsome, morose, cavilling, captious, splenetic, cynical, petulant, waiward.

PEEVISHNESS. *s.* Perverseness, chagrin, curstness, protervity.

PENDULUM. *s.* Moving as a pendulum, vibratory, oscillatory; the swing of a pendulum, oscillation; the time of performing one swing, diadrom; such vibrations of a pendulum as are performed in equal times, are termed, isochronal vibrations; term used for the pendulum, chronometrum perpendiculum, *L.*

PENSIONER. *s* Beneficiary.

PENSIVE. *a.* Meditabund. (See Thoughtful.)

PEPPER. *s.* (Jamaica pepper) pimento or pimenta, all-spice; partaking of the nature or properties of pepper, piperine.

PEOPLE. *s.* The common people, canaille; one of the common people, plebian; council or assembly of the people, folkmote; passing to the common people as fashions do in time, volgivagant; the country people, peasantry; to people a

country or increase its population, to populate; to decrease the people of a country, to depopulate or populate; incident to the people, pandemic or pandemick.

PERCH, *v.* To juke, to roost.

PERFECT. *a.* Impeccable; perfect or well drawn, graphical; not perfect, immature.

PERFECTION. *s.* Consummation, exquisiteness, complement, completion, maturity.

PERFIDIOUSNESS. *s.* Cretism, creticism.

PERFORM. *v.* To achieve or atchieve.

PERFORMANCE. *s.* Capital performance, master-stroke.

PERFORMED. *p.* Not to be performed, infeasible, unfeasible; performing more than duty requires, supererogation.

PERFUME. *v.* To cense, to fumigate, to pulvil; what perfumes, parfumatory.

PERFUME. *s.* Perfume thrown on live coals, which yields a pleasant flavour, suffitus, suffimentum; an exquisite perfume sometimes given to leather of which gloves are made, frangipane.

PERFUMED. *p.* Odoriferous, odorous, oderate.

PERFUMER. *s.* Myropolist.

PERHAPS. *ad.* Belike, peradventure, percase, verisimilar.

PERPENDICULAR. *a.* Normal, vertical; a perpendicular, such as the line, supposed to pass through the middle of a cylinder, &c. when placed on its base, cathetus.

PERPENDICULARLY. *ad.* Atrip.

PERPETUAL. *a.* Perennial, sempiternal.

PERPETUALLY. *ad.* Indesinently, incessantly, immarcessible.

PERPLEX. *v.* To beleauger, to confound, to confuse, to distract, to embarass, to bewilder, to inwrap, to nonplus.

PERPLEXED. *p.* Labyrinthian, mazy, dædalean.

PERPLEXING. *a.* Or distressing, carking.

PERPLEXITY. *s.* Intricacy, comber.

PERSON. *s.* Person who is examined, examinate; private person, idiot; grown-up person, adult; person of worth and learning, tanquam.

PERSONAL. *a.* Personal greatness, immediacy; of or belonging to personal subsistence, hypostatical.

PERSPIRATION. *s.* Obstructed perspiration, adiapneustia; free perspiration, eudiapneustia.

PERSUADE. *v.* To allure, to induce, to exhort, to excite, to incite; apt or ready to persuade, parenetic.

PERSUADED. *p.* Assured; not to be persuaded, impersuasible, or unpersuadable.

PERSUADING. *p.* Hortative, protreptical,

suasory, suasive.

PERSUASION. *s.* Persuasion or exhortation, protepticon.

PERSUASIVE. *a.* Inductive.

PERT. *a.* Flippant, alert, coxcomical, officious, dapper, procacious; pert hussey, flirt, malapert; pert fellow, prig.

PERTNESS. *s.* Dicacity.

PERVERSE. *a.* Contentious, contumacious, froward, petulant, refractory, tetrical, tetricous; perverse imitation (affectedness) cacozelia.

PERVERTED. *p.* Preposterous.

PESTILENCE. *s.* Contagion; treatise concerning the pestilence, limology.

PESTILENTIAL. *a.* Description of pestilential diseases, loimography.

PET. *s.* Tiff.

PETITION. *s.* Imparlance; of or belonging to a petition, a petitory.

PETITIONER. *s.* Suitor, suiter; female petitioner, suitress.

PETTICOAT. *a.* Petticoat-government, gynæcocracy.

PETTY. *a.* Pimping, snivelling, puisne, puny.

PHILOSOPHY. *s.* Smatterer in philosophy, philosophaster; the lectures of Aristotle in the more nice and difficult parts of philosophy, acroatics; a sect of sophists who discoursed upon matters of philosophy at supper, deipnosophists.

PHLEGM. *s.* Any medicines which draw off phlegm, apophlegmatism, hydrotic; consisting of phlegm, pituitous.

PHRASE. *s.* Locution; disused phrase, archaism; the stile and affected phrase of the citizens of Padua, in Italy, for which Livy is censured, patavinity.

PHYSIC. *s.* The taking of a doze of physic, propotisma; that particular theory of physic which refers the causes of all diseases to the chemical principles of a certain few substances, is termed the hermetical or spagirical physic. (See Medicine.)

PHYSICIAN. *s.* Pretended physician, or quack, pseudomedicus; the principal or chief physician, archiater, or archiatrus; physician who cures by unction and friction, iatroleptic; physician who cures by chemical prescriptions and applications, iatrochymic; physician who proceeds mathematically, iatromathematic; physician who studies to help or mend the complexion, cosmetick; physician who keeps close to experience, and excludes the theoretical part of physic, empiric; physician who lays down principles, and reasons from these principles and experience, is called, the dogmatical physician; physician who visits patients in bed to examine into their cases, clinical physician; physician who follows the method of Galen, and prescribes things gentle, natural, and ordinary, is called a Galenical physician; physician who proceeds in a certain regular method founded upon reason, deducing consequences therefrom to particular cases, is called the methodical physician; physician who prescribes according to chemical principles, spagirical physician; and lastly, the physician who only attends those in health, and that in order to preserve the same, and to prevent diseases, &c. (See hygienists in Quincy) hygieniacal physician.

PHYSIOGNOMY. *s.* Metoposcopy.

PICK. *v.* To cull, to excerpt, to select, to elect, to garble, to glean; to pick pockets, to manticulate; to pick or eat by little, to piddle.

PICK-POCKET. *s.* Cutpurse.

PICKED. *a.* Select.

PICK-AXE. *s.* Mattock, or mattoc.

PICKLE. *v.* To pickle, to condite, to souce.

PICKLE. *s.* Partaking of the nature of pickle, garous, muriatic; the pickle fish, &c. is preserved in, garum; West India pickle, potardo or potargo.

PICKLED. *a.* The pickled spawn of fish, caviare; pickled meat, marinade; fried in oil and pickled, marinated; that may be pickled, conditaneous.

PICTURE. *s.* Picture drawn in a very small compass, miniature; a picture or representation of any thing, icon; to dash or strike out of a picture, to dislimn; a writing or drawing of pictures on a large scale, megalography; picture done in lines only, i. e. of one colour, is called a monographic picture; picture done of one colour only, without mixture, such as one done in black and white, monochroma; picture representing naked figures, nudity; picture representing the figure at full length, portrait, or portraiture; the first draught of a picture, catagraph; sort of thin transparent stuff, to trace the outlines of a picture through, tammy. (See Figure.)

PIECE. *s.* Fet, cantlet; the act of tearing in pieces, discerption; to dash in pieces, to elide; piece cut off, frustrum; shapeless piece of any thing, mammoc.

PIERCE. *v.* To broach; to pierce through, to perforate, to permeate; to pierce, to terebrate, to thrill, to transfix.

PIERCED. *p.* Foraminous; not pierced, imperforate, unpierced; not to be pierced, impervious, impierceable, impenetrable; that may be pierced, penetrable.

PIERCING. *p.* Piquant, pungent; act of

piercing, pertusion ; a swimming, piercing, or flying ovet, tranation. (Bailey.)

PIETY. *s.* Sanctitude, sanctity, sanctimony.

PIGS. *s.* Litter of pigs, farrow ; roast made
up of the inmeat of a pig, harselet ; the
feet of a sucking pig, pettitoes ; little pig,
grice ; the least of the pigs that a sow
has at a litter, cadma ; sucking pigs are
called, nefrendes.

PIGEON. *s.* Wood pigeon, culver ; beautiful species of pigeon called the ring-dove,
palumbus ; pigeon-hole, lockyer ; pigeon-
house, columbary.

PIKE. *s.* (Pointed instrument of defence,)
hasta, *L.*

PIKE. *s.* Full grown pike-fish, luce ; young
pike, pickerel.

PILE. *v.* To pile up, to coacervate, to accumulate, to acervate.

PILE. *s.* Funeral pile, pyre ; pile of building, constructure ; the act of enclosing
ground with piles, palification.

PILES. *s.* The piles, hemorrhoides, emer-
oids or emerods, marisca.

PILFER. *v.* To lurch, to purloin ; to pilfer or draw away funds, to embezzle or
imbecile.

PILL. *s.* Large pill, bolus ; pill to be swallowed without chewing, catapotium.

PILLAGE. *v.* To depredate.

PILLAGE. *s.* Rapine, ravin, exuviæ, booty.

PILLAGER. *s.* Freebooter, piqueerer.

PILLARS. *s.* Row of pillars, colonnade ;
space between pillars, intercolumniation ;
circular range of pillars, peristyle ; a
square pillar, pilaster ; the foundation
or base of a pillar, plenth ; the base or
pedestal on which a pillar stands, stylo-
bata ; a walk under a roof supported by
pillars, piazza, portico, piache ; pillar
composed of triangles ending in a point
at the vertix, pyramid ; an inscription on
a pillar, stellography.

PILOT. *s.* The hire to a pilot for conducting a ship, lodemanage.

PILLORY. *s.* Put upon the pillory, collis-
trigiated.

PIMP. *s.* Cockbawd, purveyor, mackerel,
pander.

PIMPLE. *s.* Pustule ; tubercules, or tubercula ; full of pimples, pustulous ; the state
of being full of pimples, papulosity ; pimples which break out on the skin by reason of the winter's cold, psydracium.

PIN. *s.* Large pin, corking pin ; the pin of
a dial, gnomon ; the pin of a wheel on
which it turns, pivot ; wooden pin, peg.

PINCERS. *s.* Formed like pincers, forcipat-
ed.

PINCH. *v.* To bepinch, to tweng or tweak,

PINCH. *s.* Pinch or extremity deadlift.

PINE. *v.* To pine or waste, to emaciate, to
tabefy ; to pine or long for, to hone.

PINING. *p.* (Starving), marcid, phthisi-
cal.

PIOUS. *a.* Devotional, heremetical. (See
Holy.)

PIPE. *s.* Tube ; pipe to draw off liquors
with, siphon, syphon, crane ; pipe or
squirt for injecting liquors into the urethra, &c. syringe, metrenchytes ; relating to a pipe, tibial ; hollow like a
pipe, tubulous ; of or belonging to pipes,
auletic.

PIRATE. *s.* Buccanier, or buccaneer, corsair, freebooter, pickaroon.

PISS. *v.* (Said of cattle) to stale.

PISSING. *p.* Astalling or pissing backwards, retromingency.

PIT. *s.* Dell, gurge, abysm, abyss ; the entrance into a pit, adit.

PITCH. *s.* Bitumen, of which there are
three kinds, viz : 1st, Bitumen judaicum,
or asphaltum, which is found floating on
the Dead Sea, and in many parts of E-
gypt. 2d, Bitumen Barbadense, or Bar-
badoes tar. And, 3d, Bitumen liqui-
dum, i. e. Petroleum (see oil) ; a very
hard sort of pitch, rasis ; the finest sort
of pitch, scraped off from the sides of ships,
and tempered with wax, &c. zopissa.

PITCH-FORK. *s.* Fourche, prong.

PITH. *s.* Of or belonging to pith, medulla-
ry, parenchymatous ; to take out the pith
or marrow, to emedullate.

PITHY. *a.* (Short), Laconic, Chilonian,
Chilonic.

PITIFUL. *a.* Piteous, rueful, ruthful, servile, sordid.

PITIED. *p.* Not to be pitied, immiserable.

PITILESS. *a.* Ruthless.

PITY. *s.* Commiseration, ruth, remorse ;
one whom nobody pities, immiserable ;
to move to pity, to intenerate ; void of
pity, incompassionate.

PLACE. *v.* To place or station, to collocate ;
to place in the same age, to contempor-
ise ; to place opposite or against, to contrast ; to place or arrange, to dispose ;
to place before, to prefix.

PLACE. *s.* Peculiar to a place as some diseases, endemial, endemical, endemick ;
change of place or abode, intermigration ;
place, lieu, *F.* ; relating to place, local ;
the act of giving place to, lococession ;
the act of taking from one place to
another, transumption ; mutual exchange
of place, translocation ; to pass from place
to place, to transmigrate ; place or situation applied to the body, &c. posture ;
the description of any one place, as an
estate, &c. topography.

PLACED. *p.* Or resting on any thing, in-sistent; placed between, intercalary; placed or ranged, posited; placed above, empyrean, empyreal, supernal; placed below, infernal; the state of being plac-ed near to, juxta-position.

PLACING. *p.* A placing over against, con-traposition; act of placing, location.

PLAGUE. *s.* Contagion; good against the plague; anti-pestilential; medicines good against the plague, antilœmicæ, or anti-lomica; house or receptacle for confining those suspected of the plague, lazaretto; treatise or discourse concerning the plague, limology; plague, lues, pest; plague among cattle, murrain; the period of 40 days during which vessels are pre-vented from landing goods or men, when suspected of the plague, quarantine.

PLAIN. *v.* To plain or polish, to planish.

PLAIN. *a.* Evident, apert, apparent, blunt, demonstrable, dilucid, discernible, dis-tinct, perceptible, downright, unequivo-cal, (See Clear); plain, explicit, fau-nic, legible, luculent, notorious, obser-vable, obvious, palpable, perspicuous; plain surface, plane; that may be made plain, manifestible; plain speak-ing, planiloquy; plain proof, or evident demonstration, apodixis; not plain, im-manifest, imperspicuous, inevident; plain on one side and hollow on the other, pla-no-concave; plain on one side and round on the other, plano-convex; plain on one side and conical on the other, plano-conical.

PLAIN. *s.* A plain between woods, lawn, or laund; to make, plain, to elucidate, to evince, to evict; to make plain or smooth, to levigate.

PLAN. *v.* To meditate, to devise, to machi-nate.

PLAN. *s.* Contrivance, design, examplar.

PLANE. *s.* The art of measuring all sorts of planes, planimetry.

PLANET. *s.* The place of a planet nearest the earth, perigee, perigeum; farthest from the earth, apogee, apogœon, apo-geum; when nearest the sun, perehelii-um; when most remote, aphelion; the two points in the orbit of a planet, the nearest and farthest from the sun, are termed the apsides; the shortest diame-ter of the elliptical orbit of a planet, diacentros; the longest diameter is cal-led paracentros; that part of a curve in which a planet is, which is nearest to the earth, epigæum; planet-struck, syderose, sphacelated, astrobles, or astrobolismos; curve line described by a planet, trajec-tory; the passage of a planet just by, or under any fixed star, transit; said of two planets when they are 180° from each o-

ther, tredicile.

PLANK. *v.* To plank or floor with boards, to contabulate.

PLANTS. *s.* Treatise on plants, herbal; description of plants, phytology; divina-tion by plants and herbs, botanomancy; general term for all plants which turn towards the sun, as the turnsol, heliotre-pia; plants of doubtful gender are term-ed hermaphrodite, or androgynous; the down of plants, lanugo, L.; the flowers of plants, petals; plants which are nou-rished by the stock of others are termed parasitical plants; that eats or lives on plants, phytivorous; little plant, plantu-la, L.; the sensitive plant is called by botanists, pudica, from its shrinking when touched, (See Barberry); general name for plants, vegetables, or vegetives; the blasting of plants or trees by an east wind, sideration; general name for all female plants, thelygona; term given to such plants as shrink on being touched, Æschynomenous.

PLANTED. *p.* Or sown, sative, radicated.

PLANTING. *p.* Act of clearing grounds for planting, emphyteusis.

PLASTER. *v.* To emplaster, to parget.

PLASTER. *s.* Name of a well known plas-ter composed principally of saffron, oxy-crocium; plaster or ointment made of such consistence as neither to adhere or ran, cataplasm; sort of plasters generally made of lapis calaminaris, which dispose wounds to cicatrize, epulotic; flattish instrument in form of a knife for spread-ing plasters with, spatula.

PLASTERER. *s.* Pargeter.

PLASTERING. *p.* The act of plastering, oblimation.

PLATE. *s.* To beat into thin plates, to fo-liate; to plate over, to loricate; covered with plates, lamellated, or laminated; thin plates, such as the plates of the skull, &c. laminæ; the act of beating into plates, lamination.

PLATFORM. *s.* Or ground-plot of a build-ing, ichnography.

PLAY. *v.* To play unfairly as with loaded dice, to cog; to play upon or mock, to illude.

PLAY. *s.* Disport; used in play, lusori-ous, or lusory; apt or disposed to play, ludible; maker or writer of plays, play-wright; introduction to a play, prologue; the height of a play, counterturn.

PLAYER. *s.* Befitting a stage-player, his-trionic.

PLAYFUL. *a.* Ludescent.

PLAYING. *p.* Or waving about as flame, lambent.

PLEA. *s.* An encourager of a plea, barrator.

Q

PLEADER. *s.* Counsel, barrister, causidic ; pleader at the bar, who having taken a bribe feigns himself sick, such sickness is called argentangina, i. e. silver quincy, (Bailey).

PLEADING. *p.* The pleading of one's cause, dicœology.

PLEASANT. *a.* Gleeful, jocund, gustful, jovial, joyous, chromatic, lepid ; very pleasant smell, fragrance, aromatic.

PLEASANTNESS. *s.* Jucundity, amenity ; to look on with pleasantness, to arride ; pleasantness of temper, suavity.

PLEASANTRY. *s.* Hilarity, humour, or humor.

PLEASING. *s.* Diverting, luscious, boon, delectable, elegant, becoming, plausible.

PLEASINGLY. *ad.* Amicably, alluringly.

PLEASURE. *s.* Complaisance, fruition, glee, gratification, oblectation, solace ; pleasures, delices ; one addicted solely to pleasure, voluptuary, agapet ; the feigned goddess of pleasure, Volupta.

PLEDGE. *v.* To deposit, to impawn, to impignorate, to mortgage, to oppignorate, to pignorate ; to pledge or warrant, to plight.

PLEDGE. *s.* Earnest-money, hostage, depositum ; one who is pledge or security for another person, mainpernor, or mainprize.

PLENTEOUS. *a.* Exuberant, fertile.

PLENTIFUL. *a.* Fecund, feracious, copious, uberous.

PLENTY. *s.* Great plenty, glut, numerosity, uberty ; plenty, affluence, foison, or foizon, profluence ; the horn of plenty, cornucopia ; to make or render plenty, to uberate.

PLIANT. *a.* Compliant, flexible, limber, lithe, lithesome, sequacious, tractile.

PLOT. *v.* To brew, to cabal, to combine, to complot, to machinate.

PLOT. *s.* Designment, conjuration, conspiracy ; to oppose one plot to another, to counterplot.

PLOUGH. *v.* To plough, to ear, to till ; to plough in order to a second ploughing, to fallow.

PLOUGHING. *p.* The act of ploughing, aration, arature, exaration ; ploughing tackle of all kinds, gainage ; that which contributes to tillage or ploughing, aratory.

PLUCKING. *p.* The act of plucking, vellication ; the act of plucking away, divulsion ; the act of plucking out, evulsion.

PLUM. *s.* Plum dried in the sun, prune ; producing plums, pruniferous.

PLUME. *v.* To beplume.

PLUMP. *v.* Carnose, fat kidneyed, findy, jolly, pinguid ; plump ruddy wench, blowze.

PLUNDER. *v.* To depredate, to fleece, to forage, to gut, to harrow, to peculate, to pickeer, to ransack, to spoliate.

PLUNDER. *s.* Booty, excoriation, rapine, ravin ; living by plunder, predacious ; practising plunder, predal.

PLUNDERER. *s.* Corsair, marauder, freebooter, picaroon, poller, prowler.

PLUNDERING. *p.* Act of, direption.

PLUNGE. *v.* Suddenly into water, to douse, to submerge, or submerse.

PLUNGING. *p.* Act of, mersion, immersion.

POCKET. *s.* To pick pockets, to manticulate.

POCKET-BOOK. *s.* (Any book that is portable), manual, or manuel, enchiridion, encheridium.

PODS. *s.* The being formed in or like pods, siliquose, siliquous.

POEMS. *s.* In which the speakers assume the character of shepherds, pastorals, idyls, bucolicks, idyllions, or eclogues ; a funeral song or poem, epicedium, clegy ; that part which deities, angels, or demons, act in a poem, is called the machinery ; poem sung by one person not in dialogue, monody ; poem in which the native words in a language are made to end in latin terminations, is called a macaronic poem ; sort of poem or verses, so arranged that the initial letters form the name of some person or thing, acrostic ; confused collection of poems, rhapsody, (Bailey) ; A farewell speech or poem, apobaterion.

POET. *s.* Ancient British poet, bard ; the king's poet, laureat, or poet-laureat ; female poet, poetess, or poetress ; general name for poets, metricians ; pitiful poet, poetaster, versifier, rhymer, or rhymster ; the murder or murderer of poets, vaticide.

POETRY. *s.* Rage for reciting poetry, metromania. Under this article in Quincy's Lexicon, the following remarkable circumstance is told. " In the *Acta Societatis Medicæ Hauneinsis*, published " in 1779, is an account of a Tertian, attended with remarkable symptoms ; one "of which was the metromania, which " the patient spoke extempore, having " never before had the least taste for po-" etry ; when the fit was off, the patient " became stupid, and remained so till " the return of the paroxysm, when the " poetical powers returned again." Divination from any detached piece of poetry, orthomancy, or rhapsodomancy ; of or belonging to verse or poetry, metrical ; poetry, poesy ; pieces of comic poetry, silli, G. ; of or belonging to the wanton and obscene poetry sung by the ancient

Romans at weddings, Fescennine poetry; there are five kinds of metrical modulation in poetry, viz. Iambic, Trochaic, Dactyle, Anapæstic, and Alexandrine.

POINT. *v.* Or sharpen, to acuate; to point out, to denote, to indigitate.

POINT. *s.* Mucro, L. jot, tittle, jota; point of meeting, juncture; point or top of a pyramid or cone, apex; term used for the points or horns of the moon, cusps; tending to a point, convergent; proceeding from a point as rays, divergent; point or period of time to date from, epocha, or æra; point of support, fulcrum, fulciment, hypomochlion; chief point or end, goal; narrowed to a sharp point, mucronated; a nice point or subtilty, quodlibet; any weapon or instrument with three points, trisulcus; point of the heavens exactly above the head, zenith; exactly below the feet, nadir.

POINTING. *p.* Indicant, indicative.

POISON. *v.* To envenom, to impoison, or empoison, to venenate.

POISON. *s.* Bane; what is capable of counteracting the effects of poison, antidotal; special preservative against poison, mithridate, or mithridatum, so named from a doze taken every morning by Mithridates, king of Bithynia; an electuary good against poison, orvietan, so named from a mountebank at Orvieto, in Italy, who pretended to resist poisonous dozes be feigned to swallow on the stage; name for the poison tree, or amyris, toxicodendrum; medicines good, against poison are termed alexipharmics, elixiterics, bezoartics; charm against poison worn about the body, phylactery; any remedy against poison, antipharmacum; any medicine good against poison, or the bite of poisonous animals, theriaca, or theriace; acting by poison, veneficial; poison or love-doze used by the ancients, hippomanes; an amulet or charm against poison, alexicacon.

POISONING. *p.* The act of poisoning water by casting any thing into it to spoil it, lourgulary, (Bailey); the act of poisoning, veneation.

POISONOUS. *a.* Mephitical, venene, venenose, toxical, virulent, venetic, venomous, venemous; poisonous particles or atoms, miasma, or miasm,

POISE. *v.* To librate. (See Weigh.)

POLE. *s.* Boom; not according to the direction of the poles of the world, impolarily; flatted at the poles, oblate. (See *Prolate Spheroid*, under article *Figure*); pole used by a rope dancer, poy, from poids, F.

POLISH. *v.* To burnish, to furbish, to plainish, to gleen.

POLISHED, *p.* Limid; that may be polished, polishable.

POLISHING. *p.* Act of, limation; the gloss given by the act of polishing, politure.

POLITE. *s.* Courtlike, courtly, delicate; polite literature is termed, Belles Lettres.

POLITELY. *ad.* Complimentally.

POLITENESS. *s.* Politure, urbanity.

POLLUTE. *v.* To contaminate, to contemerate, to imbrute, to inquinate, to turpify, to conspurcate.

POLLUTION. *s.* Defædation, desecration.

POND. *s.* For keeping young fish alive, nurse pond.

PONDER. *v.* To muse, to perpend. (See Think.)

POOL. *s.* Of fresh water, freshet.

POOR. *a.* Flimsy, limber, immartial, inane, infertile, infecund, orbate, paltry, paultry, hedgeborn, indigent, insipid, marcid, sterile; to make or render poor, to depauperate, to impoverish; poor sickly appearance, peaking; extremely poor or indigent, egestous; poor, low, or weak, (wanting a head,) acephalous.

POPE. *s.* Pontiff; Pope's ambassador, legate; of or belonging to the Pope, papal.

POPPY. *s.* Resembling or partaking of the nature of poppy, papaverean, or papaverous; the syrup of poppies is named diacodion, or diacodium.

POPULAR. *a.* Democratic, plebian.

POPULATION. *s.* The same as depopulation, (Bailey)

PORCH. *s.* Of a temple, &c. propyleum, prothyrum, vestible, or vestibule.

POROUS. *a.* Parenchymatous, parenchymous.

PORT. *s.* Having no port or harbour, importuous.

PORTER. *s.* Pylorus, janitor.

PORTION. *s.* Fet, endowment, or indowment; small portion, modicum, pittance.

POSITIVE. *a.* Assertive, confident, dogmatical, categorical, peremptory.

POSITIVELY, *ad.* Absolutely, affirmatively, point blank.

POSSESS. *v.* To occupate, to pervade. (See Possession.)

POSSESSION. *s.* To put in possession, to instal, to invest, to enfeoff; to put in possession again, to revest; to put in possession of a benefice, to induct; one put in possession, feoffee; one who puts another in possession, feoffer; possession or enjoyment, fruition; possession, occupancy; the act of putting into possession, investiture, livery; having possession, possessive, possessory; the first or previous possession, preoccupancy; term in the law of Scotland when a tenant holds possession after the expiry of his lease, without a new one, he is said to hold it by tacit relocation.

POSSESSER. *s.* Of a benefice, proprietary, incumbent.

POSSIBLE. *a.* Feasible, practicable. (See impossible.)

POST-HORSE. *s.* Post hackney.

POSTSCRIPT. *s.* Hypogram.

POTATOES. *s.* Drink made from potatoes, mobby.

POVERTY. *s.* Destitution, indigence, necessitude, penury, ruination; extreme poverty, egestuosity; poverty (want of matter), jejuneness.

POULTICE. *s.* Cataplasm, malagma; poultice for horses, remolade.

POUND. *v.* To contund, to bray, to triturate; to pound or work with a hammer, to tudiculate.

POUNDING. *p.* Act of pounding, pestillation, pistillation, trituration.

POWDER. *v.* To comminute.

POWDER. *s.* To reduce to an impalpable powder, to levigate; reduce into powder, to triturate, to pulverize; that may be reduced to powder, comminuible; powder of a metal subjected to great heat, calx, (old chym.) now termed the oxyd of the metal; cases for charges of gunpowder used by soldiers, bandoleers; the act of breaking or bruising into powder, contrition; what is easily converted into powder, friable, pulverable; powder or filings of any metal, limature; powders grossly pounded, tragea.

POUR. *v.* To pour out, to diffuse, to effuse, or effund; to pour one thing upon another, to affuse; to pour back as water stopped in its course, to regurgitate; to pour from one vessel into another, to transvasate, to transfuse; to pour between, to interfuse.

POURING. *p.* A pouring round about, circumfusion; a pouring upon from above, superaffusion; a pouring together or confusion of humours, synchysis.

POWER. *s.* Function, ability, availableness, competence, control, dint, dominion, competency, energy, enforce, compass, efficacy; power or faculty, hability; power, masterdom, mastery, vigor, vigour, influx, potency, puissance; power of conviction, cogency; to have equal power, to countervail; the power of the will deduced into an act or deed, elicitation; having equal power, equipollent; the power of acting without dependence, immediacy; having great power, multipotent; invested with full power, plenipotent; having superior power, prepotency, predominance; the mechanic powers are, the balance, lever, wheel, wedge, screw, and pully.

POWERFUL. *a.* Drastic, effective, imperious, lusty, inflective, potential, prevalent, sinewy, virtual; powerful in many things, multipotent; all powerful, pancratic, pancratical, omnipotent, omnivalent; to render powerful or efficacious, to virtuate.

POWERLESS. *a.* Inefficacious; the state of being powerless, impotence, or impotency.

POX. *s.* The French pox, syphilis, lues venerea; medicines good against the French pox, antiphroditics, antivenereals.

POX. *s.* The small pox, variolæ; afflicted with the small or great pox, pockified, (see Cow); relating to them, variolous; any eruption resembling the small pox, exanthemata, or exanthema.

PRACTICE. *s.* Or custom, guise, ure, inurement; one who practises, practisant, practitioner.

PRACTISING. *p.* Or following a calling, exercent; long practised, veteran.

PRAISE. *v.* To extol, to applaud, to carol, to celebrate.

PRAISE. *s.* Encomium, laud, eulogy, or elogy, commendation; shout of praise, acclaim, or acclamation, plaudit; unmerited praise, adulation; tending to praise, epainetic, plauditory; the setting forth one's praise, euphemism.

PRAISER. *s.* Encomiast, panegyrist.

PRAISING. *p.* To join in praising, to collaud; a praising or speaking well of, eulogy.

PRANK. *s.* Curvet, vagary, freak, entrechat, F.

PRAY. *v.* To pray for pardon and mercy, to deprecate; to pray unto, to invocate, to invoke, to implore.

PRAYER. *s.* Entreatance, obsecration, obtestation, oraison, or orison; short prayer, collect; the last act of worship or prayers at night, compline; prayer against evil, deprecation; prayer or sudden effusion of the spirit, ejaculation; prayer for the dead, februation, requiem; evening prayers, vespers; morning prayers, matins; formulary of prayers, euchology; the Turkish common prayer, namaz.

PREACH. *v.* To evangelise, to sermocinate, to sermonize.

PREACHER. *s.* Sermocinator.

PRECEDE. *v.* See to go.

PRECEDENCE. *s.* Anteriority, proception, preoccupation.

PREGENTOR *s.* Accentor.

PRECEPT. *s.* Hest, aphorism, institute; giving precepts, didactick, didactical; consisting of precepts, preceptial; precept or instruction, parænesis.

PRECISE. *a.* Prim, finical, definite; want of precision, imprecision.

PREDICTION. *s.* (See Divination).

PREFACE. *v.* To premise.

PREFACE. *s.* Preamble; done by way of preface, prefatory; preface, exordium, proem, prologue, protology; prefaces, or preliminary discourses, prolegomena.

PREFER. *v.* To aggrandize, to dignify, to promote.

PREFERENCE. *s.* Prelation; preference of one thing to another, predilection.

PREGNANCY. *s.* Gestation, gravidity, ingravidation.

PREGNANT. *a.* Procreant, teemful.

PREJUDICE. *s.* Preopinion, prepossession, scath, impierment. (See hurt, mischief, wrong.)

PRELUDE. *s.* Preludium, prelusion.

PREPARATION. *s.* The want of due preparation, impreparation, unpreparedness; preparation (sacrament's eve) parasceve; complete preparation for action, procinct.

PREPARATORY. *a.* Preludious, prelusive, proemial.

PREARPE. *v.* To dispose, to habilitate; to prepare ground for planting, to pastinate.

PREPARED. *p.* (Shortened) succinct; not prepared or digested, inconcocted or unconcocted.

PRESAGE. *s.* Abodement, bode.

PRESAGEMENT. *s.* Prognostic, omen.

PRESENT. (Gift) boon, donation; present, gratuity, largess; to make or render present in a place, to presentiate; present, as present payment, prompt payment; God, or the being who is every where present, Ubiquitary, the Omnipresent.

PRESERVATION. *s.* Conservation.

PRESERVE. *v.* To condite, to retain; what has power to preserve, preservative, prophylactic or prophylactick.

PRESERVED. *p.* That may be preserved, conditaneous.

PRESIDENT. *s.* Preses, moderator, prolocutor; president or head of the religious matters among the Turks, iman.

PRESS. *v.* To press close, to compress; to press down, to depress; to press out, to express; to press on, to impel; to press hard, to scruse.

PRESS. *s.* Press made by means of a screw, torcularis.

PRESSED. *p.* Incapable of being pressed into less space, incompressible; not pressed into less space, uncompressed; pressed hard, serried,

PRESSING. *p.* Punishment of pressing to death, formerly inflicted on those who stood mute, *pain forte et dure*, Fr.; a pressing or impressing of horses, teams, men, ships, &c. for the public use, angaria, from angarie, F.; a pressing or squeezing out, ecthlipsis; it is used when speaking of swelled eyes when they dart forth sparks of light (Quincy); act of pressing, pression, pressing, (not to be dispensed with) urgent, indispensible; pressing (forcible) vive.

PRETENCE. *s.* Colour, flam, pretext, prophasis, stalking-horse.

PRETEND. *v.* To dissemble, to obtend, to simulate.

PRETENDED *p.* (False) pseudo, as pseudo adelphus, a false brother, &c.

PRETENDER. *s.* Superficial pretender, coxcomb; pretender, similar.

PRETTY. *a.* Bonny, quaint.

PREVAIL. *v.* To dominate; to prevail on, to induce, to predominate.

PREVENT. *v.* To anticipate, to forfend, to intercept, to obviate, to preclude, to prevene, to repel; to prevent or hinder the advantage that one should gain from another, to interlope.

PREVENTING. *p.* The cause of preventing or intercepting, intercipient; a preventing or intercepting, apolepsia.

PREVENTION. *s.* Circumvention, preoccupation. (See Cheat.)

PREVENTIVE. *s.* Prophylactic or prophylactick.

PREVIOUS. *a.* Precedaneous, preliminary, preludious, prelusive, preparatory; previous or introductory observations, prolegomena, præcognita; previous or antecedent to objections, proleptical.

PREY. *s.* The nest of a bird of prey, aerie or eyry; of or belonging to prey, manubial; living by prey, predacious; prey taken by violence, ravin or rapine (See Plunder); to go in search of prey, to prowl.

PREYING. *p.* Predal, predatory, rapacious; of a preying nature, prædatitious.

PRICK. *v.* To goad, to stimulate.

PRICK. *s.* Puncture; prick or sting of conscience, synteresis.

PRICKING. *p.* Piquant, pungent.

PRICKLES. *s.* Set with prickles, eschinated; the prickles of certain plants and animals, aculei.

PRICKLY. *a.* Acuate, muricated; prickly as a thistle, acanacious.

PRIDE. *s.* Imperiousness, lordliness, fastidiosity, arrogance, crest, disdain, elation, tumour; great pride, superciliousness, surquedry; full of pride, overweening.

PRIEST. *s.* Turkish priest, dervise; imam,

mofti ; to make confession to a priest, to
shrive ; the servant of a Roman Catholic
priest, acolothist ; priest's cap, pluvial ;
an ornament worn about the neck of a
priest, and across his breast, denoting the
yoke of Christ and the cord that bound
him, stole, (Bailey) ; gulled or managed
by priests, priest-ridden ; of or belonging
to a priest, sacerdotal.

PRIMARY. *a.* Primogenial ; primary disease, protopathy.

PRIME. *a.* Diagnostic, incomposite.

PRIMITIVE. *a.* Primordial ; primitive
word, prototypon, etymon ; primitive or
radical names are termed, imposititious.

PRINCE. *s.* Potentate ; sovereign prince or
ruler, dygnastic ; petty prince, princeling.

PRINCIPAL. *a. s.* Metropolitan, metropo-
litical, premier, primal, prime, cardinal,
especial, fundamental, pre-eminent.

PRINCIPLE. *s.* Institute, dogma, rudiment,
element, tenet ; principle assumed without proof, postulation ; that universal
principle which pervades all space is called, the hylarchic principle ; that active
principle in medicines, by which they
operate, hæcceity ; similar or like principles which are found in organised bodies,
are called, homoeomerical principles ;
principles (in arts and sciences) are ele-
ments and rudiments ; the Aristotelian
principles are : Water, Air, Earth, and
Fire ; the Epicurean are : Magnitude,
Figure, and Weight ; mathematical principles, are, definitions, axioms, and postulates ; the three chymical principles, viz :
salt, sulphur, and mercury, were called by
Paracelsus, the hypostatical principles.

PRINT. *u.* To print another's copy, to the
prejudice of the rightful owner, to com-
print.

PRINTER. *s.* Typographer ; printer's ink-
balls, pompets.

PRINTING. *p.* The plate of a printing-
press, platen or platin ; thin pieces of metal used in printing to fill up the void
spaces at the end of short lines, quadrates ;
thin ledge of wood used in printing, reg-
let or riglet ; the art of printing, typo-
graphy ; an instrument used in printing,
to which a leaf of copy is fixed for the
compositor's more convenient seeing, vi-
sorium ; the workmen or members of a
printing-office after they have paid their
entry-money, are called, chapelonians,
from the first printing-house having been
in a chapel in Westminster Abbey.

PRIOR. *a.* Anterior, primeval, procatarctic.

PRISON. *s.* Durance, limbo, goal, lob,
jail ; prison-fees, carcilage ; to put in
prison, to engaol, to incarcerate ; a cus-

tomary sum given by one to his fellow-
prisoners on his first committment, garnish.

PRISONERS. *s.* Agreement for an exchange of prisoners, cartel.

PRIVACY. *s.* Hugger-mugger.

PRIVATE. *a.* Latent, auricular, clancular,
dormant, opertaneous, privy ; private person, idiot ; private friend, privado ; private post or station where one or more lie
to surprise others, ambuscado or ambuscade ; kept private or secret, *in petto*
(Ital.) ; travelling in a private manner,
incog. or incognito ; private entertainment, junket ; to convert to private use,
to impropriate.

PRIVATELY. *ad.* Privily, clandestinely,
under the rose.

PRIVILEGE. *s.* Franchise, immunity, indult or indulto ; to deprive of privilege,
to disfranchise.

PRIVY. *a* (Secret) clancular ; one whose
privy parts are not perforated, atretus ;
privy counsellor, symmysta.

PROBABLE. *a.* Verisimilar.

PROBABLY. *ad.* Belike. (See likely and
perhaps.)

PROBE. *s.* A term which frequently occurs in the works of Hippocrates for a
search made into wounds by the specillum or probe, melosis. (Quincy)

PROBLEM *s.* Effection.

PROCEEDING. *p.* Gradient ; a proceeding or flowing from, emanation.

PROCESS. *s.* Term used for the time a law-
process is depending, litispendence.

PROCLAIM. *v.* To announce, to divulge,
to enunciate.

PROCLAMATION. *s.* Indletion, edict,
placart, manifesto, programma.

PRODIGAL. *a.* Profuse ; prodigal spending
of one's means in eating and drinking,
abliguration.

PRODIGALITY. *s.* Prodigality or intemperance, asotia.

PRODIGIOUS. *a.* Portentous, teratical.

PRODIGIOUSLY. *ad.* Prodigiously great
or large, immane, immense.

PRODUCE. *v.* To educe, to propagate ; able
to produce, effective ; to produce with
labour, to elaborate.

PRODUCE. *s.* Increment.

PRODUCED. *p.* That may be produced,
generable, productile, productive ; produ-
duced of the earth, terrigenous.

PRODUCING. *p.* Producing young alive,
viviparous ; producing young by eggs, oviparous ; producing young, fetiferous, ge-
nerant ; producing only one at a birth,
uniparous ; the producing of perfect living animals, zoogonia.

PRODUCT. *s.* Product of two numbers,
factum.

PROFANE. *v.* To unhallow, to exaugurate.

PROFANE. *a.* Irreligious, impious.

PROFANED. *p.* Not to be profaned, inviolable, unviolable.

PROFESSOR. *s.* Professor of civil law, jurist, civilian; professor of divinity, theologist, theologue, theologer, theologian.

PROFIT. *v.* To bestead.

PROFIT. *s.* Avail, emolument, behoof, lucre, vantage; to arise by profit, to accrue; profits of lands, mises (Bailey); profit (advantage or use) utility; the temporary use or profit of any thing, usufruct; the person who has the temporary use or profit of money, &c. usufructuary or usucaptor; studious of profit, questary.

PROFITABLE. *a.* Behooveful, beneficial, lucrative, lucrific, lucriferous, lucrous.

PROFOUND. *a.* (Abstruse) recondite.

PROFUSE. *a.* Prodigal.

PROFUSENESS. *s.* Prodigence.

PROGRESS. *s.* Gradation, profluence.

PROGRESSION. *s.* Progression or advance, profection.

PROHIBIT. *v.* To inhibit, to interdict.

PROJECT. *v.* Project or jut out, to beetle, to belly, to bouge.

PROJECTION. *s.* The orthographic projection of the sphere upon the plane of the meridian, analemma; projections are, stereographic, orthographic, gnomonic, cylindric, scenographic, globic, mercatoric, and helicosophic or helicometric, to which some add the anamorphous or perspective projection, so delineated, that at one point of view any figure, viz. the human face, shall appear deformed, but in another, an exact representation shall be produced.

PROMISE. *v.* To behight; to promise solemnly, to plight.

PROMISE. *s.* Voluntary and oral promise, assumpsit or assumsit; one who makes a promise for another, particularly at the sacrament of baptism, sponsor.

PROMOTE. *v.* Promote or assist, to adjute, or adjuvate, to avail, to conduce, to contribute, to promove.

PRONE. *a.* Procumbent. (See Lying.)

PRONOUNCE. *v.* To articulate, to prolate, to accent; to pronounce fully, to aspirate.

PRONOUNCIATION. *s.* Pronunciation or utterance, prolation; a stammering in the pronunciation of a word by the repetition of the first letter of it, as in abaft when pronounced a-a-a-baft, this fault is termed, traulismus. (See Stammering.)

PROOF. *s.* Approof, assay, eviction, evidence, probation, symptom, tentation; concurrent proof, comprobation; capable of proof, evincible; position assumed without proof, postulatum, hypothesis; proof without the possibility of a doubt, apodixis; incapable of proof, indemonstrable or undemonstrable.

PROP. *s.* Buttress, fulcrum, fulciment, hypomochlion, erisma, substruction, obex.

PROPER. *a.* Adviseable, behoveable, competent, correspondent, meet, expedient, legitimate, applicable, equinecessary, apposite, idoneous, opportune; more proper, fitlier;. most proper, fitliest; proper or useful, proficuous; a proper distribution of things, or the act of setting things in order, diacosmesis; the proper disposition or temperament of a natural body, best fitting it to perform its functions, idiocracy.

PROPERTY. *s.* Moveable property, chattel.

PROPHECY. *s.* The communication of the power or spirit of prophecy, afflatus.

PROPHECY. *v.* To predict, to prognosticate.

PROPHETIZE. *v.* To vaticinate.

PROPHESYING. *p.* The prophesying or foretelling by casting of lots, cleromancy.

PROPHETS. *s.* Murder or murderer of vaticide.

PROPHETESS. *s.* Pythoness, divineress.

PROPHETICAL. *a.* Fatidical, prophetick, prescient, prescious.

PROPORTION. *v.* To adapt.

PROPORTION. *s.* Analogy; reducible to some proportion, commensurable; proportion to be made up by one or more, contingent, quota; mean proportion, medium, average; the regular proportion of victuals in a college or society, commons; instrument for finding mean proportionals between any two lines given, mesolabium; proportion, omology, parility; proportion or relation, rapport; proportion or rate which several quantities of the same kind have to each other, ratio; the share or proportion of meat, drink, or forage, given to seamen or soldiers for a day, ration; just proportion of members symmetry, eurythmy.

For proportion among mathematicians, Euclid gives the following definitions.

" 1. *Permutando* or *alternando*, by " permutation, or alternately; this word " is used when there are four proportion- " als, and it is inferred, that the first has " the same ratio to the third, which the " second has to the fourth, or that the " first is to the third as the second to the " fourth. 2. *Invertendo*, by inversion : " When there are four proportionals, and " it is inferred, that the second is to the " first as the fourth to the third. 3. *Com-*

" *ponendo*, by composition, when there are
" four proportionals, and it is inferred that
" the first together with the second, is to
" the second as the third, together with
" the fourth, is to the fourth. 4. *Divi-*
" *dendo*, by division; when there are four
" proportionals, and it is inferred, that the
" excess of the first above the second, is
" to the second as the excess of the third
" above the fourth, is to the fourth.
" 5. *Convertendo*, by conversion; when
" there are four proportionals, and it is in-
" ferred, that the first is to its excess a-
" bove the second, as the third to its ex-
" cess above the fourth. 6. *Exequali*
" (*sc. distantia*) or *ex æquo*, from equa-
" lity of distance, when there is any num-
" ber of magnitudes more than two, and
" as many others, so that they are pro-
" portionals when taken two and two of
" each rank, and it is inferred that the
" first is to the last of the first rank of
" magnitudes, as the first is to the last of
" the others. Of this there are the two
" following kinds, which arise from the
" different order in which the magnitudes
" are taken two and two. 7. *Ex æquali*,
" from equality: This term is used simply
" by itself, when the first magnitude is to
" the second of the first rank, as the first
" to the second of the other rank; and as
" the second is to the third of the first
" rank, so is the second to the third of the
" other, and so on in order, and the in-
" ference is as mentioned in the preced-
" ing definition, whence this is called or-
" dinate proportion. 8. *Ex æquali, in*
" *proportione per turbata, seu inordina-*
" *ta ;* from equality, inperturbate or dis-
" orderly proportion: This term is used,
" when the first magnitude is to the se-
" cond of the first rank as the last but
" one is to the last of the second rank, and
" as the second is to the third of the first
" rank, so is the last but two to the last
" but one of the second rank; and as the
" third is to the fourth of the first rank,
" so is the third from the last to the last
" but two of the second rank; and so on
" in a cross order; and the inference is as
" in the 18th definition." (See Reasoning.)

PROPOSAL. *s.* Proposition, overture; one
who makes a proposal, proponent.

PROPOSE. *v.* To exhibit, to motion, to
proffer, to propound.

PROPOSED. *p.* Proposed and determined,
pight.

PROPOSITION. *s.* The name of an intricate proposition discovered by Pythagoras,
on which occasion he sacrificed an ox to
the gods, dulcarnon, (See Difficulty) pro-

position, effection; a proposition previous
to another serving to demonstrate what
follows, lemma; self evident propositions
are called, axioms, postulates, porimes;
an antecedent proposition, premiss; a
maxim or proposition, protasis; proposition composed of four or five previous
ones, and which is to be demonstrated by
their means, epicherema.

PROPPED. *p.* Propt.

PROPRIETOR. *s.* Proprietary; female
proprietor, proprietress.

PROPRIETY. *s.* Adequateness, pertinence,
pertinency.

PROSE. *s.* Relating to prose, prosaic or
prosaick; to turn prose into verse, to
transprose.

PROSECUTE. *v.* To prosecute at law, to
implead.

PROSPECT. *s.* Term used for a fine or
pleasant prospect, Belvidere, being the
name of one of the pope's palaces in
Rome, so situated; prospect through
trees, vista or visto.

PROSPER. *v.* To secundate.

PROSPEROUS. *a.* Auspicious; eagerness
acquired from a prosperous beginning,
fleshment.

PROSTITUTE. *s.* Bonaroba, courtesan or
courtezan, night-walker, punk; Thais
is a name given also to a prostitute, from
Thais a famous courtezan at Athens;
trade of a prostitute, putanism, putage.

PROTECT. *v.* To enguard, to enshield, to
sanctuarise, to shroud.

PROTECTION. *s.* Auspice, conservation,
patrocination, tuition, tutelage, guardian-
ship.

PROTECTOR. *s.* Guardian; one in the
hands of a protector or guardian, ward.

PROUD. *a.* Masterly, tumid, dictatorial,
imperious, luciferian, fastidious, intoler-
ant, ostentatious, arrogant, cavalier;
pompous, supercilious, uppish, orgillous;
proud through learning, pedantic; to
make proud, to elate; to be proud of, to
glory; a making proud, superbific; the
growth of proud flesh, hypersarcosis;
proud dame, minnekin, minx; uncommon-
ly proud, misproud.

PROVE. *v.* To convince, to assay, to deraign, to evidence, to evince; to prove to
be the same, to identify; to prove any
thing true, to verificate, to verify; to
prove an argument false, to refute, to
refel.

PROVED. *p.* Enforced, attested; what is
asserted without being proved, gratuitous.

PROVENDER. *s.* Pabulum, aliment.

PROVERB. *v.* (See Maxim.)

PROVIDER. *s.* Proveditor, provedore, pro-
visor, purveyor, caterer; female who

provides, cateress.

PROVISION. *s.* Forage, grist ; provisions for a journey, viaticum ; place where provisions are kept, buttery ; to shift for provisions, to prog ; one who sells provisions to soldiers in camp or garrison, sutler ; provision or providing clause, purview or proviso.

PROVOKE. *v.* To aggravate, to egg, to enchafe, to exasperate, to incense, to irritate, to pique, to shagrin or chagrin ; one who provokes to anger and passion, incensor.

PROVOKING. *p.* Provoking to anger, lacession.

PROVOST. *s.* Belonging to a provost, provostal. (Bailey.)

PROW. *s.* Prore.

PRUDENCE. *s.* Policy, prospicience, sapience.

PRUDENT. *a.* Advisable, matronly, circumspect, considerate, sapient, discreet, judicious ; not prudent, undiscreet.

PRUNING. *p.* The act of pruning trees, surcu ation.

PSALMS. *s.* The act or practice of singing psalms, psalmody ; the 15 psalms from the 118th to the 184th, or from the 119th to the 184th, which were wont to be sung by the Levites as they ascended the 15 steps of Solomon's temple, one psalm being sung on each step, are called, gradual psalms.

PUBLIC. *a.* Public road or level walk, estrade ; public (not suppressed) extant ; public or open, apert ; public rates, cense ; public notice given of any thing, ban ; robber of the public, peculator or depeculator ; to become public, to transpire.

PUBLICLY. *ad.* What is publicly known, notorious, apparent.

PUBLISH. *v.* To announce, to blaze, to blazon, to divulge, to notify, to promulgate, to promulge.

PUBLISHED. *p.* Published abroad, propaled.

PUBLISHER. *s.* Promulgator, promulger.

PUFF. *v.* To puff up, to elate, to inflate, to sufflate, to tumify, to vesicate ; to puff or blow through, to perflate.

PUFFED. *p.* Tumid ; puffed up as in an emphysema, emphysematous.

PUFFING. *p.* A puffing or blowing away, diffiation.

PUFFY. *a.* Flatulent, flatuous.

PULL. *v.* To tug or pull, to tew ; to pull off the bark of trees, to delibrate ; to pull with violence, to lug ; to pull back, to abduce ; to pull down, to dilapidate ; to pull up by the roots, to eradicate, to aberuncate ; to pull by way of signal, to hob ; to pull asunder, to rend, to touze ;

to pull or pluck, to vellicate.

PULLEY. *s.* Trochlea ; the wheel of a pulley, truckle ; that part of mechanics which treats of pulleys or wheels, trochilics.

PULPIT. Rostrum.

PULSE. *s.* An intermission in a pulse, which is denied by some to be perceptible in people in health, but in dying persons is distinctly felt, perisystole (Quincy) ; term used for a pulse that beats double, and which is reckoned a certain sign of an approaching hæmorrhage from the nose, dicrotus ; pulse not suitable to a person's age, pararythmus ; pulse not modulating or beating in a natural manner, arythmus, and is the contrary of eurythmus or eurythmia, which signifies an orderly pulse ; pulse proper for one period of life, changing into one proper for another, is called, heterorythmus, and, lastly, if it passes into a modulation proper to no age, it is then called, ecrythmus (Quincy) ; term used for time, motion, or modulation of the pulse, rythmus or rythm ; that part of physic which treats of the pulse, sphygmica ; the pulse or beating of the heart and arteries, sphygmus ; an unequal fluctuating pulse is called, cymatodes ; that natural heat which is measured or perceived by the pulse, thermometron.

PULSE. *s.* i. e. Seeds not reaped, but gathered by the hand, is called, legume or legumen.

PUMP. *s.* What acts as a sucker of a pump, embolus, piston.

PUN. *s.* Clinch, quodlibet.

PUNCH. *v.* (To beat,) to pommel.

PUNCH. *s.* (Hole made by a punch) pertusion.

PUNCH. *s.* (Beverage) a mixture of acid, sugar, and water, used in making of punch, sherbet ; name sometimes used for punch as consisting of five ingredients, diapente. Punch had its origin in 1682 or 1683, from a Captain of an English ship in the East Indies, adding to the sherbet used there, which was composed of water, fruit, sugar and nutmeg, a fifth ingredient, viz. spirits ; the natives asked the new liquor, and afterwards when they were to drink sherbet, called for *panch*, which in their language signifies the *fifth*. The Captain on his return taught his countrymen the composition, calling it *punch*, and it was immediately celebrated by a poem, wherein it was feigned to be made by the gods, who contributed the several ingredients.

PUNISH. *v.* To trounce, to chasten, to chastise, to dicipline, to inflict, to venge,

R

PUNISHMENT. *s.* Avengeance, avengement, castigation, infliction, punition, supplice; exemption from punishment, impunity; liable to punishment, obnoxious; denouncing or enacting punishment penal, punitive, punitory, vindicatory, defensory, justificatory.

PUNY. *a.* Ailing, puisne.

PUPIL. *s.* Pupil or disciple, sectator.

PUPPET. *s.* Mammet, moppet, or mopsy, punchinello.

PURBLIND. *a.* One who is purblind, myops; state of being purblind, eluscation.

PURBLINDNESS. Myopy, poreblindness.

PURCHASER. *s.* Chafferer.

PURCHASING. *p.* The act of purchasing, emption; the act of purchasing up the whole of any commodity, coemption. (See to Buy.)

PURE. *a.* Impeccable, incorrupt, inculpable, innocuous, essential, ethereal, ethereous, immaculate, ethical, intelligential, meracious; pure as clear water, limpid, pellucid; pure style of language, as Cicero's, Ciceronian.

PURGATIVE. *a.* Diarrhœtic.

PURGE. *s.* To defecate, to depurate; to purge a hawk, to enseam; such medicines as purge downwards, catacathartics or catocathartics; the lesser and weaker purges are termed by physicians, minerativa; medicines which purge gently, aperienta, eccoprotica.

PURGING. *p.* Cathartic; a purging or purgation, coprophory; a purging gently by stool, hypocatharsis; medicines which had the virtue ascribed to them of purging all humours alike, panchymagogues.

PURIFICATION. *s.* Purification by means of water, lustration.

PURIFY. *v.* To clarify, to defecate, to depurate, to mundify.

PURIFYING. *p.* A purifying liquors by means of skimming, despumation.

PURITY. *s.* (Chastity) pudency or pudicity.

PURPLE. *s.* Of a purple colour, puniceous, murrey; the purple standard of St Dennis, borne against infidels, lost in Flanders, auriflamb or auriflambe; to tinge with purple, to impurple; purple spots which appear sometimes in putrid fevers, petechiæ.

PURPOSE. *s.* Nonce, intent, destination; final purpose, goal, crownet; just to the purpose, pertinent, apposite, significant; a propos, F. purpose, aforethought, precogitation.

PURPOSELY. *ad.* Advisedly.

PURSE *s.* Crumenal.

PURSUE. *v.* To course, to ensue, to exagitate.

PURSUER. *s.* Questrist.

PURSUIT. *s.* Pursuit after a thief, hue and cry.

PUS. *s.* Pyon or matter discharged from a wound which is not tainted, is called, laudable pus or matter; consisting of pus, purulent.

PUSH. *v.* To push off, to foil, to ward; to push forward, to propel, to protrude.

PUSH. *s.* (In fencing) passade or passado; push or tilt, veney.

PUSHING. *p.* The act of pushing forwards, trusion.

PUT. *v.* To put off, to dally, to fub, to postpone, to procrastinate, to prolong, to suspend; to put off or delay, to respite, to retard (see delay); to put in possession, to infeoff; to put or insert in a writing with an intent to defraud, to foist; to put on by way of ornament, (or to fetter,) to garnish; to put on as a duty, to impose; put (placed) posited; put between, intercalary; to put down, to repress or suppress; to put away, to repudiate; to put aside, to reposite, to sequestrate; to put off or set aside, to supersede; to put in or inject, to immit.

PUTREFACTION. *s.* Good against putrefaction, antiseptic; what accelerates putrefaction, septic.

PUTRIFIED. *p.* Putrified from being over ripe, fracid; putrified or rotten as a bone, carious.

PUTTING. *p.* A putting or thrusting away, depulsory; the act of putting off, divesture; a putting off or delay, prorogation, crastination, procrastination, dilatoriness.

PUZZLE. *v.* To pose, to oppose, to buffle, to empuzzle, to nonplus.

PUZZLE. *s.* Conundrum, trangram.

PUZZLED. *p.* Moidered.

PYRAMIDS. *s.* A description of the pyramids, pyramidography.

Q

QUACK. *s.* Charlatan, empiric, medicaster, mountebank, pseudo-medicus, saltimbanco ; general name for quacks, agyrtæ ; the immethodical manner of quacks, is called amethodica.

QUAKE. *v.* To frill, to quappe. (See to Shake)

QUAKING. *p.* Horrent, trepid.

QUALIFIED. *a.* Apt, capable, competent. (See Fit.)

QUALIFY. *v.* To habilitate, to legitimate.

QUALITY. *s.* Of the same quality or kind, homogeneous : of a different kind, heterogeneous ; void of all sensible qualities, apoeum. (See Kind and Nature.)

QUANTITY. *s.* Fet ; small quantity, iota, quantum ; that may be estimated according to quantity, quantitive.

QUARREL *v.* To litigate, to aggress.

QUARREL. *s.* Fray, affray, bate, brangle, broil, tiff, rixation, brawl, cavil, feud, contention.

QUARRELLING. *p.* Act of quarrelling, rixation, velitation.

QUARRELSOME. *a.* Action-taking, litigious, contentious, controversial, fractious, pugnaceous.

QUARTER. *v.* To quarter as a traitor, to excarnificate.

QUARTERING. *p.* The act of quartering and living in one's house, against the will of the householder, sorning (*L. T.*)

QUELL *v.* To obtund. (See to crush.)

QUENCHING. *p.* The act of quenching, restinction.

QUESTION. *v.* To interrogate, to appose, to catechise.

QUESTION. *s.* Examen, interrogatory, problem, erotema ; a dark and obscure question, enigma ; answering a question in law, redditive ; an earnest question or interrogatory, pusma. (Rhet.)

QUIBBLE. *s.* Conundrum, quillet, subtilty, trangram, gimcrack, quirk.

QUICK. *a.* Expedient, fleet, glib, subtile, subtle, vegete, expeditious, apace, presentaneous, vivid, prompt, rapid, inventive, percipient, perspicacious ; quick-sighted person, lynceous ; quick (cutting) trenchant ; quick or nimble, volant ; quick in thought or scent, sagacious ; quick and witty answer, repartee.

QUICKEN. *v.* To actuate, to excite, to incite, to vivify.

QUICKENED *p.* Quickened motion, accelerated motion.

QUICKNESS. *s.* Velocity ; quickness or cleverness, adroitness, dexterity ; quickness (diligence) impigrity ; quickness of intellect, acumen, vivacity, gnavity.

QUICKSAND. *s.* Syrtis.

QUICKSILVER. *s.* Of or belonging to quicksilver, hydrargyral.

QUIET. *v.* To quiet, to appease, to compose, to becalm, to hush, to placate.

QUIET. *s.* Placid, indisturbance, mund, halcyon, quiescent, sedate, serene, temperate, tranquillous, tranquil ; quiet (rest) repose ; want of quiet, intranquillity ; one who devotes himself to a state of quiet, hesychastes ; in a quiet state, undisturbed.

QUIETED. *p.* That may be quieted, mulcible.

QUIETING. *p.* Sedative. (See Sleep.)

QUILL. *s.* Quill of the wing most remote from the body of a fowl, pinion.

QUIRK. *s.* Quiddity, quodlibet, conundrum, trangram. (See Quibble.)

QUIT. *v.* To abandon, to abdicate, to absist, to evacuate, to relinquish, to renounce, to vacate.

QUITTING. *p.* Act of quitting, exit, exodus.

QUOTA. *s.* Contingent.

QUOTATION. *s.* Citation, cital ; false quotation, miscitation.

R

RABBIT. s. Coney, cony; stocked with rabbits, coniculose or cuniculous; box where rabbits are kept, hutch; to bring forth rabbits, to kindle; park or enclosure for rabbits, warren.

RABBLE. s. Canaille, mobility, posse, varietry.

RACE. s. Kidney, clan, sept, pedigree, genealogy, progeny, stirp; race or course, career.

RACEHORSE. s. Courser; race-ground or course for the running of horses, hippodrome.

RACK. s. A sort of rack used anciently for extorting confession, equuleus.

RADICAL. a. Radical or primitive names are called, imposititious.

RAGE. v. To rage as the sea, to estuate.

RAGE. s. Transport or transportation, chafe, exasperatedness, fume, incensement, ire, rigour; in a rage, fumingly.

RAGGED. a. Ragged fellow, tatterdemalion, tippo.

RAGING. p. Furious, indignant, infuriate; a raging or madness, debacchation.

RAIL. v. To inveigh, to illatrate or allatrate, to oblatrate, to convitiate, to exclaim against.

RAIL. s. Rail or fence before a door, diathyrum, L.; rails on the top of a cart, raers.

RAILER. s. Insectator.

RAILING. p. (Scandal) probrosity, scurrility; railing speech, invective, banter; a railing match, rating, lerry.

RAILLERY. s. Raillery or drollery, mimiambus. (Bailey.)

RAIN. v. To rain in small drops, to misle or mizzle, to drizzle.

RAIN. s. Umbrella for keeping off the rain, parapluye.

RAINBOW. s. Iris.

RAINY. a. Pluvial, pluvious, impluvious.

RAISE. v. To levy, to muster; to raise the price, to enhance; to raise or build, to extruct, to fabricate (see to build); to raise in esteem, to extol; to raise or exalt, to promote, to promove; that which raises up, atollent; to raise or rouse, to exuscitate, to resuscitate, to suscitate; to raise as a blister, to vesicate.

RAISED. p. Raised or bunched, protuberant; that cannot be raised or exalted illeviable.

RAISING. p. Act of raising, elevating; a raising up again, relevation; raising up, act of, sublation, sublevation.

RAKE. v. To lecher, to wench.

RAKE. s. Ronyon, blood.

RAM. s. Act of generation between a ram, and ewe, blissoming; animal produced between a ram and she-goat, musimon; ram half castrated, ridgel or ridgil.

RAMBLE. v. To transcur, to pilgrim, to roam, to spoliate.

RAMBLE. s. Evagation, excursion, digression, deviation.

RAMBLER. s. Idle rambler, gadder.

RANDOM. a. Done at random, habnab; floating at random, adrift.

RANK. a. Fetid, fulsome, nauseous, olid, olidous; rank smell of meat, fumette; holding the same rank or degree, coordinate.

RANGE. v. To assert, to expatiate, to roam, to spatiate, to transcur; to range troops for battle, to darrain.

RANT. v. To rodomontade.

RAPE. s. Constupration, defloration, stupration.

RAPTURE. s. Rapture or extraordinary elevation of the mind, anagoge. (Bailey)

RARE. a. Admirable, infrequent, unfrequent.

RASCAL. s. Ruanion, scroyle, skellum, varlet, rascallion, rampallion.

RASH. a. Desperate, festinate, heady, hot-spurred, inconsiderate, unconsidered, indeliberate, unpremeditated, undeliberated, indeliberated, precipitant, precipitous, temerarious.

RASHLY. ad. A-head.

RASHNESS. s. Headiness, incogitancy, temerity.

RAT. s. What is fatal to rats, ratsbane, sminthean; name for the water rat, crabber.

RATE. v. To appreciate, to compute, to assess, to cess, to estimate.

RATES. s. Public rates, cense, quota.

RATTLESNAKE. s. Crotalopharous. (Zool.)

RAVENOUS. a. Gormandizing, rabious, subvulturian.

RAVING. p. Delirious, lymphated.

RAVISH. v. To vitiate, to construprate,

to deflour, to efforce, to stuprate, to violate ; to ravish or transport with joy, to inwrap, to rapture.

RAVISHER. *s.* Raptor, violator.

RAW. *a.* Crude ; a growing raw again as a wound, recrudescent ; raw or unexperienced sailor, fresh water.

RAYS. *s.* The darting forth of rays, irradiation, or radiation.

REACH. *v.* To continge.

REACHED. *p.* That cannot be reached, inaccessible, or unaccessible.

REACHING. *p.* Reaching to, pertingence, pertingency.

READILY. *ad.* Extempore, *L.*

READINESS. *s.* Kelter, adroitness, proclivity ; readiness to be taught, docility ; readiness of speech combined with elegance, facundity ; readiness of wit, vivacity ; readiness or dexterity in dissections, enchiresis or epichiresis ; want of readiness, inaptitude, unaptness, unreadiness.

READING. *p.* Lection ; the act of reading over, prelection, perusal ; a double reading as in several scripture texts, dittology.

READY. *a.* Acute, expedient, expert; fleet, glib, agile, feat, apt, pat, presentaneous, procinct, prompt, remuable, proclive, subtle or subtile, tidy ; ready to break forth, erupturient ; ready to oblige, obsequious ; ready (sea term) predy, as a predy ship is, when she is cleared for engagement ; ready to fall off, as ripe fruit, succiduous ; ready (dextrous) yare.

REAL. *a.* Extradictionary, implicit, natal, incontestible, uncontestable, uncontrovertible or incontrovertible, immanent, ingenerated, intern, internal, intrinsic, intrinsical, indubious, indubitable, indubitate, material, positive, absolute, virtual, innate or innated.

REALITY. *s.* Identicalness, identity.

REALLY. *ad.* Actually, affirmatively, intrinsically, de facto, *L.*, agood.

REAPING. *p.* Of or belonging to reaping, messorious.

REASON. *v.* To argue, to expostulate, to ratiocinate,

REASON. *s.* (Propriety) congruity ; used or done with reason, ratiocinable ; the giving a reason why, etiology ; deprivation of reason, infatuation, irrationality ; performed without the deduction of reason, intuitively. Reason (in arithmetic) is the rate betwixt two numbers, and is a certain proportion, especially the quotient of the antecedent divided by the consequent.

Reason in the above sense, of a greater quantity to a less, as well as a less to a greater, is five-fold, viz: "First, " *Multiple* ; Secondly, *Superparticular* ;

" Thirdly, *Superpartiens* ; Fourthly, " *Multiple-superparticular* ; Fifthly, and " lastly, *Multiplesuperpartiens.* The " three first of which are called simple, " the two last, mixt reason, or habitude : " to give a name to their opposites or con- " traries, we join the preposition sub, " then they are called, *submultiple, sub- " superparticular,* &c.

" 1*st, Multiple* reason is, when the an- " tecedent, or greater number, contains " the consequent or less number, some " certain number of times without a re- " mainder, as 6 to 3 commonly called, " *Duple* ; 21 to 7, commonly called *tri- " ple* reason, their opposites are of the less " to the greater, as 3 to 6, 7 to 21, that " is subduple, subtriple reason.

" 2*d, Superparticular* Reason, is when " the antecedent or greater number con- " tains the consequent or less number " but once with a fraction, whose nume- " rator is always unity ; such are 3 to 2, " 4 to 3, 5 to 4, &c., commonly called, " *sesquialtera, sesquitertia, sesquiquar- " ta,* reason or proportion. Its opposite " is *subsuperparticular,* as of 2 to 3, 3 to " 4, 4 to 5, &c. commonly called *subses- " quialtera, subsesquitertia, subsesqui- " quarta,* &c.

" 3*d, Superpartient* Reason is, when " the antecedent or greater number con- " tains the consequent or less number " once with a fraction, whose numerator " is always more than unity ; such as " 5 to 3, 7 to 4, &c. commonly called, " *superdupartiens tres,* and *supertripar- " tiens quarta,* &c. Its opposite is *sub- " superpartiens,* as of 3 to 5, 4 to 7. or " *subsuperdupartiens tres, subsupertri- " partiens quartas,* &c.

" 4*th, Multiplesuperparticular* Rea- " son, is, when the antecedent or greater " number contains the consequent or less " number divers times with a fraction, " whose numerator is always unity, such " as 9 to 4 ; or *Duplasesquiquarta,* 9 to 2 ; " or *Quadruplasesquialtera,* 26 to 5 ; or " *Quintaplasesquiquinta,* &c. Its op- " posite is *Submultiplesuperparticular,* " as 4 to 9, 2 to 9, 5 to 26, &c.

" 5*th, Multiplesuperpartiens* Reason, " is when the antecedent or greater num- " ber contains the consequent or less " number divers times with a fraction, " whose numerator is always greater than " unity, as 8 to 3, commonly called *Du- " plasuperdupartiens tertia* ; 19 to 5 " is termed, *Triplasuperquadripartiens " quinta,* &c. Its opposite is *Submul- " tiplesuperpartiens,* as 3 to 8, 5 to " 19, &c. Under some of these five spe-

" cles are comprehended all the variety
" that can happen betwixt two numbers,
" in respect of quantity ; the same holds
" also in fractions, as well as mixt num-
" bers." Hill's Arith.

REASONABLE. *a.* Equitable, rational ;
reasonable account or explanation of a
thing, rationale.

REASONER. *s.* Disputant, polemick.

REASONING. *p.* Principle of reasoning or
theorem, philosopheme ; a false or deceitful way of reasoning, paralogism ; sophistical argument or reasoning, pseudomenos ; reasoning is either *à priori, à posteriori, à fortiori,* or *apagogic.* (See Demonstration.)

REBEL. *s.* Malecontent, runagate, apostate, renegade or renegado, revolter.

REBELLION. *s.* One who rises up in rebellion, insurgent.

REBOUND. *v.* To recoil, to repercuss.

REBOUNDING. *p.* Resilient.

REBUKE. *v.* To jobe.

REBUKE. *s.* Countercheck, epitemesis,
increpation, objurgation. (See Reproof.)

RECALL. *v.* To recant, to reclaim, to retract, to retrieve, to revocate, to repeal.
(See to Start)

RECALLED. *p.* Not to be recalled, irre-
vocable, unrevokable.

RECANTATION. *s,* Palinode or palinody,
retractation, retraction.

RECEIPT. *s.* Acquittance, recipe.

RECEIVE. *v.* To admit, to imbibe ; apt
or fit to receive, receptive.

RECEIVED. *p.* Generally received or admitted, receptory.

RECEIVER. *s.* Accipient, recipient.

RECEIVING. *p.* Receiving or recovering ;
also an interruption, apolepsia.

RECENT. *a.* Recent or late, neoterick or
neoteric.

RECKON. *v.* To addeem, to annumerate,
to compute, to calculate, to suppute,

RECKONED. *p.* Wrong reckoned, miscast;
reckoned or reputed, putative.

RECKONER. *s.* Accomptant or accountant, countercaster.

RECKONING. *p.* (Share) scot.

RECLUSE. *s.* Anchorite.

RECLUSE. *a.* Ascetic.

RECOILING. *p.* Resilient. (See Start,)

RECOLLECT. *v.* To bethink. (See Remember.)

RECOLLECTION. *s.* Reminiscence. (See
Memory.)

RECOMPENCE. *s.* Amends, indemnification, meed, gratuity, guerdon ; the law
of recompence, which renders one good
or ill turn for another, lex talionis, *L.* recompence, reguerdon, requital, compen-
pensation, equivalent.

RECOMPENCE. *v.* To requite. (See Reward.)

RECONCILE. *v.* To conciliate, to placate. (See Agree.)

RECORD. *v.* To chronicle, to memorize.

RECORDED. *p.* Not to be recorded or
remembered, irrecordable, unrecordable.

RECORDS. *s.* Book of records, repertory ;
ancient records, archives.

RECOVERABLE. *a.* Recuperable ; not
recoverable, irrecoverable, irrecupera-
ble, irretrievable ; a recovering or retaining, apolepsia.

RECOVERY. *s.* Recovery, or regaining,
readeption ; recovery of life, reviviscency,
resuscitation.

RED. *a.* Flushed with red, florid ; colour
produced by red and white mixed, gridelin ; of the colour of red lead, minious ; dark red, murrey ; red paint used
for the face, rouge ; of a red colour, rubious, rubid, sanguine ; making or turning red, rubific ; to make red, to rubify,
to rubricate ; the red breast (in Ornith.)
rubecula.

REDDISH. *a.* Spadiceous, erubescent.

REDEEMED. *p.* Not to be redeemed, ir-
repleviable, or irreplevisable, (L. T.)

REDEMPTION. *s.* Of or belonging to redemption, or ransoming, redemtory.

REDNESS. *s.* Erubescence, or erubescen-
cy ; inclined to redness, rubicund, rubi-
form.

REDUCE. *v.* Or weaken, to enerve, to
enervate ; to reduce .into smaller space,
to epitomise ; to reduce or lessen, to retrench.

REDUCED. *p.* That cannot be reduced,
irreducible.

REDUCTION. *s.* Reduction into principles, principiation.

REEDS. *s.* Abounding with reeds, arun-
dineous.

REEL. *v.* To vacillate.

REFERENCE. *s* Appeal, compromise, allusion, rapport ; one to whom reference
is made, referee.

REFINED. *p.* Abstruse, abstracted ; highly refined, empyreal ; refined (possessed
with elevated ideas as Plato,) platonic.

REFINING. *p.* The refining of metals, affinage ; refining of liquors, clarification,
(See to clear.)

REFLECT. *v.* To bethink ; what reflects,
reflector.

REFLECTED. *p.* Reflected light, doctrine
of, anacampticks, or catoptrics

REFLECTION. *s.* Retrospection ; reflection or blame, imputation ; moral reflection, epiphonema.

REFORM. *v* To amend, to reclaim.

REFORMING. *p.* Redressive.

REFRESH. *v.* To recreate, to refect, to regale; to refocillate, to focillate; to re-.fresh or cool, to refrigerate.

REFRESHMENT. *s.* On a journey for man or beast, bait.

REFUGE. *s.* Asylum, girthol, L. T.

REFUSAL. *s.* Denay.

REFUSE. *v.* To refuse or reject, to recuse, to renege, to repudiate; to refuse or deny, to abnegate, to nill; one who refuses to communicate, recusant.

REFUSE. *s.* Mulloc, coom, orts, offal, recrement, strigment.

REGAIN. *v.* To retrieve.

REGAINING. *p.* Act of, readeption.

REGARD. *v.* To advert, to reck.

REGARD. *s.* Deference, spectation.

REGARDLESS. *a.* Of circumstances, irrespective.

REGENERATION. *s.* Palingenesia, renascibility.

REGISTER, *s.* Calendar, catalogue; chief register, or notary, prothonotary.

REGISTERED. *p.* Ascriptitious, conscript.

REGULAR. *a.* Discursory, gradual; a regular progression, graduation.

REGULARITY. *s.* Or constancy, insiture, (Johnson,)

REGULATE. *v.* To adjust, to attemper, to discipline. (See Order.)

REGULATING. *p.* The art of regulating or managing household affairs, oeconomicks.

REJECT. *v.* To oppugn, to recuse; to reject or disallow, to reprobate; to reject put away, or divorce, to repudiate.

REJECTED. *p.* That ought to be rejected, repudious.

REIGNING. *p.* Regnant, predominant.

REINS. *s.* Such medicines as are good against diseases in the reins, nephritics.

REJOICE. *v.* To rejoice greatly, to guade, to exult, to glory, to gratulate, to congratulate.

REJOICING. *p.* A rejoicing together, congratulation; a rejoicing above measure, exultation,

RELAPSE. *s.* Relapse into a disease, palindrome.

RELATE. *v.* To historify, to narrify, to recount; to relate to, or belong, to pertain, to appertain.

RELATED. *p.* Related to, affined, cognate; the state of being nearly related, propinquity; related by the father's side, consanguinean; by the mother's, uterine; by both, German; the cohabitation of parties too nearly related, incest; that cannot be related or told, ineffable, inenarrable; that may be related or told, narrable.

RELATING. Relating to, appertaining, pertingent.

RELATION. *s.* Rapport, recountment, recital, habitude, kin, ally; relation or report, narrative, enarration, narration; having a reciprocal relation, correlative.

RELAXING. *p.* Relaxing medicines are termed syncritica.

RELIEF. *s.* Subvention, succour, opitalarion; relief from labour, respiration, recreation.

RELIEVING. *p.* Assuaging, sedative, redressive, relevant.

RELIGION. *s.* The opinion of individuals in matters of religion, differing from that of the catholic and orthodox church, heresy; the mutual communication in the exercise of religion, intercommunity; one converted to any religion, proselyte; a teacher of religion, hierophant; the abandoning or renouncing one's religion, apostacy.

RELIGIONIST. *s.* Conventual.

RELIGIOUS. *a.* One who gives himself up to religious contemplation, hesychastes; religious brotherhood, confraternity; the act of kneeling during religious worship, genuflection; externally religious, pharasaical.

RELIGIOUSLY. *ad.* Religiously disposed, eremetical, or heremetical, devotional, recluse.

RELISH. *s.* Palate, gusto.

REMAINDER. *s.* Remnant, residue, residuum; having a remainder, aliquant.

REMAINING. *p.* Remanent, residual.

REMAINS. *s.* Relics, reliques; relating to what remains, residual, residuary.

REMARK. *s.* Annotation.

REMARKABLE. *a.* Observable, signal.

REMARKABLY. *ad.* Conspicuously, eminantly.

REMEDIED. *p.* Not to be remedied, irremediable, irremissible, unremediable.

REMEDY. *s.* Universal remedy, catholicon, panacea, alexicacon, præsidium; affording a remedy, remediate; not admitting of a remedy, remediless.

REMEMBER. *v.* To bethink, to con, to occur.

REMEMBERED. *p.* That cannot be remembered, irrecordable.

REMEMBRANCE. *s.* Moniment, reminiscence; tending to keep in remembrance, commemorative.

REMORSE. *s.* Causing remorse, compunctive; remorse or sting of conscience, synteresis.

REMOVABLE. *p.* Remuable.

REMOVAL. *s.* Ablation, estrangement, alienation, migration, transition, transmigration, transportance; removal, or transposition, metathesis; removal or change of one disease into another, metaptosis, which is distinguished into a *diadoche* when the removal proves salutary; or a *metastasis*, when the change is to the worse.

REMOVE. *v.* To absist, to abstract, to emigrate, to amove, to transmigrate, to demigrate; to remove in a body, to commigrate; to remove from body to body, to metemsychose; to remove again, to remigrate; to remove from a place, (to banish), to relegate; to remove or set aside, to sequester.

REMOVING. *p.* Act of, remotion.

REND. *v.* To abscind, to lacerate, to lancinate, to laniate.

RENEW. *v.* To renovate, to revive; to renew, or begin again, to interpolate, to redintegrate, to reintigrate.

RENEWAL. *s.* Renewal of health, convalescence; renewal of life, reviction, reviviscency.

RENEWED. *p.* That which is renewed every year, restible.

RENOWN. *s.* Lustre, celebrity, renome.

RENT. *s.* Disruption, scissure.

RENTS. *s.* Or revenues, obventions.

RENUNCIATION. *s.* Or positive denial, abnegation.

REPAIR. *v.* To reintegrate, to retrieve; to repair loss, to reimburse; to repair the strength, to refect.

REPAIRED. *p.* That which is repaired every year, restible.

REPAST. *s.* Collation, refection.

REPAY. *v.* To refund, to reimburse, to remunerate, to retaliate, to requite, to retribute.

REPAYING. *p.* Retributive, retributory.

REPEAT. *v.* Or double, to ingeminate; to repeat by frequent admonitions, to inculcate; to repeat or tell, to relate; to repeat again, to recapitulate, to reiterate. (See to tell.)

REPEATING *p.* Iterant; a repeating of the same meaning by different words, tautology.

REPETITION. *s.* Iteration.

REPELLING. *p.* Repelling by elastic force, renitent.

REPENTANCE. *s.* Compunction, contrition, penitence, resipiscence; void of repentance, impenitent, obdurate.

REPETITION. *s.* Of words, crambe, Gr.

REPLY. *v.* To respond; to reply quickly and sharply, to recoupe.

REPLY. *s.* Replication, response, responsion; reply to an answer, rejoinder; witty and sharp reply, repartee.

REPORT. *s.* Bombilation, (Bailey), bombulation, (Johnson), brait; report, (commendation) præconomy, præcony; the spreading abroad a report, rumigeration.

REPOSE. *s.* Recubation, recumbency.

REPOSITORY. *s.* Promptuary, repertory.

REPREHEND. *v.* To increpate. (See Blame.)

REPRESENTATION. *s.* Effigy, effigies, emblem, hieroglyphic, icon.

REPRESENT. *v.* To personate.

REPRIMAND. *s.* Or chide, (term used at the University), to jobe, (Bailey), magisterial reprimand, lecture; reprimand given in bed by a wife to her husband is termed, a thoral or curtain lecture.

REPROACH. *v.* To gibe or gybe, to conviciate, to revile, to vilify, to upbraid.

REPROACH. *s.* Attaint, attainture, calumny, censure, discommendation, discredit, exprobation, ignominy, imputation, disparagement, obloquy, medisance, reflexion, or reflection; public reproach, ostracism; bitter reproach, sarcasm; term of reproach for an impudent scolding woman, a Billingsgate; without reproach, irreprehensible.

REPROACHFUL. *a.* Ludibrious, opprobrious, probrous, scurrilous; reproachful accusation, invective.

REPROACHFULLY. *ad.* Contumeliously, injuriously, ignominiously, scurrilously.

REPROACHING. *p.* Or reproving in an elegant and easy way, which at the same time tends to convince one of his fault, epiplexis, (Rhet).

REPROOF. *s.* Admonition, reprehension, sneap, increpation; reproof with correction, castigation; reproof or chiding, correption, objurgation; gentle reproof, epiplexis; to deserve reproof, to demerit.

REPROVE. *v.* To reprehend, to increpate, to lecture, to sneap; to reprove or reprimand, (term at the Universities), to jobe.

REPROVING. *p.* In an elegant and easy way, which at the same time tends to convince one of his fault, epiplexis, (Rhet.)

REPUTATION. *s.* Good reputation, eudoxy, euphemism.

REQUEST. *s* Postulate, entreatance, rogation; to obtain by earnest request, to impetrate.

REQUIRED. *p.* Bounden; things required, desiderata; that cannot be required again, irreposcible.

RESEMBLANCE. *s.* Effigies, effigy, analogy, parility, conformity, parity, semblance, similitude; giving a slight resemblance as a shadow, adumbrant.

RESEMBLE. *v.* To emulate, to savour. (See like.)

RESEMBLING. *p.* Semblative.

RESERVE. *v.* To appropriate; to reserve or keep in one's breast, is termed, *keeping the matter in petto.*

RESERVE. *s.* Reserve or silence, taciturnity.

RESERVED. *p.* Coy.

RESERVEDNESS. *s.* Unsociableness, insociableness, incomity.

RESIDE. *v.* To reside for a while, to sojourn; one who resides in the same place with others, cohabitant; to reside under another's roof, to hospitate.

RESIDENCE. *s.* Resiance, biding, commorance.

RESIDENT. *a.* Residentiary, resiant.

RESIGN. *v.* To abdicate, to abandon. (See to Yield.)

RESIST. *v.* To oppugn, to reluct or reluctate.

RESISTANCE. *s.* Oppugnancy, reluctation; that resistance in solid bodies, when they press upon, or are impelled one against another, renitency.

RESOLVE. *v.* To solve. (See Determine.)

RESOLUTE. *a.* (Steady or obstinate) pertinaceous. (See Obstinate.)

RESOLUTION. *s.* Analysis; final resolution or determination, ultimatum.

RESOUND. *v.* To reverb, to reverberate.

RESOUNDING. *p.* Rebation, reverberation.

RESPECT. *s.* Respect or courtesy, abaisance; respect or regard, spectation.

REST. *v.* To center or centre.

REST. *s.* Cessation; rest or quiet, mund, repose, requiem; rest (death) quietus; lying at rest, quiescent; state of lying at rest, quiescence; rest or support of wood placed in a wall on which a beam is to be laid, torsel.

RESTING. *p.* Resting on any thing, superincumbent, implicit, insistent.

RESTITUTION. *s.* Reddition, rendition.

RESTLESS. *a.* (Deprived of sleep) insomnious.

RESTLESSNESS *s.* Jactitation, pandiculation; that sort of restlessness which accompanies several disorders, or the approach of them, blestrismus.

RESTORATION. *s.* Restauration, reddition.

RESTORE. *v.* To reintegrate, to redintegrate, to renovate, to reflect, to revive; to restore (or repay), to refund, to remit.

RESTRAIN. *v.* To inhibit, to prohibit (see to Forbid) to scant, to stint.

RESTRAINED. *a.* Not restrained, latitudinarian.

RESTRAINT. *s.* Abstention or abstention, coarctation, coercion, controul.

RESULTING, *p.* Eventual. (See Accidental.)

RESURRECTION. *s.* Resuscitation; those heretics in the 4th century who denied the resurrection of the dead and the general judgment, Procliniatæ. (Bailey.)

RETIRE. *v.* To recede; to retire or retreat from view, to abscond.

RETIRED. *p.* Cloistered, friarlike, heremitical, recluse; retired farm-house, grange. (Johnson.)

RETIREMENT. *s.* Privacy, secrecy, solitude, recess.

RETIRING. *p.* A retiring or separating, secession.

RETREAT. *v.* To recede; to retreat by inches, to inch; retreat, harbour, privacy, haven.

RETURN. *v.* To revert, to regress; to return a remark wittingly, to retort; to make a return of good or evil, to retaliate, to retribute.

RETURN. *s.* Return to life, reviction; return to health, convalescence; the return of a piece of ordnance, recoil; admitting of no return, irremeable.

RETURNING. *p.* Returning from time to time, recurrent, revertive.

REVELATIONS. *s.* The book of Apocalypse.

REVENGE. *v.* To avenge, to vindicate.

REVENGE. *s.* Choler, wreak; goddess of revenge, Nemesis.

REVENGEFUL. *a.* Vengeful, vindictive, vindicative.

REVENUES. *s.* Obventions.

REFERENCE. *v.* To hallow; to venerate, to revere.

REVERENCE. *s.* Adoration, deference, homage, observance; act of rising together by way of respect or reverence, consurrection; want of reverence, irreverence, unreverend.

REVIEW. *v.* To muster, to reconnoitre.

REVIEW. *s.* Retrospection, revisal, recognition.

REVIVAL. *s.* Reviction.

REVIVE. *v.* To resurge, to resuscitate, to recreate.

REVIVED. *p.* That cannot be revived, irredivivous.

REVIVING. *p.* Analeptic, analeptick, consoling, corroborating.

REVOLTER. *s.* Renegade, renegado, apostate.

REVOLUTION. *s.* Vicissitude; one revolution of the moon, lunation.

REWARD. *v.* To remunerate, to reguerdon.

REWARD. *s.* Desert, gratification, remuneration, recompence, premium, meed, gratuity, guerdon; done without reward, gratuitous, impensible, gratis, *L.*; reward given to a guide, guidage; relat-

S

ing to a reward, munerary, requital.

REWARDED. *p.* Not to be rewarded, irremunerable ; fit to be rewarded, remunerable.

REWARDING. *p.* Retributive, retributory.

RHAPSODY. *s.* Arnodi. (See Song.)

RHYME. *s.* To berhyme ; the making of rhymes, mimology.

RHYMER. *s.* Mimologer.

RIBAND. *s.* Ribbon ; knot of ribands worn on the head, favor, favour, fontange.

RIBS. *s.* Of or belonging to the ribs, costal ; placed between the ribs, intercostal ; the fleshy or muscular parts between the ribs, mesopleuria.

RICH. *a.* Fecund, fertile, fragrant, generative, luscious, locuplete, opulent, prolific, prolifical, sumptuous, gorgeous, racy.

RICHES. *v.* Affluence, mammon, pelf ; one who doats on riches, mammonist ; proud by riches, purse-proud ; the god of riches, Plutus.

RICKETS. *s.* The disease called the rickets, rachitis.

RID. *v.* To get rid of, to doff ; not to be got rid of, inexpedible.

RIDDLE, *v.* To ree.

RIDDLE. *s.* (Perplexing question) rebus, enigma, syntheme, ænigma ; riddle (sieve) divination by means of a riddle, coscinomancy.

RIDE *v.* To ride up and down, to obequitate.

RIDGE. *s.* Balk ; ridge of a hill, ambe.

RIDICULE. *v.* To ridicule, to rally, to scoff, to deride ; to ridicule by imitating, to mime or mimic.

RIDICULE. *s.* Banter, burlesque ; any object of ridicule, butt ; using delicate ridicule, subderisorious.

RIDICULING. *p.* A ridiculing or bantering with good nature, subderisorious.

RIDICULOUS. *a.* Grotesque, ludicrous, ludibrious, risible ; any work so dressed up and altered from the original as to become ridiculous, travested, travestile, travesty.

RIDING. *p.* A riding towards, adequitation ; term used for such disorders as are incident to much riding on horseback, hippuris.

RIG. *v.* To rig out, to dizen, to bedizen. (See to Adorn.)

RIGHT. *s.* Equity, impartiality ; to make right, to rectify (see to Correct) ; the state of being right, rectity ; right to present to a benefice, advowson ; situated on the right hand, dextral or dexter.

RIGHT-ANGLED. *a.* Orthogonal, rectangular.

RIGHTLY. *ad.* Aright.

RING. *s.* Encirclet, gyre or gire ; the rings on which a mariner's compass is hung in the binnacle, gymbals or gimbalds ; ring or bracelet, manille ; motto wrote on a ring, posy or posey ; divination by means of rings, dactyliomancy or dactiliomancy.

RINGING. *p.* Ringing with an echo, resonant.

RINGLETS. *s.* Ringlets of a beautiful woman, are called, heart-breakers.

RIOT. *v.* To riet in gluttony, to engorge.

RIOT. *s.* Hubbub, revel, tumultuation.

RIOTOUS. *a.* Nepotal, nepotine, tumultuary, deboist ; riotous living, abligurition.

RIOTOUSNESS. *s.* Chambering. (Bailey.)

RIP. *v.* To rip open the belly, to eventerate.

RIPE. *a.* Fracid, mature ; too early ripe, premature, præcox, præcocious ; the state of being too early ripe, precocity ; not ripe, immature, inconcocted, unconcocted.

RIPEN. *v.* To mature, to mellow, to maturate.

RIPENING. *p.* Maturative ; the ripening of preternatural humours, pepasmos.

RISE. *v.* To rise or swell, to tumulate, to fester, to tumify, to rankle ; to rise out of, to emerge ; to rise again, to resurge ; to rise above, to transcend.

RISING. *p.* Rising up together by way of reverence, consurrection ; rising or setting with the sun, cosmical ; just rising or beginning, incipient ; rising out of, exortive ; parts rising above the rest, extancy ; the time of one rising in the morning, levee ; rising as a planet or star, ortive ; rising up anew, renascent ; rising up (swelling) tumid ; rising or springing up, ecphysis.

RISK. *s.* Hazard, jeopardy, risque.

RIVAL. *v.* To rival, to emulate.

RIVAL. *s.* Opponent, aspirant, competitor, co-rival, antagonist.

RIVALSHIP. *s.* Rivalry or rivality, competition.

RIVER. *s.* A river is said to disembogue where the mouth of it enters into the sea ; such places where a river falls with noise and violence, as at the great fall of Niagara, catadupes or cataracts ; the mouth of a river, lade, ostiary ; bred near a river, amnigenous ; of or belonging to rivers, fluminous, fluviatic.

ROAD. *s.* Public road, estrade ; of or belonging to the road or highway, viary.

ROAR. *v.* To bluster, to fulminate.

ROAR. *s.* Boation.

ROARING. *p.* Mugient, bellowing.

ROAST. *v.* To roast on a gridiron, to grill.

ROAST. *s.* Roast made of the inmeat of a pig, harselet.

ROASTED. *p.* Roasted oysters, escalop ; roasted as ores are in reverberating furnaces, torrified.

ROASTING. *p.* Assation.

ROB. *v.* To depredate, to despoil, to filch, to pilfer, to spoliate, to harry, to pill or peel, to prog, to peculate; to rob by trick, to defraud.

ROBBERS. *s.* Gang of robbers in Italy, banditti; robber, brigand, *F.* picaroon, piqueerer, padder, freebooter, poller; sea-robber, pirate; robber of the public, depeculator or peculator.

ROBBERY. *s.* Robbery when the value exceeds a shilling, is termed, great larceny; when below a shilling, is termed, petty larceny; robbery of the church, sacrilege; practising robbery, predal.

ROBBING. *p.* Act of robbing, expilation, grassation.

ROBE. *s.* (Dress) palliament; royal robe, stole (hence groom of the stole.)

ROBUST. *a.* Athletic or athletick.

ROCK. *s.* Breaker, cliff; steep rock, precipice; the state of abounding with rocks, scopulosity

ROCKY. *a.* Scopulous.

RODS. *s.* Rods which were carried before the Roman Consuls, &c. fasces, *L.* rod or beam for raising weights, lever; divination by means of rods or wands, rhabdomancy; the method of computing by Napier's rods, rhabdology.

ROGUE. *s.* Scellum or skellum; the cant word used by rogues, gibberish (this sort of language is sometimes called slang.)

ROLL. *v.* To roll round, to circumgyrate, to circumvolve; to roll up, to coil; to roll together, to convolve, to roll into a ball, to glomerate, to conglomerate.

ROLL. *s.* To roll of jurymen on a trial, empannel; roll or list, file, matricula.

ROLLED. *p.* Rolled upon itself, convoluted.

ROLLING. *p.* Act of rolling or tumbling, volutation; a rolling towards, advolution.

ROME. *s.* Name of the feigned deity worshipped by the ancient Romans, that frightened Hannibal from Rome, Rediculus.

ROOF. *s.* That part of the roof of a house which hangs over the wall, eaves; situated under the roof, subtegulaneous; sloping roof hanging out from the main wall or gabel of a house, penthouse, pentice or mantlet; pieces of wood used sometimes in place of slates for the covering of roofs, shingles.

ROOFED. *p.* Testudinated.

ROOM. *s.* Room in a church where the priest's gowns, &c. are kept, vestry or revestiary, sacristry; room in a ship, cabin (from cabane, *F.*); lodger in the same room, chum; room or space, lati-

tude; room (instead of any thing else) lieu, *F.*; room used to dress in, tiring-room; room used to wash and dress linens in, laundry; upper room or garret, sollar; dining-room, zeta; close room in a ship, pullet.

ROOT. *v.* To root up, to aberuncate or averruncate, to deracinate, to eradicate, to erase, to extirpate; to root out, to exterminate.

ROOT. *s.* (Generation) stirp (see Race and Set) to take root, to radicate; having round roots, to radicate; cutter of roots, rhizotomist; having many roots, radicose.

ROOST. *v.* To juke, to perch.

ROPE. *s.* One turn of a rope, bight, fake, kenk; old rope, junk; ropes of all descriptions, cordage; ropemaker, knacker; rope or thong for holding dogs, hawks, &c. leash; the turn of a rope in the act of veering out, kneck; the art of dancing on a rope, schoenobatica, funambulation; small sort of rope used to secure others from fretting, sinnet; rope by which a ship's boat is dragged after the vessel, gift-rope.

ROPY. *a.* Mucous, muculent, sizy, glutinous, viscid, lentous, mucilaginous.

ROSE. *s.* (Disease) erysipelas, St Anthony's fire; of, or belonging, or afflicted with the rose, erysipelatous; an infusion of rose flowers made in warm water with sugar added, mucharum.

ROSIN. *s.* Resin; yielding rosin, resinaceous.

ROSY. *a.* Roseate,

ROT. *v.* To fester, to rankle, to gangrene.

ROT. *s.* Rot among cattle, murrain.

ROTTEN. *a.* Addle, gangrenous, marcid, putredinous, putrid; rotten from being over ripe, fracid.

ROTTENNESS. *s.* Putrefaction, putridness, putridity; rottenness of the bones, cariosity, teredum; rottenness from too much moisture, mydesis. (See Putrefaction.)

ROTTING. *p.* State of rotting, putrescence.

ROUGH. *a.* Abrupt, impolite, or unpolite, uncourteous, discourteous, inclement, hirfute, hispid, villose, villous, asper, faxed, horrent, austere, gothic, inelegant, salebrous; rough (shrubby) frutescent; rough, (ugly) ill-favoured; rough or tempestuous, gusty; rough or wrinkly, rugose; sounding harsh and rough, halsening; rough (scaly) squamose, squamous; rough or hilly, tumulose; rough (full of clods), glebous, gleby; rough (harsh to the ear) immusical or unmusical, scabrous; rough in stile, Hudibrastic; rough (unshapely) informous; rough fellow, hedgeborn, agrestic, knuff; rough (set with bristles) setaceous; rough (hairy) sili-

R 2

cious; rough (husky) siliculose; rough or rich in flavour as old wine, racy; rough or sandy, sabulous, tophaceous; rough and ungovernable in temper, intractable or untractable; rough (untrodden) invious; rough (not effeminate) masculine; rough (rocky) scopulous; rough (clownish) agrestic or agrestical; rough or prickly, acanacious; rough (sour and bitter) acerb.

ROUGHNESS. *s.* Pilosity, salebrity, shagginess.

ROUND. *a.* Rotund, annular, globated, globose, globous, spherical; round and hard body, conglobation; round rooted, bulbous; rising in a round form, convex; round on one side and hollow on the other, concavoconvex or convexoconcave; round on one side, and plain on the other, planoconvex; half round, semi-annular, hemispherical; bent round in the inside, incavated; round on both sides, (applied to optical glasses) omphaloptic, or omphaloptick. (See Glass.)

ROUNDNESS. *s.* Circularity, endlessness; approaching to roundness, subrotundous.

ROUNDING. *p.* Act of rounding, circination.

ROUSE. *v.* To awake, to excite, to exsuscitate or exsuscitate, to incite, to suscitate; ro rouse a beast of prey, to imprime.

ROUT. *s.* (The mob) mobile, mobility.

ROVE. *v.* To expatiate, to forage, to peragrate, to pilgrim, to roam, to prowl, to spatiate.

ROVING. *p.* Discursive, errant, migratory, rantipole, vagous, vagrant.

ROW. *s.* Cordon, file, stratum, enfilade; row of trees planted against a wall, espaliers.

ROWING. *p.* Rowing match, regatta, remigation.

ROYAL. *a.* Imperial, palacious, regal, regifical, basilical.

ROYALTY. *s.* Regality, kingship.

RUB. *v.* To curry, to fret, to fray; to rub off, or rub under, to suffricate; to rub off, to abrade, to corrade; to rub a diseased part with an unguent, to embrocate; to rub out, to erase, to expunge; to rub up, to burnish, to furbish; to rub over, to perfricate.

RUBBING. *p.* The act of rubbing one thing upon another, affriction, friction, frication; a rubbing together, confrication; the rubbing in of any volatile and penetrating fluid for the purpose of relieving pains, embrocation; a wiping or rubbing out, extersion; a rubbing in, infrication or infriction; rubbing or wearing off, detrition.

RUBBISH. *s.* Mulloc; of or belonging to rubbish, ruderary.

RUDDY. *a.* Blowsy, rubious, fulvid, fulvous.

RUDE. *a.* Uncourteous, discourteous, uncomplaisant, churlish, contumelious, disrespectful, faunic, rustic, rustical, gothic, impolite, unpolite, incondite, incult, uncultivated, royaish, salvage; rude man, carle, macaroon, churl; rude (churlish) cynical; rude language, ribaldry.

RUDENESS. *s.* Abusiveness, impertinence.

RUDIMENTS. *s.* The first rudiments of grammar, accidence.

RUEFUL. *a.* Ruthful.

RUFFIAN. *s.* Myrmidon.

RUFFLE. *v.* (Ruffle or tease) to harry, to hare.

RUGGED. *a.* Scabrous, asper, frampold, hirfute, hispid. (See Rough.)

RUIN. *v.* To dilapidate, to dirk, to raze or rase, to ruinate, to subvert, to sap, to shend, to stuprate.

RUIN. *s.* Labefaction, demolition, devastation, extirpation, excision, extermination, havoc, perdition, peremption, pest, subversion.

RULE. *v.* To dominate, to regulate, to preside; to rule with insolence, to domineer.

RULE. *s.* Domination, dictate, enjoinment; rule or form, module, precept, reglement; moral rule or maxim, aphorism; any settled or fixed rule, ascertainment; rule of conduct, cynosure (Metaph.); rule or law such as that of the Holy Scriptures, canon; general rule, porism, precedent; without rule, anomalous, erratic or erratick; not subject to rule, extra-regular; rule or command, masterdom, mastery; rule or principle laid down, position; easily subjected to rule, regible.

RULER. *s.* Mandator; ruler or principal of a school, rector; ruler or depute-king, regent. (See Master and Governor.)

RUMBLING. *p.* Rumbling of the guts, borborygmus.

RUMOUR. *s.* Bruit; the spreading abroad a rumour, rumigeration.

RUN. *v.* To course, to career, to run off, to decamp, to elope, to desert, to elapse; to run as the blood through the veins, to thrill; to run through, to lancinate, to transfix; to run a stake through the body, to empale; to run to and fro, to transcur; to run away through fright, to scamper, to scud.

RUNNING. *p.* Careering; the act of running down, decursion; a running to and fro, discursion; act of running or flowing out, emanation, effluxion; a flowing or running out, effluence; flowing or running into, influent; running between, intercurrent; a running between as an interposition of a tide, &c. interluency;

running or rushing in, as the Atlantic ocean does into the Mediterranean at the straits of Gibraltar, irruent; running back recurrent, refluent; running over, (issuing as waters from a spring) scaturient.

RUPTURE *s.* General name for a rupture, hernia; rupture in the groin, bubonocele; watery rupture, hydrocele; rupture wherein the intestines and caul fall into the scrotum, oscheocele, hydrocele or oscheophyma; rupture when the bowels pressing through the peritoneum fall down in to the groin, enterocele; rupture of the intestines at the navel, enteromphalus; rupture of the navel, omphalocele; rupture occasioned by wind alone, physocele, pneumatocele; rupture occasioned by hard matter retained in the intestines, &c. parocele; rupture occasioning a fleshy swelling of the testicles, sarcocele; rupture of the scrotum or membrane containing the male testicles, scrotocele; rupture or tumour of the scrotum of a fatty consistence, steatocele or steatoma; rupture or falling down of the womb, hysterocele; troubled with the rupture, hernious; bandage for ruptures, truss, amma. (For a more full list of ruptures, see Hernia in Quincy's Lexicon.)

RUSTY. *a.* Eruginous, ferruginous, rubiginous, ærugineous.

S

SABBATH. *s.* Those who deny the holiness of the Sabbath, antisabbatarians; of or belonging to the Sabbath, dominical, sabbatical.

SACK. *s.* Satchel.

SACRAMENT. *s.* The sacrament of the Lord's supper, eucharist, synaxis, housel; not having taken the sacrament, unhouseled; heretics, (followers of one Montanus, disciple of Quintilla a prophetess) who took bread and cheese, in place of bread alone, on that solemn occasion, Quintilians, Artotyrists (Bailey); the bread used at the sacrament of the Lord's supper after being consecrated, hostia; sacrament given by Roman Catholic priests to dying persons, viaticum.

SACRED. *a.* The head of a sacred order, hierarch; sacred writing, hierogram or hierography; to make sacred, to consecrate.

SACRIFICE. *v.* To offer as a sacrifice, to victimate, to delibate, to immolate.

SACRIFICE. *s.* Victim; sacrifice for the dead, februation; sacrifice of one hundred oxen, hecatomb; any sacrifice or offering, oblation; a sacrifice which is wholly burnt on the altar, holocaust; the act of killing beasts for sacrifice, mactation; a sacrificing, litation; an atoning or purging by sacrifice, piation; a tasting or offering up of sacrifices, elibation.

SACRIFICED. *p.* The name of the place where the Ammonites sacrificed their children to their god Moloch, causing drums to be beat to drown their cries, Tophet, i. e. a drum.

SAD. *a.* Deplorable, disconsolate, dumpish, fatal, feral, lachrymal, lugubrious, rueful or ruthful, tragic, tragick or tragical, funebral or funebrous; that which makes or renders sad, mestifical; sad (thoughtful) pensive; sad (lamenting) plaintful, plaintive; sad (of a cloudy appearance) nubilous, nubilose.

SADDEN. *v.* To contristate, to dole, to discomfort.

SADDLE. *s.* An ornamental piece of cloth put under a saddle, housing (from houscaux, F.); saddle on which a woman sits, pad, pillion; the protuberance on the fore part of a saddle, pommel; saddle or harness of any kind for a horse, ephippium.

SADNESS. *s.* Modicity, ruth.

SAFE. *a.* Inviolate, invulnerable, mund; safe (healthful) salubrious, salutary.

SAFE. *s.* Safeguard, defensive (Bacon); safeguard or safety of a city, &c. palladium, so named from the famous statue of *Minerva* or *Pallas* at *Rome*, on which the safety of the city was supposed to depend.

SAFETY. *s.* Surance; place of safety, harbour, haven; state of safety, immobility, impregnability, invincibility, incolumity.

SAFFRON. *s.* Of or belonging to saffron, croceous.

SAIL. *v.* To navigate, to sail in search of plunder, to cruise; to sail round about, to circumnavigate; to sail across or on different courses, to traverse; canvas of which sails are made, mildernix, pouldavis; bearing sails, veliferous; the state of being ready to sail, afloat; term used among mariners when a ship is coming forwards with all sails set, booming.

SAILED. *p.* That cannot be sailed upon,

innavigable or unnavigable.

SAILER. *s.* Sailor, mariner, navigator; of or belonging to a sailor or sailing, nautical or nautick; a thorough-bred sailor is termed, a tarpaulin or tarpawling.

SAILING. *p.* The art of oblique sailing, lexodromics or loxodromicks; the sailing of a ship neither before the wind nor by it, but quartering, is termed, lasking; the art of sailing in the arch of a great circle of the globe, orthodromicks or orthodromics; the art of sailing, histiodromia; a sailing-match, regatta; a sailing before the wind with the foresail set, as is done in great storms, spooning; a sailing back, renavigation; a sailing forward, velification.

SAINT. *s.* The act of declaring a saint, canonization.

SALARY. *s.* Having a salary, salarated; salaries or gifts given by great men, sportula.

SALE. *s.* Licitation, vendition, mart; one who is appointed to call passengers into a sale, klicker.

SALEABLE. *a.* Vendible.

SALMON. *s.* Head of a salmon, jowl; little salmon, samlet, skegger.

SALT. *v.* To brack. (Perry.)

SALT. *s.* Salt melted in water to the point of saturation, brine, garum; rolled in salt, cored; of the nature of salt, garous; the vessels in which salt is set to drain, leach-troughs; house where salt is prepared by boiling, bullary, saltern; salt-petre (among the Paracelsians) halini-ton; an excessive duty formerly exacted on salt in France, gabelle, or gabel; of the nature of salt, saline, salsuginous; full of salt, salinous; abounding with salt, salsamentarious; to season or impregnate with salt, to salite.

SALTING. *p.* Salting or pickling, salsure.

SALTISH. *a.* Brackish, salsuginous.

SALTNESS. *s.* Salsitude; partaking both of saltness and sourness, salsoacid.

SALUTE. *v.* To accost, to greet, to hail.

SAME. *ad.* Of the same kind or origin, congenerous, congenite; the very same person, thing, &c. identick, or identical.

SAMENESS. *ad.* Indentity.

SANCTUARY. *s.* Asylum, adytum, girthol.

SAND. *s.* Sand-bath in which the feet of dropsical persons are placed, psammismus; sand or gravel which sometimes breeds in the bodies of men and animals, psammos; a quick-sand, syrtis.

SANDY. *a.* Tophaceous, arenaceous, arenose, calculous, gritty, sabulous.

SARCOLOGY. *s.* Is that part of anatomy which treats of the doctrine of the integu-

ments, and includes myology, or description of the muscles; splanchnology, or description of the viscera; angiology, or description of the arteries, veins, lymphatics, &c.; neurology, or description of the nerves.

SASH. *s.* Cincture, shash, (Bailey).

SATAN. *s.* Belial. (See Spirit).

SATISFACTION. *s.* Atonement, contentation, expiation.

SATISFIED. *p.* Not to be satisfied, insatiable, insatiate, unsatiable.

SATISFY. *v.* To replenish, to requite, to cloy, to satiate, to stanch.

SAUCE. *s.* Condiment.

SAUCY. *a.* Arrogant, frontless, malapert, pert, petulant, pragmatical, procacious; saucy fellow, prig; saucy and abusive language, scurrility, dicacity.

SAVAGE. *s.* Leonine, remorseless, fell, ferine, ferocious, rapacious, belluine, rustical, salvage.

SAVAGENESS. *s.* Savagery, ferity.

SAVE. *v.* (Lay up,) to intreasure, or oeconomize; to save, (to shelter), to sanctuarise, to shroud.

SAVED. *p.* The possibility of being saved, salvability.

SAVIOUR. *s.* Ancient heretics, followers of one *Marcion*, a stoic, who denied that our Saviour was the Son of God, Marcionists; heretics in the 4th century who denied the incarnation of our Saviour, Proclinitæ: ceremony performed in the church of Rome on the Wednesday, Thursday, and Friday before Easter, in representation of the agony of our Saviour, and darkness in the garden, tenebres, or tenebræ.

SAW. *s.* Having teeth like a saw, serrated.

SAY. *v.* To advance, to broach, to prolate.

SAYING. *p.* Old saying or maxim, adage; any remarkable or witty saying, apothegm.

SCAB. *s.* Scab in dogs or cattle, mange; running scab, petigo; sort of scab or itch which sometimes affects the scrotum, psoriasis; such medicines as are good against the itch or scab, psorica; scab on the eyes attended with inflammation, psorophthalmy.

SCABBINESS, *s.* Psora.

SCALD. *s.* Scald or burn, ambustion.

SCALE. *v.* To scale off, to exfoliate.

SCALE. *s.* Flake, lamen; scales which fall from the head, furfures, dandriff; consisting of thin scales, foliaceous.

SCALY. *a.* Furfuraceous, squamose, squamous; scaly disease, leprosy, or leprosity.

SCANDAL. *s.* Obtrectation, probrosity, traducement, reproach.

SCANDALISE. *v.* To detract.

SCANDALOUS. *a.* Ignominious, libellous; scandalous language, scurrility; scandalous reports circulated against a peer of the realm, or great officer of state, is termed *scandalum magnatum.*

SCANTY. *a.* Neap, penurous. (See Want.)

SCAR. *s.* Cicatrix, or cicatrice. (See Wound.)

SCARE. *v.* To intimidate. (See Fright.)

SCARIFYING. *p.* A scarifying of the gums, &c. encharaxis.

SCARLET. *a.* Of a scarlet dye, coccinion.

SCATTER. *v.* To diffuse, to disperge, to disperse, to disseminate.

SCATTERED. *p.* Easily scattered, dissipable; scattered between, interfused.

SCENT. *s.* Odor, or odour; having or possessing no scent, inodorate, inodorous; sweet scent, redolence; yielding a sweet scent, redolent; such ingredients as give medicines a good scent, hedysmata.

SCENTED. *a.* Strong scented as butter or oil too long kept, rancid; strong scented, rank, or stinking, graveolent.

SCHEME. *s.* Contrivance, device, enterprise; any silly scheme, fangle; malicious scheme, machination; a treatise on the method of drawing schemes, troposchematology.

SCHOLAR. *s.* Disciple, pupil, humanist, sectator; money given by scholars at entrance, minerval; of or belonging to the state of a scholar, pupilage, pupilary; scholar appointed by the master to oversee the rest, prepositor; scholar of the lowest rank at Cambridge, sizer, and is one of the same description who is called at Oxford servitour; scholar in the university of Oxford appointed to make jesting and satirical speeches, *terræ filius.*

SCHOOL. *s.* Seminary; money paid at entrance to school, minerval; one of the school appointed by the master to oversee the younger scholars, prepositor; the nodification of some speech or ceremony to be performed in a school or public seminary, programma.

SCHOOLFELLOW. *s.* Bookmate.

SCHOOLMASTER. *s.* Pedagogue; the chief schoolmaster or principal of a colledge, gymnasiarch.

SCIENCES. *s.* The knowledge of many sciences, polymathy; the circle of arts and sciences, cyclopædia, or encyclopædia; the seven liberal sciences are grammar, logic, rhetoric, arithmetic, geometry, astronomy, and music; of or belonging to arts and sciences, or terms used in them, technical. (See Arts.)

SCOFF. *v.* To jeer.

SCOFF. *s.* Foutra, gibe, glike, sarcasm,

(See Bark and Rail.)

SCOFFER. *s.* Contemnor, derider.

SCOLD. *v.* To berattle, to chide, to jobe, to objurgate.

SCOLD. *s.* Vixen, termagant.

SCOLDING. *p.* A scolding match, lere; act of scolding, rixation; scolding woman, termagant, vixen.

SCORCH. *v.* To adure, to parch, to torrify.

SCORCHED. *a.* Adusted, torrid.

SCORCHING. *p.* Act of, adustion, torrefaction.

SCORN. *v.* To contemn, to deride, to disregard, to spurn.

SCORN. *s.* Contempt, disdain, irrision, misprision, meprise.

SCORNFUL. *a.* Indignant, (See Angry.)

SCORNFULLY. *s.* Askew.

SCOUNDREL. *s.* Losel, skellum, fustilarian, loon, poltron, or poltroon, varlet; a beggarly scoundrel, bezonian, (Perry.)

SCOURING. *p.* Possessing a scouring or cleansing quality, abstergent; souring medicines, rhyptics; place for scouring and washing kitchen utensils, &c. scullery; any substance that scours or cleanses as soap, smegma.

SCOUT. *s.* Emissary, antecursor, precursor, explorator; scout sent out on horseback, vidette.

SCOURGING. *p.* Act of scourging, flagellation, (See Whip.)

SCRAP. *s.* Mammoc; scraps collected from authors, analecta, aanlect, cento.

SCRAPE. *v.* To scrape out, to erase, to expunge; to scrape together, to corrade.

SCRAPINGS. *s.* Scrapings or shavings, raments, rasions, strigment.

SCREAM. *s.* Scream or noise made by an insect, fritinancy.

SKREEN. *s.* (Pretence) stalking-horse; screen or fence of boards, diathyrum.

SKREW. *s.* Skrew-press, torcularis; resembling a skrew, spiral.

SCREWED. *a.* Cockleated.

SCRIPTURAL. *a.* Canonical.

SCRIPTURES. *s.* One versed in the scriptures, textuarist, or textuary.

SCROPHULA. *s.* Scrophula or scrofula; good against the scrofula or king's evil, antistrumatick or antistrumatic.

SCULPTURE. *s.* The science of sculpture, toreumatography, insculpture, taillée-douce, F.

SCUM. *v.* To despumate.

SCUM. *s.* Scum of liquors, mother, spume.

SCURFY. *a.* Furfuraceous.

SCURVY. *s.* Diseased with the scurvy, scorbutic; good against the scurvy, antiscorbutic.

SCURVY. *a.* Scurvy mean wretch, runnion

SEA. *s.* The abyss, the profound ; the open or high sea, offing ; the feigned god of the sea, Neptune ; robber at sea, pirate ; a river is said to *disembogue* where it empties itself into the sea ; passage made over sea, transfretation ; ruling the sea, salsipotent ; lying towards the sea, seaward : lying under the sea, submarine ; name for any shelf, quicksand, or dangerous part of the sea, syrtis, G. ; commander at sea, (Admiral), thalassiarch ; description of the sea, haliography ; belonging or relating somewhat to the sea, semimarine ; belonging to two seas, bimarical ; of or belonging to the sea Æquorean, or Equorean ; coming from beyond the sea, transmarine ; appearing as a ship at sea, looming ; mouth or arm of the sea, estuary ; goods floating on the sea, flotson ; the recess or ebb of the sea, ampotis ; a description of the seas, hydrography ; lands recovered from the sea, innings ; relating to the sea shore, littoral ; sea fight, naumachy ; sea sick, nauseabund ; of or belonging to a seaman, nautical.

SCYTHE. *s.* Bent like a scythe, falcated.

SEAL. *s.* The king's seal, signet.

SEALED. *p.* (Closed up as the upper end of a barometer,) hermetically sealed.

SEAM. *s.* Commissure ; seams or sutures of the skull are four. 1. The Lambdoidal, so named from its form resembling the Greek letter Lambda. 2. The Sagittal, from its figure resembling that of an arrow. 3d. The Caronal Suture, which reaches transversely from one temple to the other over the crown of the head. And, 4th, The Squamose, or scaled suture, so named from the bones being laped over each other ; seam next the keel of a ship, garboard strake ; seams between the planks of a ship, rends.

SEARCH. *v.* To search after, to explorate, to quese, (Milton) to explore, to indagate ; to search, to vestigate ; to search out in the dark, to poke ; to search by means of a surgical instrument, to probe ; to search for the sake of curiosity, to pry.

SEARCH. *s.* Search, inquest, scrutiny, quest ; an inquiry or search, interrogatory ; diligent search, pervestigation, perquisition, perscrutation, rummage.

SEARCHED. *p.* Not to be searched out, inscrutable ; that may be searched out, scrutable.

SEARCHER. *s.* Scrutator, scrutineer.

SEARCHING. *p.* Inquirent, investigating ; a searching out, scrutation.

SEASON. *v.* To savour, to condite ; to season the mind with good principles, to imbue, (Bailey).

SEASONABLE. *a.* Tempestive.

SEASONABLY. *ad.* Betimes, tidily, opportunely.

SEASONED. *p.* That may be seasoned or pickled, conditaneous.

SEASONING. *p.* Condiment.

SEAT. *s.* The seat of a disease, *minera morbi* (among Physicians) ; seat in a church, pew ; seat in a garden where trees and twigs are cut and plaited over it, topiary work, (from Topiaria, L.) large long seat with a back to it, settee, settle ; seat or throne of a bishop within the chancel, faldisdroy.

SECOND. *a.* A second marriage, deuterogamy ; a second disease proceeding from the first, deuteropathy ; the second intention or design, deuteroscopy.

SECRECY. *s.* Taciturnity ; *under the rose*, privacy ; secrecy or bye place, huggermugger ; to lie flat on the belly in a place of secrecy for the purpose of surprise, to lie *perdue*.

SECRETARY. *s.* Symmista, archigrapher.

SECRET. *s.* Clandestine, auricular, occult, cabalistical, covert, clancular, inly, cryptic, cryptick, cryptical, intestine, inscrutable, opertaneous, mystic, latent, talismantic, recondite ; a secret (what is not yet discovered particularly in Arts and Science), arcanum, L. ; revealer of secrets, blabber ; secret place from which one may annoy or fall upon an enemy, ambuscade ; one intrusted with a secret, confident ; secret assembly, conventicle ; secret agent, emissary ; secret writing, steganography, cryptography ; secret malice, heart-burning ; secret feast or entertainment, junket ; to skulk or remain in secret, to miche ; to keep a matter secret is termed keeping it in *petto* (Ital.) to speak or impart a matter as a secret, to *speak under the rose* ; secret friend, privado ; admitted to secrets, privy ; apt to betray secrets, proditarious, leaky ; to keep secret, to suppress ; a secret mode of conveyance or carriage, subvection ; a secret place of retirement, adytum.

SECRETLY. *ad.* Clandestinely ; put or placed secretly for some thing else, subdititious.

SECURE. *v.* To ensconce, to secret, to munite.

SECURE. *a.* Salutary.

SECURITY. *s.* Assurance, bulwark, palladium, surance ; security against loss, indemnification ; one who is security or bail for another, mainpernor, or mainprize.

SEDUCING. *p.* The act of seducing women, thelypthora.

SEE. *v.* To perceive ; to see at a distance,

to espy, to ken, to descry ; to see before-
hand, to presage. (See Foretel.)

SEED. *s.* To scatter or spread seed, &c. to
disseminate ; fruit which contains only
one seed, monopyrerous ; having only one
seed vessel, unicapsular ; belonging to
that class of plants which have but one
seed in the seed vessel, enangiomonosper-
mous ; bearing four seeds, tetraspermous ;
having five seed vessels, pentacapsular ;
having many seeds, polyspermous ; having many seeds in one seed vessel, mo-
nangiopolyspermous, (Bot.) ; such plants
as bear their seeds on the back part of
their leaves, being the same with capil-
laries, are termed epiphyllospermous ; resembling seeds or grains, granulary ; of or
belonging to seed, seminal, spermatical,
or spermatic ; an involuntary emission of
the seed during sleep, exonerrosis ; the seed
of the elm, samara ; of the oak, acorn ;
of the beech, mast.

SEEING. *p.* Seeing (not barely believing),
intuitive, (Hooker) ; difficulty in seeing
objects distinctly, dysopia ; formed in the
act of seeing, visive.

SEEK. *v.* To query, to quese, to vestigate ;
to seek after diligently, to investigate or
evestigate.

SEEKER. *s.* Questrist.

SEEKING. *p.* Seeking or investigating, zetetick or zetetic.

SEEM. *v.* It seems to me, methinks.

SEEN. *a.* In contradistinction to mere theory, autoptical ; easily to be seen, con-
spectable, (See Discern) ; not to be
seen, indiscernable, or undiscernible ;
difficult to be seen, inaspicuous.

SEIGNOR. *s.* The title of the Grand Seignor, paudishaw, (i. e. an expeller of
princes or injuries), (Bailey) ; the palace
where his concubines are kept, seraglio,
(Ital,) ; the foot guards of the Grand
Seignor, about 300 in number, who are
armed with bows and arrows, solachs.

SEIZE. *v.* To fang, to arrest, to distrain, to
excuss, to bend, to intercept, to occupate.

SEIZING. *p.* Cause of seizing intercipient ;
the act of seizing or taking possession,
occupancy ; seizing by violence, rapacious ; seizing, prehensile ; a seizing by
way of recompence, reprisal, reprise.

SELF-LOVE. *s.* Philauty.

SELFISH. *a.* Mercenary.

SELL. *v.* To vend ; to sell or enslave, to
mancipate, (Bailey) ; to sell wine or
victuals, to cauponate ; to sell, to alien,
to alienate.

SELLER. *s.* Seller of provisions by retail,
higgler ; seller of yarn by retail, jour-
ney-chopper, (Bailey.)

SELLING. *p.* A selling and buying, chaffe-

ry ; an auction or selling, licitation ; of
or belonging to selling, mercative ; a
selling of timber, &c. for building, mate-
riation, (Bailey.) ; act of selling, vendition ; a kind of crime which is committed
by a deceitful selling of a thing otherwise
than it really is, as if a man should sell
that for his own, which is actually the
property of another, stellionate, (Johnson.)

SEND. *v.* To send for, order, or summon,
to accite ; to send in, to intromit ; to send
away another upon an embassy, to delegate ; to send out or issue, to emit ; to
send away or banish, to relegate ; to send
back, to remand.

SENDING. *p.* The act of sending from one
place to another, transmission ; the sending away one or more on any business or
matter, mission, legation ; a farewell or
sending away, propempticon.

SENIORITY. *s.* Primogeniture.

SENSATION. *s.* Fault in sensation, dysæs-
thesia.

SENSELESS. *a.* Brute, (from Brutus, *L*)
insensate.

SENSES *s.* A deprivation of the senses, accompanied with trembling, tromoesis or
tromos. (Bailey.)

SENSIBILITY. *s.* Sensility. (Bailey.)

SENSITIVE. *a.* Plants of the sensitive kind
are termed, æschynomenous plants, from
the Greek word αισχυνομαι, I am ashamed.

SENT. *p.* That which may be sent, missive,

SENTENCE. *v.* To pass sentence by con-
signing to punishment, to adjudge.

SENTENCE. *s.* A delay of sentence generally in criminal affairs, reprieve, respite ;
sentence, award, decree, doom, verdict,
crisis ; the final or decisive sentence of an
arbiter, laudum ; a term for two sentences
alike in length, isocolon, *G.* ; change of
sentence or decree, reversal ; full of sentences or short observations, sententious ;
the due construction of words into sentences, syntax ; a short instructive sentence, gnoma ; such sentences as are short
and pithy, Chilonian or Chilonic ; choice
collection of sentences, anthology.

SENTIMENT. *s.* Discourse or treatise concerning sentiment, gnomology.

SEPERABLE *a.* Exemptitious.

SEPARATE. *v.* To abduce, to abstract ;
to separate or cut, to incide ; to separate
or distinguish good from bad, to discrimi-
nate, to garble ; to separate or rot, to
fester, to rankle ; to separate, to divaricate, to divorce, to decouple, to disunite,
to disjoin, to disperse, to dissociate, to dissolve, to detach, to discontinue ; to separate or set apart, to besort, to individuate ;
one who separates from the church, schis-
matick or schismatic ; to separate fine

T

matter from gross, to secern; to separate or set apart, to segregate, to seposite, to sequester, to sejugate, to abgregate, to separate by force; to sever.

SEPARATED. *p.* Disjunct, incontiguous; that cannot be separated, indiscerptible, indissolvable, undissolvable, insoluble; part that is separated, secrement.

SEPARATION. *s.* Distraction, avulsion, disgregation, elision, disunion; separation by straining, excernment; separation or ejection of animal substance, excretion; the separation of juices in an animal body, secretion; a sudden separation, abruption; separation of parts or resolution, analysis.

SEPARATELY. *ad.* Apart, asunder, distinctly.

SEPARATING. *p.* Parting or pulling asunder, sejunction; a distinction, dividing, or separating, diastole (Bailey); a separating or cutting, dissevering.

SEPULCHRES. *s.* Memoriæ, *L.*; an empty sepulchre set up in honour of the dead, cenotaph or cenotaphium.

SERIOUS. *a.* Composed, meditative, pensive.

SERIOUSNESS. *s.* Gravity.

SERMON. *s.* Prelection; sermon (in contempt) preachment; to make a sermon, to sermonize.

SERPENT. *s.* Serpent said to kill by looking, which from the crest on its head is called, basilisk, or, little king; the cast skins of serpents, reduviæ or exuviæ, *L.*; eating or feeding on serpents, ophiophagous; a huge serpent found in both the East and West Indies, the largest of the serpent kind, said to be forty feet long, and is accounted excellent food, boiguacu; serpent which seems to have two heads, from its faculty of moving forwards with either end, amphisbœna; a serpent the bite of which is said to produce unquenchable thirst, dypsas or causus. (Quincy)

SERVANT. *s.* Servant employed in all sorts of business, factotum; servant employed in a shop, clicker; household servants, meiny; belonging to the train of servants, menial; domestic servant, manupastus, *L.*; servant-maid, miskin frow; (Bailey); servant who does not dwell in one's house, but only bears his livery, retainer (Johnson); servant (laquey) skipjack, skip-kennel; money given to servants by strangers, vails or vales; the servant who gathers up the fragments after dinner, analectes, *G.*

SERVE. *v.* To serve under, to subminister.

SET. *v.* To set on or incite, to alloo; to set off or display, to apparel, to embellish; to set off or adorn, to dizen, to garnish, to impaint; to set apart, to appropriate; to set up, to constitute; to set right or un-

deceive, to disabuse; to set in gold, silver, &c. to enchase; to set down anthoratatively, to prescribe; to set free, to manumit; to set aside, to sequester.

SET. *s.* Covey, junto, fraternity, horde, posse, *L.*; set (party) cabal, cabala; set of letters for printing, font, (see Type), set (placed) posited; set (planted) sative; those stars which never set, are termed, inocciduous.

SETTING. *p.* Setting and rising with the sun, cosmical; setting (western) ponent; never setting (said of some stars) inocciduous.

SETTLE. *v.* To adjust; to settle or establish, to affear, to determine; to settle or dwell in a place, to domiciliate; to settle privately, to concert; to settle, rest or light upon, as birds, to juke, to perch; to settle or repose in security, to nestle; to settle or arrange before hand, to preconcert; to settle terms, to stipulate.

SETTLED. *p.* Settled or fixed, statary; settled or determined, pight; not settled or determined, pending; settled or agreed upon in marriage, combinate.

SETTLING. *p.* Settling or easing, sedative; a settling again, reposition.

SEVEN. *a.* The space of seven weeks, years, &c. hebdomade; seven-sided figure, heptagon; seven times as much, septuple; the possessing or having seven sounds, heptaphony; consisting of seven different ways or sorts, septifarious; of seven leaves, septifolious; of seven shapes, septiform; of sevensides, septilateral; of seven ounces, septuncial; of the order of seven (as a week) septimane, septuary; belonging to the number seven, septenarious, septenary; of the space of seven years, septennial. (See One, Two, Three, &c.)

SEVENNIGHT. *s.* As this word is generally used only in *one* sense, the following authority is quoted from Johnson. It happened on Monday was *sevennight*, that is, *on the Monday before last Monday*: it will be done on Monday *sevennight*, that is, *on the Monday after next Monday*. Addison.

SEVENTH. *a.* Containing 1-7th part, subseptuple.

SEVENTY. *a.* Of or belonging to seventy, septuagesimal.

SEVERAL. *a.* Divers (See Sundry.)

SEVERE. *a.* Inclement, piquant, poignant, pungent, rigid, stern, vindicatory, punitory; severe or biting to the taste, acerb; severe (rigid) austere, breme, agelastic; severe (religiously scrupulous) monachal; severe (taunting) sarcastic or sarcastical. (See Sharp.)

SEVERITY. *s.* Rigor, rigour; severity or

bitterness of treatment, amaritude; severity or sternness of countenance, tetricity, torvity; severity of treatment by constraint, duresse.

SEVERN. *s.* The raging of the river Severn below the city of Gloucester, higra. (Bailey.)

SEW. *v.* To sarcinate; to sew slightly, to baste; to sew up a rent with so much nicety that it is not perceived, to finedraw.

SEWED. *p.* Sewed together, consutile.

SEXES. *s.* Possessing both sexes, androgynous, hermaphroditical; the intercourse between the sexes, aphrodisia, coition; common to both sexes, epicene; change of sex, transexion.

SEXTON. *s.* Sacristan, sacrist.

SHABBY. *a.* Shabby ragged fellow, tatterdemalion, jippo.

SHACKLE. *v.* To immanacle, to inthral, to manacle; to shackle or bind the elbows behind the back, to pinion.

SHACKLES. *s.* Gyves.

SHADE. *v.* To obumbrate, to opacate.

SHADE. *s.* Umbrage, fraicheur, fresco; retreat or arbour where one may retire into the shade, bower.

SHADINESS. *s.* Fraicheur, F. (See Shade.)

SHADOW. *s.* Umbrage; to cast a shadow upon, to inumbrate, to adumbrate; an imperfect shadow, penumbra; resembling a shadow, umbratile; battle with a shadow, sciamachy; divination by shadows, sciomancy; art of finding out the hour of the day or night by a shadow, sciagraphy; investigating shadows, sciotheric, such as the mathematical instrument used for adjusting clocks and watches, called the sciotheric telescope; those inhabitants of the torrid zone, who have no shadow at noon, which happens when their respective latitude is equal to the sun's declination, ascii; the inhabitants of the torrid zone, whose shadows are cast both north and south, which happens according as the sun is in the northern or southern signs, viz: when he is in the southern, the shadow falls northward, &c. *econtra,* amphiscii; the inhabitants living between the tropics and polar circles, whose shadows fall northwards in north latitude, and southwards in south latitude, heteroscii; the inhabitants of the frigid zones, whose shadows go round them in a day, Periscii. (See Inhabitants.)

SHADY. *a.* Bowery, silvan, umbratile, umbrose, umbrageous, umbraical; shady bowers, walks, &c. frescades.

SHAFTS. *s.* The shafts of a carriage are termed thills; hence the horse that draws between the shafts is called the thiller-horse.

SHAGGY. *a.* Crinose, hispid, hirfute, villose, villous.

SHAKE. *v.* To brandish, to conquassate, to didder, to frill, to exagitate; to shake or infeeble, to infirm; having power to shake, concussive; to shake with cold or fear, to quake, to quiver, to quappe, to quassate, to vacillate, to vibrate.

SHAKING. *p.* Vibrissant; a shaking or nodding, nutation; shaking off, decutient; a shaking as one in an ague, tremor or tremour; violent shaking or jolting, succussion, succussation or incussion; a shaking again, recussion.

SHAME. *s.* Reproach; shame attending a villainous action, opprobrium.

SHAMEFACED. *a.* Pudibund, verecund.

SHAMEFUL. *a.* Ignominious, arrant, dedecorose, dedecorous, egregious, ludibrious, profligate.

SHAMELESS. *a.* Frontless, brazenfaced, irreclaimable.

SHAMELESSNESS. *s.* Effrontery, impudicity.

SHANKER. *s.* Therioma or theriodes, i. e, malignant ulcers, from their effects resembling the havoc done by wild beasts.

SHAPE. *v.* To modify.

SHAPE. *s.* Having many shapes, multiform, omniform, variform.

SHAPELESS. *a.* Inform or informous.

SHARE. *s.* Commons, dividend, dole, impartance, purparty, quota; small share, modicum; share or proportion of meat, drink, or forage, given to seamen and soldiers for one day, ration; having a share with others, participant.

SHARER. *s.* Sharer or partner, puefellow, skainsmate.

SHARP. *a.* (Prickly acanacious; sharp (bitter or sour) acerb; sharp (hot and bitter) acrid; sharp (sour) acid; sharp (quickness of intellect) acumen, sagacity; sharp or thin undigested humour resembling serum, ichor; sharp (witty or subtile) argute; sharp (piercing or chill) breme; sharp-sighted, eagle-eyed, lynceous, perspicacious; sharp (or rough) horrent; sharp (cutting) trenchant, incisive; sharp (cunning) subtle, subtile, subdolous; sharp (biting) mordicant, pungent, mordacious; full of sharp points, muricated; very sharp, peracute, piquant, poignant; sharp (quick or ready) prompt; sharp (eager) vehement.

SHARPEN. *v.* To sharpen, to acuate, to exacuate.

SHAVE. *v.* To barb.

SHAVING. *p.* Act of shaving or erazing, abrasion; shavings or scrapings, raments, rasions, strigment; the act of shaving the hair, tonsure. (See Hair.)

SHEATHING. *p.* Act of sheathing, vagination.

SHEATHS. *s.* Such insects as have their wings in sheaths, are termed, vaginipennous.

SHED. *v.* To effuse, to effund ; to shed or cover, to hovel; not liable to be shed, indeciduous.

SHED. *s.* Shed hanging out a-slope from a wall or the gable of a house, pent-house, pentice, or mantelet.

SHEEP. *s.* Old toothless sheep, croan ; sheep two years old, hoggerel, hoggrel ; the wool taken from the skin of a dead sheep, morling or mortling.

SHEET. *s.* Sheet of paper divided into two leaves, folio ; into 4, quarto, and is wrote thus, 4to ; into 8, octavo, thus, 8vo ; into 12, duodecimo, thus, 12mo ; into 18, octodecimo, thus, 18mo ; besides these, there are 24mo, and 32mo ; waste printed sheet, maculature.

SHELLS. *s.* Fish having two shells, as oysters, bivalvular ; shell of a fish, conch (from choncha, *L.*) ; of or belonging to shells, testaceous ; the little hollows in the shells of fishes, formed for the fastening the tendons of their muscles, vestigia ; shell fruits of all kinds are termed, acrodrya ; to shell off as the scales of a corrupt bone from the sound part, to exfoliate.

SHELTER. *v.* To nurse, to hovel, to sanctuarise, to shroud.

SHELTER. *s.* Cove, creek, coverture, harbour, haven ; the shelter or place of rest of a boar or wild beast, lair ; shelter or obscurity, concealedness.

SHELTERING. *p.* Protective, (see Covering.)

SHEW. *v.* (See Show.)

SHIELD. *s.* Buckler ; large shield which covers the whole body, povese or pavise ; bearing a shield, scutiferous.

SHIFT. *v.* To shift one's dress, to doff ; to shift off, to evade, to fend ; to shift or play off, to tergiversate ; to shift, to dodge, to palter ; to shift for provisions, to prog ; to shift one's place, to demigrate.

SHIFT. *s.* Expedient, far-fetch, subterfuge ; woman's shift, smicket.

SHINE. *v.* To beam ; to shine together, to constellate ; to shine forth, to effulge ; to shine from heat or polish, to gleen, to glister, to glisten, to radiate.

SHINESS. *s.* Prudery, coyness.

SHINING. *p.* Beamy, effulgent, fulgent, fulgid, lucent, lucid, luminous, lustrous, nitid, relucent, resplendent, scintillating, splendent, shining round, circumfulgent ; shining between, interfulgent, interlucent ; act of shining between, intermication ; shining through, tralucid, translucid, tralucent.

SHIP. *s.* Money borrowed on a ship, bottomry ; place for repairing or building of ships, dock ; to put or go on board ship, to embark, to inship ; any swift sailing ship which scours the seas, dromo, *G.* ; goods saved from the wreck of a ship, jetsam or jetsom ; the account of articles, brought by a ship, invoice ; said of a ship when her bolts, &c. are so rusted, as to cause her to leak, iron-sick ; when she has just got out of sight of land, land-lay'd ; said of a ship going right before the wind, going large ; the sailing of a ship neither before the wind or by it, but quartering, is termed lasking ; to steer a ship irregularly, to laveer ; the appearance of a ship in the offing, looming ; of or belonging to ships, naval ; belonging to ships or mariners, nautic or nautical ; said of a ship when it inclines more to one side than another, lust, hence the sea phrase of a ship lusting more to this side than that ; pertaining to a small ship, navicular ; that will bear or float a ship, navigerous ; said of a ship when she is moored with her head to the shore with two cables, one of which is belayed on shore, the other attached to an anchor in the water, moored *à proviso* ; the lowest plank of a ship next the keel, is called the garboard plank ; the lowest seam is called, the garboard strake.

SHIPWRECK. *s.* Goods thrown overboard when in danger of shipwreck, lagan. (Saxon.)

SHIRT. *s.* An attack made by soldiers with their shirts over their apparel, in order to be known to each other, camisade or camisado.

SHOCK. *v.* To jolt ; to shock or fright, to gast.

SHOCK. *s.* Brunt, concussion, succussion, rejolt.

SHOCKING. *p.* Ghastly, hideous, horrent, horrible.

SHOD. *p.* Shod or fitted with shoes, calceated, soleated.

SHOES. *s.* Shoes fitted with, calceated, soleated ; the act of pulling off the shoes, discalceation ; deprived off shoes, excalceated ; old fashioned shoes, leripoops (Bailey) ; shoes without heels, pinson ; border or seam of a shoe, rand ; the winged shoes of Mercury, talaria ; upper leather of a shoe, vamp.

SHOEMAKER. *s.* Cordwainer (from cordonnier, *F.*)

SHOOT. *v.* To shoot or dart out, to ejaculate ; to shoot or put forth, to germinate ; to shoot or spring, to pullulate ; to shoot in rays, to radiate.

SHOOT. *s.* Shoot of a tree, bough, sprout,

imp; young shoot, scion; shoot, surcle; full of shoots, frutescent.

SHOOTING. *p.* A shooting into the form of flowers, efflorescence; act of shooting or throwing, projection.

SHOP *s.* Of or belonging to shops, tabernarious, officinal.

SHORE. *s* Beach, rivage; of or belonging to the shore, littoral; to put on shore, to disembark,

SHORT. *a.* Compendious, succinct, concise, laconic, summary, transient, momentary; the short and brief manner of speech for which the Lacedæmonians were noted, laconism; short or brittle as glass, &c. fragile; short and fat, squab; short and pithy sentences are termed, Chilonian or Chilonic sentences; the act of cutting short, decurtation.

SHORTEN. *v.* To abbreviate, to abridge, to abstract, to epitomise, to contract.

SHORT-HAND. *s.* The art of short-hand writing, brachygraphy.

SHORTNESS. *s.* Conciseness, syntomy, briefness; shortness of speech, brachylogy.

SHORTSIGHTED. *p.* Purblind or pore-blind.

SHOT. *p.* That which may be shot or darted, missile or missive, jaculable.

SHOULDER. *s.* Of or belonging to the shoulder, humeral, scapular, scapulary; shoulder-knot, epaulette, (from epaule, F. the shoulder); placed between the shoulders, interscapular; the shoulder-blade, omoplate; gout in the shoulder, omagra.

SHOUT. *v.* To vociferate.

SHOUT. *s.* A shout of praise, acclaim or acclamation; the shout of a multitude, conclamation.

SHOUTING *p.* Jubilant.

SHOVEL. *s.* Peel, from pelle, F.

SHOW. *v.* To evict, to display, to exhibit, to explicate, to interpret, to monstrate, to ominate, to evince, to exhibit, to display, to purport, to reveal, to disclose, to ostentate; to show or prove, to approve (Johnson); to show or point out as with the finger, to indigitate; to show or tell unlucky things, to obnunciate; to show or lay open, to expound, to illustrate, to explicate; to show before hand, to premonstrate, to prognosticate.

SHOW. *s.* Enforce, ostent, pageantry, pretence, pretext, colour; false show, feint; show or representation, gest; show of wild beasts anciently let loose to the Roman people, pancarpus; show or equipage, aparatus, eclat; show (beauty and comeliness) pulchritude; show (or lustre) sheen; fair show, semblance.

SHOWING. *p.* Indicant, indicative; a showing or indication, endeixis.

SHOWN. *p.* That may be easily shown, manifestible.

SHOWY. *a.* Flashy, gaudy, garish or gairish, gorgeous, janty or jaunty, plausible; any showy trifle, gewgaw.

SHRILL. *a.* Argute; shrill and loud noise, clangour.

SHRINK. *v.* To shrink, to blench, to constrict, to cower, to flinch, to recoil; to shrink through pain, to queck.

SHRUB *s.* Arboret; abounding with shrubs, frutescent, arbustine; place full of shrubs and briars, queach.

SHUDDER. *v.* To shudder, to quake, to quiver.

SHUFFLE. *v.* To prevaricate, to tergiversate, to evade, to shuffle or trick, to shark.

SHUFFLER. *s.* Equivocator, prevaricator.

SHUFFLING. *p.* Jesuitical, equivocating.

SHUN. *v.* To absonate, to evitate, to loathe or lothe.

SHUT. *v.* To shut up, to occluse, to occlude, to seclude, to pen, to portcullis; to shut in, to immure, to bay, to block or blockade, to cloister, to embar, to incloister, to encompass, to engoal, to imbound; to shut up in a pinfold, to impound; to shut up as dogs are, to kennel; to shut up as hawks, to mew; to shut up in prison, to incarcerate; to shut up or inclose, to interclude; to shut out, to exclude, to fend, to preclude.

SHUT. *a.* Shut up or retired, recluse.

SHUTTING. *a.* A shutting up (smearing) obturation; a shutting up with lock or bolt, obseration.

SHY. *a.* Recluse, coy, inconversable, incommunicative, unconversable.

SICK. *a.* Clinical, distempered; apparatus necessary for the care of a sick person in bed, lectisternium; said of sick people, whose distemper requires them to keep in bed, lectual; sea sick, nauseabund, queasy; to feign one's self sick, to egrate, or ægrate.

SICKISH. *p.* Mawkish.

SICKLY. *a.* Peaking, ailing, crazy, puny, puling, valetudinary; sickly, sallow, (Rowe.)

SICKNESS. *s.* Sickness produced on shipboard is properly termed nausea, (Quincy); sickness owing to intemperance, crapulence, or crapulent; the falling sickness, *epilepsy* or *caducus*, it is also called *Morbus Herculeus*, from the violence of its attacks; any long sickness, macronosia; a lingering sickness, or deep consumption, syntexis, (Bailey); sickness, (green sickness), pica, chlorosis, malacia; sickness or grief, egritude.

SIDE. *s.* Confine, latus, L.; having equal sides or legs, equicrural, isosceles, equilateral; side or margin, margent; side (lip or brim) labra; of or belonging to the side, lateral; making or composing sides or walls, parietal; having three sides, trilateral; four sides, quadrilateral; five sides, pentaedrous, or pentedral; six sides, hexaedrous; having many sides, multilateral, polyedrous, or polyedrical, polygonal; situated or pressing on every side, undequaqual; side by side, abreast, collateral; situated on the right side, dextral; on the left, sinister, (see Figure.)

SIDEWAYS. *ad.* Askance or askaunce, obliquely, askaunt, askew.

SIEGE. *s.* Of or belonging to a siege, obsidional.

SIEVE. *s.* Bolter, sarse, searse; sieve through which a liquor to be refined is poured, colander; corn sieve, cribble; to strain as through a sieve, to percolate; to strain through a sieve, to transcolate; divination by means of sieves, coscinomancy.

SIFT. *v.* To garble, to bolt, to canvass, to discuss, to delve, to eventilate, to fish, to episcate, to excern, to ree, to sarse, to searse; to sift as meal, to succernate.

SIFTED. *p.* Thoroughly sifted or searched, enucleated.

SIFTING. *p.* Act of sifting, cribration.

SIGHING. *p.* Act of, suspiration.

SIGHT. *s.* Ken; sight or view, spectation; privation of sight, ablepsy, (Bailey); immediate sight or perception of the mind, intuition; shortness of sight, myopy; total privation of sight in the night time, otherwise called *night blindnefs,* nyctalopia; of or belonging to the sight, visual.

SIGN. *v.* To make a sign with one's finger, to beckon or becken; to make a sign, to betoken, to presignify; to sign under any other person, to subsign.

SIGN. *s.* Characteristic, characteristick, indication, symptom, vestige, crisima; signs (particularly those used in algebra and arithmetic,) symbols; a discoursing or talking by signs made by the fingers, dactylogy; the undoubted and certain signs of a disease, distinguishing it from all others, are termed diagnostic signs; good or bad sign, omen, prognostic; a bad sign, portent; a talking by signs made by the hands, chirology; the 12 signs of the zodiac, dodecatemory.

SILENCE. *s.* Obmutescence, taciturnity; concealment by silence, reticence; the feigned god of silence, Harpocrates; interjections denoting or commanding silence, mum, hist, hush.

SILENT. *a.* Tacit; (almost silent) pacilo-quous.

SILK. *s.* Cloathed in silk, sericated; untwisted silk, sleave; made of silk, bombycinous.

SILLINESS. *s.* Silliness of the imagination or judgment, paraphrosyne. Quincy reckons this word synonimous with mania.

SILLY. *v.* To grow silly, to dote.

SILLY. *a.* Addlepated, apish, irrational; tilly-valley, brainless, futile, infantile, injudicious, nias; silly fellow, zany, wiseacre, noody, widgeon.

SILVER. *s.* Luna, (old chym); silver and lead as found in their native mixed state, plumbagine; silver in mass, bullion; the act of covering over with silver, inargentation; the art of making silver, argyropea.

SIMILAR. *a.* Adjaphorous, or adiaphorous, akin, geminous, homologous.

SIMILARITY. *s.* Similarity or proportion, omology; similarity of parts in an organized body, homoeomery, or homoeomeria.

SIMPLE. *a.* Futile, incomplex, incomposite, inept, bardous, elemental, single-fangle, frivolous; irrelative, ludicrous, indiscreet, or undiscreet, mawmish, nias, puerile.

SIMPLETON. *s.* Nizy, asshead, capochia, dopdle, jackalent, jobbernowl, loon, mooncalf, widgeon, wiseacre, nincompoop, or nincumpoop. (See Fool.)

SIMPLENESS. *s.* Simpleness or doting in the imagination, paraphrosyne. Quincy says this word is synonymous with mania.

SIMPLY. *ad.* Impolitically, impoliticly.

SINCERE. *a.* Cordial, frank. (See Real.)

SIN. *s.* Liable to sin, peccable; full of, or abounding in sin, peccaminous; sorrow for sin, penitence, contrition, compunction; heretics who taught that sin rather deserved reward as punishment, Antitactes. (Bailey); exemption from sin, impeccability.

SINCERITY. *s.* Probity. (See Honest.)

SINFUL. *a.* Vitiable. (See Faulty.)

SING. *v.* To carol.

SINGING. *p.* Any entertainment of singing, ridotto, or opera; a singing a hymn, called *nunc dimittis,* and performing other superstitious ceremonies to recommend and dismiss a dying person is termed among Roman Catholics, missura.

SINGLE. *v.* To single out, to individuate.

SINGLE. *a.* Irrelative; single life, celibacy.

SINGULAR. *a.* (Notable or excellent), eximious.

SINK. *v.* To debase, to depress, to descend; to sink (diminish or lessen), to abate; to sink voluntarily under water, to dive;

to sink or plunge under water, to immerge, or immerse; to sink as the heavier part of a fluid, to subside; to sink under, to succumb; to sink or lose spirit. to jade; to sink to brutality, to imbrute.

SINK. *s.* Sink or drain, jakes.

SINKING. *p.* A sinking or falling off in a sentence in which the last part is lower than the first, anticlimax; sinking, cadent.

SIRENS. *s.* (See syrens.)

SIR. *s.* (Good sir,) (or old sir,) gaffer.

SIROP. *s.* Sirup made of the tops of poppies, diacodium.

SISTER. *s.* Sister by the father's side is named sister-consanguinean; by the mother's side, sister-uterine; by both father and mother, is sister german; the murder or murderer of a sister, sororicide.

SIT. *v.* To sit over, to brood; to sit as a bird, to perch, to juke; to sit on eggs, to incubate.

SITTING. *p.* A sitting down by one, assession; time passed in sitting, sedentary, as a sedentary life.

SITUATED. *a.* Posited, (see Placed.)

SITUATION. *s.* Posture, position, predicament, site; relative situation, bearing; the situation in which any thing is placed with respect to the sun or air, exposition; situation with regard to place, location.

SIX. *a.* Six-sided figure, hexagon, or exagon; six-eyed, cenocular; consisting of the number of six, senary, (see One, Two, Three, &c.)

SIXFOLD. *a.* Sextuple.

SIXTH. *a.* One sixth part, subsextuple.

SIXTY. *a.* Of or belonging to the number sixty, sexagenary; those fractions which have 60 for their constant denominator, are termed sexagesimal fractions.

SIZE. *s.* Dimension; of an enormous size, huge, immane, (see Big.)

SIZINESS. *s.* Viscosity, glutinousness; that siziness of the blood which sometimes obstructs the vessels, lentor.

SKETCH. *s.* Sketch or faint shade, adumbration.

SKILFUL. *a.* Adroit, cunning, dædalian, discerning, expert, feat, judicious; intelligent, masterly. yare; skilful management, manœuvre; a very skilful person, masterhand.

SKILFULLY. *ad.* Skilfully made, affabrous.

SKILL. *s.* Ability, address, discernment, cunning, intelligence, mastery; complete skill in all matters, panurgy; trial of skill, or contention for a prize, agonism.

SKILLED. *a.* Sapient, erudite; one skilled in his calling or profession, adept.

SKIM. *v.* To rase.

SKIN. *v.* To flay, to disease; to skin over a sore, to cicatrize.

SKIN. *s.* Fell, pelt, integument; thin skin, film, pellicle; skins or fleeces of the stag wolf, inserns, (Bailey); the skin of a dead sheep, morling, or mortling; the cast skins of serpents, lizards, &c. exuviæ, reduviæ; dealer in skins, fellmonger; of or belonging to the skin, cutaneous, cuticular; lying under the skin, subcutaneous; medicine to smooth the skin with, tetanothra, G.; hardness of the skin occasioned by much labour, tylus; the true skin, derma, or *Cutis vera*, L.; the outer scarf skin, epidermis; spots under the skin proceeding from extravassated blood, as when a blow has been inflicted, ecchymoma, or ecchymosis.

SKIP. *v.* To gambol, to caper.

SKIRMISH. *v.* To bicker, to quiver, to hurtle; to skirmish as light horsemen, to pickeroon.

SKIRMISH. *s.* Rencounter.

SKIRMISHING. *p.* Velitation.

SKULL. *s.* Pannikel, scalp; the plates of the skull, laminæ; the scaly sutures of the skull are called lepidoides, (Anat.); the membrane which covers the skull, pericranium; a laying open the fore part of the skull from one temple to another, formerly practised when a considerable inflammation or defluxion of the eyes was present, periscyphismus; surgeons instrument used in fractures of the skull, trepan. (See Seam.)

SKY. *s.* Welkin; sky coloured, azure, cerulean, or ceruleous.

SLACK. *a.* Lax, remiss.

SLACKEN. *v.* To slacken, to relax.

SLANDER. *v.* To slander, to asperse, to calumniate, to infame, to traduce, to belie, to bespatter, to defame, to detract.

SLANDER. *s.* Obtrectation, obloquy; personal slander, lampoon.

SLANDERER. *s.* Famicide, insectator; slanderer, abydocomist, from Abydos, the inhabitants of which were famous for inventing slanders, and boasting of them.

SLANDEROUS. *a.* Slanderous libel posted up for public view, pasquil, pasquin, or pasquinade, so called from a place in the centre of Rome called *la piazza di Pasquino*, where an old broken statue stood on which such were fixed.

SLAUGHTER. *s.* Carnage, Internecion.

SLAVE. *s.* Thrall (Shakesp. Milton); female slave, neif, or naif; the act of releasing or emancipating slaves, manumission.

SLAVER. *v.* To drivel.

SLAVERY. *s.* Bondage, mancipation, servitude, thraldom, captivity; predominancy of slaves, dulocracy.

SLAVISH. *a.* Servile.

SLAY. *v.* To butcher, to immolate, to laniate, to contrucidate, to perempt.

SLAYER. *s.* Occiser.

SLAYING. *p.* Act of slaying, peremption.

SLEEP *s.* Dead sleep, caros, coma, lethargy; medicines which prevent sleep anthypnotics or antihypnotics; driving away sleep, somnifugous; inability to sleep, insomny; medicines which cause sleep, hypnotics, narcotics, opiates, somnifera, paregorics; medicines which can ease pain, by procuring sleep, anodynes; producing sleep, soporiferous, soporific, soporative; causing sleep, somniferous, somnific; the act of laying to sleep, consopiation; laid to sleep, sopited; a particular affection of the eyes which makes the patient sleep with them open, lagophthalmy; to sleep with one's eyes open, to corybantiate; to raise from sleep, to exuscitate; person who walks about in his sleep, noctambula, or noctambulist; the act of walking in one's sleep, noctambulation, or oneirodynia; term for the occasional emission of the semen during sleep, oneirogonos, G.; sleep or nap taken in the afternoon, zest; constant propensity to sleep, cataphora.

SLEEPINESS. *s.* Doziness, drowsiness, somnolence, or somnolency.

SLEEPING. *p.* Dormant; a sleeping place generally for several people, dormitory; the common sleeping room of all the friars of a convent, dorter, dortoir, or dorture; a sleeping together, consommation.

SLEEPY. *a.* Inert, oscilant, lethargic; sleepy song used for infants, lullaby.

SLENDER. *a.* Exile, gaunt, meagre, minute, lank, tenuous, tenuious, gracile; slender or weak either in mind or body, imbecile; a making or rendering slender, attenuant.

SLICE. *s.* Slice of bacon, rasher.

SLIDE. *s.* Apt to slide, labile.

SLIGHT. *v.* To disregard, to disvalue; to slight or lightly esteem, to floccify.

SLIGHT. *s.* Flimsy, limber, frivolous, gaunt, meagre; slight in texture, leasy, flimsy; slight of hand, legerdemain, F.; slight or contempt, misprise; slight, (careless), perfunctory; slight and ill made cloth, &c. sleazy.

SLIGHTLY. *ad.* Cursory, cursorily.

SLILY. *ad.* Cautelously.

SLIME. *s.* Full of slime, limous, or limose, oozy.

SLIMY. *a.* Limous or limose, mucid, mucilaginous, viscous, mucous, ropy, uliginous, muculent, oazy; slimy ground, oaz.

SLINK. *s.* Castling.

SLIP. *s.* Apt to slip, labile; slip, as slip of the tongue, lapse.

SLIPPERS *s.* Pantofles (from pantoufle, F.); sort of slippers tied on the feet, anciently worn, sandal.

SLIPPERY. *a.* Glib, volubile, labile, lubrie, lubricous; to make slippery, to lubricate; the act of making slippery, lubrifaction.

SLITS. *s.* Scissure; having many slits or chinks, multifidous.

SLOPE. *v.* To incline.

SLOPE. *s.* Pendence.

SLOPING. *p.* Prone.

SLOTH. *s.* Sloth or laziness, accidie.

SLOTHFUL. *a.* Remiss, inergetical, retchless.

SLOTHFULNESS. *s.* Segnity, pigritude, inertitude.

SLOW. *a.* Deliberate, dilatory; that slow and continued fever to which consumptive people are subject, hectic, or hectical; to make a slow and protracted noise, to intone; slow, listless, livelong, torpid; to move slow, to lag; a very slow person, malthorse; slow digestion, bradypepsia.

SLOWLY. *ad.* Moving slowly tardigrade, or tardigradous.

SLOWNESS. *s.* Irksomeness, lentitude, lentor; slowness of speech, tardiloquy.

SLUGGARD. *s.* Bed-presser, (see Idler.)

SLUGGISH. *a.* Inert, lag, lither, inergetical; sluggish fellow, lob.

SLUGGISHNESS. *s.* Lentor, lentitude, inertitude.

SLUICE. *s.* Sluice or lock in a river, sasse.

SLUMBER. *s.* Slumber accompanied by dreams, agripnia, G.

SLY. *a.* Insidious, clandestine, designing, crafty, vulpinary, jesuitical, shrewd, subdolous, subtile, subtle, vaprous; sly fellow, fox, lorel, reynard.

SMALL. *a.* Exiguous, exile, miliary, diminutive, miniken, minute, pedling, gracile, dwarfish, pygmean; small body, crepuscle; infinitely small body or quantity, monad or monade, differential, driblet; small particles or atoms, minima; any thing petty or small, pigmy, pigwidgeon; small portion or share, modicum; small allowance or portion, pittance; any small work, opuscle; small being or dwarf, minim; description of small objects, micrography; small, (inferior), puisne; small part, jot, jota, title, Iota; small pocket, volume, enchiridion, maual; having small cords or fibres, funicular; small cattle, tits, G.

SMALLNESS. *s.* Parvitude, parvity, pancity, tenuity.

SMART. *a.* Clever, lepid, pert, shrewd; very smart, (said of a child,) perilous.

SMATTERER. *s.* Smatterer in art or science, sciolist.

SMEAR. *v.* To anoint, to oint; to smear with gore, to ensanguine.

SMEARING. *p.* Act of smearing, obturation.

SMELL. *s.* Smell or scent, essence, odor, or odour; sweetness of smell, fragrance, or fragrancy; the rank smell of meat, fumette; resembling the smell of roasted meat, nidorose, or nidorous; to have a smell or flavour of, to savour; fetid smell emanating from the body, dysodes; having a strong or rank smell, graveolent; bad smell, fetor or foetor; having no smell, inodorate, inodorous; without smell, opposed to fetid, anodmon, G.

SMELLING. *a.* Smelling strong, olid, or olidous; possessing the sense of smelling, olfactory.

SMILE. *v.* To smile affectedly and deceitfully, to leer or fleer; to smile upon, to arride; to smile in a simple innocent manner, to simper.

SMILING. *p.* A smiling, subrision, arrision.

SMITH. *s.* The trade of a smith, smithery; smith's work shop, smithy.

SMOKE. *v.* To besmoke, to fumigate; to smoke underneath, to suffumigate.

SMOKE. *s.* Like or resembling smoke, fumid, halitous; divination by means of smoke, capnomancy.

SMOKED. *p.* Smoked fish, fumado.

SMOKY. *a.* Fuliginous, fumid.

SMOOTH. *v.* To blandish, to complane, to lubricate; to smooth by rubbing on a stone with water, to levigate; to smooth, (term used by artificers in hammering of metals by repeated small strokes), to planish.

SMOOTH. *a.* Glib, voluble, lubric, lubricous; smooth or calm, serene; smooth or cleanly written, terse.; smooth speech, tolutiloquence; smooth and level walk, estrade.

SMOOTHED. *p.* Smoothed as with a pumice stone, pumicated.

SMOOTHING. *p.* Act of smoothing, levigation.

SMOOTHNESS. *s.* Glabrity.

SMOTHER. *v.* To suffocate.

SNAIL. *s.* Nursery of snails, escargatoire; of or belonging to snails, limaceous.

SNAKE. *s.* Names for the water snake, natrix, or torquata; rattle snake, creta-

lophorous.

SNAP. *v.* To knap.

SNAPPED. *p.* (Caught) Raught, (Ent.)

SNAPPISH. *a.* Canine, captious, snarling, carping, cynical.

SNARE. *s.* Engle, gin, springle, illaqueation, springe, laqueus, lees, (Ent.)

SNARL. *v.* To growl.

SNARLER. *s.* Cynic, momus, (Bailey.)

SNARLING. *p.* Latrant.

SNATCH. *v.* To snatch or sweep off, to raff.

SNATCHED. *p.* Snatched off, raught, arreptitious.

SNATCHING. *p.* A snatching away by force, ereption, correption.

SNEER. *v.* To gleek.

SNEER. *s.* Sneer, foutra, gibe, glike.

SNEEZE. *v.* To neese, (Johnson.)

SNEEZING. *p.* Medicines which cause sneezing, ptarmics, or ptarmica, sternutatories, errhines; the act or effort of sneezing, sternutation.

SNORTING. *p.* Any noise made which resembles snorting, ronchisonant.

SNOUT. *s.* Snout or trunk of an elephant, proboscis.

SNOW. *s.* Abounding with snow, nival, niveous.

SNOWY. *a.* Ningid.

SOAK. *v.* To drench, to imbrue, to indrench, to irrigate, to macerate.

SOAP. *s.* Smegma; soap and water froth made from, lather; of or belonging to soap, smegmatic.

SOB. *v.* To suspire.

SOBER. *a.* Abstemious, abstinent, demure, sane, temperate.

SOBERNESS. *s.* Gravity.

SOCIAL. *a.* Homiletical.

SOCIETY. *s.* Fraternity, guild, sodality, community; of or belonging to society, sodalitious; living in society, cenobitical; fellows of the same society, confreres, coterie.

SOCKET. *s.* Socket wherein a tooth grows, mortariolum, L. alveolus, L.

SODOMY. *s.* Buggery, pederasty.

SODOMITE. *s.* (See Ganymede.)

SOFT. *n.* Soft, (not bony) exosseous; soft (mild of temper) meek; soft, (mitigating) balsamick, or balsamical; soft or mild, bland; soft (tame or gentle) sade; soft, feminine, effeminate; soft (easily bent), flexible, limber; soft hair or down, flex or flue; soft as wool, lanarious; soft or pliant, lither; soft or spungy, fungous; the soft internal part of trees, pith, medulla; soft with some degree of tenacity, mucilaginous; term in ichthyology for such fishes as have soft

U

fins, with bones not pointed, malacopterygious; soft ground, oaz or oazy; soft as pap, papescent; soft as flesh, parenthymatous, or parenchymous; soft as feathers, plumous; soft or nice, tid; soft (meek) pigeon-livered, placid; soft (easily drawn) tractile, ductile; soft or muddy, uliginous; soft or tender, emolid.

SOFTEN. *a.* To lenify, to mellow, to modify, to mitigate, to assuage, to appease, to relent, to soothe, to flatter, to attemper, to effeminate; to soften or melt as metals, to fuse; to soften or knead to softness, to malaxate; to soften the passions, to humanize, to intenerate; aptness to soften or melt, liquescency; to soften by working in the hand, to tew.

SOFTENED. *p.* That may be softened, mollifiable.

SOFTENING. *p.* Demulcent, emollient, epicerastic, lenient, humific, assuasive, paregoric, mollient, assuaging; act of softening, emolition, humectation; softening medicines, malactica, emulsions.

SOFTNESS. *s.* Delicacy; softness or effeminacy, muliebrity.

SOIL. *v.* To dirty, to bedaggle, to befoul, to bemire, to bemoil, to grime, to besmear.

SOIL. *s.* Compost, glebe; the method of enriching the soil by labour, emponema.

SOILED. *a.* Dingy.

SOLD. *p.* That may be sold, mercatable or mercable, venal, vendible; one to whom any thing is sold, vendee.

SOLDERING. *p.* A soldering together, ferumination, (Bailey).

SOLDIER. *s.* Campaigner, veteran; Irish horse-soldier, hobler; Irish foot-soldier, kern; Turkish soldier, janissary; German foot-soldier, lansquenet; private soldier in artillery, matross; soldier, militarist, (Shakesp.); one mustered as a soldier though not enlisted, passevolant; soldiers on horseback, cavalry; lodgings for soldiers, barracks; to enslave or oppress with soldiers, to dragoon; soldier's trull, doxy; one who has the command of 10 soldiers, lancepesade; the place where soldiers are mustered and paid, diribitory; band of 10 soldiers, decury; handful or very small band of soldiers, maniple; small square body of soldiers, platoon; square battalion of soldiers closely embodied, phalanx; to fill up the number of a band of soldiers, to succenturiate.

SOLE. *s.* Sole of the foot, belonging to, plantar.

SOLEMN. *a.* Awful; the act of taking a solemn oath, dejeration; a solemn declaration, protestation, asseveration.

SOLEMNITY. *s.* Gravity; investing with solemnity into an office, inauguration.

SOLICIT. *v.* To subagitate, (Bailey); to canvas. (See to ask.)

SOLID. *a.* Findy, massive, massy; solid or cogent, (said of arguments) nervous or nervy; solid or firm, compact, consistent; the solid contents of any magnitude, cubature; the centre of a solid, centrum; the art of measuring the contents of solid bodies, stereometry.

SOLILOQUY. *s.* Monologue, dialogismus.

SOLITARY. *a.* Cloistered, monial, heremitical.

SOLVED. *p.* That cannot be solved, insolvable; that is not solved, unsolved.

SON. *s.* Son born in wedlock, with relation to one born before it, of the same father and mother, *mulier*, L. T. (Bailey).

SONG. *s.* Lay, air, canto, chant, descant; little song, canzonet, arrietta; pastoral songs, madrigals, bucolics; the songs of Solomon, Canticles; song of devotion or joy, carol; song sung in succession, catch; mournful song, elegy; funeral song, epicedium; nuptial song, epithalamium; sort of song in form of a rhapsody, arnodi, (Bailey); song of triumph, pæan; song of triumph after victory, epinicion, G.; uttering songs of triumph, jubilant; sleepy song used for infants, lullaby; the burden of a song or ballad, refret, from refrein, F.; composer of songs, asmatographer.

SOON. *ad.* Betimes; very soon, eft; done too soon, immaturely; what is soon past, transient, fleeting.

SOONER. *ad.* Sooner than, ere.

SOOT. *s.* Soot of an oven, coom.

SOOTH. *v.* To balm, to cajole, to fawn, to glaver.

SOOTHSAYERS. *s.* A sort of chair on which the Roman soothsayers sat when they were taking their observations, *sella solida*, (Bailey).

SOOTHSAYING *s.* Ariolation, sortilege. (See Divination.)

SOOTY. *a.* Fuliginous; made or rendered sooty, collied.

SORCERY. *s.* Sortilege. (See Magic.)

SORDID. *a.* Avaricious, venal; sordid wretch, hunks.

SORES. *s.* Medicines which dry up sores, epulotics; salve for every sore, panchrestos; a growing sore again, recrudescent; medicines which bring sores to an eschar, synulotics; lint for a sore, pledget, spledget, tent.

SORROW. *s.* Dump, stound; grief or sorrow, sollicito, (Ital.); sorrow or misery, bale, condolence, dole, dolor, or dolour; deep sorrow, heart-ache; sorrow for sin, attrition, contrition, compunction, penitence; producing sorrow, luctiferous, or luctific; sounding out sorrow, luctisonous; to sorrow for, to bewail or wail; name given to any opiate which lulls care and sorrow, nepenthe.

SORROWFUL. *a.* Dampy, disconsolate, elegiac, lugubrious, luctificable, luctuous, pensive, piteous, plaintful, plaintive, rueful, ruthful; to make or render sorrowful, to contristate; that which makes sorrowful, mestifical.

SORT. *v.* To collate.

SORTS. *s.* Possessing many sorts, multifarious; comprising all sorts, omnifarious, omnigenous; of all manner of sorts, omnimodus, L.

SOT. *s.* Bibber, toper.

SOTTISH. *a.* Alabandical; the state of being sottish through drink, perpotation.

SOVEREIGN. *s.* or *a.* Liege.

SOVEREIGNTY, *s.* Regality.

SOUGHT. *p.* Things sought for, *desiderata.* L.

SOUL. *s.* Ghost, (Sandys) discourse concerning the soul, psychology; heretics who followed Lucifer, Bishop of Cagliari in Sardinia, A. C. 365, who held that the soul of man was propagated out of the substance of his flesh, Luciferians; the transmigration of souls from body to body, or doctrine held by Pythagoras and Plato, metemsychosis, G.; magnanimity or greatness of soul, megalopsychy; combat between soul and body, psychomachy; conveyance or translation of the soul from one body to another, transanimation, transmigration.

SOUNDS. *s.* The doctrine of sounds, acoustics, phonicks; void of sound, inaudible; possessing the power of inflecting or altering sounds, phonocamptic; a grave and deep sound, bass; Great sound or noise, bombulation; agreement of sound, consonance; agreeable sound, euphony; that part of music which treats of the differences and proportions of sounds, harmonics; to form sounds to a key or note, to modulate; the harmony of sound, melody, (Hooker); instruments for magnifying sounds, microphones, G. The inarticulate sound of the voice, which persons utter in apoplexies and such like distempers, mugitus; having many or various sounds, multisonous; giving a loud and full sound, sonorous; a succession of loud sounds, peal; the effect of sound in the ear, percussion; multiplicity of sounds, polyphonism; instruments contrived to multiply sounds, polyacoustics, polyphones; an undulation of sounds proceeding from a center, actinobolism;

graceful sound or voice, euphony; agreement or harmony of sounds, symphony; the science which explains the doctrine of refracted sounds, diacoustics.

SOUNDING. *p.* High sounding words, bombast, (see Words); sounding harshly, halsening; sounding or uttering sorrow, luctisonous; sounding again with an echo, resonant; sounding terribly, terrisonous, horrisonous; sounding high, altisonous.

SOUNDNESS. *s.* Soundness or healthiness, sanity; soundness or healthiness of an animal body, ulomelia; soundness, staunchness; soundness of doctrine, orthodoxy; being in a state of soundness, vegete.

SOUR. *a.* Acerb, austere, dogged, eager, glum, morose, cynical, crabbed, tetrical, tetricous, torvous.

SOURING. *p.* Souring for punch made of the juice of unripe grapes, omphacium.

SOURCE. *s.* Source or origin, etymon, (see Word)); the source of a disease, (among physicians) *minera morbi.* L.

SOURNESS. *s.* Sourness and saltness, partaking of the nature of, salsoacid; a sourness of the stomach proceeding from bad digestion, apepsy, or apepsia; sourness of aspect, torvity, tetricity.

SOUTH. *a.* One of the cardinal points; the south wind, Notus. L.

SOUTHERN. *a.* Antarctic or antarctick, meridional, austral.

SOW, *v.* To seminate.

SOWING. *p.* Relating to sowing, sative.

SPACE. *s.* Compass, expanse, or expansion; intermediate space, intermedium, interstice; space of seven weeks, &c. hebdomade; space between two or more pillars, intercolumniation.

SPANIARDS. *s.* The offspring of Spaniards with native Americans, Mestisos.

SPANISH. *a.* Spanish flies, Cantharides, of which the largest and best are brought from Italy. Quincy.

SPAR. *s.* Spar, (among miners) in the form of icicles, stalactites; spars in the form of drops, stalagmites.

SPARE. *s.* Spare horse, (horse not mounted), leer-horse.

SPARE. *a.* (Lean,) guant, meagre.

SPARED. *p.* Not to be spared, indispensable or indispensible.

SPARING. *p.* Economical, lenten, illiberal, parsimonious, penurious.

SPARINGNESS. *s.* Parcity.

SPARK. *s.* To throw out sparks; to scintillate.

SPARKLE. *v.* To glister, or to glisten; to radiate; to scintillate.

SPARKLING. *p.* Brilliant, act of sparkling, emication.

SPATTERDASHES. *s.* Gambade or gambado, huseaus, from houseaux. F.

SPAWN. *s.* Spawn of the sturgeon salted, caviare.

SPEAK. *s.* To speak first, to accost, to address; to speak in a slow and indifferent manner, to drawl; to speak bitterly of one, to inveigh; one who speaks as it were from the belly, gastromyth, ventriloquist.

SPEAKER. *s.* (Chairman,) prolocutor.

SPEAKING. *p.* Difficulty in speaking, dysphony; a speaking of the truth, veriloquy; foolish speaking, morology; speaking but few words, pauciloquous; plain speaking, planiloquy; speaking terrible things, terriloquous; the speaking as if it proceeded from one's belly, ventriloquism; a person who has that faculty, is called engastrimythos; speaking holy things, sanctiloquent; a speaking gracefully, charientismus, G. speaking of the truth, veriloquent; speaking craftily, versutiloquent; a speaking to one's self as though it were to another, dialogismus; a preposterous way of speaking, putting that first which should be last, hysterology, hysteron-proteron; a speaking between, or when another is speaking, interlocution; a mode of speaking peculiar to a language or dialect, idiom.

SPEAR. *s.* Hasta, L. spear or harpoon used for striking fish with at sea, tren.

SPECTACLES. *s.* Lunettes.

SPECKLED. *a.* Peckled, motly or motley, pied; the state of being speckled, nevosity.

SPECTRE. *s.* Spectre or spectrum, apparition. (See Spirit.)

SPEECH. *s.* Loss of speech, obmutescence; fluency of speech, volubility; slowness of speech, tardiloquy; a prolixity in speech, macrology; sharpness or conciseness of speech, brachylogy; the close of a speech, peroration; the notification of an intended speech concerning something to be performed in a public seminary, programma; discourse or speech consisting of two parts, dilogy; of three, trilogy; of four, tetralogy; a set speech made to one or more, address; speech made in public, oration, harangue; speech or discourse, loquela; a peculiar phrase or manner of speech, locution; speech or discourse made by one in solitude to himself, soliloquy, monologue; speech of a general to his soldiers animating them to fight or avoid sedition, allocution; speech or address to the passions, declamation; speech of praise or thanks, panegyrick, encomium; farewel speech, apobaterion, valediction; a peculiar phrase or turn of speech in any language

idiom, idiotism; one who has an impediment in his speech, mogilalos; one who has an impediment in his speech from being tongue-tied, ancyloglossus; to stammer in one's speech, to balbutiate; stammering in speech, blesiloquent; the scholar in the university of Oxford appointed to make jesting and satyrical speeches, is called *terræ filius*; speech at the end of a play, epilogue; speech before a play, prologue; mean and low speech of no value, micrology; one who has lost the use of speech, but retains his voice, anaudos; this is not to be confounded with aphonia, which signifies the loss of the voice altogether. (See Stammering.)

SPEED. *s.* Pernicity, celerity, dispatch or despatch, rapture or rapidity, velocity; at full speed, tantivy or tivy.

SPEEDY. *a.* Festinate.

SPELL. *v.* To spell a syllable wrong, to mis-spell. (Bailey.)

SPELL. *s.* Spell or charm, amulet, incantation. (See Charm.)

SPELLED. *a.* Rightly spelled, orthographical.

SPELLING. *p.* The art of spelling properly, orthography.

SPEND. *v.* To spend or bring to an end by waste, to absume; to spend or lay out money, to disburse or dispurse, to dispend; to spend money profusely and unnecessarily, so dissipate, to mispend, to palter.

SPEW. *v.* To disgorge, to puke, to endew (said of a hawk.)

SPHERE. *s.* Sphere with its lines projected on a plain, planisphere; half a sphere, hemisphere; of or belonging to half a sphere, semispherical; title of a treatise of the sphere written by Ptolemy, almagest.

SPICES. *s.* One who sells spices, aromatopola.

SPICY. *a.* Fragrant, aromatic, aromatical or aromatick.

SPIDER. *s.* Lycos (Zoology); full of or abounding in spiders, araneous; name of a spider found near Tarento, the bite of which is cured by music, tarantula; a distemper arising from the bite of the tarantula, tarantism; those who are so bit are termed tarantali: Of this very odd effect with its cure, Baglivi, an Italian physician, hath wrote a very rational account, whereby it appears that the odd effects of this bite, and its method of cure by music, are by no means fabulous as some have supposed (Quincy); the name of a little venomous spider, resembling the stone of the black grape, rha-gion; spinning webs like a spider, telary.

SPIKE. *v.* To spike ordnance (among gunners.) to cloy.

SPINE. *s.* Spine or backbone, chine; an incurvation of the chine, hyboma.

SPIRAL. *a.* Spiral line, helix; of or belonging to a spiral form, peristaltic (see Guts); spiral or twisted, turbinated; that art which teaches how to draw or measure spiral lines upon a plane, and show their respective properties, helicometry or helicosophy.

SPIRIT. *s.* (Boldness) audacity; spirit, crest; spirit (zeal) fervour or fervor; meanness of spirit, micropsychy, pusillanimity; rectified spirits, i. e. any spirit, completely dephlegmated, alcohol; any subtle spirit or vapour, gas; rectified spirit of wine, pyrenus or pyroenus; that universal spirit or principle pervading all space is called the hylarchic principle; spirit (devil) demon or dæmon; spirit (fairy) ouphe, puck, sprite; spirit (or ghost) spectre, cacodæmon; spirit, hobgoblin, empusa, goblin, apparition, manducus, phantom; spirits or ghosts, lemures, L.; frighted with spirits, larvated; to cast out evil spirits, to exorcise, to adjure; treatise on evil spirits, demonology; the doctrine of the existence of spirits, pneumatology; a lowness or depression of the spirits, hyp, or hypochondria; a fainting or swooning from too great a decay or waste of the spirits, lepothymia; a dejection of the spirits accompanied with anxiety, *athymia*; some use this word as synonymous with *melancholia* (see Madness); the generation of the animal spirits in the cortical substance of the brain, pneumatosis (Bailey); a familiar or prophesying spirit, or one endued with it, Python.

SPIRITLESS. *a.* Exanimated, flimsy, hypochondriac; spiritless or flat, vapid or insipid; spiritless person, mop or mopus.

SPIRITUALLY. *a.* Incorporeally immaterially.

SPIT. *v.* To spit or eject saliva by hawking, to excreate, to expectorate; to spit profusely, to salivate.

SPITE. *s.* Malevolence, malignity; in spite of, maugre.

SPITEFUL. *a.* Vindicative, vindictive, rancorous.

SPITEFULLY. *ad.* Obstinate, pervicacious.

SPITTING. *p.* A discharge by spitting exspuition; which may be discharged by spitting, screable; a spitting, screation.

SPLEEN. *s.* Good against the spleen or melancholy, antisplenetic.

SPITTLE. *s.* Saliva, L.; a discharge of spittle, either natural or promoted, ptya-

lism, ptyalon, ptisma, ptysmagogue, salivation; relating to the spittle, salivous.

SPLENDID. *a.* Gorgeous, pompous, refulgent, resplendent.

SPLENDOUR. *s.* Brilliancy, eclat, effulgence, fulgor, nitidity, refulgence, sheen, (See Brightness.)

SPLIT. *v.* To dispart; that may be split, fissile.

SPOIL. *v.* To blast, to blend, to depredate, to dirke, to embezzle, to taint, to vitiate, to deprave; to spoil or spot, to maculate or mackle; to spoil or plunder, to pillage, to shend, to spoliate.

SPOIL. *s.* Spoil, booty, exuviæ; taken as spoils in war, manubial.

SPOILING. *p.* The act of spoiling or laying waste, vastation, grassation.

SPONGE. *s.* Spunge.

SPONGY. *a.* Fungous, excrescent, parenchymatous or parenchymous.

SPORT. *s.* Disport, pastime, diversion, gambol.

SPORTIVE. *a.* Lusorious, lusory.

SPOT. *v.* To bespot, to maculate or mackle, to pip, to sully; to mark with small spots, to punctulate.

SPOT. *s.* Tainture, blemish, macula, maculation, blot, blotch; act of freeing from spots, emaculation; black and blue spots on the body, as the effects of blows, molopes, G.; spots resembling flea bites which appear in some fevers, erythrommata, petechiæ from petechia, *Ital.*; spots on the skin from a extravasation of the blood, ecchymoma or ecchymosis; spot or freckle on the skin occasioned by the sun, ephelis; spots on the face of the sun which appear brighter than the rest of his body, faculæ.

SPOTLESS. *a.* Immaculate.

SPOTTED. *a.* Distinct (Milton); spotted, grisly, (Bailey) liard, roan, pied.

SPOUSE. *s.* Relating to a spouse, sponsal.

SPREAD. *v.* To diffuse, to dilate, to dispand, to display, to disseminate, to propagate, to bespread, to expand; to spread with leaves, to infoliate; to spread over, to besprinkle, to perfuse; to spread over as in blushing, to suffuse.

SPREADING. *p.* Spreading round, circfusile.

SPRIGS. *s.* Full of sprigs, fruticose.

SPRIGHTLINESS. *s.* Lustihood, alacrity, vivacity.

SPRIGHTLY. *a.* Vivid, blythesome, crank, jocund, blithe, mercurial, parlous, vegete, vivacious, debonnair.

SPRING. *v.* To bounce, to bound, to volt; to spring or bud, to pullulate, to egerminate; to spring or start back, to resile.

SPRING. *s.* Elasticity; spring or effort,

nitency (Johnson); spring (among mechanics) resort, from resort, F.; full of water-springs, scaturiginous; bubbling up like water from a spring, scatebrous; of or belonging to the spring, vernal; flourishing as in the spring, vernant.

SPRINGING. *p.* The act of springing out suddenly, exilition; springing up anew, renascent; springing or shooting with a quick motion, salient; springing out under another, subnascent, subsultive; a rising or springing up, ecphysis. (Bailey.)

SPRINGY. *a.* Elastic.

SPRINKLE. *v.* To bespatter, to disperge, to insperse, to irrorate, to perfuse, to besprinkle, to bestrew, to sprinkle, to moil. (Bailey.)

SPRINKLING. *p.* Act of sprinkling, aspersion, rigation, spargefaction.

SPROUT. *v.* To burgeon, to chit, to germinate; to feed on sprouts, to browse.

SPROUT. *s.* Cion or scion; sprout growing out of a branch which grew out itself but one year before, malleolus (Bot.)

SPROUTING. *p.* A sprouting again, regermination.

SPUE. *v.* To disgorge; excitement to spue, emetic. (See Vomit.)

SPRUCE. *a.* Finical, gimmy, gent.

SPUNGE. *s.* Sponge.

SPONGY. *a.* Bibulous; spungy as a rotten bone, carious.

SPUR. *v.* To goad; to spur on, to incite, to excite, to stimulate.

SPUR. *s.* Artificial spurs put on cocks, gaffles, gablocks; cock's spur, gauntlet.

SPURNING *p.* A spurning or trampling under foot, proculcation.

SPY. *v.* To descry, to espy.

SPY. *s.* Emissary, escout, scout, espial, vedette, explorator.

SQUALL. *s.* Squall or whirlwind, tornado.

SQUANDER. *v.* To palter.

SQUARE. *v.* To square or lye at right angles with any thing else, to conquadrate.

SQUARE. *s.* Square, tetragon; coverlet wove in squares, counterpoint; of or belonging to a square, quadratic; variegated by squares, tesselated.

SQUARED. *p.* That may be squared, quadrible.

SQUARING. *p.* Term used among geometricians for the squaring of a circle, tetragonism.

SQUEAMISH. *a.* Mawkish, queasy. (See Sickness.)

SQUEEZE. *v.* To squeeze betwixt the fingers, to tweag, to tweak; to squeeze out oil or the essence of any plant, to express.

SQUEEZING. *p.* The act of squeezing out, ecthlipsis; a squeezing or crushing,

thlipsis.

SQUINT. *v.* To gloat, to pinker, to skew, to leer.

SQUINTING. *p.* A squinting, squintifego, (Dryden) strabism or strabismus.

SQUIRT. *v.* To squirt in, to immit.

SQUIRT. *s.* Squirt for injections, s ringe.

STAB. *s.* Stab or thrust with any weapon, stoccado.

STABLE. *s.* Ecurie, hostry; to keep up as at stable, to stabulate; the state of being kept up at a certain rate, as horses are at stable, livery. (Spencer.)

STAFF. *s.* Staff or baton used by public officers, truncheon; the snaky staff of Mercury, caduce, (from caduceus, L.); ring put on the end of a walking-staff, verrel, verril or ferrule.

STAG. *s.* Stag or male deer which hath cast his horns, pollard; the horn of a stag, beam.

STAGE. *s.* List of stages in travelling, gest.

STAGE. *s.* Of or belonging to, or befitting a stage-player, histrionic, histrionick or histrionical; to hiss off the stage, to exsibilate.

STAGE. *s.* The last stage or state of any thing, ultimity.

STAGGERING. *p.* A staggering or faultering, titubation, vacillation.

STAIN. *v.* To distain, to maculate, to mackle, to taint; to stain with blood or gore, to insanguine.

STAIN. *s.* Attaint, attainture, blur, inquination, macula or maculation, solure, pollution, tainture.

STAKE. *v.* To put to death on a stake, to empale or impale.

STAKE *s.* Stake, bet.

STAIR. *s.* Spiral stair, cockle stair; any ascent by means of the steps of a stair, gradatory; the upright post of a spiral stair, newel or nuel.

STALE. *a.* Frouzy.

STALK. *s.* (Foot-stalk) pedicle; stalk or branch, stirp; full of stalks, fruticose.

STALL. *s.* Stall before a shop, bulk; stall or tent, booth; stall for a cow, boose.

STALLION. *s.* (Bully) leaman (from l'aimant, F.)

STAMMER. *v.* To hesitate, to maffle, to balbutiate.

STAMMERER. *s.* Mogilalos, ancyloglossus.

STAMMERING. *p.* A stammering in the attempt to pronounce a word by the repetition of the first letter of it, as a-a-a-abaft, traulismus; stammering or lisping in speech, blæsiloquent, *psellismus*; stammering or a faulty articulating and uttering of words. Of this defect Dr Cullen distinguishes seven species: *psellis-*

mus hæritans, when there is difficulty to pronounce the first syllable of some words, and which is not effected but by frequent repetition. 2. *Psellismus ringens,* in which the letter *R* is aspired and sounded as if it was doubled. 3. *Psellismus lallans,* in which the letter *L* is sounded too liquid. 4. *Psellismus emolliens,* in which the hard letters are sounded too soft, and the letter *S* is too much used. 5. *Psellismus balbutiens,* in which from a too large tongue the labial letters are too much heard. 6. *Psellismus acheilos,* in which the labial letters are with difficulty uttered. 7. *Psellismus lagostomatum,* in which, from a faulty palate, the guttural letters are all pronounced. (Quincy.)

STAMPING. *p.* Stamping with the feet, supplosion.

STANCH. *v.* To stanch blood, &c. by fire or heat, to ensear, to cauterize. (See to Stop.)

STAND. *v.* To stand off or leave off, to absist; to stand off (lurk) to miche; to stand as water in a pool, to restagnate, to stagnate.

STANDARD. *s.* Gonfalon or gonfanon, banner, guidon; St Dennis's purple standard borne against infidels, auriflam, auflambe, or orifleme; standard (what may be judged by) criterion; whatever is above the common standard, hypermeter.

STANDING. *p.* Resting or standing upon, insistent; standing as water in a pool, stagnant, restagnant.

STAR. *s.* Placed between the stars, interstellar; a blazing star resembling a torch, lampadias; instrument for finding the motion of the north star round the pole, nocturlabe; instrument for taking the height or depression of the pole star, nocturnal; the science of describing the stars, astrography; of or belonging to the stars, sideral, sidereal, siderean; relating to the stars, stellar or stellary; said of those stars which never set, inocciduous.

STARCH. *s.* Sort of grain of the nature of rice of which starch is made, amelcorn.

START. *v.* To start or leap fantastically, to gambol; to start back, to blench, to resile, to recoil, to boggle or bodge.

STARTS. *s.* Moving by starts, subsultory.

STARTING. *p.* A starting asunder, dissilition; starting-post, goal.

STARVE. *v.* To clamm, to famish; to starve with cold, to infrigidate.

STARVED. *p.* Meagre; starved fellow, jackalent, atrophus.

STATE. *s.* Habit, habitude, posture, predicament; single state, celibacy; living in a single state, monial; good state of the body, euchrasy; state (grandeur) regality; last state or stage of any thing, ultimity.

STATELY. *a.* Sumptuously, gorgeously, augustly, lordly, portly, regifical, pompous.

STATION. *v.* To station or place, to collocate.

STATUE. *s.* Statue representing the head, breast, and shoulders, bust or busto; inscription on a statue, epigraphe; wooden statue used by painters which may be put in any required attitude, layman; cavity or hollow made in a wall to receive a statue, niche or nice; name of a famous statue in Rome not far from the Capitol, on which commonly answers to the satyrical questions fastened on the latter are fixed, Marforio.

STATURE. *s.* Height of stature, procerity.

STAY. *v.* To stay or dwell in a place, to abide; to stay or dwell in a place for a while, to sojourn.

STAY. *s.* Stay or habitation, abode, biding; stay (support) fulcrum, fulciment, retinacle.

STEADFAST. *a.* Perseverant, resolute.

STEADFASTNESS. *s.* Immobility.

STEADY. *a.* Fiducial, persistive, pertinacious, resolute, stable.

STEAL. *v.* To prig, to prog, to nim (cant) to purloin; to steal privately, to crib, to embezzle, to filch, to pilfer; to steal (among tailors) to cabbage; to steal children for the purpose of transporting them, to kidnap; having an inclination to steal, furacity.

STEALING. *p.* A private withdrawing or stealing, subterduction; a stealing of sacred utensils from the church, sacrilege; act of stealing, suppilation, surreption.

STEALTH. *s.* Got by stealth, furtive, surreptitious, abacted.

STEAM. *s.* Exhalation, gas.

STEEL. *s.* Mars (Old Chym.) impregnated with steel chalybeate.

STEEP. *v.* To drench, to imbrue, to macerate.

STEEP. *a.* Steep hill, cliff; steep rock, precipice.

STEEPLE. *s.* Steeple which rises to a point, spire.

STEEPNESS. *s.* Steepness of a hill descending, declivity; the steepness of a hill ascending, acclivity; steepness, inclination or slope, pendence, proclivity.

STEER. *v.* To steer or conduct a ship in different irregular courses, to laveer.

STEP. *s.* Step (march) procession; step (manner of walking) gait; done step by step, gradual, gradatory; flight of steps, greeze, grice or grise; proceeding by steps, scallary; ascending step by step as a ladder, climacterical.

STEPMOTHER. *s.* Of or belonging to a stepmother, novercal.

STEPPING. *p.* Stepping stones, sarn.

STERN. *s.* Stern, poop (from poupe, F.; towards the stern of a ship, abaft or aft.

STERN. *a.* Having a stern aspect, truculent.

STEW. *s.* Bordel, brothel.

STEWARD. *s.* Caterer; steward of a college, purveyor, manciple; steward of a great man's house, major-domo; the lord high steward, seneschal or seneshal.

STICK. *v.* To adhere, to cleave, to cohere.

STICKING. *p.* Act of sticking or cleaving to, inhesion.

STICKY. *a.* Glutinous, viscid, viscous, gelatine, gelatinous, depectible.

STIFF. *a.* Stiff (surly or rugged) budge; stiff or gluey, gelatine, gelatinous; stiff (close drawn) tense; stiff (incommunicative, inconversable, uncommunicative, unconversable; stiff (obstinate) opiniatre, pertinacious, precise, rigid, stern.

STIFENESS. *s.* Inflexibility, inflexibleness; stiffness (lightness) tension.

STIFFLE *v.* To suffocate.

SON. *s.* Belonging to, or becoming a son, filial; Irish or Erse name for a son, mac.

STILE. *s.* Old and new stile, (see Year); high and bombastic stile of language, fustian; using a high and affected stile, grandiloquous; stile or language, lingo; (Portuguese); the affected stile of language for which the Paduans were censured, Patavinity. (See Style.)

STILL. *a.* Serene, tranquillous; still (quiet) halcyon, tranquil, quiescent; still as standing water, restagnant, stagnant.

STILL. *s.* Limbec or alembic; place or receptacle for a still, stillatory.

STILTS. *s.* Scatches.

STING. *s.* Having a sting (prickly) aculeate; sting or prick of conscience, synteresis.

STINK. *s.* Fetor; stink or rank smell of meat or fish long kept, fumette, hogo or hogoo.

STINKING. *a.* Fetid, foisty, mephitical; stinking noisome, olid, olidous, putid, putredinous, rancid, putredness or putridness; a stinking exhalation from the whole or any part of the body, dysodia; strong scented or stinking, graveolent; stinking or rotten tobacco, mundungus.

STIR. *v.* To budge, to excite, to incite, to coil, to emmove; to stir up, to exagitate, to exuscitate or exsuscitate, to extimulate, to stimulate, to vivify; to incense, to exasperate, to instigate, to suscitate; to stir up anew, to resuscitate;

to stir up flame, &c. to accend.

STIR. *s.* Stir (tumult) ado, fuss, pother, pudder, romage, turmoil, utis; unwilling to stir, restiff, restive, resty.

STIRRING. *p.* Act of stirring up, concitation.

STIRRUP. *s.* The person whose office it is to hold the stirrup to the king when he mounts on horseback, is called a gentleman of the queiry (from ecuyer, F.)

STITCHED. *p.* That is stitched or sewed together, consutile.

STOCK. *v.* To replenish.

STOCK. *s.* Private stock of goods, money, &c. hoard.

STOCK. *s.* Person who owns or is possessed of actions, shares or stock in a company, actionary, actionist; stock or store, budget, pelf.

STOCKS. *s.* Stocks in which the feet are put as a punishment, bilboer.

STOLEN. *a.* Cribbed, furtive; stolen in an artful and cunning manner, obreptitious.

STOMACH. *s.* Stomach of a bird, craw, choule, crop, ingluvies, gizzard, maw, pannel; the stomach, gaster (Bailey); the lower orifice of the stomach, janitor, pylorus; of or belonging to the breast or stomach, stomachic (Bailey); of or belonging to the stomach, gastric or gastrick (Quincy); to throw aliment, &c. into the stomach, to ingest; to fill an empty stomach, to exaturate; canal leading from the mouth to the stomach, oesophagus; wind broke from the stomach, eructation; sour belch from the stomach, oxyregmia; balls filled with hair, sometimes found in the stomachs of animals, ægagropili; instrument made of whale-bone used in surgery for cleansing the stomach, provango; the stomach of ruminating animals is reckoned divisible into four distinct ventricles, viz. venter, reticulum, omasum or omasus, and abomasum.

STONE. *s.* The loadstone, adamant (Bacon); the whet-stone, cos (Perry); to clear from stones, to elapidate; flat stone for paving, flag; one who cuts in stone, lapicide, sculptor, lithoglyphic; to turn into stone, to inlapidate, to petrify; to stone to death, to lapidate; one who deals in stones or gems, lapidary; the art of carving in stone, colaptice, G.; lumps or fragments of stone or marble rounded by the action of the sea, &c. bowlderstones; the middle stone of an arch, keystone; resembling stones, lapideous; that which turns any thing into stone, lapidescent; forming stones, lapidific, lapidifical; act of engraving on stone, also a description of precious stones, lithography; prediction by the casting of stones, lithomancy; stone pavements of Mosaic work, i. e. in small pebbles, cockles, shells, &c. of different colours, lithostrota; the stone of a cherry, plumb, &c. oesicle; stone said to be of great virtue for uniting of broken bones, osteocolla; growing into stone, petrescent; a turning into stone, petrifaction, or petrification, lapidification; ancient names of engines used for casting great stones, espringold, and catapulta; free-stone as it comes from the quarry, ashlar; stepping-stone, sarn; full of gravel stones, scrupose; cement for fastening of stones, lithocolla; name of the fabled robber whose punishment was to roll a stone up hill, which perpetually recoiled on him, Sisyphus; stone which is pretended to be an antidote to drunkenness, Dionysias; the name of a surgical instrument used in extracting a stone out of the bladder, lapidilium; a surgeon who cuts for the stone, lithotomist; the operation of cutting for the stone, lithotomy or cystotomy; the breeding of the stone in the human body, lithiasis; medicines which dissolve the stone in the bladder, lithontriptics; medicines good against the stone, nephritics; any medicine for breaking the stone in the bladder, calcifragous; medicines which break or dissolve the stone in the bladder, saxifraga; the old chemical name for a stone which dissolves gravel in the human body, serphera; the stones of a dunghill cock, waddles, to cut the stones from the males of an animal, to geld, to castrate, to evirate, to emasculate, to eunuchate, to glib; to cut the stones from the female of an animal, to spay.

STONING. p. A stoning to death, lapidation.

STONY. a. Tophaceous, calculous; to make or render stony, to inlapidate; stony concretions found at the bottom of some mineral waters, tophus; the faculty in a human body of turning things to a stony substance, lapillation.

STOOL. s. Stool, dejection, discharge by stool, ejectment; the frequent desire of going to stool with an inability of voiding the faeces, tenesmus.

STOOL. s. Stool, or seat with three feet, tripod or tripos; ducking stool, tymborella, trebuck, tribucket, or tumbrell.

STOOP. v. To courb, to coor, to condescend.

STOP. v. To instop, to arrest, to clamm, to constipate, to countercheck, to obstipate, to desist, to discontinue, to impede, to land-dam, to intercept, to interclude, to obviate, to preclude, to repress, to retard; to stop the procedure of an undertaking, to procrastinate; to stop or put off an affair, to supercede; to suspend; to stop by force, to coerce; to stop by fire or heat, to ensear, to cauterize; to stop or stammer in speech, to maffle; to stop blood, to stanch.

STOP. s. Cessation, check, suspense, let, barrier; order or command given in sea language to stop, avast; stop or low fence, aha; stop in speech, hesitancy; that never stops, indesinent; stop or hinderance, Remora, L.; stop, (doubt or difficulty) quandary.

STOPPAGE. s. Stoppage or interruption, intercision; cause of stoppage, intercipient; stoppage of urine, ischuria or ischury.

STOPPER. s. Stopple, fipple; stopper of a great gun, tampion, tamkin, tomkin, tompion.

STOPPING. p. Escharotic, searing, caustic, obstruent; cause of stopping or hindering, interception; act of stopping up by smearing, obturation; stopping of obstructive, oppilative; medicines of a stopping nature, obstruentia, stiptics or styptics.

STORE. s. Great store, affluence, profluence.

STOREHOUSE. s. Promptuary, buttery, reconditory, repository, repertory, reservatory.

STORM. s. Violent storm, hurricane; that brings storms or tempests, nimbiferous; storm (attack), onslaught; storm (whirlwind), tornado, travado.

STORMY. a. Boisterous, gusty, nubiferous, nimbose, procellous.

STORY. s. Story or flat placed on the top of another, intersole, mezanine.

STORY. s. Device; an invented or fabricated story, fiction, legend.

STOVE. s. Zeta, zeticula, hypocaustum; stove or sweating house, balneary; stove where moisture is driven off, vaporary.

STOUT. a. Bony, chopping, hardy, lusty, squab, valorous, virile.

STRAIN. v. As a joint, to eluxate; to strain off, to decant, to deprome, to elutriate, to excern, to filter, to defecate; to strain through a sieve, to transcolate; to strain or vomit, to retch.

STRAIN. s. Flexure, contortion.

STRAINER. s. Colander; strainer for decoctions, syrups, &c. made of a piece of flannel or woollen cloth joined by the corners, Hippocrates's sleeve.

STRAINING. p. Art of straining, sola-

X

tion, colature, filtration, percolation.

STRAIT. *a.* The act of making narrow or strait, angustation.

STRANGE. *a.* Informous, legendary, uncouth, extraneous, extrinsic, fractious, marvellous, necromantic, peregrine, preternatural, queer.

STRANGELY. *ad.* Strangely or miserably, elengelic.

STRANGENESS. *s.* Infrequency, unfrequency, novity.

STRANGER. *s.* Guest, allophylus; inn or place of entertainment for strangers, xenodochy; the murder or murderer of a stranger, hospicide.

STRAPS. *s.* Straps of leather, laines.

STRATAGEM. *s.* Finesse, ruse.

STRAW. *s.* Haulm or haum; formed of, or like straw, festucous; straw-coloured, festucine.

STRAY. *v.* To deviate.

STRAYING. *p.* Discurrent.

STREAKED. *a.* Brinded, dappled.

STREAM. *s.* Stream of fresh water, freshet, rill, or rillet; islets formed by a stream or shifting of the tide, alluvia; of or belonging to streams or rivers, fluminous.

STREAMER. *s.* Bandrol, banner.

STREET. *s.* Parish-officer who cleans the street, scavenger.

STRENGTH. *s.* Efficacy, brawniness, lustihood, pithiness, potency, puissance, vigour, energy, vigorosity; strength or power to convince, validity; want of strength, atony; one who is soon restored to health and strength, when weakened by disease, euanasphaltos; to take away the virtue or strength of any thing, to evertuate.

STRENGTHEN. *v.* To insinew, to enforce, to invigorate, to munite; to strengthen (chemical language), to concentrate.

STRENGTHENING. *p.* Strengthening medicines are termed, roborantia or analeptics.

STRESS. *s.* The stress laid upon a particular part of a word denoted by a little mark, as thus' in the word *pi'teous,* &c. accent; a remarkable stress laid on a word or sentence, emphasis.

STRETCH. *v.* To distend, to elongate; to stretch forth, to protend.

STRETCHED. *p.* Stretched or increased, intensive; stretched, tense; capable of being stretched, tensible, tensile.

STRETCHING. *p.* Stretching or restlessness, as in some fevers, pandiculation; the act of stretching a thing, intension; a stretching out, porrection, tensure; act of stretching out, tension.

STREW. *v.* To bespread, to bestrew.

STRICT. *a.* Disciplinarian, precise, rigid, stern, rigorous.

STRIFE. *s.* Bate, contention, dissension, discord, vitiligation; strife (wrangling by words), logomachy; promoter of strife, make-bate.

STRIKE. *v.* To buffet, to lamm, to verberate, to pash; to strike against, to bob; to strike together, to collide; to strike or knock out, to elide; to strike gently, to dab; to strike back, to counterbuff; to strike out, to efface; to elicit, to excogitate; to strike against, to impinge, to allide; to strike out, to rase or erase, to expunge; to strike hard, to thwack.

STRIKING. *p.* Striking, percutient; the art of striking against any thing, appulse; the act of striking one thing against another, allision, collision, percussion; striking or pleasing, plausible; striking or forcible, emphatical.

STRIP. *v.* To dedecorate, to denude or denudate, to despoil, to disrobe, to divest, to doff; to stripe off the skin, to excoriate, to fleece; to strip off the bark, to excorticate; to strip or plunder, to forage; to strip naked, to connudate; to strip or spoil, to spoliate.

STRIPE. *s.* Stripe (blow), verberation.

STRIPT. *a.* Stript of, bereft, discased, dismantled.

STRIVE. *v.* To conflict, to contend, to cope.

STRIVING. *p.* A striving, struggle, or effort, luctation.

STROKE. *s.* Occursion, appulse, bar, brunt, dint, bang, concussion, percussion; violent stroke of one body against another, impetus; stroke in fencing, butt.

STROLLING. *p.* Vagrant.

STRONG. *a.* Athletic, bony, brawny, drastic, meracious, cogent, depressive, emphatical, energetic, hardy, lusty, masculine, nervous, nervy, perdurable, ponderous, potent, robust, puissant, sinewy, stable, stanch, tendinous, valid, vehement, vive; strong as a wall, mural; strong (flavorous), said of wine, racy.

STRUGGLE. *v.* Against, to reluct, to reluctate.

STRUGGLE. *s.* Reluctation, renitency, luctation, colluctation, conflict, effort.

STRUMPET. *s.* Concubine, harlot, nightwalker, prostitute, punk, quean; worn out strumpet, harridan.

STUBBLE. *s.* Eddish, haulm, or haum.

STUBBORN. *a.* Contumacious, glum, heady, obdurate, opiniatre, pertinacious, petulent, pervicacious, perverse, refractory, restiff, restive, resty.

STUBBORNESS. *s*. Refragability.

STUDENT. *s*. Academician, tyro; student in medicine, philiatros; student of two years standing, soph or sophister; student of the lowest order, sizer, servitour.

STUDY. *v*. To con, to apply, to meditate, to evigilate, to ruminate; to study by candle-light, to lucubrate, to elucubrate; improvement in study, proficiency.

STUFF. *v*, To accloy, to satiate, to surfeit, to suffarcinate.

STUFF. *s*. (Nonsense), jargon, gibberish.

STUFFING. *p*. Act of stuffing, infarction.

STUMBLING. *p*. Stumbling or faultering in speech, titubation.

STUPID. *a*. Fatuous, illusory, impotent, bardous, conceitless, doltish, dozy, humdrum, dronish, insensate, maudlin; stupid fellow, clumps, moone, buffle-head, bull-head.

STUPIDITY. *s*. Fatuity, oscitancy or oscitation, stolidity, surdity, torpor, insulsity; the goddess of stupidity, Moria.

STUPIFY. *v*. To besot, to doze, to hebetate, to mope; to stupify by drink, to inebriate.

STUPIFYING. *p*. Obstupefactive, narcotic.

STYLE. *s*. Style of a dial, gnomon; short and emphatic style of language, Chilonian or Chilonic, from Chilo, one of the seven wise men of Greece; eloquent and pure style, as Cicero's, is termed a Ciceronian style. (See Stile.)

STYLED. *a*. Styled or named, ycleped.

STYPTIC. *a*. Astrictive. (See Stanch and Stop.)

STYE. *s*. Stye on the eye-lid, crithe.

SUBDUE. *v*. To mate, to quash, to suppress, to debellate.

SUBJECT. *s*. Subject of consideration, carpet; subject or accountable to, responsible.

SUBJECTION. *s*. Captivity; to be in subjection, to truckle.

SUBMISSION. *s*. Deference, fealty, compliance.

SUBMIT. *v*. To acquiesce, to condescend, to knuckle, to consign.

SUBSCRIPTION. *s*. Subscription or writing under, hypogram.

SUBSTANCE. *s*. To change into another substance, to transubstantiate; of the same substance, consubstantial; the real substance of any thing, essence.

SUBSISTING. *p*. incapable of subsisting together, incompossible.

SUBSTITUTE. *v*. To subrogate, to surrogate.

SUBSTITUTE. *s*. Proxy, succedaneum.

SUBSTITUTING. *p*. A substituting, suffection.

SUBTLE. *a*. Acute, quaint, shrewd, vaprous, vulpinary, subtile, machiavilian, tenuous, tenuious; to render subtle, to subtiliate.

SUBTILITY. *s*. Panurgy, policy, quillet, quodlibet.

SUBTRACTION. *s*. Substraction (Johnson), subduction, deduction; the least term in subtraction, subtrahend.

SUBURBS. *s*. Inhabiting the suburbs, suburbine, suburban, suburbian.

SUCCEED. *v*. To ensue, to fadge, to fare.

SUCCESSION. *s*. Succession (change), vicissitude, diadoche; joint succession to an inheritance, coparceny or coparcenary; having a right in succession, reversionary.

SUCCOURING. *p*. (Relieving from pain), redressive.

SUCK. *v*. To suck up, to absorb; to suck back again, to resorb.

SUCKER. *s*. Imbiber; what acts as a sucker of a pump, embolus; bloodsucker, sanguisuga; sucker (shoot), surcle.

SUCKING. *p*. A sucking or drawing up, imbibition, suction, lactation; disposed or capable of sucking up, bibulous, lactant; sucking infants are termed sububeres, or nefrendes.

SUDDEN. *a*. Ejaculatory, emergent; indeliberate, unpremeditated, inopinate, undeliberate, repentine, subitaneous; sudden attack, illapse, superchery, rencounter, onslaught; done of a sudden, tumultuary; done of a sudden without premeditation, extempore, or extemporary.

SUDDENLY. *a*. Coming on suddenly, unawares, superadvenient, supervening.

SUET. *s*. Sevum. L.

SUFFER. *v*. To tolerate, to brook.

SUFFERABLE. *a*. Patible.

SUFFERANCE. *s*. Endurance.

SUFFERING. *p*. An impatience in suffering, dysphory; an easiness in suffering, eupathy or euphoria; suffering, (affection or disorder), pathema; incapable of suffering, impassable or impassive; a suffering or undergoing, perpession.

SUFFICIENT. *a*. Capable, competent, relevant; more than sufficient of any commodity, glut.

SUGAR. *s*. Name of an instrument invented for ascertaining the quantity of sugar present in wort, in the science of brewing, sacchorometer; refined sugar, otherwise called pearl sugar, *Manus Christi*, L.; of or belonging to sugar, saccharine; drink made of sugar, wine,

X 2

&c. taken as a whet, propoma.

SUIT. *v.* To accommodate, to accord, to adapt, to beseem, to besort, to correspond, to fadge; to suit or agree, to quadrate, to respond, to tally.

SUITABLE. *a.* Matchable, meet, idoneous, compatible, conformable, applicable, competible, decorous, apposite, pertinent, condign, congruous, omological, pat, pertinent, semblative; more suitable, fitlier; most suitable, fitliest; not suitable, misbecoming.

SUITING. *p.* Harmonical, concordant; not suiting, discordant.

SUITS. *s.* The debating of law-suits, actitation.

SULLEN. *a.* Dogged, morose, glouty, glum, reserved.

SULLENNESS. *s.* Dudgeon, mulligrubs, mumps.

SULPHUR. *s.* Kibrit.

SUMMER. *s.* Relating to the summer, estival or æstival; the passing the summer in a place, as migratory birds do, estivation.

SUMMON. *v.* To accite, to convocate, to convoke, to evoke.

SUMMONS. *s.* Cital, citation, interpellation, subpœna, vocation.

SUMPTUOUS. *a.* Opiparous.

SUN. *s.* Phœbus, G.; mock sun, parhilium or parelium, parhelion G.; covering from the sun, generally used aboard ships, awning; appearing or seen from the sun, heliocentric; rising and setting with the sun, cosmical; the face of the sun or planet, disc or disk; to dry in the sun, to insolate; of or belonging to the sun, solar; the sun's least distance from the earth's centre, perigœum or perigee; the sun's greatest distance from the equator, either north or south, when he appears for some days stationary, is termed the summer or winter solstice; warmth in the sun, apricity; a basking in the sun, aprication; an umbrella, to keep off the sun, parasol; glass for viewing the body of the sun through, helioscope.

SUNBURNT. *p.* Blowzy.

SUNDAY. *s.* Of or belonging to Sunday, dominical.

SUNDRY. *a.* Divers, omnifarious.

SUNSET. *s.* Rising at sunset, or setting at sunset, acronical.

SUPPER. *s.* Of or belonging to supper, cenatory; supper given to labourers at the bringing in of harvest, medsyppe; the consecrated bread used at the Lord's Supper, hostia; the sacrament of the Lord's supper, eucharist, synaxis, housel; heretics who took water alone, aquarians; a sect or company who discoursed of philosophical matters at supper, deipnosophists. (See Sacrament.)

SUPPING. *p.* Act of supping up, sorbition.

SUPPLICATION. *s.* Obtestation, oraison or orison, rogation.

SUPPLY. *v.* To indue, to subminister, to succour, to suppeditate.

SUPPLY. *s.* Grist, subvention, subsidy.

SUPPORT. *v.* To abet, to escot, to bolster, to foster, to cherish, to buoy, to propugn; to support, suffer or bear, to abide.

SUPPORT. *s.* Adminicle, coadjuvancy, munition, sustentation, approbation, fulcrum, fulciment, prop, torsel, behalf, buttress, retinacle, substruction, hypomochlion, obex; support or care, tuition, tutelage.

SUPPOSE. *v.* To conjecture, to deem, to presume, to surmise; to suppose before hand, to presuppose, to presurmise.

SUPPOSED. *p.* Putative; that may be supposed, supposeable.

SUPPOSITION. *s.* Hypothesis.

SURE. *a.* Cocksure, evident, stable. (See Clear)

SURELY. *ad.* Forsooth.

SURETY. *s.* One who is surety for another, manucaptor, mainprize; one who is surety in baptism, sponsor.

SURFACE. *s.* Superficies, area, expansion; to extend in surface, to distend; any irregular and small surface, facet or facette; lying within the surface, intime; divided into small surfaces, scutillated.

SURFEIT. *s.* To accloy, to cloy; medicines good in relieving a surfeit, acrapula.

SURGEON. *s.* Chirurgeon, bonesetter; the name of a famous surgeon who was said to have made a new nose to one of his patients, out of a piece of another man's flesh, Tagliacotius or Taliacotius.

SURLY. *a.* Bluff, budge, canine, chuffy, crusty, glouty; surly fellow, churl, carlo.

SURMOUNTED. *p.* That cannot be surmounted, insuperable.

SURNAME. *s.* Cognomen.

SURPRIZE. *s.* Flurry, alarm, surreption; done by surprise, surreptitious; got by surprise, subreptitious; coming by surprise, supervenient.

SURPRISED. *p.* To stand surprised, to stand aghast.

SURRENDER. *s.* Dedition, reddition, rendition.

SURROUND. *v.* To hend, to inviron, to invest, to imbay, to begird, to blockade, to encircle, to encompass, to engird, to enguard, to envelope, to environ, to enwheel.

SURROUNDING. *p.* Ambient, circumambient; a surrounding with a trench, obvallation.

SURVEY. *v*. To lustrate, to traverse, to perambulate. (See Examine.)

SURVEYING. *p*. The art of surveying countries, chorometry, geodesia; instrument used in taking angles when surveying large tracts of country, theodolite. (See Angle.)

SUSPEND. *v*. To interdict, to respite, to supercede.

SUSPENDED. *p*. Pendulous, pensil or pensile

SUSPECT. *v*. To surmise; to suspect before hand, to presurmise.

SUSPENSE. *s*. Irresolution, pendence.

SUSPENSION. *s*. Suspension of arms, armistice.

SUSPICION. *s*. Surmise, umbrage; free from suspicion, indubitous, indubious, indubitable or indubitate, undubitable.

SUSPICIOUS. *a*. Apprehensive.

SWALLOW. *v*. To swallow up, to absorb, to englut, to gorge, to flap-dragon, to ingurgitate, to lurch; to swallow eagerly, to regorge; to swallow down as into an abyss, to gurgitate; to swallow up again, to resorb.

SWALLOWED. *p*. Any medicine which is to be swallowed without chewing as a pill, catapotium.

SWALLOWING. *p*. Act of swallowing deglutition; a difficulty in swallowing, dysphagia.

SWAN. *s*. Young swan, cygnet.

SWAMPY. *a*. Boggy, quaggy.

SWATCH. *s*. Swatch or the first specimen or taste of a thing, libation. (Bailey.)

SWEAR *v*. To depone. (See Pledge.)

SWEAT. *v*. To transude.

SWEAT. *s*. A provocation to sweat, by making the patient approach the fire, or by placing him in a sweating room, paroptesis; exciting sweat, diaphoretic; bloody sweat, hæmatopedesis; causing sweat, sudorific.

SWEATING. *p*. Act of sweating out, exsudation or exudation, extillation; an inordinate sweating, desudation; a sweating again, resudation; a sweating through, transudation; sweating houses, hummums (Turk.); act of sweating, sudation; sweating medicines, areotics, hydrotics or diaphoretics; sweating-bath, sudatory, hypocaustum; critical judgment of distempers formed from sweating, hydrocritics.

SWEATY. *a*. Sudorous.

SWEEP. *v*. To sweep or snatch away, to raff; to sweep or scour by means of shot, the whole length of an enemy's line, to enfilade.

SWEET. *a*. Grateful, delicious, fragrant, luscious, nectarian, odoriferous, odorous, odorate, fragrant; sweet to the palate or

ear, melodious, harmonious, dulcet (Milton, Shakes.); the sweet or fragrant smell of some plants, &c. aroma; yielding sweet smell, redolent.

SWEETEN. *v*. To adduce, to disembitter, to dulcify, to dulcorate, to edulcorate.

SWEETHEART. *s*. Leman (from l'aimant, *F*, paramour.

SWEETMEAT. *s*. Confiture.

SWEETNESS. *s*. Sweetness of smell, fragrance, fragrancy, redolence or redolency; sweetness of temper, suavity.

SWELL. *v*. To bloat, to bouge, to bunt, to estuate, to tumify, to tumulate, to vesicate; to swell with wind, to inflate.

SWELLED. *p*. Turgid, tumid; swelled state, turgescence, edematose; swelled or knotted, geniculated; swelled as with an emphysema, emphysematous; swelled into a convex irregular figure, gibbous; swelled in the legs, gourdy; swelled or raised into protuberances, embossed.

SWELLING. *p*. Turgent; swelling or bunching out, protuberant; swelling without pain, callosity; swelling on the eye-lid, called the stye, crithe; a swelling or tumour, intumescence or intumescency, inturgescence; any swelling or inflammation, phlegmon; act of swelling, tumefaction, turgescence; a swelling by wind, suflation; little swellings on any part of the body, tubercles, tubercula; full of little swellings, tuberose, tuberous.

SWIFT. *a*. Fleet, pernicious, rapid; swift-footed, alipede; any swift-sailing vessel which scours the seas, dromo, *G*.

SWIFTNESS. *s*. Celerity, pernicity, velocity; to pass on with great swiftness as a ship before the wind, to spoon.

SWIMMED. *p*. That cannot be swimmed over, innatable.

SWIMMING. *p*. Goods found swimming on the sea, and which the lord-admiral claims by his letters patent, flotson or flotzam; act of swimming, natation; term in heraldry when fishes are drawn in an escutcheon, lying at length as if swimming, naiant or natant; swimming above, supernatant; the act of swimming above, supernatation; the act of swimming across or over, transnatation, tranation; an escape by swimming, enatation; swimming or dizziness of the head, scotomy.

SWIMS. *p*. That swims, or can swim, natatile.

SWINE. *s*. A swine in America said to have its navel on its back, javaris.

SWING. *s*. The time a pendulum takes in performing one swing, diadrom; swing of a pendulum, vibration, oscillation.

SWIVEL. *s.* Swivel gun, pederero, patere-ro, pattererro, (from *Pedrero,* Spanish.)

SWOONING. *p.* A swooning from too great a waste of the spirits, lipothymia or apsychia.

SWORD. *s.* Bilbo; King *Edward* the Confessor's sword without a point (an emblem of mercy) which is carried before the kings and queens of England at their coronation, curtana or curteyn; combat with swords, degladiation; bearing a sword, ensiferous; sword-player, gladiator, scrimer; handle of a sword, hilt; a fatal and deadly sword, morglay, (from *mortglaive,* F.); the knob that balances the blade of a sword, pommel; sword-bearer, port-glaive; small sword used only in thrusting, rapier; broad-bended sword, sabre, cimeter or scimeter, faulchion, glaive or glavie.

SYLLABLE. *s.* A word of one syllable,

monosyllable; of two, dissyllable; three-trissyllable; four, quadrisyllable; more than four, pollysyllable; any word having eleven syllables, such as the word honorificabilitudinity, is termed a hendecasyllabon; that part of grammar which teaches the quantity and accent of syllables, prosody. (See Grammar.)

SYMPATHY. *s.* The act of moving to sympathy, inteneration.

SYMPTOM. *s.* Indication, minnings; having bad symptoms, cachetic or chachetical.

SYRENS. *s.* The Syrens are called by some Aglaepe, Pisinoe, and Thelxiopia, by others, Thelxiope, Molpe, and Aglaophones; they are also named, Leucoise, Ligea, and Parthinope.

SYRINGE. *s.* Syringe for injecting a medical liquor into the nostrils, rhinenchites; into the womb, metrenchytes.

T

TABLE. *s.* Trapeza; belonging to the table, mensal; to serve at table, to skink; table fellowship, commensality; to eat at the same table, to intercommon; written on tables, intabulated or tabulated; to lie at table after the manner of the ancients, to accumb; board used by waiters, for carrying dishes, &c, off a table, voider; astronomical tables calculated to shew the diurnal motion of the planets, ephemerides; astrological table, erected publicly, containing an account of eclipses, &c. parapegma or parapegmata; astronomical tables framed by Erasmus Rheinoldus, for finding the motion of the heavenly bodies, *Prutanic tables,* so called, as being dedicated to Albert duke of Prussia, hence also the astronomical tables called, Alphonsine, got their name from their framer Alphonsus king of Arragon; tables of money, weights, measures, &c. having denominations generally known and understood in a country, in contradistinction to those having multifarious denominators, are termed, geodetical tables; tables in which the Greek Church inrolled the names of persons baptised, &c. diptychs.

TADPOLE. *s.* Porwigle.

TAIL. *s.* Cue; tail of a hare, scut; tail of a horse cover for, trousequeue; tail of a fox, holy water sprinkle. (Hunt. term)

TAINT. *v.* To defile, to leaven.

TAINT. *s.* Contagion, tainture, catch.

TAKE. *v.* To arrogate, to excuss; to take away, to abstract, to bereave, to divest, to evict; to take away or divert the affections, to alienate; to take or receive, to accept; to take away guns from a fort, to disgarnish; to take from, to besume; to take by assault, to expugn; to take by inches, to inch; to take off the top of any thing, to decacuminate; to take in a net, to immesh, to mesh; to take away, to steal) to prog, to purloin (see to steal); to take up again (to renew) to resume.

TAKEN. *p.* Apprehended; not to be taken, impregnable, invincible; that cannot be taken by assault, inexpugnable.

TAKING. *p.* Act of taking away, ablation, ademption; a taking away by force, ereption; a taking from one place to another, transumption.

TALE. *s.* Legend, fiction, relation.

TALK. *v.* To commune, to confabulate; to talk much of one's self, to egotize; to talk fondly, to honey; to talk idly, to prate; to talk, to sermocinate; to talk low, to buzz; that talks of dreadful things, terriloquous.

TALK. *s.* Foolish talk, liplabour, lipwisdom, preachment; nonsensical talk, jargon; mutual talk, interparlance; full of talk, loquacious, linguacity, linguose; talk loquela, parle or parley, predication; too much talk, polylogy; talk of doubtful meaning, ambilogy.

TALKATIVE. *a.* Very talkative, multiloquous; talkative, flippant, futile, loquacious, garrulous, leaky, verbose, polyloquent, rantipole.

TALKATIVENESS. *s.* Dicacity.

TALKER. *s.* Great talker, tongue-pad.

TALKING. *p.* Talking aloud, bawling; talking too much, polylogy; a talking to, allocution; talking to one's self, soliloquy; vain talking, vaniloquy, vaniloquence, inaniloquent, inaniloquous; talking dreadful things, terriloquent.

TALL. *a.* Tall drowsy fellow, lungis; tall girl, maypole.

TALLNESS. *s.* Celsitude, procerity, properness.

TALLOW. *s.* Sevum.

TALON. *s.* Clutch, pouncer.

TAME. *v.* To cicurate, to reclaim, to subdue.

TAME. *a.* Bland, cade, mansuete, pigeonlivered, meacock; tame lamb, corset.

TAMED. *p.* Capable of being tamed, domable; incapable of being tamed, incicurable, indomable.

TAMENESS. *s.* Mansuetude, domesticity.

TAMING. *p.* Act of, cicuration.

TAMPERING. *p.* Act of tampering with a jury, or the witnesses, imbracery, *L. T.*

TAN. *s.* Tan colour, auburne.

TANNER. *s.* Tawer.

TANNING. *s.* Tanning of leather, alutation.

TAPER. *s.* Wax taper, bougie.

TART. *a.* Acrimonious, parlous, acescent.

TASTE. *v.* To savour, to delibate.

TASTE. *s.* Gout, libation, gust or gusto, sapor, palate; void of taste, insipid; possessing a hot and biting taste, acrid; resembling the taste or smell of roasted meat, nidorous or nidorose; having a good taste, sapid; loss of taste, apogeusis.

TASTELESS. *a.* Ingustable, intastable.

TASTING. *p.* First act of tasting, pregustation.

TAVERN. *s.* Of or belonging to taverns, tabernarious; the act of frequenting taverns, popination.

TAUGHT. *p.* Erudite; self-taught, automath; readiness to be taught, docile; incapable of being taught, indocile.

TAUNT. *s.* Exacerbation, gibe or gybe, sarcasm.

TAWNY. *a.* Cervine, olivaster, swarthy; tawny colour, minim.

TAX. *s.* Assess, cess, escot; subsidy; tax on salt, gabel.

TAYLOR. *s.* Fashioner; nickname for a taylor, prick-louse.

TEACH. *v.* To disciple, to indoctrinate.

TEACHABLE. *a.* Docile.

TEACHER. *s.* Pedagogue, usher; pertaining to a teacher, didascalic; teacher of religion, hierophant.

TEACHING. *p.* Lore; entrance-money given by scholars for teaching, minerval.

TEAR. *v.* To lancinate, to rend, to dilacerate; to tear in pieces, to lacerate, to laniate, to mammoc, to elacerate: to tear, to touze; to tear up, to exterminate, to deracinate.

TEARING. *p.* Tearing in pieces, discerption.

TEARS. *s* Brine; generating tears, lachrymal; medicines that provoke tears, apodacritics; things which excite tears by their acrimony, such as onions and the like, dacryopoeos.

TEAZE. *v.* To chagrin, to grill, to harrow; to teaze with solicitation, to importune, to irritate.

TEATS. *s.* Having teats, mammeated.

TEDIOUS. *a.* Live long, operose, prolix, prolixious, verbose; tedious discourse, diatribe.

TEDIOUSNESS. *s.* Tediousness in discourse, periphrasis.

TEETH. *s.* The gnashing of the teeth, through pain or otherwise, bryamus, frement; having two teeth, bidental; loss of teeth dedentition; belonging to the teeth, dental; speaker through the teeth, dentiloquist; breeding of teeth, dentition; dog-teeth, cynodentes, *dentes canini*; fore teeth, incisors; uttered jointly by the teeth and tongue, linguadental; sound pronounced by the teeth and lips, labiodental; the broader part of the teeth or grinders which chew and mince the meat, mensa (Anat.); belonging to the teeth, odontic; itching of the gums when children breed teeth, odaxismus; instrument for drawing teeth, odontagogos, odontagra; stony concretion that grows on the teeth, odontolithos; medicine to rub the teeth with, odontotrimma; the hindermost teeth of the head, generally appearing in those come to years, *dentes sapientiæ*; to grind harshly between the teeth, to scranch; teeth that appear after one is full grown, sophronestores; a numbness of the teeth by any acid, hæmoida; the large teeth of a boar which stand out, tushes or tusks, razors; the sockets of the jaws in which the teeth are inserted, alveoli, præsepia, mortariolum; a discourse or treatise on the teeth, dendrology; a distemper of the teeth when they are loose and ready to fall out, gomphiasis; a painful numbness of the teeth, hæmodia; term used for those children or old people who have no teeth, nefrendes; an epithet for the four middle fore teeth, because they are seen in the act of laughing, gelasinos; formed like teeth, dentiform ; the large teeth or grinders are called, molares, L.

TELL. v. To advertise, to advise (see to Buzz) to convey, to enunciate, to histofify, to interpret, to indicate ; to tell or show ill tidings, to obnunciate ; to tell before hand, to premonstrate ; to tell, to prompt, to propagate, to recount, to relate, to disclose, to reveal; to tell, (to reckon) to suppute, to compute.

TELL-TALE. s. Buzzer.

TEMPER. v. To anneal; to contemper; to temper by fire, to neal.

TEMPER. s. Sourness of temper, acerbity; difficulty in keeping one's temper, dyspathy ; sweetness of temper, suavity ; a peculiar temper or turn of mind, idiosyncrasy ; malignant and bitter temper, virulency.

TEMPERAMENT. s. Good temperament of body, euchrasy or euchymy ; temperament of body fitting it best to perform its functions, idiocracy ; that part of physic which teaches how to acquire a good temperament of body evectica.

TEMPERATE. a. Abstemious or abstinent, continent.

TEMPEST. s. Violent tempest, hurricane; that brings tempest, nimbiferous.

TEMPESTUOUS. a. Gusty, procellous.

TEMPESTUOUSNESS. s. Procellosity.

TEMPLE. s. Fane ; temple supported only by pillars, monopteron ; temple of all the heathen gods, pantheon ; temple of the Chinese, pagoda ; porch of a temple, propyleum.

TEMPLES. s. Bones of the head strengthening the temples, parietal bones.

TEMPT. v. To seduce ; to tempt to do evil, to instigate, to incite.

TEN. a. Sum of ten, decade ; figure of ten equal sides, decagon ; ten commandments, decalogue ; ten years continuance, decennial ; numbered by tens, decimal ; tenfold, decuple : commander of ten men, decurion ; commander of ten thousand men, myriarch ; tenth part, containing 1-10th part, subdecuple, disme, denary. (See, One, Two, Four.)

TEND. v. To tend as the range of a coast, to trend.

TENDER. a. Cade, clement, compassionate, effeminate, feminine, pathetic, piteous, puny, tid, emolid; tender (full of passion) sensuous, sympathetic ; to make tender or soften the feelings, to intenerate, to humanize.

TENDENCY. s. Aptitude, bent, proclivity, propension. propensity.

TENDERLY. ad. Gingerly.

TENDERNESS. s. Bosom, brittleness, lenitude, lenity, muliebrity, pathos, pitifulness; tenderness (feeling for a fault) remorse ; tenderness (mercy) ruth.

TERM. s. Appellation, condition; antecedent term, premiss ; terms belonging to, and used in arts and sciences, technical ; to surrender upon terms, to capitulate ; the monthly terms of women, menses, catamenia, menstrua.

TERMED. p. Termed (called) ycleped.

TERRACE. s. Walk, solarium.

TERRIBLE. a. Alarming, dread, formidable, tremendous, horrible, horrent; any thing terrible. gorgon ; terrible of aspect, truculent, formidulous.

TERRIBLY. ad. Sounding terribly, terrisonous.

TERRIBLENESS. s. Dirity.

TERRIFIED. a. Afeard.

TERRIFY. v. To affright, to confound, to dastard, to dismay, to hare, to amaze, to appal, to astonish, to gallow, to gast.

TERROR. s. Affright, hideousness, horror, trepidation ; causing terror, terrific ; striking terror, fulminatory ; the standing up of the hair through terror, horripilation.

TESTAMENT. s. Dying without a testament, abintestate, intestate ; supplement to a testament, codicil ; disqualified from making a testament, intestable ; authentic copy of a testament, probat or probate.

TESTAMENT. s. Greek version of the Old Testament, Septuagint.

TESTICLE. s. A man who has but one testicle, monorchis ; membrane which contains the male testicle, scrotum ; the testicles, cullions, didymoi, or didymi.

TESTIMONY. s. Attestation, evidence, probation.

THEATRICALLY. ad. Histrionically.

THEFT. Got by theft, furtive; petty theft, larceny, pilfery ; literary theft, plagiary, plagiarism.

THEOREM. s. Philosopheme, porism ; theorem almost self-evident, porime.

THICK. v. To make thick, to incrassate, to inspissate.

THICK. a. Halitous, crass, callous, condense, dense, gourdy, grumous, hazy; thick (muddy) mucous, muculent; thick, impervious, impertransible, pail-mail, spiss, squab, turbid.

THICKEN. v. To congeal, to constipate, to incrassate, to inspissate ; medicines that thicken the blood and juices, incrassatives, pycnotics.

THICKET. s. Brake, holt, hoult.

THICKNESS. s. Crassitude, spissitude.

THIEF. s. Cutpurse, filcher, laron, lurcher;

ses article a thief steals, meinour or meinour; thief, parenticide, from *pere* a purse, and *cede*, to cut; thief, picaroon, picker, piqueerer.

THIEVE. *v.* To purloin.

THIEVISH. *a.* Light-fingered; goddess of thieves, Laverna.

THIEVISHNESS. *s.* Furacity.

THIGH. *s.* Of or belonging to the thigh, femoral; machine for placing a broken thigh in, solea.

THIN. *a.* Aqueous, dispersed, flimsy, gaunt, meagre, ichorous, lank, leasy, macilent; thin (pure) subtile, subtle, tennous, tenuious, halituous; thin part of the blood serum; medicines which thin viscous humours, leptuntics; to make thin, to attenuate, to dilute, to extenuate; consisting of thin scales, foliaceous.

THINK. *v.* To cogitate, to conceive, to opine, to surmise; to think close, to muse, to ruminate; to think differently, to dissent; to think, to ponder; to think before hand, to premeditate, to presurmise; to think over again, to recogitate; I think, methinks.

THINKING. *s.* Imaginant.

THIRD. *a.* One-third part, subtriple; the performing of a thing the third time, tertiation.

THIRST. *s.* Total exemption from thirst, insitiency; an excess of thirst, polydipsia; serpent whose bite produces an unquenchable thirst, dipsas, or causus. (Quincy)

THIRSTY. *a.* Adry; very thirsty, sitibund, siticulous.

THIRTY. *a.* Belonging to the term of thirty years, tricennial.

THISTLE. *s.* Carduus, polyacantha.

THONGS. *s.* Thongs of leather, laines, leashes.

THORNS. *s.* Bearing thorns, spiniferous.

THORNY. *a.* Spinous.

THOUGHT. *s.* Conception, excogitation, device; want of thought, absence, incogitancy, insensate; deep thought, farfetched, brown study; previous thought, precogitation, preconception; thought of before hand, propense, premeditated.

THOUGHTFUL. *a.* Cogitable, considerate, contemplative, meditabund, pensive, wistful, cogitabund.

THOUGHTLESS. *a.* Brainless, hightytighty, conceitless, artless, improvident, inconsiderate, insensate, incogitable, incogitant.

THOUSAND. *a.* Chiliad; figure of a thousand sides, chiliaedron; consisting of a thousand, millenary or millesimal; one who holds that Christ will reign a thousand years on earth, chiliast, millenarian; the number of ten thousand,

myriad; commander of ten thousand men, myriarch, chiliarch.

THRALDOM. *s.* Servitude.

THRASH. *v.* To thwack. (See to beat.)

THREADS. *s.* Consisting of threads, filaceous; slender thread, filament; lock of thread or hair, fleak; thread-bare, napless; a certain length of thread, skain, skein; untwisted thread, sleave; to part into threads, to sley or sleave.

THREAT. *s.* Intermination, menace, bravado, commination, denouncement, denunciation.

THREATEN. *v.* To hector, to deter.

THREATENING. *s.* Of or belonging to threatenings, comminatory; threatening danger, imminent, impendence; threatening harshly, minacious, minatory; threatening, minacity.

THREE. *a.* The number of three, ternary, ternion; having or possessing three, trigeminous; a division into three equal parts, tripartition, trichotomy; having three fangs or prongs, tridental; having three grains or kernels, tricoccous; having three horns, tricornigerous; having three bodies, tricorporal; of three days continuance, triduan; of three years continuance, triennial; the having three husbands or three wives, trigamy; having three sides, trilateral; discourse of three parts, trilogy; of or belonging to the number three, trine; of or belonging to three nights, trinoctial; three names or terms, trinomial; musical composition of three parts, trio; divided into three parts, tripartite; three feet in length, width, or depth, tripedal; consisting of three leaves, tripetalous, tryphillous; three-footed stool or standard, tripod, tripos; three-cornered figure, triquetra; division into three parts, trisection; any piece of machinery worked by three pullies, trispast; pike or weapon with three points, trisulc; having three syllables, trisyllable; doctrine of three Gods in the Trinity, Tritheism; any thing supported by three feet, trivet; office of three men in equal authority, triumvirate. (See One, Two, Four, &c.)

THREEFOLD. *a.* Tergeminous, ternary, trible, trifarious; the quality of being threefold, triplicity.

THRESHOLD. *s.* Threshold of a door, groundsel or groundsil.

THRIFTY. *a.* Economical.

THROAT. *s.* Gullet; belonging to the throat, guttural, jugular; of or belonging to the throat, bronchial; to cut the throat, to jugulate; medicine for washing the throat, gargarism, or gargle;

Y

that operation where the fore and upper part of the wind-pipe is divided, to assist respiration, during the time that large tumours are upon the upper parts of the throat, as in quinsey, &c. laryngotomy; dangerous inflammation of the throat, quinsy or squinancy.

THRONE. s. Time a throne is vacant, interregnum, interreign; throne or seat of a bishop within the chancel, faldistroy.

THROW. v. To throw down, to precipitate, to dilapidate; to throw open, to disafforest; to throw out unlawfully, to disseize; to throw out, to egest, to eject, to reject, to endew, to project; to throw, to ejaculate, to elance; to throw off, to extrude; to throw into the stomach, to ingest; to throw up, to puke; to throw back (to return an answer) to retort; to throw back as water stopped in its course, to regurgitate; to throw one headlong on iron spikes from a high place, as is practised in Turkey on malefactors, to ganch or gaunch.

THROW. s. Throw or throe, anguish of childbearing.

THROWING. p. Act of throwing a missive weapon, jaculation.

THROWN. p. That may be thrown, missile, missive trajectile.

THRUMS. s. Mockadoes.

THRUST. v. To scruse, to protrude; to thrust away from, to abstrude; to thrust off, to extrude; to thrust into by force, to obtrude.

THRUST. s. Passade or passado, tierce, tilt; thrust, stoccado, longe, allonge; a thrust back, retrase.

THRUSTING. p. Act of thrusting forwards, trusion.

THUMB. s. Pollex.

THUMP. v. To belabour.

THUMP. s. Bang. (See Blow.)

THUNDER. s. To make a noise like thunder, to fulminate; discourse on thunder, brontology.

THUNDERING. p. Thundering or blasting with lightning, fouldring.

THURSDAY. s. Thursday next before Easter, Maunday-Thursday.

TICKLE. v. To titillate.

TIDE. s. One rising above another, eagre; backward motion of the tide, ebb; recess or ebb of the tide, ampotis; ebbing and flowing of the tide, estuation; a place where the tide works up, fleta; low tide or slack tide, neap tide; islets or banks formed by the tides, alluvia, L.

TIE. v. To mancipate, to coss; to tie together, to band, to connect, to constringe, to fagot; to tie again, to renodate; to tie the feet close together, to hopple.

TIE. s. Tie or band, ligature; tie or shackle, syndesmus; any thing which ties or connects the parts of a body, ligament.

TIEING. p. Alligation, constriction, ligation; act of tieing up with a bandage, fasciation; a tieing back, religation.

TIGHTEN. v. To brace.

TIGHTNESS. s. Tenseness, tension.

TILE. s. Large sort of tile, pantile or pentile; covered with tiles, imbricated.

TILLAGE. s. Agriculture. (See Ground.)

TILL. v. To ear.

TIME. s. Time-measurer, chronometer, chronoscope; time-piece, horologe; art of measuring time by hours, horometry; art of accounting or reckoning of time, horography or horologiography; instrument for measuring time by means of water, clepsydra; error of calculating time, anachronism; a setting down things before the real time they happened, prochronism; happening of events at the same time, synchronism; the science teaching how to compute the time from the creation, &c. for the use of history, chronology; time inserted, embolism; period of time to date from, epocha, era; time between any two events, interlapse; performed in equal times, isochrone; length of time, diuturnity or diuternity; belonging to this present time, hodiernal; change of time, air, or symptoms (among physicians) metabole; done in time, tempestive, timeously; out of time, intempestive.

TIMELY. a. Tidy.

TIN. s. Ore of tin, calamine; tin (among chymists) Jupiter; tin-works or mines, stannaries.

TINNED. a. Tinned iron, latten or lattin.

TINGE. v. To colour, to suffuse, to imbue; to tinge red, to incarnadine.

TINCTURE. v. To impregnate, to perfuse; to tincture deep, to imbue.

TINGLE. v. (To quiver) to thrill.

TIRE. v. To defatigate, to jade.

TIRED. p. Not to be tired, indefatigable, infatigable.

TIRESOME. a. Irksome, prolix, prolixious.

TIPSY. a. Maudlin.

TITHES. s. Dismes; to take or value tithes, to addecimate; exempt from tithes, indecimable; a receiving tithes, in kind, pernancy; one who is an enemy to tithes, adecat.st.

TITLE. s. Appellation; ancient title, munition; to confer a title to dub; possessing only a title, titular, titulary; title at the top of a leaf, protocol; method practised with books having a bad sale, of giving them a new but different title, is termed; *quacking of titles*.

TOAST. *s.* Briadice.

TOBACCO. *s.* Tobacco that is stinking, mundungus; sort of tobacco sent from Portugal to France by John Nicot, in 1560, Nicotain; tobacco from South America, Oronoko or Oranoko, so named from the great river of that name.

TOES. *s.* The great toe, pollex (Quincy); toes of a hawk, pettysinglers.

TOIL. *v.* To mail, to plod, to tew, to turmoil; relief from toil, respiration.

TOILET. *s.* Lady's toilet, levee.

TOILSOME. *a.* Penile.

TOKEN. *s.* Prognostic, recognizance, characteristic, emblem, symptom, indication, omen, token, oeilad; token of ill, portent.

TOLD. *p.* Depicted; that may be told, narrable, effable, predicable; that may not be told, ineffable, inenarrable.

TOLERABLE. *a.* Mandible, patible.

TOLL. *s.* Impost, hedagium; toll man, thelonianouse, (old law term.)

TOMB. *s.* Sepulchre; tomb, empty one set up in honour of the dead, cenotaphium or cenotaph; inscription on a tomb, epitaph.

TONE. *s.* Uniformity of tone, monotony; half tone, semitone.

TONGUE. *s.* Uttered jointly by the tongue and teeth, linguadental; tongue (speech) lingo; tongue-tied, elinguid; one who is tongue-tied, ancyloglossus.

TOOL. *s.* One employed as a tool to bring about a business, stalking-horse.

TOOLS. *s.* Apparatus, implements.

TOOTH. *s.* (See Teeth.)

TOOTHACH. *s.* Odontalgia, dentagra; belonging to the toothach, odontalgic; medicines for the toothach, odontics; stony concretions that form on a tooth, odontolithes.

TOP. *ad.* Acme, apex, vertex, summit; belonging to the top of the head, coronal; to take off the top off any thing, to decacuminate.

TOPSY-TURVY. *ad.* Arse-versy, or arsy-versy.

TORCH. *s.* Lighted torch, flambeau, link, tead or tede; boy who lights passengers, link-boy.

TORMENT. *v.* To excruciate; to hag.

TORMENT. *s.* Torsion.

TORMENTERS. *s.* Tormenters of guilty consciences are termed, Dirae; and such are the furies, Megara, Alecto, and Tisiphone.

TORMENTING. *p.* One who is possessed with that idiosyncrasy or peculiar turn of mind, by which he is constantly tormenting himself, heautontimorumenos.

TORN. *p.* Torn away, erased, disrupt; torn, that may be torn in pieces, discerptible; that cannot be torn, illacerable, indiscerptible.

TORTOISE. *s.* Relating to a tortoise, testudinous.

TORTURE. *v.* To contort, to cruciate, to excruciate.

TOSS. *v.* To betoss, to touze.

TOSSED. *p.* Tossed about, amphibolous; tossed by the waves, fluctivagous.

TOSSING. *p.* Tossing motion, jactitation. (See Restlessness.)

TOTAL. *a.* Versal, aggregate, oecumenical, plenary.

TOUCH. *v.* To continge; to touch lightly, to perstringe, to attinge; to touch by way of signal, to bob.

TOUCH. *s.* Contact; imperceptible to or by the touch, impalpable, intactible.

TOUCHED. *p.* That may be touched, tactile, tangible.

TOUCHING. *a.* Adjoining; touching, pertingent, attiguous; a touching softly, palpation.

TOUGH. *a.* Cartilaginous, findy, mucilaginous, ropy, sclerotic, sequacious, sizy, depectible.

TOWER. *s.* Barbacon; watch-tower, pharos.

TOY. *v.* To faddle.

TOY. *s.* Gaudery, gewgaw, jiggum-bob, whim-wham, trangram. (See Trifle.)

TRACE. *v.* To investigate, to vestigate.

TRACING. *p.* Act of tracing, vestigation.

TRACE. *s.* Vestige.

TRACK. *s.* Track of a buck, fusee; track, lead; track of a wheel, orbit; track, to follow by the track, to vestigate.

TRADE. *v.* To negociate, to chaffer.

TRADE. *s.* Calling, chaffery, commerce, function, mercat, mercature; one who engrosses a trade to himself; monopolist; jack of all trades, alpheg, factotum.

TRADING. *p.* Mercantile.

TRAFFIC. *s.* Chaffery, commerce, mercht, mart, mercature.

TRAIN. *v.* To train (teach) to indoctrinate, to nurture; train of consequences, consecution; solemn train of persons, procession, retinue, attendance.

TRAITOR. *s.* Betrayer, infidel, proditor.

TRAMPLE. *v.* To exculcate, to deculcate.

TRAMPLING. *p.* Act of trampling upon, occultation, proculcation.

TRANQUILLITY. *s.* Tranquillity of mind, ataraxy or ataroxia.

TRANSFER. *v.* To alien, to assign, to consign.

TRANSFORM. *v.* To transmew.

TRANSLATION. *s.* Translation of a natural body from one place to another in a right line (among philosophers) lation metastasis; literal translation, metaphrase; translation, traduction; belonging to a translation, tralatitious.

TRANSLATIVE. *a.* Metaleptic.

TRANSLATOR. *s.* Metaphrast.

TRANSMIGRATION. *s.* Transmigration of souls, metemsychosis.

TRANSPARENCY. *s.* Diaphaneity.

TRANSPARENT. *a.* Limpid, luculent, pellucid, relucent, tralacent, tralucid, translucid, translucent, transpicuous; half transparent, diaphanous, semitransparent, semidiaphanous; not transparent, undiaphanous.

TRANSPORT. *v.* To transport with delight, to inwrap.

TRANSPOSITION. *s.* Metathesis; transposition of letters, anagram (which see in Johnson.)

TRANSVERSE. *a.* Metaleptic, as the *metaleptic motion* of a muscle, (Anat.)

TRAP. *v.* To illaqueate, to induce.

TRAP. *s.* Engle, gin.

TRAVEL. *v.* To travel about, to peragrate; to travel into far countries, to peregrinate.

TRAVAILING. *p.* Travelling or travelling (being in labour) parturient.

TRAVELLING. *p.* List of stages in travelling, gest; travelling, itinerant; the science of travelling, oditology (Kotzebue.)

TRAVELS. *s.* Book of travels, itinerary; of or belonging to travels, viatic.

TREACHEROUS. *a.* Insidious, deceitful, perfidious, proditorious, punic.

TREACHERY. *s.* Duplicity, gullery, infidelity, prodition.

TREACLE. *s.* Molosses or molasses; of or belonging to treacle, theriacal.

TREAD. *v.* To tread under foot, to conculcate, to deculcate, to exculcate.

TREASON. *s.* Prodition; concerted treason, conspiracy.

TREASURE. *s.* Finance; secret treasure, hoard; to lay up treasure, to thesaurise.

TREASURER. *s.* Treasurer of a college, bursar.

TREASURY. *s.* Hanaper, repertory.

TREAT. *v.* (To entertain) to juncate; to treat with, to regale, to negotiate; to treat with contempt, to disparage.

TREAT. *s.* Banquet, repasture, regalio.

TREATISE. *s.* Dissertation, syntagma, tractate; treatise on medicine, dispensary; treatise concerning the plague, limology; treatise concerning the art of preparing medicines, pharmacology; treatise on opium, meconology; treatise on the method of drawing schemes, troposchematology; treatise concerning the mind or soul, psychology; treatise on customs and manners, ethology; treatise on fevers, pyretology; treatise on diseases, nosology; treatise on flowers, antholy; treatise concerning the entrails of the human body, splanchnology; treatise on evil spirits or devils, daemonology; treatise on trees, dendrology; treatise on living animals, zoology; treatise on the glands, adenography; on the bowels, enterology; on the veins, arteries, &c. angiology; on eruptive fevers, exanthematologia; treatise on sentiment, gnomology. (See Description.)

TREATY. *s.* Oral treaty, parle or parley.

TREES. *s.* Discourse concerning trees, dendrology; belonging to trees, arborary, arboreous, arborous; arm of a tree, bough; wood of low trees, coppice; trees kept low by cutting, dottard, pollard; trees planted against a wall, so as to touch each other, espaliers; divination by writing on the bark of a tree, sycomancy; the act of pruning trees, sarculation; branches of trees, ramage; blasting of trees by an east wind, sideration; syderation; trees reserved at the felling of wood for the growth of large timber, standels, standils, standards; the clearing of a tree from moss, emuscation; prospect through trees, visto, vista; mode of fencing trees with earth, tumping; a disease in which trees lose their bark, defluvium; an excrescence like mushrooms on some trees, agaric or agaricon; graft stuck into the clefts of trees, enthemata.

TREMBLE. *v.* To quake, to quiver, to quappe.

TREMBLING. *p.* Tremulous, quivering; trembling with fear, trepid; trembling or shaking as in an ague, tremor; state of trembling, trepidation; trembling with the deprivation of the voluntary motion of the senses, tromoosis, tromma.

TRENCH. *s.* Trench round a place, circumvallation; encompassing with a trench, obvallation.

TRIAL. *s.* Adventure, assay, bout, attempt, essay, test, exploration, probation, tentation, tentative; trial ordeal or ordeal, of which there were four particular ways that persons accused of crimes were to clear themselves, viz: Ordeal by combat, by fire, by cold water, and by warm water; trial of skill, agonism; of or belonging to a trial, judicial.

TRIANGLE. *s.* Trigon; having two of the sides or legs equal, isosceles; having three acute angles, oxygon; having all its sides unequal to each other, scalenous; act of measuring triangles, trigonometry; the two legs of a right-angled triangle, containing the right angle, are termed, tuchical or trigonum ; the longest side of a right-angled triangle, hypothenuse ; right-angled triangle, orthogon. (See Figure.)

TRIANGULAR. *a.* Any triangular figure triquetra.

TRIBE. *s.* Horde. (See Clan.)

TRIBLE. *s.* Tergeminous.

TRICK. *v.* To dodge, to dupe, to jockey, to cozen, to fub, to gull, to shark.

TRICK. *s.* Device, finesse, artifice, stratagem, gimcrack, bite, evasion, feat, fourbe, juggle, legerdemain, malversation, gambol, deception, hocus-pocus, imposture, stratagem, subterfuge, tach or tache, trangram ; relating to tricks, gestic.

TRICKER. *s.* Trickster, hiccius-doccius, hocus-pocus, fourbe.

TRIFLE. *v.* To dally, to dandle, to fribble, to fuddle, to fettle, to palter, to piddle.

TRIFLE. *s.* Ado, kickshaw, whimwham, bagatelle, gewgaw, fingle fangle, jiggumbob, impertinence ; trifles, trumpery.

TRIFLER. *s.* Doodle, nincompoop.

TRIFLING. *p.* Gewgaw, jejune, inconsistent, importless, inept, nugatory, airy, exile, fingle-fangle, frivolous, futile, peddling, minute, tidly-valley, puerile, trivial ; trifling talk, nugacity, nugality.

TRIM. *v.* To decorate, to dizen, to embellish, to preen, to prain, to prune, to dight.

TRIMMING. *p.* Trimming of old things, mangonism.

TRINKET. *s.* Jiggum-bob. (See Trifle.)

TRINITY. *s.* Trinity, triad ; the subsistence of the three persons of the Trinity, hypostasis ; one who denies the Trinity, Antitrinitarian.

TRIUMPH. *v.* To exult, to gaude, to glory.

TRIUMPH. *s.* Palm ; uttering songs of triumph, jubilant ; the lesser kind of triumph, ovation.

TRIUMPHAL. *a.* Triumphal song, curule, epinicion.

TRIUMPHANTLY. *ad.* Triumphantly mounted, cock-horse.

TRIUMPHING. *p.* Insulture.

TROOP. *s.* Belonging to a troop, agminal ; troops of horse, cavalry ; to range troops for battle, to darrain.

TROTTING. *p.* (Jolting) succussion, succussation.

TROUBLE. *s.* Trouble or bustle, ado, discommodity, disquiet ; full of trouble, aerumnous, incommodity, intranquillity, thraldom, comber ; full of trouble, operose, solicitous ; unnecessary trouble, periergy ; to involve one's self in trouble, to fall into or incur a premunire ; trouble and affliction, thlipsis, tribulation, turmoil.

TROUBLESOME. *a.* Cumbersome, importune, irksome, plaguy.

TROUGH. *s.* Trough used by plasterers, bricklayers, &c. for carrying lime on the shoulder, hod.

TRUCE. *s.* Armistice ; belonging to a truce, induciary.

TRUE. *a.* Extradictionary, irrefragable, incontestable, uncontrovertible, uncontestible, categorical, orthodox, stanch, veracious, veritable ; to prove any thing true, to verificate ; very true, undefeasible.

TRULY. *ad.* De facto, *L.* infallibly, logically, actually, forsooth, intrinsically, categorically, cordially.

TRUMPET. *v.* To tubicinate ; to blow a trumpet, to buccinate.

TRUMPET. *s.* Clarion ; speaking trumpet, stentorophonictube ; blast or lesson ou the trumpet, levet.

TRUNK. *s.* Trunk of an elephant, proboscis.

TRUST. *v.* To confide in, to desponsate ; to betrust ; to trust in the hands of another to deposite.

TRUST. *s.* Reliance, affiance, commission.

TRUSTY. *a.* Fiducial, fiduciary, liege.

TRUTH. *s.* Verity, veracity ; telling the truth, veridical ; a speaking of truth, veriloquy ; observant of the truth, veracious ; undoubted truth, truism.

TRY. *v.* To assay or essay, to explorate, to explore, to probe ; to try exactly, to perpend.

TRYING. *p.* Tentative. (See Trial.)

TUBE. *s.* Bent tube used in drawing off liquors, siphon, syphon, crane.

TUFT. *s.* Dallop, clump. (See Heap.)

TUG. *v.* To tew. (See Pull.)

TUMBLING. *p.* Act of volutation.

TUMULT. *s.* Padder, romage, sedition, turbulency, garboil, hubbub, hurly-burly, misrule, affray, broil, bustle, combustion, coil, fuss ; to make a tumult, to deray ; exciter of tumult, incendiary ; tumult in the night, night-rule ; tumult, commotion, confusion, faction.

TUNE. *v.* To accord. (See Agree.)

TUNEFUL. *a.* Canorous. (See Agreeable.)

TURF. *s.* Glebe ; the privilege of digging turf, turbary ; of or belonging to turf, glebous, gleby.

TURGID. *a.* Bloated, burly, tumid, caricous.

TURN. *v.* To convert, to convolve ; to turn as milk among an acid, to posset ; to turn back, to retrogade ; to turn or wind, to sinuate ; to turn aside, to tralineate, to traverse ; to turn aside, to avert, to deflect, to intort, to wind ; to turn round, to circinate ; to turn from the subject, to digress; to turn or bend, to inflect; to act by turns, to reciprocate; to turn out, to degrade; to turn often in a course, to laveer; to turn upwards, to obvert; to turn or fold round about, to obvolve.

TURN. *s.* (Bout) veney, turnstile, tournequet; turn, creek, flexion or flexure, gipe, or gyre; turn of a rope or cable, fake; one of a peculiar turn of mind, genio.

TURNED. *p.* That may be turned, vertible; turned backwards, anacamptic, (said of echoes.)

TURNING. *p.* Turning aside, diversion; turning up the ground, fodient; act of turning round, gyration, rotation; a turning back of humours, revulsion; the art of turning in a lathe, toreutice; the power of turning, verticity; turning round, vertiginous, versatile; consisting of four turnings, quadrivial; full of turnings and windings, amfractuous, anfractuous.

TURPENTINE. *s.* Mixt with, or like turpentine, terebinthine.

TWEEZERS. *s.* Volsella, vulsella.

TWELFTH. *a.* Containing one twelfth part, dodecatemorion, or dodecatemoron.

TWELVE. *a.* Consisting of twelve, duodecuple; the twelve signs of the zodiac, dodecatemary; twelve-sided figure, dodecaedron, or dodecagon; book of twelve leaves to a sheet, duodecimo; twelve dozen, gross. (See One, Two, Four, &c.)

TWENTIETH. *s.* Vigesimal; a custom among the Romans, in which every twentieth man was put to death, vigesimation.

TWENTY. *a.* Of or belonging to twenty, vicenary.

TWICE. *a.* Twice told, bifarious, bifold.

TWIG. *s.* Scion, surcle; of or belonging to twigs, viminal; made up of twigs, vimineous; full of twigs, sarmentous.

TWILIGHT. *s.* Crepuscle.

TWINS. *s.* Gemini, didymoi, or didymi.

TWINED. *p.* Tortile, tortive.

TWINKLE. *v.* To Nictate.

TWINKLING. *p.* Twinkling with the eye, connictation.

TWIST. *v.* To contort, to crisp, to intort, to wreathe.

TWIST. *s.* Lock of twist or hair, flesk.

TWISTED. *p.* Helical or helical, tortile, tortive, tortuous, turbinated.

TWISTING. *p.* Twisting of the guts, vermiculation.

TWO. *a.* Two in gaming, deuce, doublet; belonging to two, binarian, binarious, binary, bimarical; having two parts or terms, binominal; two names, binominous; two verses, distich; divided into parts, bipartite; words of two syllables, disyllable; belonging or denoting two, dual; having two heads, bicipital or bicipitous; two bodies, bicorporal; two teeth, bidental; two feet, bipedal, &c. (See One, Three, Four, &c.)

TYPE. *s.* (Resemblance or representation) antitype; set of types for printing, font; the types used in printing are the following: 1. French Canon. 2. Two lines Double Pica. 3. Two lines Great Primer. 4. Two lines English. 5. Two lines Pica. 6. Double Pica. 7. Paragon. 8. Great Primer. 9. English. 10. Pica. 11. Small Pica. 12. Long Primer. 13. Bourgeois. 14. Brevier. 15. Minion. 16. Nonpareil. 17. Pearl: And, 18. Diamond.

TYPICAL. *a.* Metaphorical.

TYRANNY. *s.* Arbitrariness, domination. (See Power.)

U

UGLY. *a.* Evil-favoured, ill-favoured, haggard, inform; any thing ugly and hideous, Gorgon; ugly old woman, hag; ugly-faced, hatchet faced.

ULCER. *s.* Virulent ulcer, cancer, chancre; act of the regeneration of flesh in an ulcer, granulation; term given to ulcers which are of difficult cure, dysepulotica; epithet given to such persons whose ulcers are difficult to heal, dyselchia, or dyselches; lint put into a wound or ulcer, turunda, dosil; ulcerous, chancrous, (Wiseman.)

UMBRELLA. *s.* Umbrella to keep off the sun, parasol, F.; to keep off the rain, parapluye, F.

UNACCUSTOMED. *a.* Insolite.

UNAFFECTED. *a.* Impregnable, (Johnson.)

UNAFFECTING. *a.* Jejune.

UNANIMOUS. *a.* Unanimous voice; Latin term in Parliament when any matter is carried with universal assent, *nemine contradicente*, generally contracted *nem. con.*

UNAVOIDABLE. *a.* Avoidless, inevitable, unevitable.

UNBAR. *v.* To unbar, to reclude. (See Bar.)

UNBECOMING. *a.* Indecorous, indign, misbecoming.

UNBELIEVER. *s.* Infidel, miscreant.

UNBEGOTTEN. *a.* Ingenerated, innate, ungenerated.

UNBLAMABLE. *a.* Inculpable, unculpable.

UNBODIED. *a.* Intelligential.

UNBLUNTED. *a.* (Determined) unrebated, (Hakew.)

UNBOUNDED. *a.* Interminable, interminate. (See Endless.)

UNBOUNDEDNESS. *s.* Immensity, infinitude.

UNBROKEN. *a.* Integral, inviolate, unviolated.

UNBURIED. *a.* Inhumated, intumulated.

UNCEASING. *a.* Incessant.

UNCERTAIN. *a.* Irresolute, amphibological, variant, contingent, equivocal, ambiguous, erratic, flexuous, fortuitous, vague, fugitive, precarious, problematical; uncertain case, moot case; speech of uncertain meaning, ambilogy.

UNCERTAINLY. *ad.* Hesitancy, incertitude, lubricity.

UNCERTAINTY. *s.* Ambiguity, quandary, vacillation, incertitude, suspense.

UNCHASTE. *a.* Lecherous, ruttish, bawdy, jadish, incontinent, libidinous, salacious.

UNCHASTITY. *s.* Incontinence.

UNCIVIL. *a.* Uncourteous; uncivil turbulent fellow, rudesby, macaroon.

UNCIVILIZED. *a.* Barbarian, uncivil, inurbane, discourteous, disgracious, disrespectful, impolite, unpolite.

UNCLEAN. *v.* To make unclean, (to defile) to turpify.

UNCLE. *s.* Eam or eme.

UNCOMELY. *a.* Uncomely likeness, caricature, anamorphosis.

UNCOMMONNESS. *s.* Infrequency, unfrequency.

UNCOMPOUNDED. *a.* Incomposite.

UNCONFINED. *a.* Latitudinarian.

UNCONNECTED. *a.* Incoherent, irrelative, rigmarole.

UNCONQUERABLE. *a.* Insuperable.

UNCONSTANT. *a.* Remuable.

UNCONSUMABLE. *a.* Incremable, incombustible, asbestine.

UNCOVER. *v.* To disvelop, to develope.

UNCOUTH. *a.* Gothic, inform.

UNCULTIVATED. *a.* Boorish, incult.

UNCTUOUS. *a.* Adipose, balsamic. (See Fat, Greasy, Clammy.)

UNDEFILED. *a.* Immaculate, intemerate.

UNDER. *ad.* Placed under, subjacent.

UNDERGOING. *s.* An undergoing, perpession.

UNDERMINE. *v.* To sap, to subvert, to supplant.

UNDERMINING. *p.* An undermining, suffossion.

UNDERSTAND. *v.* To comprehend, to penetrate; able to understand, intellective.

UNDERSTANDING. *s.* Maturity, brain, intellect, intelligence; quickness of understanding, sagacity; failing in the understanding, moria, (with physicians.)

UNDERTAKER. *s.* Pollinctor.

UNDERSTOOD. *p.* That may be understood, deprehensible.

UNDERVALUE. *v.* To depreciate, to vilify, to debase, to postpone.

UNDESERVING. *a.* Indign.

UNDIGESTED. *a.* Ichorous, unconcocted.

UNDISTINGUISHABLE. *a.* Indiscriminate.

UNDISTURBED. *a.* Sedate.

UNDO. *v.* To feaze.

UNDRESS. *v.* To disrobe, to doff.

UNDRESS. *s.* Dishabille.

UNDULATING. *p.* Undulating like a flash of lightning, crispisulcant.

UNEASINESS. *s.* Tribulation, turmoil.

UNEASY. *a.* Homefelt, perturbid, plaintful, solicitous; to make uneasy, to concern, to discomfort, to disquiet.

UNEQUAL. *a.* Inequable, or unequable; unequal pulse, cymatodes; triangle composed of unequal sides, scalene or scalenous.

UNEQUALLED. *a.* Unparagoned.

UNEQUALLY. *ad.* Anomalously, disproportionately, inadequately.

UNEVEN. *a.* Acanacious, prickly, inequable, asper, aifform, salebrous, anomalous.

UNEVENNESS. *s.* Imparity, salebrity, imparility.

UNEXPECTED. *a.* After clap, inopinate, subitaneous.

UNEXPECTEDLY. *ad.* Superadvenient, unawares.

UNFADED. *a.* Virent.

UNFADING. *a.* Immarcessible.

UNFAILING. *a.* Indefectible.

UNFAIR. *a.* Insiduous, sinister, uningenuous, disingenuous.

UNFAITHFUL. *a.* Infidious.

UNFAVOURABLE. *a.* Malign, averse, disgracious, inauspicious.

UNFEATHERED. *a.* Callow, deplumated.

UNFERMENTED. *a.* Azimous.

UNFINISHED. *a.* In embryo.

UNFIT. *a.* Disallowable, disproportionate; illicit, incommodious, inadequate, incompetent, inept, inapplicable, inapposite, incapacitated ; to make unfit, to disqualify : unfit to be desired, ineptable.

UNFITLY. *ad.* Inadequately, incompatibly, incompetibly.

UNFLEDGED. *a.* Callow.

UNFOLD. *v.* To decypher, to develop or disvelop, to evolve, to explicate, to interpret, to enucleate.

UNFORTUNATE. *a.* Adverse, disastrous, inauspicious, infortunate, luckless, misadventured, sinister.

UNFRUITFUL. *a.* Infecund, infertile, sterile, infructuose, teemless, unfertile.

UNGODLY. *a.* Irreligious.

UNGRATEFUL. *a.* Ingrate.

UNGUARDED. *a.* Unchary.

UNHANDSOME. *a.* Maladroit.

UNHANDY. *a.* Aukward, clumsy, inexpert, unexpert.

UNHAPPINESS. *s.* Infelicity.

UNHAPPY. *a.* Luckless, improsperous, unblest ; unhappy conclusion, catastrophe.

UNHEALTHY. *a.* Insalubrious.

UNIFORM. *a.* Equable, homotonous.

UNHURT. *a.* Inviolate or unviolated ; to maintain unhurt, to indemnify.

UNINJURED. *a.* Inviolate, unviolated.

UNION. *s.* Accord, admixion, or admixtion, adunation, agglutination, brotherhood, coalescence, cohesion, communion, catenation, concatenation, concrescence, junction, coalition, juncture, inosculation, confederacy, conjugation, conjunction, connexion, contact, convention ; union by marriage, &c. alliance ; union of the sexes, coition ; union of circumstances, conjuncture ; union of two against one, syncratism ; without union, inconnexedly, unconnected

UNITE. *v.* To accord, to adjoin, to adjugate, to affix, to immix, to immingle, to inosculate, to ally, to cabal, to cleave, to combine, to confederate, to band, to cement, to coalesce, to compact, to conglutinate, to congree, to conjoin, to conjugate, to incorporate, to incorpse, to connect, to consociate, to consolidate ; to unite as male and female, to copulate; to unite in any office, to colleague ; to unite in one substance, to consubstantiate, to contex.

UNITED. *p.* Federate, conjunct ; united help, coadjuvancy.

UNITING. *p.* Uniting of rays, corradiation ; act or power of uniting, unition.

UNITY. *s.* Monad or monade.

UNIVERSAL. *a.* Versal, epidemical, catholic, oecumenical ; universal disease, *morbus pandemius*, L. ; universal wisdom or knowledge, pansophy, perspicience ; universal conception of things, transcen-

dentals ; universal medicine, catholicon, or diacatholicon ; universal dissolvent, ignisaqua, alkahest, ignisgehennæ.

UNIVERSE *s.* Macrocosm, mc scosm, mond.

UNIVERSITY. *s.* Relating to an university, academical ; notification of some speech or ceremony to be performed in an university, programma ; university of Oxford ; a scholar in this university appointed to make jesting and satyrical speeches, is called, *Terræ filius*; the form of expelling a member from the university, *bannimus.*

UNJUST. *a.* Partial, sinister, illegal, iniquitous, injurious.

UNKIND. *a.* Bowelless, disgracious, invidious, ungenial.

UNKNOWN. *a.* Occult.

UNLEARNED. *a.* Illiterate, unlettered.

UNLEAVENED. *a.* Azimous.

UNLIKE. *a.* Disparate, dissimilar, heterogeneous, diverse, extraneous.

UNLIKELY. *ad.* Unplausibly.

UNLIKENESS. *s.* Disparity.

UNLIMITED. *a.* Indefinite, undefined, indeterminate, undeterminate, discretionary, illimitable, immense, inconditionate, inconditional, unconditional, latitudinarian ; unlimited state or quantity, indefinitude.

UNLOAD. *v.* To exonerate, to desarcinate. (Bailey)

UNLOCK. *v.* To reclude.

UNLOCKING *p.* An unlocking, reseration.

UNLOOSED. *a.* Not to be unloosed, inenodable.

UNLUCKY. *a.* Funereal, inauspicious, infaustous ; act of making unlucky, infausting, (Bacon.)

UNMAN. *v.* To effeminate, to emasculate, to evirate, to castrate, to geld.

UNMANLY. *a.* Unmanly delicacy, effeminacy.

UNMANAGEABLE. *a.* Intractable, untractable.

UNMANNERLY. *a.* Rustical.

UNMARRIED. *a.* Unmarried state, celibacy.

UNMATCHED. *a.* Unparagoned.

UNMEANING. *a.* Vague.

UNMERCIFUL. *a.* Inclement, relentless, remorseless.

UNMOVEABLENESS. *s.* Immobility, impregnability.

UNMOVED. *a.* (Careless) reckless.

UNMUSICAL. *a.* Immusical, inharmonious.

UNNATURAL. *a.* Adventitious, affected, grotesque, insitive, preposterous, ungenial.

UNNECESSARY. *a.* Superfluous, supervataneous ; unnecessary caution or trouble in an operation, periergy.

UNPASSABLE. *a.* Impervious, impertransible.

UNPATRIOTIC. *a.* Ineivic.

UNPITYING. *a.* Relentless.

UNPLEASANT. *a.* Infestive, injocund, illepid, injucund.

UNPLEASANTNESS. *s.* Insuavity.

UNPOLISHED. *a.* Inurbane ; unpolished, (rugged) scabrous.

UNPOLITE. *a.* Discourteous, impolite, uncourteous.

UNPOLLUTED. *a.* Immaculate, intemerate.

UNPRACTISED. *a.* Initiate, (Shakesp.)

UNPREJUDICED. *a.* Imprejudicate, unprejudicate.

UNPREPARED. *a.* Inconcocted, unconcocted.

UNPROFITABLE. *a.* Supervacaneous, bootless, frustraneous, inutile.

UNQUIET. *a.* Anxious, intranquil.

UNRAVEL. *v.* To decypher, to develop, to disentangle, to disvelop.

UNREASONABLE. *a.* Absonant, or absonous, absurd, exorbitant ; unreasonable zeal, bigotry.

UNREASONABLENESS. *s.* Alogy.

UNRESOLVED. *a.* Irresolute.

UNRESTRAINED. *a.* Latitudinarian.

UNRIPE. *a.* Cunde, immature, inconcocted, unconcocted.

UNRULY. *a.* Misadventured, heady, jadish, refractory, sinister, waiward.

UNSAFE. *a.* Insecure, unsecure.

UNSALEABLE. *a.* Invendible.

UNSEASONALE. *a.* Importune, inopportune, intempestive.

UNSEARCHABLE *a.* Inscrutable, impervestigable.

UNSETTLED. *a.* Mutable, pending, vagous.

UNSERVICEABLE. *a.* Inutile.

UNSHAPEN. *a.* Inform.

UNSHEATHING. *p.* Evagination.

UNSKILFUL. *a.* Inexpert, unexpert.

UNSKILFULLY. *ad.* Rawly.

UNSKILFULNESS. *s.* Tyrociny.

UNSOCIALNESS. *s.* Insociableness, incomity.

UNSOCIAL. *a.* Incommunicative, inconversable, unconversable.

UNSPEAKABLE. *a.* Ineffable, immemorable.

UNSTABLE. *a.* Fugitive, volatile, labile.

UNSTEADY. *a.* Lubric, lubricous, flexuous.

UNSTEADINESS. *s.* Fugacity, volatility.

UNSTOP. *v.* To reclude.

UNSUCCESSFUL. *a.* Improsperous.

UNSUITABLE. *a.* Inapposite, incompatible, incompetible.

UNSUITABLENESS. *s.* Incongruence, incongruity, inconsistency, ineptitude, inexpedience, unexpedience.

UNSUPPORTED. *a.* Aidless.

UNTAMEABLE. *a.* Indomable.

UNTAUGHT. *a.* Illiterate, unlettered.

UNTHANKFUL. *a.* Ingrate, ungrateful.

UNTHOUGHT. *a.* Unthought of, inopinate.

UNTIMELY. *ad.* Abortive.

UNTILLED. *a.* Incult, uncultivated.

UNTIE. *v.* To renodate.

UNTIED. *p.* Not to be untied, inenodable.

UNTIRED. *a.* Indefatigable.

UNTOUCHED. *p.* Intact.

UNTRACTABLE. *a.* Intractable.

UNTRODDEN. *a.* Invious.

UNTWIST. *v.* To fease, to sley, or slease.

UNVARIABLE. *a.* Invariable.

UNUTTERABLE. *a.* Ineffable.

UNUSUAL. *a.* Infrequent, unfrequent, uncouth, insolite.

UNWARY. *a.* Incautious, uncautious, unchary.

UNWEARIED. *a.* Indefatigable ; that position of a limb which is equally distant from flexion and extension, which position the part can longest bear unwearied, acamatos, G.

UNWIELDY. *a.* Bellyed, abdominous.

UNWHOLESOME *a.* Insalubrious.

UNWISE. *a.* Injudicious.

UNWIND. *v.* To eglomerate.

UNWILLING. *a.* Averse, loath, or loth, reluctant.

UNWILLINGNESS. *s.* Nolition.

UNWORTHY. *a.* Illaudable, indign.

UPBRAID. *v.* To exprobate.

UPBRAIDING. *p.* A peculiar manner of upbraiding, tending at the same time to convince, epiplexis.

UPHOLD. *v.* To buoy.

UPPER. *a.* Attic.

UPRIGHT. *a.* Inculpable, unculpable, innocuous, irreprehensible.

UPRIGHTNESS. *s.* Rectitude.

UPROAR. *s.* Garboil, hubbub.

UPSTART. *s.* Coxcomb, skip-jack.

UPWARDS. *ad.* To lye with the face upwards, to resupinate ; act or posture of lying, &c. upwards, supinity.

URGE. *v.* To urge, to enforce, to extimulate, to excite, to incite, to goad, to impel, to inculcate ; to urge to do evil, to instigate.

URGENT. *a.* Importune, vive.

URGING. *p.* Act of urging on, instimulation.

2

URINE. *s.* Excessive discharge of urine, diabetes; what provokes urine, diuretic; difficulty of making urine, dysury, ischuria, ischury, strangury; an insensible discharge of urine, diamnes; medicines which provoke urine, ischuretics; stale urine, lotium, lie; a suppression of urine from the urethra being imperforated, aspadialis; passage of the urine, urethra; bottle for the receiving of urine in bed, urinal; sediment in urine like vetches, eroboides; urine which seems to have little leaves or scales in it, petalodes; the making of urine backwards, retromingency; examination of urine, uroscopy; a judging of diseases by the sight of urine, urocriterium, uromancy; those contents of the urine which float about in the middle, resembling a cloud, enearema; the sediment of urine, hypostasis.

USAGE. *s.* Assuetude, consuetude.

USE. *v.* To use, to adhibit, to apply; to bring into use, to inure, to habituate.

USE. *s.* Lucre, behoof, increment, practice, usance; worn out of use, obsolete, exolete; to convert to private use, to impropriate; the temporary use of a thing, usufruct; the person who has the temporary use of money, &c. usufructuary; the use of goods, &c. for a length of time, usucaption.

USEFUL. *a.* Advantageous, proficuous, subservient; a pertinent and useful observation, gnome.

USEFULLY. *ad.* Behoveable, fructuous.

USELESS. *a.* Bootless, effectless, frustraneous, fallacious, inane, ineffective, inept, inutile, teemless.

USUAL. *a.* Customary, habitual.

USURY. *s.* Feneration.

UTTER. *v.* To broach, to ejaculate, to probate.

UTTERABLE. *a.* Effable.

UTTERANCE. *s.* Elocution, prolation; power of utterance, vocality, vocalness.

UTTERED. *p.* That cannot be uttered, nefandous, ineffable; that may be uttered, effable.

V

VAGABOND. *s.* Fugitive, gipsy, landloper.

VAGRANT. *a.* Fugitive, vagous.

VAGUE. *a.* Indeterminate, lax, undeterminate.

VAIN. *a.* Lere, tumourous, ineffective, frustraneous, impracticable, unattainable, infeasible, ambitious, boastful, bootless, nugatory, ostentatious, pedantic; vain glory, kenedoxy; vain talking, vaniloquence, vaniloquy, inaniloquent, inaniloquous; vain discourse, mateology; vain science, mateotechny; vain imagination, phantasm; vain, (ostentatious in religion) pharisaical.

VALLEY. *s.* Dale, dell, dingle; valley where the Ammonites sacrificed their children to their god Moloch, and caused drums to be beat to hinder their cries from being heard, is called Tophet, which in Hebrew signifies a drum.

VALIANT. *a.* Valorous; most valiant, prowest.

VALOUR. *s.* Prowess, puissance, valor.

VALUABLENESS. *s.* Preciosity.

VALUE, *v.* To admire, to pique, to appraise, to estimate, to appreciate; to value high, to reck.

VALUE. *s.* Equal in value, equivalent; of no value, immoment, tralatitious.

VALVES. *s.* Having two valves, bivalvular; having one, univalvular.

VAN. *s.* Avantguard.

VANE. *s.* (Weathercock) triton.

VANISH. *v.* To vade.

VANISHING. *p.* Vanishing away, evanescent, evanid, ponent.

VANITY. *s.* Flatulency, (Glanville), flatuosity, levity, pageantry.

VANQUISH. *v.* To debellate.

VAPOUR. *s.* Vapor, exhalation; cool vapour, aura; to resolve into vapours, to evaporate; relating to vapour, halitous, meteorous, fumous; flying about as vapour, lambent; act of passing into vapour, vaporation.

VAPOROUS. *a.* Halituous,

VARIABLE. *a.* Variant, versatile.

VARIEGATE. *v.* To freak, to bespot, to chamblet, to dapple, to diversify.

VARIEGATED. *a.* Dædalian, dædal.

VARIETY. *s.* Diversity; having great variety, multifarious.

VARIOUS. *a.* Multiplicious, multitudinous; streaked with various colours, dædal, dapple.

VARY. *v.* To chamblet, to infleet, to revoke, to transmew.

VARYING. *p.* Heteroclitical.

VAST. *a.* Enormous, huge, immane, immense, infinite, interminable, interminate, nimious.

VAULT. v. To vault over, to concamerate, to imbow.

VAULT. s. Vaults, catacombs; a raising in the form of a vault, camarosis; vault where bones are kept, charnel-house.

VAULTED. a. Camerated.

VEGETABLES. s. That feeds on vegetables, phytivorous.

VEHEMENT. a. Fervent, fervid, impetuous, intense.

VEIL. v. To intricate.

VEINS. s. Discourse on the veins, &c. angiology; an opening the mouths of veins, exanastomosis; the inosculation or mutual joining of veins, anastomosis. (See Sarcology.)

VELLUM. s. Fine vellum made of the skin of a cast lamb or calf, abortive, (Bailey.)

VENERY. s. What incites to venery, aphrodisiacs, philters, or philtron, G.

VENT. s. Emission, spiracle, suspiral.

VENOMOUS. a. Virulent.

VENUS. s. (Relating to the rites or secrets of Venus,) thoral; the planet Venus when it rises before the sun, Lucifer.

VERBAL. a. Verbal translation, metaphrase.

VERBALLY. ad. Verbally declared, nuncupative, nuncupatory.

VERILY. ad. Actually, forsooth, defacto, L.

VERMILION. s. Cinnabar, minium; vermilion colour, minious; painted with vermilion, miniated; one who writes or paints with vermilion, miniographer.

VERMINE. s. Tendency to breed vermine, verminous; to breed vermine, to verminate.

VERSE. s. A foot in verse, consisting of two syllables, the first long and the other short, trochee; a foot in verse consisting of three long syllables, trimacrus; verse consisting of three measures, trimeter; verse in poetry consisting of three long syllables, molossus; verses that are composed of a long and a short syllable alternately, iambic; of two short syllables, pyrrhichius; a foot in verse consisting of four syllables, proceleusmaticus; stanza of four verses, tetrastitch; stanza in a poem consisting of five verses, pentastich; verses of eleven syllables are termed phalecian; a verse that has a syllable wanting at the end, brachycatalecton; any composition of one single verse, monostick; verse with complete syllables, acatalectic; art of composing verse, orthometry, poesy; to change or turn from verse to prose, to transprose; to make verses, to versificate; divination from any detached piece of verse, orthomancy; a rage for reciting verses, metromania, (Quincy), (See Poetry); Alexandrian verse, chronogram; couple of verses, couplet; licentious verse, dithyrambic; mean verses, doggerel; half a verse in poetry, hemistic; verses for epitaphs or monuments, are termed lapidary, verses; epigram consisting of eight verses, ogdastic; verses consisting of five feet, pentameter; of six, hexameter; verses so called from the famous poetess Sappho, Sapphic verses; verses beginning and ending with the same word, serpentine verses; a verse which reads the same way backwards as forwards, as subidura, arudibus, palindrome; poetical verses are either iambic, trochaic, dactyle, anapoestic, or Alexandrine; verses so arranged as the initial letters form the name of some person or thing, acrostic; little verse, versicle.

VERSED. a. Well versed in arts and sciences, adept; the being versed in many sciences, polymathy.

VESSEL. s. Conceptacle, receptacle, recipient; to draw out a vessel, to deprome; large vessel of drink, meaker; full of vessels as an organized body, vascular; obstruction of the vessels, infarction; an eruption of the blood through the vessels, persultation.

VESTRY. a. Sacristy.

VEX. v. To vex, to afflict, to irritate, to discompose, to aggrieve, to chagrin, to despite, to disaster, to disoblige, to disquiet, to distract, to enchafe, to malign, to exasperate, to goad, to grate, to harass, to infest, to pique, to pester, to perplex, to perturbate, to shagreen.

VEXATIOUS. a. Plaguy, perverse.

VEXING. p. Grating.

VIBRATION. s. Vibration of a pendulum, the time of performing a single one, diadrom; vibrations of pendulums in equal times, isochrone vibrations; vibration, (shaking,) titubation, (Perry.)

VICE. s. Vitiosity, perversion, pravity.

VICEROY. s. Exarch.

VICINITY. s. Confinity.

VICIOUS. a. Defective, disordinate, jadish.

VICTORY. s. Palm; song of triumph after a victory, epinicion.

VICTUALS. s. Prog, viands; provider of victuals, caterer, cateress, purveyor; victuals eaten between meals, nunchion, lunchion; double allowance of victuals to students on holidays, gaudies; one who buys victuals in one place, and carries it to another, badger.

VIEW. s. Ken, perception, perspec-

sive, aspect; view, (sight) spectation; view or prospect through trees, vista visto ; general view of a subject, synopsis ; circle that terminates our view, horizon ; certain oblique view of the eye, leer ; act of discovering to the view, retection ; view or sense of seeing, conspectuity.

VIGOROUS. *a.* Vegete, animated, drastic, energetic, sanguine.

VIGOUR. *s.* Mettle, prowess, vigor; vigour, (health), invalescence ; to endue with vigour, to invigorate.

VILE. *a.* Abject, abominable, naughty, arrant, contemptible, degenerous, errant, notorious, execrable, ferine, facinereous, flagitious, gory, grubstreet, heinous, homicidal, horrible, horrid, ignoble, impious, incorrigible, indefensible, inexpiable, infidel, iniquitous, intolerable, irreligious, libellous, notorious, obscene, odious, approbrious, peccaminous, plaguy, miscreant, proletarious, scurrilous, tricobolar ; rakehelly, reprobate ; vile, (lewd) salacious, scelerate, tartarean; vile wretch, miscreant ; vile verses are termed doggerel.

VILENESS. *s.* Vility, turpitude.

VILLAGE. *s.* Belonging to villages, villatic ; small village, hamlet, villa, vill.

VILLAIN. *s.* Cozener, pander, scelerate, skellum, varlet.

VILLANOUS. *a.* Flagitious, nefarious, repudious.

VILLANY. *s.* Turpitude.

VINDICATE. *v.* To avenge, to assert, to propugn, to avouch.

VINE. *s.* That pertains to a vine, vitigeneous ; bearing vines, vitiferous ; to lay a vine stock or branch in the ground, so as it may take root, to provice.

VINEGAR. *s.* Eisel ; vinegar and water mixed, oxycrate ; vinegar and honey boiled up together, oxymel.

VINTAGE. *s.* Relating to vintage, vindemial.

VINTNER. *s.* Oenopolist.

VIOLATE. *v.* To constuprate, to efforce, to contemerate, to deflower, to infract, to infringe, to profane, to ransact, to stuprate.

VIOLENCE. *s.* Esture, aggression, brunt, compulsion, enforce, rapine, vehemence, orgasm ; to drive with violence, to foupe; getting by violence, extorsive ; seizing by violence, rapacious ; drawn away by violence, abacted.

VIOLENT. *a.* Turbulent, furious, impetuous, outrageous, mail-mail ; very violent, peracute, precipitous, splenic ; violent commotion, estuation ; those taken away by violent deaths, biothanati ; a grow-

ing violent, or painful again, recrudescent.

VIOLENTLY. *ad.* (Vigorously) amain, boisterously, perforce.

VIOLETS. *s.* Resembling violets, violaceous.

VIOLIN. *s.* Player on the violin, violonista, violist.

VIPER. *s.* Belonging to a viper, viperine, viperous.

VIRGIN. *s.* Pure virgin, vestal ; to play the virgin ; to virgin (Shakesp.); worshippers of the Virgin Mary, Marianalatrists.

VIRTUE. *s.* To take away the virtue or strength, to evertuate ; wanting virtue, unvirtuous, virtueless ; the cardinal virtues are : Prudence, Temperance, Justice, and Fortitude.

VIRTUOUS. *a.* Chaste, homiletical, laudable ; virtuous habits requisite and absolutely necessary for every individual towards the well-being of the community, are termed, homiletical virtues.

VISAGE. *s.* Phiz.

VISCOUS. *a.* Lentous.

VISIBLE. *a.* Apparent, aspectable.

VISION. *s.* Phantasm, phasma ; interpreter of visions, oneirocritic ; one who pretends to see visions, and predict thereby things impossible, visionary, visionist ; to be troubled with visions, to corybantiste; doctrine of reflected vision (in optics) catoptrica.

VISIT. *s.* Late visit, couchee ; morning-visit, levee.

VISITER. *s.* Guest, visitant.

VITAL. *a.* Vital flame or heat of animals, biolychnium.

VOICE. *s.* Voice (vote) suffrage ; in one voice, univocal ; want of voice, aphony ; to form into voice, to vocalize ; by the voice, vocal ; bad tone of voice, cacaphony ; lowness of the voice proceeding from an ill constitution, asaphy ; one who has a strong voice megalophonos ; voice of Stentor, a Greek mentioned by Homer, which was louder than 50 men together, Stentorian voice ; depravity of voice, paraphonia, of which there are six species, viz : 1. *Paraphonia puberum,* is that disagreeable change of voice observable about the age of fourteen. 2. *Paraphonia rauca,* when the voice is coarse and rough. 3. *Paraphonia resonans,* when besides the disagreeable voice, it whistles as it were, through the nose. 4. *Paraphonia palatina,* in which the voice is obscure, confused, and hardly conveys an intelligible sound. 5.*Paraphonia clangens,* a shrill or squealing sound. 6. *Paraphonia comatosa,* when the voice is sent out during inspiration, and resembles the snorting of people asleep, (Quincy.)

VOID. *v.* To mute.

VOID. *a.* Frustraneous, inane, devoid, indigent, invalid, vacant, vacive; made void, aniented; void space, inanity, vacuum, vacuity; void of, destitute.

VOID. *s.* To make void, to abolish, to cancel, to disannul, to evacuate.

VOIDING *p.* Voiding superfluities out of the body, apocrisis or apocrisia.

VOLUNTARY. *a.* Gratuitous, ultroneous.

VOLUNTARILY. *ad.* Done voluntarily, spontaneously.

VOLUPTUOUSNESS. *s.* Philosarchy.

VOMIT. *v.* To disgorge, to endew, to parbreak, to puke; to vomit up, to regorge, to retch; to have an inclination to vomit, to nauseate.

VOMIT. *s.* Vomitive, vomitory, emetic; discharge by vomit, &c. ejectment; root of the Indian plant commonly used to produce a vomit, ipecacuhana; what tends upwards as a vomit, anadosis; apt to vomit, queasy; term or epithet given to those who vomit with difficulty, dysemeti; one who vomits up his excrements, copriemetos.

VOMITING. *p.* Good against vomiting, antiemetics; act or power of vomiting, vomition.

VOTE. *v.* To vote with or for, to suffragate.

VOTES. *s.* Solicitation for votes, canvass.

VOTER. *s.* Poller.

VOW. *s.* Protestation; given or done by a vow, votive.

VOYAGE. *s.* Account or journal of a voyage, itinerary.

VULGAR. *a.* Plebeian, mobbish, popular, proletarious, trivial.

VULTURE. *s.* Living by rapine like a vulture, subvulturean.

W

WAGER *v.* To bet.

WAGER. *s.* Depositum, deposite; wager of law, leygager.

WAGERER. *s.* Bettor.

WAGGISH. *a.* Arch, jocund, jocose, jocular, parlous.

WAGGON. *s.* The pole which stops the wheel of a waggon from going too fast down a steep place, trigon.

WAGGONER. *s.* Auriga.

WAIT. *v.* To await.

WAIT. *s.* In wait, *perdue;* one who lies in wait, insidiator.

WAITER. *s.* Board used by waiters for carrying off dishes, &c. from a table, voider.

WAITING. *p.* Waiting place from which one may dart on his enemy, ambuscade, ambush, ambushment; the act of waiting on, assecution.

WAKE. *v.* To wake, to arouse.

WALK. *v.* To walk up and down, to obambulate, to perambulate; to walk round about, to circumambulate; to walk in the cool air, to walk in *fresco.*

WALK. *s.* Excursion, gait; walk leading to a house, &c. avenue; walk shaded by trees, grove; walk in a church, ile, aisle isle; walk under arches, piazza, portico; walk in the fields, promenade; walk on the flat roof of a house, terrace; cool and shady walks, frescades.

WALKING. *p.* Ambulatory, gradient; a walking, ambulation; a walking about from inquietude of mind, deambulation; a walking up and down after the manner of Aristotle's followers, peripatetic; a particular manner in walking, gait; a walking in the night-time in one's sleep, noctambulation.

WALL. *v.* To wall in or up, to mure, to immure.

WALL. *s.* Wall which is indented, or has interstices for cannon, &c. battlement; the act of scaling walls, escalade; situated betwixt walls, intermural; low wall of an enclosure, gison; the end wall of a building, gable; the filling of walls with mortar, lorication; of or belonging to walls, mural, parietal; money paid to keep walls in repair, murage; wall which is breast high, parapet; to inclose by walls, to immure.

WALLED. *a.* Walled round, circummured.

WALLET. *s.* Budget; wallet in which a soldier holds his provisions, *gardeviante,* Fr.

WALLOWING. *p.* The act of wallowing, volutation.

WAN. *a.* Bleak, lurid, maidpale, pallid.

WAND. *s.* Divination by a wand, rhabdomancy.

WANDER. *v.* To deviate, to exorbitate, to roam, to peragrate, to pilgrim, to traverse.

WANDERING. *p.* Fugitive, volatile, deviating, itinerant, sauntering, vagous, vagrant, vagabond, errant, amplivagons, circumforaneous, discurrent, emigrant; a wandering or deviating, aberration; act of wandering, evagation; wandering on the hills, montivagant; wandering by night, noctivagant; a wandering up and down, oberration, pererration; wandering alone solivagant; wandering every where, omnivagant.

WANT. *s.* Defection, derelection, exigence or exigency, indigence; state of want, destitute; want of patience or moderation, intolerance; want of ease, untranquillity; want of power, invalidity; great want, mendicity, penury, indigence, necessitude; want (emptiness) vacuity, vapidity; the want or privation of children, orbity.

WANTED. *p.* Things wanted, *desiderata, L.*

WANTING. *p.* Deficient, devoid, elleptic.

WANTON. *a.* Lascivious, lecherous, lubric, lubricous, apish, buxom, coltish, riggish, ruttish, salacious, sportive, petulant, rampant, sybaritical, waggish; wanton girl, minx, parnel, tomboy; wanton woman, gig; wanton trick, disport; of or belonging to the wanton and obscene poetry sung by the ancient Romans at weddings, fescennine; to look with a wanton air, to gloat.

WAR. *s.* To subjugate by war, to debellate; the feigned war of the giants against heaven, gigantomachy or theomachy; waging war, belligerent; state of open war, hostility; of or belonging to war, martial; aid or assistance in war, symmachy; engaged in war (fighting) militant; the war of the pigmies and cranes, pygmæageranomachy.

WARD. *v.* To ward off, to avert, to parry.

WARDROBE. *s.* Revestiary, revestry.

WARLIKE. *a.* Battallious, cavalier, hostile, agonistical; warlike stores of all kinds, habiliments.

WARM. *v.* To calify.

WARM. *a.* Fervent, ardent, eager, prurient, sanguine, vehement; warm baths, thermæ; a growing warm, incalescent; warm imagination, enthusiasm; luke-warm, tepid; a making warm, tepefaction.

WARMTH. *s.* Excandescence; warmth of temper, irascibleness.

WARN. *v.* To admonish, to caution, to monish; to warn before hand, to premonish; one who warns, monitor.

WARNING. *p.* Item, monition, precaution; warning, monitory.

WARRANT. *s.* Commission, surance.

WARREN. *s.* Viviary.

WARRIOR. *s.* Champion.

WART. *s.* Verucca; full of warts, verucose.

WARY. *a.* Cautious, circumspect, vigilant, scrupulous, wareful.

WASH. *v.* To drench; to wash clothes, to buck; to wash off, to elute; to wash out, to rinse; house where a laundress washes and dresses clothes, laundry; medical preparation commonly called a wash, lotion; any substance that washes as soap, smegma; place to wash kitchen utensils in, scullery; vessel in which any diseased part is washed, lavatory; vessel in which glasses are washed, monteth or montet.

WASHERWOMAN. *s.* Laundress. (Camden)

WASHING. *p.* Act of washing, lavation; the act of washing clean, ablution; washing and ironing house, laundry; a washing or gargling the mouth, diaclysma.

WASP. *s.* Hornet.

WASTE. *v.* To dispeople, to emaciate, to to embezzle, to impoverish, to evaporate, to exantlate, to harrass, to havoc, to absume, to mispend, to tabefy, to scath; to lay waste, to spoliate; to waste or rub off, to abrade.

WASTE. *s.* Desolation, destruction; waste printed sheet, maculature; waste of flesh, marcor, marasmus; waste meat (what is not used at table), offals (Arbuthnot); act of laying waste, vastation.

WASTEFUL *a.* Effuse, lavish, prodigal.

WASTEFULNESS. *s.* Prodigence.

WASTING. *p.* Consumptive, esurine, coroding, hectic or hectick, macerating; a wasting or destroying, collabefaction.

WATCH. *v.* To espy; to watch diligently, to evigilate, to invigilate, to advigilate; to watch and study late, to lucubrate.

WATCHFUL. *a.* Alert, cautious; watchful (want of sleep) levisomnous, vigilant.

WATCHFULNESS. *s.* (Want of sleep) insomny; want of watchfulness, (carelessness) invigilancy.

WATCH. *s.* Watch tower, barbacan, pharos, phare; private soldier on watch, sentinel or centry; watch-word, syntheme; watch, horodix, horologe; name of the greenish shell or case of some watches made of the skin of the shark or ass, shagreen; watch-pocket, fob.

WATCHING. *p.* The act of watching all night, excubation; a careful watching, pervigilation; a watching or dreaming slumber, Agripnia.

WATER. *v.* To irrigate; to put or sink under water, to immerge, to immerse; to empty water with a ladle, to lade or lave; to clear from water, to dephlegmate, to alcoholize; to plunge under water, to submerge or submerse.

WATER. *s.* Spring or fountain water, hydropege; water in which red hot iron has been often quenched, is called *apobamma*, or *aqua fabrorum* (Quincy); ordeal by water (see Fire); of or belonging to water, aquatic; running water, brook, freshet; water fall, cataract; water-pipe, conduit; the water rat, crabber; the art of conveying water by pipes, hydraulics; liquor made from honey and water, hydromel, mead; one who swims under water, urinator; water frozen in the act of dropping, icicle; the flowing in of water, interluency; an overflowing of water, inundation, cataclysm, *G.*; passage for water, lade; inland body of water, lough, loch or lake; purification by water, lustration; divination by water, hydromancy; divination by water in a bason, lecanomancy; poisoning of water by casting any thing into it, lourgulary* (Bailey); the dread of water, hydrophobia, *aqua pavor*; act of plunging in water, mersion; any animal which can live both in the water and on land, amphibious; water mixt with vinegar, oxycrate; any piece of land almost surrounded by water, peninsula, from *pene* and *insula*, L. almost an island; the conveyance of water from one place to another, hydragogy; place or receptacle where large quantities of water are kept, reservoir, conservatory, cistern; water-clock anciently used to measure time by, clepsydra, *G.*; water-drinkers, *aquæpotes*, L.; such waters as run between banks, are called, riparious; a bubbling of water as from a spring, scatebrosity; issuing as water out of a spring, scaturient; standing water, stagnant or restagnant; waterman who rows in a cock-boat, sculler; any mill or engine for forcing water upwards, forcier; lying under the water, subaquaneous; composed of land and water, terraqueous; spider which runs on the surface of water brooks, tipula (Nat. Hist.); an overflow by water, alluvion; such engines as raise water by the spring of the air, are termed, hydraulo-pneumatical engines; water organ, hydraulus; the science of weighing water, or bodies immersed in it, hydrostatics; the making water or staling backwards, retromingency; such animals, as make water backwards, are called, retromingent animals.

WATERINESS. *s.* Wateriness of the eyes, delacrymation.

WATERING. *a.* Act of watering, rigation, irrigation.

WATERY. *a.* Aqueous, hydropic, hydropical, dropsical; medicines which discharge watery humours, hydrogues, hydrotics; medicines which draw away watery humours, phlegmagogues; thin watery matter oozing out of the glands, rheum; watery rupture, hydrocele; the watery part of the blood, serum; sharp watery matter which arises from ulcers, ichor; watery underneath, as some hands, subriguous, weary.

WAVE. *v.* To brandish; to roll as a wave, to undulate.

WAVE. *s.* Surge, billow, breaker; borne by the waves, fluctigerous; tossed by the waves, fluctivagous or fluctivagant; playing as the waves, undulary or undulatory.

WAVER. *v.* To boggle or bodge, to equivocate, to fluctuate, to vacillate, to prevaricate.

WAVING. *p.* Waving or undulating like a flash of lightning, crispisulcant.

WAX. *s.* Cere; covered or done over with wax, incerated.

WAY. *s.* Way (or means) expedient; way or manner of deportment, gait; way or road, avenue; the milky way, *via lactea*, galaxy; of or belonging to a way or road, viary; consisting of four ways or courses, quadrivial; where there is no way or passage to or from, invious.

WAYLAY. *v.* To beset.

WEAK. *a.* Fatuous, illusory, impotent, feminine, effeminate, flaccid, lax, flimsy, limber, brainless, crazy, debile, decrepit, evanid, exosseous, irresolute, lithe, lithesome, fragile, imbecile, immartial, inefficacious, ineffectual, intenible, invalid, puny, cobweb (Bailey) relaxed; weak (headless) acephalous; weak or stupid, addlepated; the weak or blind side, foible; to wax weak, to vade.

WEAKEN. *v.* To infirm, to emasculate, to enervate, to enerve or uunerve, to unnervate, to incapacitate, to retund; to weaken by adding water, to dilute.

WEAKENING. *p.* Act of weakening, labefaction.

WEAKLY. *a.* Puling, valetudinary.

WEAKNESS. *s.* Blindside, lassitude, dejection, dotage, fatuity, insipience, instability, atony, impotence, impuissance, ineptitude, infatuation, enervity; weakness of the imagination, paraphrosyne; an indisposition to motion arising from weakness, acracy, acrasy or acrasia; weakness in argument, inconclusiveness, inconsequence; weakness induced by any illness, lysis.

WEALTH. *s.* Affluence, mammon; one who doats on wealth, mammonist,

WEALTHY. *a.* Locuplete, opulent, topping.

WEANING. *s.* The act of weaning a child, ablactation, delactation.

WEAR. *v.* To wear or rub off, to abrade, to obliterate ; to wear away, to corrode.

WEARIED. *a.* Not to be wearied, indefatigable, infatigable.

WEARING. *s.* A wearing or rubbing off, detrition.

WEARINESS. *s.* Medicine to take away weariness, myracopium or acopon; that position of a limb which is equally distant from flexion and extension, which position the part can longest bear unwearied, acamatos, G.

WEARISOMENESS. *s.* Irksomeness, lassitude, defatigation.

WEARY. *v.* To defatigate, to fatigate, to harrass, to lade, to moil, to turmoil.

WEATHERCOCK. *s.* Fane, triton, girella.

WEATHERGLASS. *s.* Baroscope, barometer, aeroscope, manometer (see Glass) ; the weatherglass is sometimes called the Toricellian tube, or experiment, from Toricelli the inventor.

WEAVE. *v.* To intertex, to braid, to blight ; to weave together, to contex ; to weave in a round mass, to conglomerate.

WEAVER. *s.* The yarn of a weaver's warp, abb ; a weaver's reed, slaie.

WEAVING. *p.* Relating to the act or art of weaving, textrine, textorian.

WEB. *s.* Of or belonging to a web, telary.

WED. *v.* To desponsate, to espouse.

WEDDING. *s.* Obscene poems anciently sung at the Roman weddings, fescennine poems.

WEDGE. *v.* To wedge in, to jam.

WEDGE. *s.* Gad, quoin, or coin ; formed as a wedge, cuneal.

WEDGING. *p.* Act of wedging in, cuneation, incuneation.

WEED. *v.* To weed corn, to sarcle.

WEED. *s.* Full of weeds, algous.

WEEDING. *p.* Act of weeding, sarculation ; goddess who presides over weeding, Runcina.

WEEK. *s.* The space of a week, hebdomad; of or belonging to a week, septimane, septuary.

WEEKLY. *a.* Hebdomadal, or hebdomadary.

WEEP. *v.* To beweep.

WEEPING. *p.* Incapable of weeping, illachrymable ; causing weeping, fletiferous.

WEIGH. *v.* To gravitate, to librate, to poise, to trutinate ; to weigh equally, to equiponderate, to equilibrate ; to weigh ⸏consider, to perpend, to pensitate ; to

outweigh, to preponder, or preponderate

WEIGHED. *p.* Capable of being weighed, ponderable.

WEIGHING. *p.* Weighing down, pressitant, gravitating ; an outweighing, superponderancy ; the science of weighing fluids, or any thing immersed in them, hydrostatics.

WEIGHT. *s.* Poise or poize, ponderosity, ponderousness, pression, pressure ; void of weight, imponderous ; opposite weight, (what is put in the opposite scale) counterbalance, counterpoise ; equality of weight, equiponderance, equipollence, equipoise, equilibrity ; the act of keeping the weight even, equilibration ; instrument or rod resting on a point used for raising great weights, lever ; the property directly contrary to weight, levitation, levity ; one skilled in the knowledge of weights and measures, oedastic ; a weight of cheese, wool, &c. containing 256 lbs. avordupois, waga ; estimated by weight, ponderal; the doctrine of weights, statics ; any officer who has the oversight of the weights in a market, zygostates; belonging to such an officer, zygostatic ; the neat or just weight of commodities after deducting tare, is called suttle; tables of weights where the denominations are generally known, such as money, tables, &c. in contradistinction to numbers, which have multifarious denominations, geodetical tables.

WEIGHTY. *a.* Findy, massive, massy, momentous, moliminous, nervous, nervy, valid, efficacious.

WELL. *ad.* Well or dextrously performed, adroitly ; well bred, debonair.

WELL. *s.* Growing or breeding near wells, fontigenous ; name of a remarkable well near Torbay, in Devonshire, which ebbs and flows several times in the space of an hour, bubbling now and then as a boiling pot, Laywell ; the stone laid round the brim of a well, kerb-stone.

WELSH. *a.* The Welsh tongue is called the Cymraegan tongue ; Welsh rabbit, ramekin, from Ramequin, F.

WENCH. *s.* Plump wench, blouze; bouncing overgrown wench, stammel, (Bailey) ; loose wench, doxy.

WEST. *a.* One of the cardinal points of the compass ; said of dials turned toward the west, disorientated, (see Dial) ; west or western ponent, favonian, occident, occidental, occiduous.

WET. *v.* To wet, to madefy, to bedabble, to besprinkle, to bedash, to humect, to humectate, to bedew, to imbrue, to embay, (Spencer), to irrorate, to irrigate.

WET. *a.* Oozy, pluvial, pluvious, uvid,

dank, humid, sloppy, subriguous ; wet with rain, impluvious ; the act of making wet, madefaction.

WETNESS. s. Madidity.

WETTING. p. A wetting gently, humecting ; the act of wetting, madefaction, humectation.

WHALE. s. Leviathan ; of the whale kind, cetaceous ; the jaw-bone of a whale, menker.

WHEAT. s. Wheat boiled in milk, furmenty, or frumentry ; ale made from wheat, mum ; made of fine wheat, siliginose, siligineous.

WHEEDLE. v. To cant, to coax, to cog, to glaver, to gloze, to inveigle.

WHEEDLER. s. Cajoler.

WHEEDLING. p. Parasitical, sycophantic.

WHEEL. s. Trochus, G. ; the black matter that works out from wheels, coom ; the circumference of a wheel, felloe or felly ; the middle part of a wheel in which the axle is inserted, nave, or nef ; the iron hoops about the nave of a wheel, trieks ; the iron pin which keeps on the wheels to the axle-tree, linch-pin ; the mark of a wheel, rut, orbit ; the pin on which a wheel turns in any engine, &c. pivot ; the art of wheel work, or rotatory motion, trocholics, trochilics, or trochilice ; the turning round as a wheel, rotary ; the act of whirling about as a wheel, rotation ; to stop or wedge the wheel of a carriage to prevent it's recoiling, to scoat, to scatch, or scatch.

WHEELING. p. A wheeling about, evolution.

WHET. v. To whet or sharpen, to exacuate.

WHET. s. (What excites an appetite,) propoma.

WHIM. s. Caprice, freak, whimsey, humour, or humor, phantasm, freak, vagary.

WHIP. v. To fease, to firk.

WHIPPING. p. Act of whipping, flagellation, vapulation.

WHIRL. s. A whirl of wind or water, eddy.

WHIRLING. p. Vertiginous, vertical ; whirling round, dinetical, vertiginous ; act of whirling round, circumrotation.

WHIRLPOOL. s. Gurge, vortex.

WHIRLWIND. s. Tornado, travado, typhon.

WHISKERS. s. The whiskers, mustaches, or mustachoes.

WHISKY. s. The proper Irish and Erse name for whisky, usquebaugh, (Johnson).

WHISPER. v. To whisper, to exsufflate, to sussurate.

WHISPER. s. Buzz or buz, inkling, sussurration.

WHISPERER. s. Earwig.

WHISPERING. p. A whispering, insussurration.

WHITE. a. White of an egg, glare, or glair ; white lead, ceruss, psimythium, (old chym.) ; white and red mixed, gridelin ; white as snow, nival, niveous.

WHITEN. v. To dealbate, to blanch, to bleach.

WHITES. s. The whites, fluor albus, leucorrhœa.

WHITISH. a. Subalbid.

WHITLOW. s. Agnail, paronychia.

WHITSUNDAY. s. Pentecost.

WHITSUNTIDE. s. The festival of Whitsunday.

WHOLE. a. Whole or total, versal ; the whole, aggregate ; whole, integral ; the whole or full amount, solidum ; act of making whole, integration ; relating to the whole world, oecumenical.

WHOLESOME. a. Mandible, salubrious, salutary.

WHORE. v. To whore, to lecher.

WHORE. s. Bawd, bunter, bonaroba, courtesan, or courtezan, demirep, doxy, harlot, strumpet, lacedmutton, mort, lupanatrix, night-walker, prostitute, punk, trull ; Thaïs, (after the name of a famous courtezan at Athens) ; belonging to a whore, lenonian, meretricious ; worn out whore, harridan ; life or trade of a whore, putanism.

WHOREDOM. s. Palliardise ; act of whoredom, putage.

WHOREMASTER. s. Bellswagger, lecher, ribauld.

WICKED. a. Abominable, immoral, errant, criminous, curst, impious, iniquitous, irreligious, naughty, nefandous, nefarious, paricidal, peccaminous, piacular ; very wicked, flagitious, atheous, atheistical, atrocious, Belial, facinerous, or facinorous, heinous, profligate, retchless, ungracious ; wicked wretch, scelerate ; of an extreme wicked temper or disposition, virulent.

WICKEDNESS. s. Miscreance, improbity ; great wickedness, enormity ; unbounded wickedness, enormousness.

WIDE. a. Discous, ample, capacious, expansive.

WIDEN. v. To broaden, to dilate, to distend.

WIDENESS. s. Latitude.

WIDOW. s. Relic, widowhood, viduity.

WIDTH. s. Latitude.

WIFE. s. The wife of a prince, &c. con-

A a

sort; governed by a wife, henpecked; aliment for a wife, jointure; ludicrous and disdainful term for a wife, kicksy-wicksey; goods at the disposal of a wife, parapherpalia; one very fond and sub-missive to his wife, uxorious.

WIG. *s.* Peruke, periwig; very large wig, which sdades the face, vallancy.

WILD. *a.* Desert, agrarian, gothic, antique, brute, campestral, faunic, rustic, ferine, agrestic; wild, (improbable) romantic, chimerical; wild, (lecherous) libidi-nous; wild, (relating to hunting) vena-tic; wild, (savage) salvage, dissolute, riggish; very wild, rakehelly; wild, scare, (said of boys); any thing wild or irreclaimable, haggard; the den or couch of a wild beast, lair or layer.

WILE. *s.* Farfetch, finesse, stratagem.

WILL. *s.* Will-with-a-wisp, *ignis fatuus*, L.

WILL. *v.* To bequeath. to demise.

WILL. *s.* Arbitrament; the power of the will deduced into act, elicitation; here-tics who maintained the free will of Christians, Lampetians; one who makes a will, legator, testator, or testatrix; having made a will, testate; disqualified to make a will, intestable; will made by word of mouth before witnesses, nuncu-pative will; authentic copy of a will, probat, or probate; inheriting from a person who dies without a will, abin-testate; supplement to a will, codicil.

WILFUL. *a.* Pervicacious. (See Obstinate.)

WILLING. *a.* Willing, (in good humour) accordant; act of willing, volition.

WILLINGLY. *ad.* Lief or lieve; sponta-neously, ultroneous; done willingly, im-perate.

WILLINGNESS. *s.* Allubescency.

WILLOW. *s* Osier or ozier.

WILY. *a.* Vulpine, cautelous. (See Cun-ning.)

WIND. *s.* Gentle wind, breeze, or breese, aura, zephyr, or zephyrus, loomgale; trade winds in the East Indian ocean, monsoon; north wind, boreas; wind from the east, subsolanus, eurus, or ori-ens; belonging to the south wind, aus-tral; belonging to the west, occidental, or favonian, (see Compass); name of a dry north-easterly wind that blows on the coast of Guinea, in Africa, hermitan; wind from the north-east which blows at certain seasons in the Mediterranean, and is accounted dangerous, euroclydon; description of the winds, anemography; productive of wind, subventaneous; ex-pellent of wind from the stomach, car-minative; wind broke from the stomach, eructation; consisting of wind, pneuma-tic; open to the wind, or that may be

blown through, perflable; north wind is named in Italy and the Mediterranean, tramontane; south-east or Syrian wind, siroc, sirocco; sudden gust of wind, squall; the side most distant from the wind, lee-side; the side nearest the wind, windward-side or weather-side; to bring a ship near or close to the wind, to loof or luff; when a vessel sails before the wind it is termed spooning; wind, or rather hurricane, which on some coasts blows all night *from* the shore, tornado; instrument for measuring the different strengths of wind, anemometer, anemos-cope; the wind flower anemony, or le-monia.

WIND. *v.* To wind or turn, to intort; to wind or turn often, to laveer; to wind as a serpentine road, to sinuate.

WINDINESS. *s.* Flatulency, flatuosity, flatulence, inflation, ventosity.

WINDING. *p.* Labyrinthean, meandrous, sinuous, tortuous; a winding or turning about, gyration; winding or turning spirally, helical, or heliacal; full of windings and turnings, amfractuous, an-fractuous.

WINDLASS. *s.* Capstain.

WINDOW. *s.* Window made of lath work, lattice.

WIND-PIPE. *s.* Trachea, ventiduct; top of the wind-pipe, larynx; cover of the wind-pipe, gargareon, G.

WINDY. *a.* Flatulent, flatuous, subventa-neous, ventose; windy rupture of the scrotum, pneumatocele; windy rupture of the navel, pneumatomphalus.

WINE. *s.* Repository for wine, bin; an of-fering of wine, libation; the art of mak-ing different sorts of wine, zimotechnics; wine newly pressed from the grape, must, cute; beverage made of wine, &c. ta-ken as a whet, propoma; spirit of wine, pyroenus, alcohol; said of wine which still retains its rich flavour, racy; posses-sing the properties of wine, vinose, or vi-nous; unfermented wine, stum; wine-cellar, vintry; wine in which spice and sugar have been steeped, and the liquor strained off, *vinum hippocraticum*; hymn anciently sung in honour of the God of wine, dithyrambus.

WING. *s.* Pinion; having two wings, bi-pennated; having four, as some insects, quadripennated; the wing of a church, aisle; wanting or destitute of wings, im-pennous; furnished with wings, pennat-ed; term for those insects that have their wings in sheaths, as the beetle tribe, va-ginipennous, or vaginopennous.

WINGED. *a.* Aligerous, pennated, alifer-ous; the winged horse, Pegasus, Hippo, griff; the winged shoes of Mercury, talaria.

WINK. *v.* To nictate.

WINK. *s.* Oeilliad, aeiliad, or oeilaid.

WINKING. *p.* A winking or twinkling, connictation, connivance.

WINNER. *s.* The winner at a race, or when one gains all at any game, sweepstakes, (Shakes.)

WINNOW. *v.* To eventilate.

WINTER. *s.* Relating to winter, brumal, hibernal, hybernal, hyemal; to winter in a place, to hyemate; a remaining the whole winter at any place, perhyemation, hybernation.

WIPE. *v.* To absterge, or absterse.

WIPING. *p.* A wiping or rubbing off, extersion.

WIRE. *s.* Wire-work over a window, to defend it, trellis; consisting of wires, filaceous.

WISDOM. *s.* Sapience, sageness; infinite wisdom, omniscience, pansophy; mighty in wisdom, sapientipotent.

WISE. *a.* Advised, judicious, oeconomical; provident, sapient; the wise men in Greece were accounted seven in number, viz. Bias, Chilo, Cleobulus, Periander, Pittacus, Solon, and Thales.

WISELY. *ad.* Circumspectly.

WISH. *v.* To wish ill, to execrate; to wish for, to desiderate; to wish for evil, to imprecate.

WISH. *s.* Oraison, or orison, velleity; wish, appetite.

WITCHCRAFT. *s.* A preservation against witchcraft hung on any part of the body by way of charm, phylactery.

WITCHES. *s.* Lamiæ, hags; witches supposed to fly through the air, volatica, (Bailey.)

WIT. *ad.* To wit, or namely, videlicet, L. contracted, *viz.*; wit, ingeny; to be at one's wits end, to be at Dulcarnon, so called from the intricate proposition discovered by Pythagoras. (See Difficulty.)

WITHDRAW. *v.* To revoke, to reverse, to repeal, to absent.

WITHERED. *p.* Lax, flaccid, marcid.

WITHERING. *p.* Marcescent.

WITHIN. *ad.* Interim, internal; lying within the surface, intime.

WITHSTOOD. *p.* That cannot be withstood, irresistible; that may be withstood, refragable.

WITNESS. *v.* To depose.

WITNESS. *s.* Deponent; false witness, pseudo-martyr; to induce one to bear false witness, to suborn; fit to bear witness, testable.

WITNESSED. *p.* Attested.

WITTY. *a.* Arch, apt, lepid, parlous,

shrewd, facetious, argute, cute, epigrammatic, sarcastic, witty answer, repartee; witty, perilous, (said of a child.)

WIVES. *s.* Having two wives at once, bigamy; three, trigamy; having many polygamy.

WOER. *s.* Paramour, leaman, from l'aimant, F.

WOFUL. *a.* Doleful, rueful, ruthful. (See Sad.)

WOLF. *s.* Lycos, lupus; stag-wolf, lucern; precious stone resembling the eye of a wolf, lycopthalmus; madness proceeding from the bite of a mad wolf, whence men imitate their cries, lycanthropy.

WOMAN. *s.* Woman who is commonly hired in, to do the drudgery of a house, char-woman; a ludicrous term used by Shakespeare for a woman, gallimaufry, (Johnson); worthless woman, baggage, bonaroba, demirep, doggess, beldam; little squat and fat woman, trub-tail; act of keeping a woman, concubinage; scolding woman, vixen; married woman, covert; old woman, tib, croan; relating to a woman's portion, dotal; aukward woman, doody; dirty woman, drab, drazel; woman's watch, &c. trinkets, equipage; old worn out woman, gibcat, grimalkin; ugly old woman, hag; over nice and affected woman, prude; ringlets of a beautiful woman's hair, heartbreakers; woman who deceives a man in love, jilt; grave elderly woman, matron; woman who is marriageable, viripotent, lapidable; woman in child-bed, enixa; woman who lusts after a man, virosa; womanhood, muliebrity; bold masculine woman, virago; young woman, (in joke) heifer; the old age of a woman, anility; woman who manages or conducts business, negotiatrix; old woman kept to guard a young one, duenna; tall ill made woman, gangrel; short and very fat woman, pundle, dowdy; wanton woman, parnel, gig; low worthless woman, quean, scut; the period when a girl puts on the appearance of womanhood, hebe; peevish, scolding contentious woman, shrew, termagant; negligent and dirty woman, slattern, traipse; over-grown bouncing young woman, stammel; name of an herb which steeped in drink is said to make a woman conceive a girl, thelygonum; traiterous or false woman, traitress; woman of suspicious character, demirip.

WOMB. *s.* Matrice, matrix, mother, (among physicians) hystera; belonging to the womb, uterine; animal in the womb, fetus, or foetus, embryo; act of bearing or carrying young in the womb, gestation; instrument wherewith liquors are injected into the womb, metrenchyta; medicine to be thrust into the womb upon some extraordinary occasion, pessary; instrument for drawing a dead child out of the womb, uncus, ungula; the operation of cutting a child out of the mother's womb, hysteromatocia, or Cæsarian operation, Julius Cæsar being brought into the world in that way; a cutting open the womb, gastrotomy, hysterotomy; rupture or falling down of the womb, hysterocele, metroproptosis.

WOMEN. s. A man who busies himself about women's affairs, cotquean; hater of women, mysogynist; act of debauching women, thelypthora; the longing of women with child, malacia; certain deities among the Romans supposed to be the helpers of women in their child-bed throws, Nixidii; the unlawful desire for women, mulierosity; the immoderate lust of some women, bordering on madness, furor uterinus, nymphomania; a hole in the church of Rippon in Yorkshire, where in old times the chastity of women was ascertained, by the chaste getting through, when the unchaste could not, St Wilfred's needle; such accidents as happen to, or are peculiar to women (such as the menses) gynœcia; the goddess of women in labour, Anteverta.

WONDER. v. To admire, to muse. (See Think.)

WONDER. s. Amazement, prodigy; book of wonders, mirabilary; any art that exhibits wonders, thaumaturgics; the seven wonders of the world are: 1st, The Pyramids of Egypt. 2d, The Mausoleum or magnificent tomb of Mausolus king of Caria, built by his queen Artemesia. 3d, The temple of Diana at Ephesus. 4th, The walls and hanging gardens of Babylon. 5th, The vast brazen image of the Sun at Rhodes. 6th, The rich statue of Jupiter Olympius at Greece. 7th, The Pharos or watch-tower, built by Ptolemy Philadelphus king of Egypt.

WONDERFUL. a. Admirable, marvellous, stupendous; speaking wonderful things, miradical; wonderful appearance of nature, phœnomenon.

WONDERFULLY. ad. Wonderfully done or executed, mirifical.

WOOD. s. Hyrst, hurst, hirst, boscage; small wood, grove, holt, hoult; wood for fire, kid, bavin, billet; brushwood, chat-wood; wood tied up for firing, cordwood; wood (float of) raft; to cover with thin wood as is done by cabinet-makers, to veneer; full of woods, saltuose, sylvan,

silvan; relating to woods, nemoral; abounding in woods, nemorose, nemorious.

WOODCOCK. s. Rusticula.

WOODEN. a. The art of making wooden cuts, lygnography.

WOODY. a. Ligneous.

WOOL. s. To card wool, to carminate; to comb wool, to tose; bed fitted only with the locks of wool, flock-bed; relating to wool, lanarious; stuff made of wool and linen, linsey-woolsey; making or working wool, lanificous; bearing wool or down, laniferous, lanigerous; wool stript off a dead sheep, mortling or morling; a certain weight of wool containing 40 tods or 28 lbs, sarplar, from sarpilliere, F.; quantity of wool weighing 256 lbs. waga.

WOOLLEN. a. A kind of woollen clothes, plonket.

WOOLLY. a. Made of woolly substance, tomentose; woolly substance growing on some plants, lanugo.

WORDS. s. One who is pedantical in the use of words, purist; stress laid on words, emphasis; opposition of words, antithesis; redundance of words, circumlocution; original or primitive word, etymon; the retaining an obsolete word, archaism; cant words used by rogues, gibberish; dictionary of old or obscure words, glossary; words of equivocal or ambiguous signification, homonymia, homonymous; inventor of words, logodædalist; discourse full of superfluous words, perissology; full of words, largiloquent, loquacious, verbose, prolix; words without wisdom, liplabour, or lipwisdom; dispute about words, logomachy; words of one syllable, monosyllable; of two, dissyllable; of three, trissyllable; of four, quadrisyllable; more than four, pollysyable; any word having eleven syllables, such as the word honorificabilitudinity, is termed a hendecasyllabon; declared by word of mouth, nuncupative, nuncupatory; words resembling each other, paronymous; word having a double meaning, as the verbs to cleave, dilogy; speaking few words, paciloquous; fluency of words, volubility; original word, prototypon; watch-word, syntheme; ill composition of words in a sentence, cacosyntheton; words of the same signification, synonyma, synonymous; a repeating the same words, tautology; art of spelling words properly, orthography; true derivation of words, etymology; due construction of words into sentences, syntax; true pronunciation of words, orthoepy, prosody; word for word, verbatim; comprehending divers significations under the same word, homonymous; word having divers meanings, homonyme; when divers things are signified by one word, homonymy; word at the bottom of a page which is repeated at the top of the next, catchword; word which is the same read backward as forward, as Madam, palindrome; dictionary of new and affected words is termed, a neological dictionary. (See Dictionary.)

WORK. v. To operate, to tew.

WORK. s. Small piece of work, job; day's work in plowing, sowing, reaping, &c. journey (from journée, F.); work done by candle light, lucubration.

WORKING. p. Working together, coefficient; act of working, elaboration; a working together, coefficacy.

WORKMAN. s. Opificer, artisan.

WORLD. s. Before the world, antemundane; end of the world, consummation; subsisting between two worlds, intermundane; worship paid to the world, or parts thereof, cosmolatry; citizen of the world, cosmopolite; beyond the bounds of the world, extramundane; situated beneath the world, inframundane; above the world, supramundane; world or great world, universe, macrocosm, megacosm, monad; little world, microcosm; belonging to the whole world, oecumenical; heretics who maintained the world had no beginning, Bagnolenses; figure of the world, typocosmy; a science describing the several parts of the visible world, cosmography; the mensuration of the world by degrees and minutes, cosmometry; the invisible world (state of the dead) hades.

WORLDLY. a. Terrene, terrestrial; worldly wretch, cosmodelyte.

WORMS. s. The earth worm, lumbricus, L; sicyania; tape-worm, tænia; full of little worms, vermiculous; full of worms, verminous; like or moving as a worm, vermicular; worm (like a worm) peristaltic; worm-shaped, vermiform; like an earth-worm, lumbrical; feeding on worms, vermivorous; such medicines as destroy worms in the human body, anthelmintics or antielminthus, helminthus, helminthagogues, vermifuge.

WORN. a. Worn by rubbing, frayed, attrite or obtrite; much worn, napless, contrite, decrepit; worn out, trite, effete; worn out old animal of any kind, gib or gibbe; worn out old cat, gib-cat.

WORSE. a. To make worse, to impair; making worse, deterioration.

WORSHIP. s. Worship of the devil, demonolatry; worship paid to the universe or its parts, cosmolatory; inferior worship, dulia; highest kind of worship, latria; state of those who worship out of fear, disidæmony, disidæmony; place of public worship of the Jews, synagogue.

WORST. a. Worst end of any thing, fagend.

WORTH. s. Utility, preciosity; companions of worth and learning, tanquam; want of worth, immerit, inutility.

WORTHIES. s. The nine worthies of the world were, Three Jews, viz: Joshua, David, and Judas Maccabæus; Three Heathens, Hector of Troy, Alexander the Great, and Julius Cæsar; Three Christians, Arthur of Britain, Charles the Great of France, and Godfrey of Boulogne.

WORTHILY. ad. Condignly.

WORTHLESS. a. Ignoble, futile, naught, base, abject, vile, putid, drossy, teemless, triobolar, vapid, desertless, scorious; worthless woman, baggage; worthless fellow, losel.

WORTHY. a. Condign, undisobliging.

WOUND. v. To vulnerate; to wound, (bore) to terebrate; to foment or rub a wound, to embrocate.

WOUND. s. Incisure; wounds proceeding from an outward cause, troma; useful in the cure of wounds, vulnerary; mark of a healed wound, eschar; lint for a wound, pledget, spleget, tent; lint put into wounds, turunda; any bandage for a wound, anadesma; medicines which bring wounds or sores to an escar, synulotics; of or relating to, or good for wounds, traumatic; name of a root growing in Maryland and Virginia, of great virtue in healing all manner of wounds, wichacan.

WOUND. p. That may be wound or turned any way, versatile or versable.

WOUNDED. p. That cannot be wounded, invulnerable; that may be wounded, vulnerable.

WOVEN. a. Woven, or capable of being woven, textile.

WRANGLE. v. To altercate, to bicker, to brangle, to litigate. (See Dispute.)

WRANGLER. s. Polemic or polemick; disputant, controvertist, chicaner.

WRANGLING. p. Cavillous, chicanery.

WRAP. v. To envelope, to furl, to invelope.

WRAPPER. s. Envelope.

WRATH. s. Ire, irritation.

WRESTED. p. Wrested from by force, abstorted.

WRESTLING. p. Luctation; of or belonging to wrestling, palestrical.

WRETCH. s. Abject, miscreant, scelerafe, ribald, rumion; cruel wretch, flint; hard wretch, harpy; an insignificant wretch, fopdoodle; low wretch, slubber-degullion; abandoned wretch, profligate; base and false wretch, recreant.

WRETCHED. *a.* Luckless, calamitous, dogbolt (Ent.) ærumnous, forlorn, inconsolable, prolitarious, unblest.

WRETCHEDNESS. *s.* Pandora's box. (Metaph.)

WRING. *v.* To intort, to wreathe.

WRINKLE. *v.* To corrugate.

WRINKLED. *p.* Cockled; state of being wrinkled, irrugation; full of wrinkles, rugose.

WRITE. *v.* To correspond; to write on the back, to endorse or indorse; to write unto, to address; to write in or upon, to inscribe; to write over, to transcribe; to write back, or over again, to rescribe.

WRITER. *s.* Composer, scrivener, scribe; writer of wanton matters, jests, and buffoonety, mimiographer; an inspired writer, hagiographer; writer of accounts, logographer; writer who snarls at the performance of others, latrant writer; writer of sacred things, hierographer; writer of trifling and base things, rhyparographer.

WRITING. *s.* Deed of one's own hand-writing, chirography, autography; beautiful writing, caligraphy; the art of writing in short-hand, brachygraphy, stenography or steganography (Bailey); the art of writing in sacred characters, cryptography or steganography; a writing or inscription on a statue, epigraphe; a writing or inscription on a tomb, epitaph; the copy of an original writing, estreat; word of contempt for any low poetical writing, hedge-note; divination by writing on the bark of a tree, stigonomancy; a writing on the back of any paper or deed, indorsement or endorsement; writing or study by candle-light, lucubration or elucubration; the scraping out of writing, rasure; sacred writings, hierograms; sacred writing or history, hierography; writing in cyphers, polygraphy; deed executed under the hand-writing of both parties, syngrapha; the true way of writing, orthography; the art of swift writing, tachygraphy; one's own hand-writing, holograph; false writing, pseudography, plastography.

WRITTEN. *p.* Written message, epistle; written in many languages, pollyglot; what is written by another's instruction, dictamen; neatly written, terse.

WRONG. *v.* To injure, to scathe.

WRONG. *a.* Counter, amiss, preposterous, reprehensible, tort.

WRY. *a.* To make wry mouths, to mop.

Y

YARN. *s.* Yarn on a weaver's warp, abb; certain length of yarn wound on a reel, skaine; sellers of yarn by retail, journeychoppers.

YAWNING. *p.* Oscitant; a yawning or stretching, pandiculation; act of yawning, hiation, oscitation, or oscitancy.

YEAR. *s.* That happens every year, annual; that happens every two years or lasts two years, biennial; every three, triennial; every four, quadrennial; every five, quinquennial, &c.; that which is renewed every year, restible; lasting throughout the year, perennial; space of four years, tetraeterid, olympiad; of five, lustre; of seven, hebdomade; of fifteen, indiction; of 100, secle; of or belonging to 100 years, secular; bearing twice in the year, biferous; a man aged 50 years, eincater, cinquater; the custom of going about from house to house, with warm ale, &c. the last night of the year, wassail, wassel; those who practise this are called, wassellers; the 7th, 21st, and 81st years of a person's life are termed, climacterical; the 63d and 81st are termed the grand climacterics, and every 7th and 9th is called, a climacter.

Years may be enumerated under the following, viz: The Metonic, the Sidereal, the Civil, the Lunar, the Tropical, the Julian and the Gregorean, &c.

Of the Julian (or Old Stile) the Gregorean (or New Style) and tropical years.

The Astronomers employed by Pope Gregory the 13th, believed that according to Copernicus the tropical year consisted of 365 days, 5 hours, 49 minutes, 20 seconds, and accordingly made the Gregorean approach as near as possible to the Copernican account; these astronomers allowed *three* days to every four centuries, which makes the Gregorean year to consist of 365 days, 5 hours, 49 minutes, 12 seconds exactly; and differs from the Copernican only by *eight se-*

conds yearly. Had Copernicus been perfectly correct with respect to the length of the tropical year, the Gregorean estimate would only have varied one day in 10,800 years, but the true length of the tropical year is not yet perfectly settled, as appears by comparing the opinions and observations of a few of the most celebrated astronomers, with the Julian and Gregorean accounts,

	d.	h.	m.	sec.	3ds.
1st, The Julian year, or Old Style, equals	365	6	0	0	0
2d, The Gregorean or New Style	365	5	49	12	0

and is 10 minutes 48 seconds *less* than the Julian.

The length of the tropical year, according to Copernicus, is — 365 5 49 20 0

and is *eight seconds more* than the Gregorian.

According to Street's Caroline Tables, - - 365 5 49 25 41

and is 13 seconds 41 thirds *more* than the Gregorian

According to Newton (best edition of his Principia) the tropical year consists of - - - 365 5 48 57 41

and is 14 seconds 19 thirds *less* than the Gregorian.

According to Dr Edmond Halley's Tables of 1701, the tropical year is - - - - 365 5 48 54 41

and is 17 seconds 19 thirds *less* than the Gregorian.

According to Tobias Mayor of Gottingen - - 365 5 48 51 7

and is 20 seconds 53 thirds *less* than the Gregorian.

According to Leonard Euler of Berlin, F. R. S., the tropical year consists of - - - 365 5 48 47 57

and is 24 seconds 3 thirds *less* than the Gregorian

According to Bossut's History of Mathematics, translated by Bonycastle, 1803 - - - 365 5 48 48 0

and is 24 seconds *less* than the Gregorian.

From this statement, the curious reader can easily calculate what length of time it will take before the Gregorian or New Style requires to be altered; for, were Newton's opinion correct, it would take $6034\frac{794}{859}$ years exactly, and even at that great distance of time would be an error of *one day*; but, if we were to take M. Bossut's authority, which is so late as 1803, it would take only 3600 years; and so on, for the other authorities.

The above being understood, the difference between OS. and NS. is easily comprehended, for the Gregorian year (NS.) being 10 minutes 48 seconds shorter than the Julian year (O. S.) their difference in four centuries amounts exactly to three days; to adjust this difference (and make time coincide as nearly as possible with the sun's motion) the first year of each century for three centuries successively, instead of being a leap year of 366 days, is made only a common year of 365 days, and the first year of the fourth century is a leap-year, as in the following series, where *L* denominates leap-year of 366 days; *C*, common year of 365 days, and the 1st, 2d, 3d, &c. subjoined to each century, denote the number of days to be added to the NS. to make the styles agree; thus, to first January 1806 NS., 12 days must be added, which throws the first day of January 1806 OS. on Monday the 13th NS. and so on; and it is somewhat curious that this has not been attended to, (as yet) in some of the Calendars!

Series of Centuries.

C.	C.	C.	L.	C.	C.	C.	L.
100	200	300	400	500	600	700	800
		1 d.	1 d.	2 d.	3 d.	4 d.	4 d.
C.	C.	C.	L.	C.	C.	C.	L.
900	1000	1100	1200	1300	1400	1500	1600
5 d.	6 d.	7 d.	7 d.	8 d.	9 d.	10 d.	10 d.
C.	C.	C.	L.	C.	C.	C.	L.
1700	1800	1900	2000	2100	2200	2300	2400
11 d.	12 d.	13 d.	13 d.	14 d.	15 d.	16 d.	16 d.

YEARLY. *a.* Annual, anniversary.

YELLING. *p.* The act of howling or yelling like a dog or wolf, ululation.

YELLOW. *a.* Olivaster; yellow, (sickly) sallow; of a deep yellow colour, fulvid.

YIELD. *v.* To subminister, to truckle, to afford, to mancipate, to produce, to assent, to cede, to concede, to acquiesce, to succumb.

YIELDED. *p.* Thing yielded or given up, concession.

YIELDING. *p.* Compliant, limber; having the quality of yielding, cessible; the act of yielding up, dedition.

YOUNG. *a.* Juvenile, puny; young (said of birds, pinfeathered; the quality of growing young again, rejuvenescency; the young of any beast, cub; young of any beast prematurely produced, slink; to produce young as ewes, to yean; as swine, to farrow; as rabbits, to kindle;

as beasts in general, to litter; as fishes, to spawn; as birds, to hatch; as hawks, to cast; as bees, to swarm; young person, younker, youngster; young cow, (or young woman in ridicule,) heifer; producing or bringing forth young, tetiferous; the act of bearing young in the womb, gestation; big with young, gravid, pregnant; to fill with young, to impregnate; producing many young at a birth, multiparous; a difficulty in bringing forth young, dystochy, or dystochia; those animals that bring forth their young by eggs are termed oviparous, and those that bring forth their young alive are viviparous animals. (See Bearing).

YOUNGER. *a.* Younger brother, cadet; younger, (inferior) puisne.

YOUTH. *s.* Youth, or the period after childhood, adolescence, adolescency.

YOUTHFUL. *a.* Blooming, juvenile.

Z

ZEAL. *s.* Affection, contention, ardency, ardentness, ardour, fervour, fervidness; want of zeal, lukewarm, tepidity, tepor; affected zeal, cacozelia.

ZEALOT. *s.* Bigot, enthusiast.

ZEALOUS. *s.* Eager, fervent, fervid, strenuous.

ZEST. *s.* Condiment.

ZODIAC. *s.* Baldric, mazaroth, signifer.

THE END.

JOHN MOIR, PRINTER,
EDINBURGH.

www.ingramcontent.com/pod-product-compliance
Lightning Source LLC
LaVergne TN
LVHW050719030325
804919LV00002B/348